Hunting and Weaving

Other Titles of Interest from St. Augustine's Press

James V. Schall, *The Regensburg Lecture*

James V. Schall, *The Modern Age*

James V. Schall, *Sum Total of Human Happiness*

James V. Schall, *The Classical Moment: Selected Essays on Knowledge and Its Pleasures*

James V. Schall, *Remembering Belloc*

Robert Royal, ed., *The Catholic Thing: Five Years of a Singular Website*

Rémi Brague, *Eccentric Culture*

Rémi Brague, *On the God of the Christians (and on one or two others)*

C.S. Lewis & St. Giovanni Calabria, *The Latin Letters of C.S. Lewis*

Josef Pieper, *Happiness and Contemplation*

Josef Pieper, *The Christian Idea of Man*

Josef Pieper, *The Platonic Myths*

H.S. Gerdil, *The Anti-Emile: Reglections on the Theory and Practice of Education against the Principles of Rousseau*

Gerhart Niemeyer, *The Loss and Recovery of Truth*

Roger Kimball, *The Fortunes of Permanence*

Pope Pius VI, *The French Revolution Confronts Pius VI* (in 2 vols.)

Karol Wojtyła [John Paul II], *Man in the Field of Responsibility*

Gabriel Marcel, *Man against Mass Society*

Gabriel Marcel, *The Mystery of Being* (in 2 vols.)

Peter Augustine Lawler, *Homeless and at Home in America: Evidence for the Dignity of the Human Soul in Our Time and Place*

Roger Scruton, *An Intelligent Person's Guide to Modern Culture*

Peter Kreeft, *Summa Philosophica*

Edward Feser, *Last Superstition: A Refutation of the New Atheism*

Jacques Maritain, *Natural Law: Reflections on Theory and Practice*

Hunting and Weaving
Empiricism and Political Philosophy

Edited by Thomas Heilke and John von Heyking

St. Augustine's Press
South Bend, Indiana

Manufactured in the United States of America

1 2 3 4 5 6   18 17 16 15 14 13

Library of Congress Cataloging in Publication Data
Hunting and weaving: empiricism and political philosophy /
edited by Thomas Heilke and John von Heyking.
pages cm
Includes bibliographical references and index.
ISBN 978-1-58731-374-5 (pbk.: alk. paper)
1. Political science – Philosophy. 2. Religion and politics.
3. Terrorism – Religious aspects. 4. Philosophy, Modern.
5. Voegelin, Eric, 1901–1985 – Political and social views.
6. Cooper, Barry, 1943– I. Heilke, Thomas W., 1960–
II. Heyking, John von.
JA71.H815 2013
320.01 d – c23   2012039819

∞The paper used in this publication meets the minimum requirements of the
American National Standard for Information Sciences Permanence of Paper for
Printed Materials, ANSI Z39.481984.

ST. AUGUSTINE'S PRESS
www.staugustine.net

Contents

Introduction

Thomas Heilke and John von Heyking

"So then, Glaucon, we must, like hunters, now station ourselves in a circle around the thicket and pay attention so that justice doesn't slip through somewhere and disappear into obscurity. Clearly it's somewhere hereabouts. Look to it and make every effort to catch sight of it; you might somehow see it before me and could tell me."[1]

"What's the smallest paradigm, then, with the same business as the political, that one could set alongside it and find adequately that which is sought? Do you want, by Zeus, Socrates, if we don't have any other ready at hand – well, do you want at any rate that we choose the art of weaving?"[2]

"I am by habit a westerner. . . . The first political conversation I recall was between my two grandfathers and my dad, in a log cabin on a fishing trip into the Chilcotin when I was about five. . . . I uttered my first political statement about a year later. My mother was driving my sisters and me to visit relatives on the ranch of my uncles, west of Nanton. The highway south of Calgary for most of the drive was parallel to the railway tracks. We gradually overtook a freight train and I announced proudly, "Look, Mum, it's the goddamn CPR." She reached over and whacked me on the side of the head and told me never to use that word again. After my tears evaporated, I was puzzled, not knowing I had uttered a blasphemy. I was just using what I thought was the full name of the railway, because that was what my grandfather and uncles always called it."[3]

"This is my home, here is where I belong." This intensely human statement is intelligible for its emotional appeal to nearly anyone. It seems also to be fundamentally antithetical to the attitude (recalling a nautical metaphor) of the philosopher or the scientist. The tension emerges specifically in the study of politics for two reasons. First, like any scientific or philosophical mode of inquiry, political science should be bound to scientific and philosophical standards of non-partisanship and impartiality, even while it investigates phenomena that belong, prima facie, to the most partisan of activities that often evokes the most partisan of responses. Is it possible to be a situated, concrete consciousness—a human being who belongs to a specific time and place—and yet be impartial in one's scientific studies, evaluations, and conclusions? Can a *person*, in other words—even a social scientist—be impartial or non-partisan on the one hand, while nevertheless rejecting a notion of pure scientific detachment on the other?[4] Our prejudices, as Barry Cooper once commented in a CBC radio interview, do not change the facts. But "facts," and especially *political* facts, are not self-revealing objects of perception, strewn on the ground and awaiting their serendipitous discovery at the hands of the scientist.[5] Facts, to be intelligible facts, are theory-bound. But are not theories, especially the theories of social scientists, merely sophisticated forms of prejudice? Can one be "at home," yet offer non-particularist judgments and evaluations of the political situation before us?

These questions may enmesh us in a never-ending knot of epistemological entanglements so that, like Nietzsche's Apollonian Greeks, we are inclined to take recourse to "powerful, mad, and pleasurable illusions."[6] In the case of the social scientist, these salutary phantasms may resolve into an empiricist, naively optimistic and un-reflective fact-gathering mission.[7] That, as we will discuss presently, is insufficient, and not the only recourse for the political scientist.

A second reason for the tension between a situated philosopher and her/his political-philosophical inquiry rests in the substantive nature of that inquiry. Much—perhaps too much—can be made of the tension between civic obligation and philosophical inquiry, between the truth-claims of philosophy and the truth-claims of the polity regarding its origins, goodness, and purposes, between the sources and methods of philosophical truth-telling and the sources and methods of civically engaged speaking. In one strong version of this argument, the philosopher, by dint of his myth-busting inquiries and convention-assaulting views that develop from such inquiry, perennially risks being a traitor to his polity, because *all* polities are, perforce, founded on myth, and myths are antithetical to the truth-telling ways of philosophy.[8] A deeply rooted, perhaps essential, conflict therefore exists between the myth-loving, myth-dwelling, myth-needing many and the theory-making, skeptically inquiring, philosophical few. On this understanding, insofar as "place" is given not merely by birth, but by myths that give to the inhabitants of each and any polity their home, their place in space and time,[9] the philosopher has no place to call home. This problem is as old as political philosophy itself. It makes several appearances in various guises in the Platonic corpus, where it receives no complete resolution,[10] and in Aristotle's remark, upon his decision to depart Athens when charges of impiety were introduced against him, that he would not allow the Athenians to offend against philosophy a second time.

On the other hand, the philosopher or scholar with no home has nothing, perhaps can have nothing, to say about politics. As much as thought strives to transcend opinion, it always originates in opinion, the realm of the polis. This is the conundrum of much contemporary political science, modeled as it is after the mathematical and physical sciences. Its rationalism produces a cloistered jargon and specialization that ensures merely that political scientists and their haggard graduate students are the only ones reading the products of its labours. A comparison with Swift's Laputans, whose science produces houses that cannot stand up, might be in order, if it occurred to anyone to apply their knowledge. Statesmen, however, seem to have little use for such contemporary political science. A major reason for this rejection is that statesmen do not recognize political phenomena in the categories of analysis used by political scientists. For example, whereas statesmen speak of loyalty and friendship, political scientists are prone to speak unrecognizably of systems, institutions, or rational actors, whose calculus is not the same as that of loyal friends. Contemporary political science has widely forgotten Aristotle's insight that genuine science needs to retain the phenomena.

Barry Cooper's "weaving" together of political philosophy and empiricism, of philosophy and Canadian politics, maintains those phenomena. For this reason, for example, readers from Alberta are able to read his analysis of Western Canadian political myths in his popular books like *Deconfederation* (authored with David Bercuson) and *It's the Regime, Stupid*—an analysis that is illuminated by the ideas of Plato, Giambattista Vico, F. W. J. Schelling, and Eric Voegelin—and still recognize that Cooper describes *their own* myths. Cooper's scholarship and popular writing derive from a specific place. A significant aspect of Cooper's work both as a scholar and as a public intellectual has, therefore, been to work out and to demonstrate what it means to be an impartial scientist, yet "located" or with a home from which one understands the world, not as a partisan, but as a participant in a process of becoming that is larger than oneself. This volume of essays considers both Cooper's academic scholarship and civic engagements in publications that have, for the past 40 years, spanned a continuum of topics in political science, especially in Canadian politics and political philosophy. Cooper's understanding of the empirical nature of political science in its scholarly and civic manifestations unifies the essays of this volume. The contributors assess his work, but more importantly, they consider an array of topics in the mode that Cooper has developed them.

One explanation for the continuity between place and thinking upon place in Cooper's scholarship is that his scholarly project is, of necessity, modern and takes place within the modern regime. Jürgen Gebhardt makes an argument in his contribution to this volume that political philosophy, at least in its current self-understanding as a distinct activity of inquiry, is a modern phenomenon. In a parallel vein, some, like Ronald Beiner, argue that, whatever its merits as a historical claim, the argument for the essential conflict between philosophy and the polis can no longer be true in the post-Enlightenment era of liberal toleration in western societies. The Enlightenment made available to the many the skeptical approaches of traditional philosophical inquiry, so that the classical antagonism between philosophical inquiry and religio-political myths no longer exists in its stark form. In the post-Enlightenment world, "millions of people live their lives without the consolations of either philosophy or religion, and they seem none the worse for it;" some would argue that religious belief, which is the source or co-author of most political myths and mythmaking,[11] is a greater force for unsettlement and violence in the contemporary world than the secularizing tendencies of philosophy could ever be.[12] Thus, it is true that the first recorded political philosopher was executed by his city, and that that city was, at the time of his execution, one of the first democratic polities historically known to us. It is also true that regimes that suppress political dissent and philosophical engagement exist today. It is equally true that the Canadian polity, a modern constitutional monarchy with democratic selection processes at several levels of government and of which Cooper is a citizen, is not known, for the most part, to persecute or otherwise abridge the inquiries of its philosophers and scholars or the public dissemination of their research results in any substantively meaningful way.[13] Accordingly, as a contemporary scholar of political philosophy living and working in Canada, Professor Cooper has had to worry little about persecution, the need for secret writing, or any prima facie fundamental public enmity between his activities of inquiry as a scholar and his duties as a citizen. Rather, beginning as a scholar of political philosophy, he has brought forward the concepts, categories, and analytical tools made available to him in his study of political philosophy to examine, in the role of a public intellectual, the history and current shape of the Canadian polity. The role of the political philosopher has changed.

Even so, the modern regime, which Cooper describes most recently as a tension between pride and interest,[14] poses a defined set of alternatives for the ways humans should live their lives. If understood, in its radicalized form, as the "end of history" or the "technological society," in which, again, "millions of people live their lives without the consolations of either philosophy or religion," then moderns abide by the imperative of technology.[15] This modern, radicalized and secular world is, however, a dreamworld and frequently a tyranny. Cooper's writings on the Canadian regime, especially his examinations of bureaucratic evils, illuminate how much of an annoyance post-historical life can be; the Canadian regime is not a post-historical tyranny, but its imbalance leans too heavily toward interest, with an insufficient leavening of the sort of pride that can sustain freedom and self-government. The Canadian state generally treats citizens more like the little children of Tocqueville's tutelary state than the zeks of Solzhenitsyn's *Gulag Archipelago*, although Canada's regime of secular "grasping and seizing" can get ugly and does, of course, hold up some ways of life over others.[16]

Cooper identified this "holding over" as a kind of "moralizing sadism." Such an expression of power is comprised of activities and articulations in which the political or material power of one group is accompanied by a rhetorical stance that expresses a moral superiority—rooted in innate qualities or historically given identities that the "superior" group possesses—over against another group, the members of which are classified as morally inferior. This inferiority can be exploited ad infinitum as an identity-producing device for the superior group to the disadvantage of the less powerful. Put another way, moral sadism consists in moral egoists demanding "to universalize what they are by presenting it as what they are commanded to be by the Law or elevated to by experience of the Good." This demand arises from what William Connolly has called a "transcendental egoism" that "silently takes its own fundamental identity to be the source that must guide moral life in general."[17] Exposing the sadistic qualities of this identity-formation does not make oneself beloved amongst the members of the "superior" group.[18] Even in this, as in other aspects, the Canadian regime need not persecute scholars in the same way Athens persecuted Socrates, because in a post-historical world, there is so little at risk for the regime in the disputes that animated the contest between the philosophical Socrates and his Athenian fellows.

Professor Cooper has undertaken the systematic work of a political scientist while openly and consciously being guided by an understanding of that science as articulated in the work of Eric Voegelin, supplemented with the work of Leo Strauss, Hannah Arendt, and, more distantly, Raymond Aron, Michel Foucault, and Alexandre Kojève, among others. Cooper has devoted significant interpretive effort to Voegelin's work, but, in keeping with Voegelin's own injunction that he did not want disciples but rather scholars who would try to "do better" than he had, or who would expand the investigations he advocated into areas he himself had not explored, Cooper has been far from a mere scholar of Voegelin or interpreter of Voegelin's opus. In a volume representing the leading lights of political philosophy in Canada, Cooper described his approach to political science and the connection between his two main foci of research, namely Canadian politics and political philosophy, as "weaving."[19] "My work," he wrote, "has combined analysis of the major questions in the history of political thought, especially classical political philosophy, with the immediate questions of the day. In the first enterprise, I have been guided chiefly by Voegelin, but also by [Hannah] Arendt and [Leo] Strauss. In the second, which is concerned chiefly with the place of the west in the nation, it has been more of a team effort."[20] We suggest that this "weaving" (or perhaps, as Cooper alternatively proposes, "braiding") reflects the true meaning of empirical political science, contrary to the positivist and quantitative meaning most political scientists ascribe to the term "empirical." Cooper's method of political analysis follows that of Voegelin, who opened the five-volume *Order and History* with his famous remark that the "order of history emerges from the history of order."[21] Professor Schabert's description of Voegelin's *Anamnesis* in his contribution to the present volume fits well with Cooper's self-understanding of warp and woof in his own work as a political scientist: "The entire book, therefore, is pervaded by a dual empirical process: by a movement that begins with the historical phenomena of order and leads to the structures of consciousness from which it arose, and, conversely, by a movement that begins with the analysis of consciousness and leads to the phenomenon of order."

Historically, political analysis has tended to begin in whatever contemporary crisis the analyst has found himself.[22] The analyst sifts through competing claims of political meaning asserted by the partisans in the crisis. From there he ascends to greater luminosity concerning the human condition by viewing those claims in light of the "major questions in the history of political thought."[23] Cooper characterizes the relationship between the study of Canadian politics and political philosophy as dialectical. They inform one another, since the search for order is necessarily the search for order that is conducted by a particular individual's concrete consciousness in the context of a particular community in space and time. Simply put, the biographical details of a scholar's life reflect a unique "complex of experience" that informs the questions the scholar brings to the competing claims of political meaning here and now as well as to the history and tradition of political thought. For this reason, the image of "weaving" and/or "braiding" that Cooper borrows from Plato's description of dialectic, appropriately describes his own work. Plato also compares dialectic to hunting, a "totemic rite" in which Cooper participates and upon which he has frequently meditated,[24] the metaphorical/philosophical version of which Zdravko Planinc examines to great effect in this volume. The metaphors of both hunting and weaving apply especially well to the impact Cooper's work in the political-philosophical interpretation of Canadian political-mythological symbols can have on an intelligent and imaginative, but non-philosophical reader.

The present volume is divided into two parts. Following Cooper's understanding of political analysis as "weaving," the topics addressed in the two parts necessarily relate to one another. Part One is devoted to the study of contemporary politics, including Canadian politics and modern terrorism. Scholars familiar with Cooper's analysis of various topics, including Canadian constitutionalism, Alberta politics and its relationship with the rest of Canada, the media, Quebec politics, human rights, military and defense policy, foreign policy, regionalism and self-interpretation, and terrorism reflect on his work as they advance scientific thinking in their own analyses. Part Two is devoted to the study of political philosophy. In several cases in both parts, the contributors have woven their theoretical reflections together with analyses of pragmatic politics, either in Canada or other polities. We observe in this weaving a demonstration of Cooper's argument, following a long line of thinkers before him, that the methods of political philosophy produce genuine empirical political science.

All of the contributors to this volume are familiar with Cooper's oeuvre, his methods, and the topics of analysis, and they are all scholars of standing in their own right. Each one has contributed to the "team effort" that Cooper notes as the source of his self-understanding. Accordingly, this collection constitutes a snapshot of a conversation that friends, colleagues, and students have conducted with Professor Cooper over the span of his career. Even more, it constitutes an advance in our understanding of the meaning of empirical political science and in its conduct.

An Outline of the Volume

Most of the twelve essays of this volume each focus on one or more of the key concepts that Cooper has developed in his work on political philosophy, or in his empirical, philosophically informed analysis of politics. Each writer, whether directly or indirectly, thereby seeks a critical engagement with some aspect of that analysis. Reflecting the two broad categories of Cooper's own scholarship and public engagement, we have divided the essays into two sections: one on contemporary politics and political culture, the other on political theory.

We begin with an essay by Professor Tom Flanagan that exhibits a more personal tone. A long-time colleague and friend of Barry Cooper, Flanagan reflects on Cooper's career within and without the academy, especially in relation to the emergence and identity of the so-called "Calgary School."[25] The title was coined by a journalist in the 1980s to identify, in a loose way, specific trends of thought associated with a small group of faculty at the University of Calgary in the Department of Political Science (as well as the Departments of History and Economics) who, including Cooper, rose to national prominence. Flanagan proposes to write the first-ever account of the School from the perspective of an "insider," cogently describing the contingencies and accidents that brought these scholars together. More importantly, his essay illustrates well the benefits of bringing academic perspectives to public debate amidst Canadian constitutional, political, and economic crises, thereby creating a space, in this case, for political theory and public policy to meet. As with Tilo Schabert's discussion of Eric Voegelin's "workshop" (described below), Flanagan's essay focuses on how persons conduct political science, and how the activity of persons, in making and cultivating judgment, gives political science its empirical quality, which is a major theme uniting all the essays in this volume.

The second essay, by Richard Avramenko, extends one of Cooper's signal contributions to Canadian political thought, namely a consideration of what the national story of Canada is around which Canadians form their collective identity. Avramenko's answer, following earlier work by Cooper, is that there is not, in fact, a single Canadian story: the story of Laurentia is not, for example, the story of the West, nor is the story of the Prairies the story, say, of British Columbia. The Orangeman culture of Ontario and its myths (and accompanying attitudes) of the "garrison state mentality" exist in sharp contrast to the experiences and stories of the Red River colonists or twentieth-century immigrants to the Canadian West. These differences, according to Avramenko and Cooper, have created political tension and friction in Canada, because Laurentian Canadians have, on the whole and for the most part, not considered the myths and stories arising from life on the Prairies to be stories central to the Canadian experience, if, indeed, they have considered them at all. Such an approach has led to the marginalization of Western Canadian identities and, according to Avramenko, to practices of moral sadism in central Canada. One question studies such as Avramenko's raise concerns the relationship of power and material interest with identity-forming myths and political identity generally. Here again, political theory meets political processes and policy formation.

Rainer Knopff offers us a short piece that illustrates how entities and constituencies on the "periphery" (to deliberately misuse a neo-Marxist term), can often behave within their boundaries in ways that replicate the larger metropole-periphery relationship of which they are the junior part. Some Albertans like to hunt in non-metaphorical mode. Knopff shows how this activity has included a free-rider problem that could be solved with means that Albertans usually advocate at the national level, but seem—hypocritically—to eschew in this instance. Intellectual hunting, like the non-metaphorical kind, is not free, either, even if it is safer in the Canadian polity than many others. That theme, occasionally brought to the surface in Cooper's work, returns in some of the more theoretical essays in this collection.

The focus on Canadian politics concludes with Janet Ajzenstat's essay on the Canadian version of protecting civil rights. Living, as they do, in a world that is inundated with American political ideas and debates, many Canadians have only the loosest notions of the core principles that inform their own political regime. Ajzenstat demonstrates in this essay, as does Flanagan in his, the value of bringing academic expertise to certain kinds of political debates. Using what she calls the "Calgary perspective," she begins with the question—rooted in empirical evidence—whether Canadian courts in the 1980s were "assuming an unprecedented role in the determination of public policy and . . . whether in some cases the policy in question would have been better left to Parliament." This question is offensive to her students, who, like many Canadians, harbor an anxious desire to be led by people with "training," which is a modernized version of the ancient desire for the leadership of the wise and noble. Such "training" is located in the modern Canadian instance in the expertise of parliamentary representatives and their staffs. Professor Ajzenstat's question points to the deeper question, rooted in this case in the historical evidence of regional Parliamentary debates at the time of Canadian confederation: in contrast to a dependency on courts (and regulating bureaucrats), do "legislatures run on the Westminster lines, play a role in securing rights?" Canadian parliamentary democracy has only one idea—parliamentary sovereignty—upon which everything else hangs. That idea implies a politics of motion (in a non-Hobbesian sense): there is no finality of symbols, ideas, opinions, or laws in such a regime, even while, at the same time, such a regime may have as much stability and durability and defense of human rights as a more constitutionally rigid order. The capacity to hold, paradoxically, a stable image of this movement in one's mind is the crux of Cooper's empiricism, which is to say, political judgment. Such capacity for paradox is unfathomable to the social scientist's impetus to categorize reality into static concepts. Thus, Ajzenstat defends the somewhat novel, yet entirely sensible idea that the "*parler*" of Parliament—"continuing contestation in parliament, perpetual dissent, noise, even . . . incivility"—is, in its very practice, the guarantor of Canadian civil rights and a source of socio-political stability.

The section on contemporary politics ends with Michael Franz's critical assessment of Cooper's account of terrorism in *New Political Religions, or An Analysis of Modern Terrorism*. Franz claims it "provides the most penetrating conceptual tools as well as the most illuminating analytical approach currently available." However, Franz wonders how broadly Cooper's understanding of terrorism as a "pneumopathology," whereby the terrorists knowingly advance a "secondary reality," applies. Franz suggests Michael Burleigh's assessment of terrorism in *Blood and Rage: A Cultural History of Terrorism* applies to a larger set of actual terrorists. Instead of describing terrorists in spiritual terms, Burleigh finds most of them act as if they are driven more by very worldly concerns including money, anger, sexual prowess, tribalism, and ethnic pride. Thus, Cooper's analysis "looks much more valuable as a *suggestive line of interpretation* than as a *rigorous psycho-spiritual diagnosis*" (emphasis by Franz). In a sense, Franz suggests Cooper's analysis is insufficiently empirical because he has not fully demonstrated that all terrorists are "pneumopaths," or even that its leaders are. However, Cooper's analysis describes a type of action (or anti-action, as Cooper argues) that defies the categories used by most scholars of terrorism, including those used by Burleigh. Indeed, Franz's use of Burleigh as a foil to Cooper is instructive for the themes of this volume: Empiricism and political philosophy. Burleigh explicitly avoids analyzing the ideologies of terrorists, which is the focus of Cooper's analysis (i.e., he relies on Sayyid Qutb to understand

Islamic terrorism), and looks instead to their "specific actions and choices" (Burleigh cites St. Matthew's precept, "By their fruits shall ye know them"). Franz considers Burleigh's historical method as too flatly empirical, and contends Cooper's analysis of their ideology (as found in their writings) and spiritual psychology "precisely the elements on which Cooper excels." Thus, Franz points the way in showing how Cooper's empiricism can be fully applied and extended to the study of terrorism, even if *New Political Religions* is only a start.

Leah Bradshaw's essay, the first of six to consider more distinctly a variety of themes from political theory and from the topics of political theory that Cooper has explored, takes up what he has identified as the three dimensions of empirical political science. Focusing on his analysis of technology, where thought and the object of thought sharply confront one another, Bradshaw examines Cooper's claim that "empirical political science is the bringing together of common sense observation upon and participation in the world, the reliance upon great texts for a better understanding of the reality we inhabit, and a reflection upon one's own consciousness as it participates in reality." Bradshaw argues that Cooper "braids" these three "different modes of engagement" together in such a way that none can be separated out without having the "braid" disintegrate. Bringing to hand Hannah Arendt's critique of the modern split between empiricism and theory, Bradshaw argues that this development—a split that Cooper has resisted in his own work—has been destructive for political science and civic discourse alike. Bradshaw provides a brief sketch of its origins in early modern thought and its culmination in a contemporary "stand-off between crude empiricism and ideology," whereby the ideologue purports to remake the world "by deducing patterns that are more systematic and more logical than the apparent incoherence of ordinary life, but his impact upon the world is similar to the alleged empiricist, because he attempts to remake the world according to a human construct." Bradshaw concludes with some reflections on challenges facing Cooper's call to restore empirical political science within the contemporary scientific, technological climate. She considers Cooper's and Arendt's meditations on thinking, and explains how reading and cooking (as opposed to hunting) are appropriate, mindful responses to the age.

In contrast with David Walsh's upbuilding discourse on hope that concludes this collection, Peter Emberley lays out a description of modern human beings in despair. The modern dilemma, Emberley claims, is constituted by the fact that we moderns have lost any possibility of "cosmological or metaphysical certainty, unable to extend our absolute trust to authorities whose discernments are vouched to be superior to our own," at the same time that we are "unwilling to throw and disperse ourselves into the desiccate worlds of industry, material self-interest and science." He observes that in pragmatic response to this existential circumstance, we choose, "through imagination or an act of will, to bracket out the causes of our doubt, and adopt religious possibilities which, while no longer known to be true, nonetheless conform to an aesthetic of our choice - a choice burdened with absolute gravity - and that we hope will generate real-world results." Emberley proposes what he sees as a more sustaining response in which we avail ourselves of the tools of modernity and post-modernity (however flawed those tools are) to push forward (and not merely look backward) to regain the insights of classical philosophy and of Christian thought and experience and appropriate these for our own personal and communal existence. Our modern pragmatic choice to bracket our doubt also contains within it the practical alternative of choosing "orthopraxy," those devotional and ritual practices that "give deep meaning to the ordinary routines of life." While Emberley draws on Rene Girard and Simone Weil for his analysis, the point of making a practical choice is rooted in judgment, a faculty of soul given neither to abstractions nor to crude pragmatism and which may inform empiricism properly understood.

In a penetrating textual exegesis of several well-known, much-analyzed allegorical passages in Plato's *Republic*, Zdravko Planinc uncovers the nature of Platonic philosophical "hunting" in literary dialectic. Planinc severely criticizes the reification or misplaced concreteness that arises in much of what he calls the "pseudo-technical jargon" of those scholars who are intent to unlock Socrates' accounts of the "sun," the "line," and the "cave," as though these allegories were an exploration of objectivized "ideas" in the modern, near-ideological sense. These symbols are not, argues Planinc, "keys" or even "the key" for unlocking what is likewise misnamed as "Plato's metaphysics and political theory." Such interpretive efforts are, in keeping with Cooper's own methods of textual exegesis, and consistent with Plato's hints on the matter, poor ways to read a text. Such an "Adeimantean reduction of philosophy to dogma, conviction, and opinion using Glauconian methods" will never work to achieve the ends of philosophy nor, especially, to uncover the qualities and outcomes of Socrates' investigations and meditations. In the course of his analysis, Planinc elaborates on the heart of the distinction between sophistry and philosophy, and how, in politics, geometric thinking and sophistry promotes brutality veiled with high-mindedness, as seen, for instance, in collaborations of technology with ideology. Planinc acknowledges Cooper's own scholarship on Plato as the basis for his own exegetical work in which he shows Plato's Socrates to be a post-Odyssean hero in a manner that transcends the ancient quarrel of philosophy and poetry.

The relationship between Leo Strauss and Eric Voegelin, in their thought and in their personal correspondence, has been of enduring interest to students of either political philosopher. This interest is not merely philological. For scholars and public intellectuals wanting to conduct scientifically valid and publically responsible investigations into the phenomena of politics, these two figures seem posed to serve as models for such work, as, indeed, they have for Cooper.[26] Jürgen Gebhardt begins his examination of the scope and shape of the relationship between the two with the comment that any "reflection on the legacy of Voegelin and Strauss must start from the following general questions: What is political philosophy? Why should the political scientist commit himself to it?" Barry Cooper has committed himself, as have the authors represented in this collection, to a form of that activity manifested in the widely influential work of both these thinkers (amidst their extensive disagreements, and along with a long list of others). In Gebhardt's estimation, Strauss and Voegelin share, with many other twentieth-century luminaries in political philosophy, "a pluri-morphic modality of the understanding of politics that is based on the classical paradigm of a '*peri ta anthropina philosophia.*' They are engaged in a science of politics that addresses the questions of the modern human being in terms of the perennial issues of the human condition." By seeing the roots of their inquiries in modern problems, Gebhardt shows how Strauss and Voegelin were engaged in an essentially modern mode of reflective inquiry, despite the ways they each appeared to reject or criticize modernity. Gebhardt elucidates how the two thinkers differed over the question of reason and revelation (as Strauss formulated the existential tension between order and disorder), but he contends that their differences over Plato's Parable of the Cave, on the origins of philosophy in the turning around of the soul, are similarly important. Gebhardt's essay in this volume is intended to show what those differences mean and what they imply for the proper conduct of political science.

Eric Voegelin's theory of consciousness is an aspect of his thought that has definitively set him apart from most other contemporary political philosophers. Reactions to it have spanned the gamut from affirmation to puzzlement, to rejection as merely a form of self-authentication or even "gnosticism." Jene Porter assesses Voegelin's theory in light of the work of philosopher John Searle and finds their positions similar and largely compatible, except in regard to Voegelin's use of the Platonic symbols of "Question" and "metaxy." Like Searle, Voegelin rejects dualism. Searle's theory provides a more refined account of what Voegelin called "intentionality," but Voegelin's focus on history, politics, and the "drama of humanity" is more expansive and penetrating. "It is immensely fruitful," argues Porter, "to conceive of humanity as participating in the process of reality, as understanding within the metaxy, and as pursuing the Question." In contrast, "To talk about the Background and normative considerations, as does Searle, seems flat and even puerile." Echoing the gestures toward the dimension of personal and historical existence in several other essays in this collection, Porter concludes that "At the level of pertinence and significance," Voegelin has much more in common "with those thinkers who stress human powers to seek and to understand" and who emphasize the thinking and acting person. Porter exhorts his readers to take up that cue.

Contemporary academic political philosophy is predominantly a philological enterprise in which the exegesis of texts leads to the writing of more texts. Cooper has participated in this activity with great success, but he has also moved beyond it to speak and write as a public intellectual. The former of these two activities is often taken to be a solitary activity. Tilo Schabert, however, presents a picture of what he has called "Voegelin's workshop," in which he shows how Voegelin's work was, in fact, anything but solitary. While the mechanical act of writing itself cannot, perforce, be a team effort, one need only look at the acknowledgements in most books and articles to see that writing as an intellectual activity is, indeed, a communal activity. So it was for Voegelin, as it has also been for nearly any scholar or public intellectual, including Barry Cooper. Echoing Planinc's observation that in philosophical and physical hunting alike, a track is an absence, "a static sign of a living, breathing animal that has moved on," Schabert suggests that a text is "the death mask of its creation," an object of study and contemplation "as the existing work of a creative deed that has all but vanished behind it." Such works, however, are generated by persons, by creative actors. Such creative acts mean that someone has been at work, and one can examine not only the product of such work, but the activity of creative work itself. This commonsensical but sometimes overlooked realization of the origins of science illuminates the nature of empirical political science, because it focuses on the location where empirical activity operates, namely the person. Speaking of Voegelin's *Anamnesis*, for example, Schabert writes: "The entire book . . . is pervaded by a dual empirical process: by a movement that begins with the historical phenomena of order and leads to the structures of consciousness from which it arose, and, conversely, by a movement that begins with the analysis of consciousness and leads to the phenomenon of order." That dual empirical process is a quality Cooper has sought to exemplify in his own scientific work. It is a process that, when shared, gives the contemplating, studying reader of the "products" arising from it access to reality experienced.

The collection ends with David Walsh's Kierkegaardian, upbuilding meditation on hope. Professor Walsh considers how political, moral and even economic order are rooted in hope, which means so much more than optimism, a shallow attitude "we take up when we have distanced ourselves from the imperative of action." Walsh's appeal to hope seems odd, because it is usually understood as a theological virtue, yet, "[w]ithout hope our global economy spirals downward without a break against its descent." Walsh shows how the recent economic crisis and recession are the crisis of a secular mindset; like Emberley, but in somewhat different directions and under slightly different categories of analysis, Walsh encourages us to engage that crisis closely. He warns against the political solipsism of need and interest, which entices us, because it deceives us with the thought that we can master "the conditions of our own existence." On the contrary, "calculations about need and interest are only possible because we are not simply reducible to need and interest." We are persons, and the primacy of that status or condition is indicated in "the hope through which we reach out to one another," which, in turn, is what it means to be a person: "The cooperation of an anthill does not have any theoretical underpinning," but for human beings, "the whole point of the acknowledgment of our primary drives is to construct a mode of satisfying that attests to our transcendence of them. A political community is by definition a free community for it exists, as Aristotle insisted, not merely for the sake of life but for the good life." At its first sounding, this may ring abstract and ethereal, yet Walsh begins his discourse with a firm link to empirical events, namely the recent financial near-meltdown in the United States with its many consequences for economic life world-wide. In the second step of Walsh's analysis, we are reminded of Planinc's argument concerning the transcendent, nearly ineffable qualities of what Socrates seeks in his philosophical quest, which, according to Walsh, cannot be divorced from the question of our common life any more than that common life can be reduced to material need and interest. We come again full circle to the union of material drives, which are the objects of study in one branch of empirical political science, with the human, individual as well as communal, quest for meaning and order, which are the objects of study for another. The latter is best displayed in the kind of empirical, theoretically informed political science Cooper—along with the contributors to this volume—find on offer in the political philosophy of antiquity and of our time. That is the political science which Cooper and his friends have extended in their own work, including the essays contained herein.

We both became acquainted with Barry Cooper not as a scholar of political philosophy or Canadian politics, nor a political commentator, but as a teacher. The first time Heilke ever heard Cooper speak was, ironically enough, at his job interview, when he gave a lecture on Alexander the Great in Anthony Parel's full-year introductory course in political theory. Heilke recalls the lecture as being mostly over his head: the notes he kept from that 1981 lecture reflect his recollections. Then, in one of the most memorable classes he took as an undergraduate, he sat in Cooper's honors seminar on Hannah Arendt. The majority of competent undergraduate and certainly graduate students seem to learn somewhere and early, that the most important way to read a thinker in the academy is critically, which means, to find "holes" in his or her arguments and smash away at those. Cooper's seminar, which he led in the Socratic style, was a lesson in careful, sympathetic reading, subordinated to the principled assumption that the author "is by far superior to you in head and in heart."[27] The seminar was a lesson in how to conduct oneself as a pupil of political philosophers.

Cooper was on sabbatical the year Heilke took MA graduate classes at Calgary, but late that year, while Heilke was finishing class-work and preparing to write on Weber's analysis of modern of bureaucracy, Cooper invited him into his office one day and asked, "you read German, right?" "Yes," came the hesitant reply. "Well, there are a couple of books written in German by Eric Voegelin on European racism that you might want to look at." Getting copies of the books themselves was a task in those days, but having done so, Heilke began dutifully deciphering Voegelin's dense Germano-scholarly prose and trying to make sense of what he was doing in these two books that Hannah Arendt recommended in her *Origins of Totalitarianism* (which Heilke had read in Cooper's Arendt seminar) as the two best books on European race thinking available at the time. That was the beginning of an MA thesis written under Cooper's supervision, and a still-active friendship.

Heyking, on the other hand, first heard of the daimonic Cooper when still a high school student, when his older sister was paired with Cooper at the wedding of one of the contributors to this volume. This premonition later came back to him during the first class of an undergraduate seminar, ostensibly on the topic of liberalism, when Cooper explained that he was having the students read Plato, because before there were "liberals" like John Locke or John Stuart Mill, there was Plato, whose understanding of liberal education shines much more brightly. Even so, students seeking illumination from Cooper in his office on the "seventh floor" would be startled upon entering a darkened, cavernous room lined with bookshelves and illuminated by a small desk lamp that cast shadows everywhere; there they would find him, partially hidden by bookshelves blocking the entrance, and seated at his desk, where they would sit down beside him, only to be startled again to see the stuffed head of a deer, "suddenly there" above their heads.[28] Heyking would go on to write an MA thesis on Eric Voegelin's understanding of cosmological symbolisms, which was a fitting topic for an Albertan for whose home the rhythms of the cosmos make themselves felt so strongly. Upon Heyking's departure from Calgary to do a Ph.D., Cooper's sage advice struck home: go study with a wise old man. Indeed, wise old men (and women) have good judgment.

The editors wish to thank Barb Hodgson and Merle Christie for their editorial assistance, and Tara Heilke for her assistance with some of the translations. We also wish to acknowledge numerous friends and colleagues of Barry Cooper for their financial assistance in the publication of this volume, including Sandy Soutzo, Morten Paulsen, Robert Roach, Terry Lauder, Bradley Nemetz, Melanie Timmons, the Navarro clan of Okotoks, Jake Kerr, Fred Wall, and several who wish to remain anonymous. We thank Joel Makin for his accounting expertise. Robert Cooney took the photograph that adorns the cover of this book. Finally, we wish to thank Bruce Fingerhut of St. Augustine's Press for publishing this book, with its obscure essays on political philosophy, and its even more obscure essays on Canadian politics.

Endnotes

1   Plato, *Republic*, trans., Allan Bloom (New York: Basic Books, 1968), 432b–c.
2   Plato, *Statesman*, trans., Seth Benardete (Chicago: University of Chicago Press, 1986), 279a–b.

3   Barry Cooper, *It's the Regime, Stupid: A Report From the Cowboy West on Why Stephen Harper Matters* (Toronto: Key Porter Books, 2009), 14–15.

4   The negation of this possibility in the natural sciences is a primary concern of Michael Polanyi in *Personal Knowledge: Toward a Post-Critical Philosophy* (Chicago: The University of Chicago Press, 1962): see his opening, summary statement, p. vii.

5   Alasdair MacIntyre, *After Virtue: A Study in Moral Theory*, 2nd ed. (Notre Dame: University of Notre Dame Press, 1984), 79–85; Polanyi, *Personal Knowledge*, 153-159, 166–169.

6   Friedrich Nietzsche, *Die Geburt der Tragödie*, §3, in *Friedrich Nietzsche: Sämtliche Werke, Kritische Studienausgabe*, Giorgio Colli and Mazzino Montinari, eds., vol. 1 (Berlin: de Gruyter, 1980), 37 [editors' translation].

7   Cf. Leo Strauss, "What is Political Philosophy," in Leo Strauss, *What is Political Philosophy? and other Studies* (Chicago: The University of Chicago Press, 1959), 18–27.

8   Cf. Thomas G. West, "Introduction," in Thomas G. West and Grace Starry West, trans. and eds., *Four Texts on Socrates* (Ithaca and London: Cornell University Press, 1984), 9–37, esp. 36.

9   Whether these myths are the "myths" of revealed or passed-down religion, or simply the stories of our past or of the founding of the polity, as discussed *infra* in Richard Avramenko's examination of the contrasting Laurentian and sodbuster myths, is not a distinction that is materially relevant for the relationship of the philosophical or scientific inquirer to them or to the basic laws (including constitutions) that are founded on them.

10   Cf. *Crito*, passim; *Republic*, 449c–502c, 621c–d; *Apology*, passim.

11   "[F]or the gods are at once the preservers of what one loves and the common man's substitute for rational inquiry." (West, *Four Texts*, 34)

12   Ronald Beiner, *Civil Religion: A Dialogue in the History of Political Philosophy* (Cambridge: Cambridge University Press, 2011), 199–204. On the second point, concerning the qualities of a secular life, see especially, Charles Taylor, *A Secular Age* (Cambridge: Belknap Press, 2007).

13   In response to Cooper's study of the Canadian Broadcasting Corporation, *Sins of Omission: Shaping the News at the CBC* (Toronto: University of Toronto Press, 1994), the head of the CBC at the time called on University of Calgary President Norm Wagner to fire Cooper. The Editors thank James Doak for sharing this information.

14   Cooper, *It's the Regime, Stupid*, chap. 1.

15   Cooper, *The End of History: An Essay on Modern Hegelianism* (Toronto: University of Toronto Press, 1984) and *Action into Nature: An Essay on the Meaning of Technology* (Notre Dame, IN: University of Notre Dame Press, 1991).

16   Cooper, *It's the Regime, Stupid*, chap. 5. Because "secular" is, in some of its versions, a symbol not of something real but of a secondary reality, that is, because it refers to an act of imagination, its practitioners must necessarily appeal to the common political world in order to make the symbol seem reasonable. Cooper's *The End of History* elaborates this point. Tellingly, in this regard, appeals to "religious"

experience can be seen in various "secular" constructions of Canadian political order. See Cooper, "Quebec Nationalism and Canadian Politics in Light of Voegelin's *Political Religions*," in *Politics, Order, and History: Essays on the Work of Eric Voegelin*, Glenn Hughes, et al. eds. (Sheffield: Sheffield Academic Press, 2001), 208–232. See also, John von Heyking, "Civil Religion and Associational Life under Canada's 'Ephemeral Monster: Canada's Multi-Headed Constitution,'" *Civil Religion in Political Thought: Its Perennial Questions and Enduring Relevance in North America*, Ronald Weed and John von Heyking, eds. (Washington, DC: Catholic University of America Press, 2010), 298–328 and "The Charter and Civil Religion," *Faith in Democracy?: Religion and Politics in Canada*, John F. Young and Boris DeWiel, eds. (Newcastle Upon Tyne: Cambridge Scholars Publishing, 2009), 36–60.

17 William Connolly, *The Augustinian Imperative: A Reflection on the Politics of Morality* (Newbury Park, CA: Sage, 1993), xvii; see also, Thomas Heilke, "On Being Ethical without Moral Sadism: Two Readings of Augustine and the Beginnings of the Anabaptist Revolution," in *Political Theory* 24 (August, 1996)3, 493–517.

18 Cf. Barry Cooper, *Alexander Kennedy Isbister: A Respectable Critic of the Honourable Company* (Ottawa: Carleton University Press, 1988), 49-69, 220–223, 283.

19 Barry Cooper, "Weaving A Work," in Ronald Beiner and Wayne Norman, eds., *Canadian Political Philosophy* (Oxford: Oxford University Press, 2000), 374–385.

20 Cooper, "Weaving," 383.

21 Eric Voegelin, *Order and History*, vol. 1, *Israel and Revelation* (Baton Rouge: Louisiana State University Press, 1956), ix. This phrase, along with a second explication of its meaning and an explanation of Voegelin's new interpretation of that meaning, is repeated in vol. 4, *The Ecumenic Age* ((Baton Rouge: Louisiana State University Press, 1974), 1–58. As a conceptual and methodological entrée into Cooper's work (and, of course, as fine exemplars of empirical political science done well), these Voegelinian pages repay a rereading.

22 See especially Thomas A. Spragens, Jr., *Understanding Political Theory* (New York: St. Martin's Press, 1976).

23 Cooper treats the products of such work with a certain degree of wry caution. Concerning his and his colleagues' work as young scholars, he writes, "We wrote mostly for other scholars on topics that only such oddballs could care about . . .". (Barry Cooper, *It's the Regime, Stupid! A Report from the Cowboy West on why Stephen Harper Matters* [Toronto: Key Porter Books, 2009], 244).

24 See Cooper, "Hunting and Political Philosophy: An Interpretation of the *Kynegetikos*," in *Philosophy, Literature, and Politics: Essays Honoring Ellis Sandoz*, Charles R. Embry and Barry Cooper, eds. (Columbia, MO: University of Missouri Press, 2005), 28–53 and *Suddenly There!: Twenty Years of Killing Time Around Southern Alberta, 1985–2005*, self-published book manuscript.

25 For a history of the title of Flanagan's contribution to this volume, see Cooper, *Regime*, 243–245.

26 Cooper and Peter Emberley, a contributor to this volume, translated and edited the

Strauss-Voegelin correspondence: *Faith and Political Philosophy: The Correspondence Between Leo Strauss and Eric Voegelin, 1934–1964* (Columbia: University of Missouri Press, 1993).

27   The phrase, which Cooper never uttered, but under which sentiment he conducted the seminar, is a piece of advice from Leo Strauss concerning the attitude one should take toward the craft of teaching political theory (Leo Strauss, *Liberalism Ancient and Modern* (Ithaca and London: Cornell University Press, 1989), 9). Voegelin makes a similar statement regarding the reading of great texts, which in this case are those of Shakespeare: "The interpretation of a literary work by a first-rate artist or philosopher must proceed on the assumption the man 'knew' what he was doing.... No adequate interpretation of a major work is possible, unless the interpreter assumes the role of the disciple who has everything to learn from the master" (Voegelin letter to Robert Heilman, July 24, 1956, in *Robert B. Heilman and Eric Voegelin: A Friendship in Letters, 1944–1984*, Charles R. Embry, ed. (Columbia: University of Missouri Press, 2004), 150).

28   Students could thus share vicariously the primal experience of hunting, of having the prey or insight appear, "suddenly there!" (*Suddenly There!*, 3). Cooper credits his friend and colleague, F. L. (Ted) Morton for articulating this symbol.

Chapter One

Legends of the Calgary School:

Their Guns, Their Dogs,

and the Women Who Love Them

Tom Flanagan

Barry Cooper is a formidable scholar, well known for his work in political philosophy, especially the study of Eric Voegelin, as well as for several influential books on Canadian politics. But Barry is not just an academic researcher; he has also been a significant participant in Canadian politics. Both as a scholar and a political player, he is often mentioned in the context of the so-called "Calgary School," a group of University of Calgary political scientists including, in addition to Barry, Rainer Knopff, F.L. "Ted" Morton, and me, and in a looser sense, the historian David Bercuson. Others have written about the Calgary School from the outside;[1] let me give an insider's view.

Building the Calgary School
The story begins in Durham, North Carolina, in September 1965, when Barry and I entered the political science graduate program at Duke University. Initially, Barry was chiefly interested in Canadian politics, which at Duke was categorized as part of comparative politics, while I wanted to become a political theorist. We got acquainted quickly, because we were assigned to share a carrel in the library. Because I was married, I was there only during the day, while Barry seemed virtually to live there.

Over time, we became personal friends and also developed some common academic interests. John Hallowell's courses in political philosophy caused Barry to join me as a theorist with Hallowell as supervisor, while I adopted Barry's interest in political parties and elections. We both took two courses in statistics taught by the mathematics department as well as Allan Kornberg's course in parties and elections, where we did our first voting-behaviour papers using computerized analysis—a big deal in 1966. We had to punch our SPSS commands onto IBM cards and leave them, together with the data cards, at a loading station, where they were picked up and taken by truck to the tri-university computing lab serving Duke, the University of North Carolina, and North Carolina State. If you were lucky, you got your printout back about a week later. But if you had made even one error in syntax, say substituting a comma for a period, your run would be aborted, and you would have to start over. It was a miracle that anything got done, but somehow, with Al Kornberg's help, we both produced publishable papers.[2]

In the fall of 1967, Barry and I both went to Europe. He went to Paris to research his doctoral dissertation on Maurice Merleau-Ponty, while I went to Berlin, where I had an exchange fellowship to study for a year at the Free University of Berlin. In the spring of 1968, I received a letter offering me a tenure-track job teaching political science at the University of Calgary. Having grown up in the eastern United States and never having travelled west of the Mississippi, I had never heard of Calgary. So I went to the reference room at the university, took an atlas off the shelf, opened it to Canada, and eventually found Calgary on the map. Intrigued by the city's location close to the Rocky Mountains, I accepted the offer. The only other offer I had at the time was from the University of Texas in Austin. It's a great university, but I don't like hot weather, and I figured Calgary would be a lot cooler. If I'd only known how much colder! My acceptance of a job in Calgary was the first step toward formation of the Calgary School.

The second step occurred in 1978 with the arrival of Rainer Knopff. Rainer had done his PhD at the University of Toronto under Peter Russell, specializing in Canadian political thought but also studying judicial process with Russell and political philosophy under the prominent Straussians Allan Bloom and Walter Berns. Rainer was recruited by our then Head of Political Science, Anthony Parel, a former Jesuit priest and political theorist with interests as diverse as Aquinas, Machiavelli, and Gandhi. Our department was losing its only constitutional law specialist, and Tony liked Rainer's combination of judicial process and political philosophy and thought that he could fill the void in constitutional law. I had little to do with this except that, as a member of the Staff Affairs Committee, I supported bringing Rainer to Calgary; I had previously met him at a conference and been favourably impressed.

The third step—a double step, in fact—occurred in 1981, when Barry Cooper and Ted Morton came to Calgary. Barry's first teaching job had been at Bishop's University in Lennoxville, Quebec, after which he had moved to York University in Toronto. But, having grown up in Vancouver and spent many youthful summers in Alberta, Barry dreamed of coming back to the West. Tony learned about Barry's availability and determined to bring him to Calgary, with tenure, to build up our political theory subfield. Ted Morton had been a classmate of Rainer Knopff in the Ph.D. program at the University of Toronto, with the same type of intellectual formation under Peter Russell, Allan Bloom, and Walter Berns. He was now teaching at Assumption College, a small liberal-arts institution in Worcester, Massachusetts. Ted was interested in joining a bigger university where there would be more opportunities for research and working with graduate students; and, originally from Wyoming, he also liked the idea of returning to the West. Tony Parel wanted Ted to teach American politics and also help Rainer develop our public-law offerings. We were one of only a few Canadian political science departments doing much in judicial process at that time, and Tony thought it could become one of our comparative advantages, particularly when taught philosophically, as both Rainer and Ted approached it.

Barry, Rainer, Ted, and I quickly became good friends (of course, Barry and I had been friends since graduate school, as had Rainer and Ted). We found we had a great deal in common, even apart from academic life. We all liked hiking, skiing, fishing, and hunting (count me out on the hunting), so we spent a lot of time together in the outdoors, where we would "pass the time pleasantly, speaking of laws," as Plato wrote in *The Laws*.[3] Although we were all more or less conservative, we had arrived at that position by somewhat different routes. Rainer and Ted had had some Straussian influence, but their interest in the judicial process and constitutional law kept them outside of the Straussian academic coterie. Barry and I had been schooled in the thought of Eric Voegelin, though I moved on to become a Hayekian in 1977, after I read *The Constitution of Liberty* (I now label my unique synthesis of Voegelin and Hayek "neo-Austrian").

Neither Barry nor I have ever been Straussians. Barry has a deeper interest in Strauss than I do and has edited the correspondence between Leo Strauss and Eric Voegelin, but that does not make him a Straussian.[4] I tried to read several of Strauss's books when I was a graduate student, but I could never finish them. The only one that made much sense to me was his early work on Spinoza, where he argued, as have other historians, that Spinoza had to engage in "Aesopian" writing because he lived in danger of persecution.[5] I made use of Strauss's insight on Aesopian writing when I wrote my own MA thesis on Spinoza, but I have never agreed with turning it into a general interpretive principle of political philosophy.

This is of some significance, because one of the most durable legends about the Calgary School is that we indoctrinated our prize student, Stephen Harper, in Straussianism, and that he is now following a secret Straussian path (the "Hidden Agenda") toward regime change in Canada.[6] But in fact Harper, who majored in economics, not political science, at the University of Calgary, took no courses from members of the Calgary School; and even if he had, he would not have encountered any Straussian influences there.

Das Bercuson Problem

The position of David Bercuson in this tableau requires additional explanation. David, who came to the University of Calgary in 1970, had studied labour history at the University of Toronto under Ken McNaught and Ramsay Cook. Thus, his intellectual background was liberal and social democratic, but not Marxist. Although he continued to pursue labour history for another decade and a half after coming here, he became increasingly disenchanted with the Marxist political correctness prevailing in Canadian labour history and decided to switch his scholarship to the fields of foreign policy and military history. Living in Calgary also gradually made him more economically conservative, to the point where he became a Progressive Conservative around the time Joe Clark became leader of the party.

David started a long collaboration with Barry Cooper in early 1990, proposing the book that became *Deconfederation*.[7] David didn't know Barry well at that point but thought that their views on Quebec would be similar. After the success of that book, the two did a great deal of work together in the 1990s, including another book, *Derailed*;[8] reports presenting historical and social science evidence in several lawsuits; and jointly written columns in the *Calgary Sun, Globe and Mail,* and *Calgary Herald.* Their collaboration led Barry to become interested in military issues, so that he is now teaching courses and supervising graduate students in the Centre for Military and Strategic Studies that Bercuson directs, and also publishing in the field of security studies as well as political philosophy.

Although David has had a long and successful collaboration with Barry, he isn't part of the Calgary School in quite the same sense as the rest of us. He is a historian, not a political scientist, and he teaches in a different department. His cooperative academic projects have been only with Cooper, not with other members of the Calgary School. Barry, David, and I go on an annual summer fishing trip together, but in other respects David mainly socializes with a different group of people. Most importantly, his political views are not identical with the rest of the Calgary School. Although a strong economic and foreign policy conservative, he sees himself as a social liberal—e.g., pro-choice on abortion, and in favour of legalizing gay marriage. Thus, his political trajectory has often been different from that of the rest of us. Though he later became a supporter of Stephen Harper, he was still working to defeat Harper in Calgary West in 1993 because of his friendship with the incumbent MP, Progressive Conservative Jim Hawkes. When the rest of us were supporting Ralph Klein, David was working for Liberal Leader Laurence Decore (actually, Decore was more conservative on many issues than Klein, but the rest of us could never bring ourselves to support the Liberal brand, even provincially).

Overall, then, David is not a member of the Calgary School *comme les autres*. His cooperation with Cooper has been extremely important, but in other respects he moves in his own orbit.

The 1980s: Building Academic Reputations

Broadly speaking, the 1980s were years of academic research for the Calgary School. Our writings did not initially attract much media attention, but we were working on politically charged topics that would eventually have an impact on public opinion. Rainer and Ted's research on how the Canadian Charter of Rights and Freedoms was being interpreted in the courts led to many articles as well as their influential books *Charter Politics* (1992) and *The Charter Revolution and the Court Party* (2000).[9] Rainer and Ted became perhaps the best-known critics of judicial activism in Canada and engaged in many debates with their opponents, both in academic forums and in the media. I also worked in the 1980s with Rainer on a study of human rights commissions in Canada. We published a book and several academic articles, but our work had no public impact.[10] The time wasn't right, and we weren't ready to cut through the hagiography surrounding human rights in Canada. Fortunately, one of our students, Ezra Levant, was able to accomplish what we could not. His best-selling book *Shakedown!* (2009) threw a scare into the human-rights establishment and promoted a round of legislative change that is still unfolding in both provincial and federal jurisdictions.[11] In the 1980s, Rainer and I had arrived at most of the same criticisms that Ezra has made of human rights commissions—their overly broad mandate, unfair procedures, and outrageously one-sided funding of complaints—but we didn't yet know how to drive an issue onto the public agenda, whereas Ezra is a promotional genius.

Apart from my collaboration with Rainer, most of my work in the 1980s was focused on Louis Riel and the Métis. I finished my biography of Riel, worked on the collected edition of his writings, and published a book debunking his role as hero of the North-West Rebellion.[12] My work on Riel led the Department of Justice to hire me as a historical consultant in the Manitoba Métis Federation land claims case. The case did not actually come to trial until 2006, but my book *Métis Lands in Manitoba* contained the evidence that, when I presented it in court as an expert witness, caused the Métis claims to be rejected.[13] I also served as Head of the Political Science Department in the years 1982-87, which kept my energies focused on university life.

Barry Cooper, during the 1980s, published mainly on topics in political philosophy, including the thought of Michel Foucault, Eric Voegelin, and George Grant. He wrote relatively little on contemporary Canadian politics, but did publish a biography of Alexander Kennedy Isbister, a half-breed son of the Rupert's Land fur trade who returned to England to become a Victorian gentleman, noted educator, and critic of the Hudson's Bay Company.[14] Though not as well-known as it deserves to be, Cooper's biography of Isbister illustrates the tremendous breadth of the Métis experience and the difficulty of pigeon-holing the Métis in social categories.

Two Decades of Political Activism

The Calgary School started to make a more visible impact on Canadian politics in the 1990s. They did this mainly as individuals rather than as a group, although they were all motivated by what Preston Manning used to call the "triple crisis" that Canada went through in the late 1980s and early 1990s:

* The constitutional crisis—high stakes negotiations over the constitution (the Meech Lake and Charlottetown Accords) accompanied by threats of separation by Quebec;
* The economic crisis—the accumulation of public debt due to uncontrolled federal deficit spending, accompanied by persistently high unemployment;
* The political crisis—loss of confidence in elected politicians, the disintegration of the Progressive Conservative Party of Canada, and the

rise of new federal political parties (Reform Party of Canada, Bloc Québécois).

In spite of common concerns, the members of the Calgary School became active in politics in individual and sometimes contradictory ways, thus refuting the persistent myth that they possess a coordinated group strategy for taking over Canadian politics.

Bercuson and Cooper made the biggest initial splash in 1991 when they published *Deconfederation,* arguing that Canada would be better off without Quebec. By speaking the previously unspeakable in this widely discussed book, they helped to firm up public opinion against the Charlottetown Accord, whose proponents were trying to sell it with apocalyptic arguments about the disintegration of Canada. Such arguments would hardly work with voters who believed that Canada would be better off without never-ending and ever-more-expensive demands from Quebec.

Bercuson and Cooper continued to write about politics for a broad public audience. In 1994 they published *Derailed,* a timely plea for Canada to return to its historic tradition of fiscal responsibility and balanced budgets. Around the same time, they started writing op-eds together, first for the *Calgary Sun,* later for the *Globe and Mail,* and finally for the *Calgary Herald.* Bercuson pulled out of the op-ed collaboration after a business dispute with the *Herald,* but he still writes occasional columns for the *Globe and Mail,* while Cooper continues to write for the *Herald.*

Both also became players in the world of think tanks. Cooper originally thought of founding his own organization in Calgary, tentatively entitled the Chinook Institute, but settled for becoming the director of the Fraser Institute's office in Calgary. While continuing to teach at the university, he also worked for the Fraser Institute for six years until an unfortunate dispute with Fraser Institute President Mike Walker led to his departure in 2005.[15] While working for Fraser, Barry took a special interest in climate change, inviting the Danish climate skeptic Bjorn Lomborg to speak in Calgary and later working with the Friends of Science to counter climate-change hysteria.

After serving a term as Dean of Graduate Studies at the University of Calgary, Bercuson became director of the university's Centre for Strategic and Military Studies, a node in the network of institutes funded by the Department of National Defence. He was also the prime mover in creating the Canadian Defence and Foreign Affairs Institute in 2002, an organization that specializes in commissioning research and publicizing it in the media through interviews and op-eds.[16] For two decades, David and Barry have worked tirelessly to push public opinion in the direction of fiscal responsibility, a strong national defence, close cooperation with our allies, resistance to Quebec separatism, and fair treatment for Western Canada

Meanwhile, I took a more circuitous path, going to work in early 1991 as a senior member of Preston Manning's Reform Party staff. I stayed there until I resigned my paid responsibilities at the end of 1992 and was fired from my remaining advisory role in the middle of 1993. The experience, described at length in my book *Waiting for the Wave,* was not entirely happy, because I became convinced that Manning-style populism was working at cross-purposes with the more conventional conservatism that I espoused.[17] That's what I thought then; looking back on it twenty years later, I still think I was partly right, but I also see that I was politically naïve and not ready for the compromises of practical politics.[18]

David and Barry's *Deconfederation*, plus Rainer and Ted's critique of judicial activism, plus my work with Reform, led to our group being characterized as the Calgary School by the American political scientist David Rovinsky.[19] Even earlier recognition in the media had come in 1992, when Jeffrey Simpson published a column in the *Globe and Mail* calling us the "Calgary mafia" and pointing to our influence, either direct or indirect, on the Reform Party.[20] Even though Simpson was careful to focus on the five of us and not to characterize the entire Department of Political Science, our colleagues in the department chose to read it that way and wrote a letter to the *Globe* emphasizing their lack of connection with the Reform Party. Over the years, they have had to develop thicker skins as we kept on writing and talking and attracting more publicity. However, their reaction does illustrate an important point. The Calgary School has never been more than a small part of the department of political science at the University of Calgary; the rarity of conservatives in academic institutions garners extra media attention when a small group of conservatives does get together. It's a man-bites-dog story.

In a longer-term perspective, perhaps the most important aspect of my time with the Reform Party was getting acquainted with Stephen Harper, who was then Chief Policy Officer. Contrary to what has often been written, Stephen had never been my student, nor indeed studied with any members of the Calgary School. We first met him in late 1990, when he would accompany Preston Manning to campus for "egghead lunches" with faculty members and graduate students who were sympathetic with, or at least interested in, the Reform Party. Stephen and I grew closer in fall 1992, when we were both concerned with the particular manner in which Preston was opposing the Charlottetown Accord. We kept in touch afterwards, as I went back to the University of Calgary and Stephen went on to become the Reform MP for Calgary-West and then President of the National Citizens Coalition. We collaborated on several writing projects, particularly on a plan for reuniting the shattered remains of the Mulroney coalition, which served as a virtual roadmap for Harper to merge the Canadian Alliance with the Progressive Conservatives in 2003 and defeat the Liberals in the 2006 election.[21]

As described in my book *Harper's Team,* I devoted about four years to helping Stephen get re-launched in federal politics.[22] I managed his leadership campaign against Stockwell Day to get control of the Canadian Alliance, then served for a year as his chief of staff while he was Leader of the Opposition in Parliament. I also managed his campaign against Belinda Stronach and Tony Clement for leadership of the merged Conservative Party of Canada, as well as the 2004 Conservative election campaign, in which we did not win but set the stage for a subsequent victory by bringing Paul Martin's Liberals down to a minority. After laying the groundwork for the next campaign, I went back to the university in 2005, but returned to the war room as senior communications adviser in the successful 2005-06 campaign, which finally brought the Conservatives to power.

My role working for Harper was different than what one might expect for a career academic. I had almost nothing to do with policy, strategy, and communications; Stephen effectively functioned as his own chief of staff in those areas. My remit was organization and management. I raised money, recruited people, and negotiated contracts with suppliers; I made sure all our trains ran on time. Stephen, for example, would decide what went in the campaign platform; I would make sure it got printed on time in an attractive format and in understandable English. Stephen would decide what to say during the campaign leader's tour; I made sure we had a jet, busses, campaign venues, and staff to organize all the events.

My legacy to the Conservative Party has nothing to do with policy. Rather, I take great pride in having helped build what Liberal Leader Michael Ignatieff has called "the toughest and most ruthless machine in Canadian politics."[23] You won't implement many policies unless you can form the government, and in a democracy that means defeating your opponents at election time. Indeed, the Conservatives, like the Liberals, are sometimes tough and even nasty in their attacks on opponents; but the secret of Conservative success is effective grassroots fundraising based on massive Voter ID and GOTV efforts. That's what raises the money to pay for negative ads, when they are needed.

I'm no longer involved in practical politics at the federal level, because Stephen Harper regarded publication of *Harper's Team* as a violation of confidentiality. It was not that the book was critical of him (it wasn't); he would have regarded any book as anathema. As a consequence, I've been shut out of playing any role in the Conservative government that I worked so hard to bring to power. But I shouldn't complain; I knew Stephen was obsessive about secrecy and that he wouldn't like the idea of my publishing a book about the campaigns I managed for him.

I also developed a presence in the media with interviews and op-eds, starting shortly after I left the employment of the Reform Party. Although I have never tried to keep count, I would estimate that I have been reported somewhere in the media about two hundred times a year since the mid-1990s (except for the four years when I went dark as Stephen Harper's campaign manager). At the time of writing, I publish a monthly column in the *Globe and Mail* and appear twice a week with Evan Solomon on CBC Newsnet's "Power and Politics" show. Now that I am exiled from federal politics, my presence in the media gives me a platform for contributing to public discussion, even if I can't affect public policy directly.

Also, my research has had some impact on public discussion of aboriginal issues in Canada. *First Nations? Second Thoughts* (2000) was a polemical book, challenging what I called the "aboriginal orthodoxy" deriving from the Report of the Royal Commission on Aboriginal Affairs.[24] It gored sacred cows right and left, including aboriginal self-government, land claims, and treaty rights. It won two prizes[25] and was on the *National Post* non-fiction Canadian best-seller list for eleven weeks in summer 2000. It was also vociferously denounced by almost every native leader from Phil Fontaine on down. With that level of controversy, it garnered an avalanche of media.

The book helped stiffen the resistance against aboriginal demands for more sympathy, more land, more jurisdictions, and more money without accountability. Certain arguments in the book, e.g., that band councils have an inherent trend to "family factionalism," abetted by representation without taxation, had rarely been made in public before but have now become conventional wisdom among conservatives, especially in the *National Post,* which devotes a lot of editorial attention to aboriginal affairs. At first, media accounts referenced my book, but gradually my arguments have become familiar enough that the author no longer needs to be identified—a sign that the ideas are making some headway in public opinion.

My most recent book, *Beyond the Indian Act,* is a positive attempt to bring about legislative change in the form of a proposed *First Nations Property Ownership Act,* which would allow First Nations to take over ownership of their lands from the federal Crown and to create individual titles in fee simple on as much or as little of their land as they wished.[26] Both stages of reform would be completely voluntary. The idea of private property for First Nations is a theoretically radical departure from the status quo, made incremental in practice by a voluntary opt-in approach.

Writing by myself, I could never hope to achieve legislative change; but *Beyond the Indian Act* is a collaborative effort, especially with Manny Jules, former chief of the Kamloops band and head of the First Nations Tax Commission, who contributed the "Foreword" to the book and also designed the cover. Jules virtually created the concept of voluntary, First-Nations-led legislation, beginning with the "Kamloops Amendment" of 1988, which for the first time authorized Indian bands to levy property taxes on reserve leaseholds.[27] *Beyond the Indian Act* wraps an academic gown around ideas that Jules has been developing for years. The book addresses public opinion, while Jules will work at finding First Nations to request the legislation, so that the government will be willing to introduce it into Parliament. Initial indications are positive, but we won't know for several years whether we will succeed in getting the legislation passed.

Of our group, Ted Morton has had by far the most visible political career, perhaps because both his father and his maternal grandfather were elected politicians in the United States. Ted's first venture into Canadian elective politics came in the 1988 Alberta advisory senatorial election, when he ran as a Reform candidate and finished second behind another Reformer, Bert Brown. Tiring of the wait for a Senate appointment by a Liberal government that did not recognize the legitimacy of the Alberta advisory process, Ted got elected as a Progressive Conservative candidate for the Alberta legislature in 2004. He then ran in the 2006 Alberta Progressive Conservative leadership race, finishing second to Jim Dinning on the first ballot and third behind Ed Stelmach and Dinning on the second ballot. He appealed particularly to the party's right wing, especially to members who were on the cusp between the PCs and the further-right Wildrose Alliance.

Premier Stelmach appointed Ted to the cabinet as Minister of Sustainable Resources. His showing in the leadership race might have justified a more important portfolio, but Ted was happy in Sustainable Resources because it included jurisdiction over hunting and fishing. We used to jokingly call him the "Minister of Ducks and Deer." Then the Wildrose Alliance, which won no seats in the 2008 election, surged in popular opinion as the recession took hold in Alberta and Wildrose selected an attractive new leader, Danielle Smith. In January 2010, Stelmach appointed Ted Minister of Finance in an obvious attempt to fend off the Wildrose challenge. That arrangement, however, only worked for about a year. Ted resigned as Minister of Finance when Stelmach started to back out of their agreement to put forth a balanced budget. Ted's resignation made Stelmach's own position untenable, so he too resigned, thereby opening up the prospect of a new leadership race in 2011.

Ted entered that race but finished fourth on the first ballot, so he did not get to carry on to the second ballot, which was ultimately won by Alison Redford. Ted then ran for re-election in the general election of spring 2012. The PC party was successful in winning a majority of seats, but Ted himself was defeated by the Wildrose candidate in his riding (full disclosure: I managed the Wildrose provincial campaign). Ted is now back at the university, and the Calgary School is no longer rent by internal political divisions-a reasonably happy ending, though Ted never got to live out his dream of becoming premier and steering Alberta in a more conservative direction.

Of all the Calgary School, Rainer Knopff has had the least involvement in politics. For much of the last two decades, he was Associate Dean of Research for Social Sciences and then Associate Vice-President of Research for the University of Calgary, which left him little time for politics. However, he has done a couple of quiet things behind the scenes. In 1993-95, he was on the committee to redraw federal constituency boundaries for Alberta; and in 2010 he was on the advisory committee that recommended names from among which the Prime Minister selected David Johnston as the next Governor-General.

Rainer was also one of the signatories of the notorious "Alberta Agenda" or "Firewall" letter published in the *National Post* early 2001. The other signatories were Stephen Harper, President of the National Citizens Coalition; Andy Crooks, a Calgary lawyer and President of the Canadian Taxpayers Federation; Ken Boessenkool, a consulting economist in Calgary; and three members of the Calgary School—Rainer Knopff, Ted

Morton, and me. The whole thing was Harper's idea; it was part of a long-term strategy he was developing to force the federal government back into a more narrowly circumscribed sphere of constitutional jurisdiction. He asked me to coordinate the writing, so I held the pen while I asked the others for ideas. The letter is printed here because it represents the mind of the Calgary School when speaking freely outside the constraints of political organizations—market-oriented, pro-Alberta, suspicious of Eastern domination, and open to political reform.

Dear Premier Klein:

During and since the recent federal election, we have been among a large number of Albertans discussing the future of our province. We are not dismayed by the outcome of the election so much as by the strategy employed by the current federal government to secure its re-election. In our view, the Chretien government undertook a series of attacks not merely designed to defeat its partisan opponents, but to marginalize Alberta and Albertans within Canada's political system.

One well-documented incident was the attack against Alberta's health care system. To your credit, you vehemently protested the unprecedented attack ads that the federal government launched against Alberta's policies—policies the Prime Minister had previously found no fault with.

However, while your protest was necessary and appreciated by Albertans, we believe that it is not enough to respond only with protests. If the government in Ottawa concludes that Alberta is a soft target, we will be subjected to much worse than dishonest television ads. The Prime Minister has already signaled as much by announcing his so-called "tough love" campaign for the West.

We believe the time has come for Albertans to take greater charge of our own future. This means resuming control of the powers that we possess under the constitution of Canada but that we have allowed the federal government to exercise. Intelligent use of these powers will help Alberta build a prosperous future in spite of a misguided and increasingly hostile government in Ottawa.

Under the heading of the "Alberta Agenda," we propose that our province move forward on the following fronts:

* Withdraw from the Canada Pension Plan to create an Alberta Pension Plan offering the same benefits at lower cost while giving Alberta

control over the investment fund. Pensions are a provincial responsibility under section 94A of the Constitution Act. 1867; and the legislation setting up the Canada Pension Plan permits a province to run its own plan, as Quebec has done from the beginning. If Quebec can do it, why not Alberta?

* Collect our own revenue from personal income tax, as we already do for corporate income tax. Now that your government has made the historic innovation of the single-rate personal income tax, there is no reason to have Ottawa collect our revenue. Any incremental cost of collecting our own personal income tax would be far outweighed by the policy flexibility that Alberta would gain, as Quebec's experience has shown.

* Start preparing now to let the contract with the RCMP run out in 2012 and create an Alberta Provincial Police Force. Alberta is a major province. Like the other major provinces of Ontario and Quebec, we should have our own provincial police force. We have no doubt that Alberta can run a more efficient and effective police force than Ottawa can – one that will not be misused as a laboratory for experiments in social engineering.

* Resume provincial responsibility for health-care policy. If Ottawa objects to provincial policy, fight in the courts. If we lose, we can afford the financial penalties that Ottawa may try to impose under the Canada Health Act. Albertans deserve better than the long waiting periods and technological backwardness that are rapidly coming to characterize Canadian medicine. Alberta should also argue that each province should raise its own revenue for health care – i.e., replace Canada Health and Social Transfer cash with tax points as Quebec has argued for many years. Poorer provinces would continue to rely on Equalization to ensure they have adequate revenues.

* Use section 88 of the Supreme Court's decision in the Quebec Secession Reference to force Senate reform back onto the national agenda. Our reading of that decision is that the federal government and other provinces must seriously consider a proposal for constitutional reform endorsed by "a clear majority on a clear question" in a provincial referendum. You acted decisively once before to hold a senatorial election. Now is the time to drive the issue further.

All of these steps can be taken using the constitutional powers that Alberta now possesses. In addition, we believe it is imperative for you to take all possible political and legal measures to reduce the financial drain on Alberta caused by Canada's tax-and-transfer system. The most recent Alberta Treasury estimates are that Albertans transfer $2,600 per capita annually to other Canadians, for a total outflow from our province approaching $8 billion a year. The same federal politicians who accuse us of not sharing their "Canadian values" have no compunction about appropriating our Canadian dollars to buy votes elsewhere in the country.

Mr. Premier, we acknowledge the constructive reforms that your government made in the 1990s—balancing the budget, paying down the provincial debt, privatizing government services, getting Albertans off welfare and into jobs, introducing a single-rate tax, pulling government out of the business of subsidizing business, and many other beneficial changes. But no government can rest on its laurels. As economic slowdown, and perhaps even recession, threatens North America, the government in Ottawa will be tempted to take advantage of Alberta's prosperity, to redistribute income from Alberta to residents of other provinces in order to keep itself in power. It is imperative to take the initiative, to build firewalls around Alberta, to limit the extent to which an aggressive and hostile federal government can encroach upon legitimate provincial jurisdiction.

Once Alberta's position is secured, only our imagination will limit the prospects for extending the reform agenda that your government undertook eight years ago. To cite only a few examples, lower taxes will unleash the energies of the private sector, easing conditions for Charter Schools will help individual freedom and improve public education, and greater use of the referendum and initiative will bring Albertans into closer touch with their own government.

The precondition for the success of this Alberta Agenda is the exercise of all our legitimate provincial jurisdictions under the constitution of Canada. Starting to act now will secure the future for all Albertans.

Sincerely yours,
Stephen HARPER, President, National Citizens' Coalition;
Tom FLANAGAN, professor of political science and former Director of Research, Reform Party of Canada;
Ted MORTON, professor of political science and Alberta Senator-elect;
Rainer KNOPFF, professor of political science;
Andrew CROOKS, chairman, Canadian Taxpayers Federation;
Ken BOESSENKOOL, former policy adviser to Stockwell Day, Treasurer of Alberta.

* This letter represents the personal views of its authors and not those of any organizations with which they are or have been connected.[28]

Comments

This little historical sketch shows something important about the Calgary School: we are a group of more or less like-minded academics, but not in any sense conspiratorial or even organized. We may have a common outlook, but not a common agenda. Two or more of us sometimes collaborate on particular projects, but basically we pursue our own careers, both academic and political, as individuals. As researchers and writers, we have contributed to the growth of a conservative movement in Canada, but we did not create and do not direct that movement.

The rationalism of the modern left leads leftist observers to overstate the significance of abstract ideas. Members of the Calgary School have become prominent in politics because, for other reasons, Calgary is the spiritual centre of the conservative movement in Canada. Preston Manning had to make his *hejira* from Edmonton to Calgary in order to build the Reform Party, because there were so many resources, both financial and human, to draw on in this city. For the same reason, the National Citizens Coalition had an office here while David Sommerville and Stephen Harper were presidents; and the Fraser Institute and the Frontier Centre have both set up offices, because there is so much support for conservative causes. The two most recent presidents of the Canadian Taxpayers Federation, Andy Crooks and Michael Binnion, are also Calgarians, even though the CTF head office is in Regina. The Canadian Defence and Foreign Affairs Institute is also here, partly because of David Bercuson and partly because of the financial support he can raise in Calgary.

Karl Marx would have understood better than modern leftists that the Calgary School is an intellectual reflex of the conservative movement. The city of Calgary provides a privileged position for the members of the Calgary School to meet and work together with the conservative political and business leaders who also call Calgary home. While the Calgary School did not provide an agenda for any of the political movements that have radiated outwards from Calgary—Preston Manning's Reform Party, Ralph Klein's revolution within the Alberta Progressive Conservatives, Stockwell Day's Canadian Alliance, Stephen Harper's Conservative Party of Canada, and Danielle Smith's Wildrose Alliance—members of the Calgary School, as individuals, have associated themselves with these movements, sometimes studying and writing about them, sometimes offering help as consultants, sometimes actually entering their employment.

It is important to emphasize that the political creativity has come mainly from the political and business leaders who have organized and funded all these movements, and the Calgarians and Albertans who have joined them. As researchers and writers, the members of the Calgary School have supported these movements, written about them, and helped to explain them to the public. But as thinkers we were not the prime movers. As Goethe wrote, *"Am Anfang war die Tat"* ("In the beginning was the act"), thus correcting the Gospel of John ("In the beginning was the Word").[29]

None of that, however, diminishes the importance of the intellectual sphere. Political movements cannot succeed in the long run without coherent ideas to guide their action. And the Calgary School has been in the forefront, through both academic and popular writings, in developing positions on some of the most controversial issues of the day. They have repeatedly challenged the orthodoxy and political correctness of the left in areas such as:

*Judicial activism (Knopff and Morton)
* Abortion (Morton)
* Gay marriage (Morton)
* Human rights (Knopff and Flanagan)
* Climate change (Cooper)
* Quebec (Cooper and Bercuson)
* Aboriginal rights (Flanagan)
* National defence (Bercuson)
* Fiscal responsibility (all)

Conservative political organizations and movements have flourished in the intellectual climate that the Calgary School has helped to create.

The Future of the Calgary School

All members of the Calgary School are now in their 60s, and retirements from classroom teaching will come gradually over the next few years. Of course, even after retirement, an academic may remain connected to his university as a professor emeritus, engaged in some combination of research, supervision of graduate students, consulting, and appearances in the media. The Calgary School, therefore, may carry on for another decade or so, but its institutional presence will gradually diminish. Its coalescence was largely an accident, and the University of Calgary will not, indeed should not, try to perpetuate it; for university hiring ought to be based on academic merit, not political convictions.

The real future of the Calgary School, therefore, lies in the careers of its students. The University of Calgary has never been a major centre of graduate education like, say, the University of Toronto; so the members of the Calgary School have not trained a large number of Ph.D.s who, while teaching at other universities, constitute a tight network like the followers of Eric Voegelin or Leo Strauss. But precisely because Calgary's Ph.D. program has been relatively small, the members of the Calgary School have had intense relationships with many of their BA and MA students. Some of these students, though they have gone on to study for the Ph.D. elsewhere, have kept up a close relationship with their Calgary School mentors and with other students they met when they studied here. Some have become professors at other universities; others have gone into politics, the media, law, and the civil service. There exists, therefore, a sort of loose network of Calgary School alumni, including several of the contributors to this volume, who are today making their own mark in Canadian public life. To mention only a few of the most prominent:

* Chris Manfredi, Professor of Political Science and Dean of Arts at McGill, now a senior figure in the study of the Canadian judicial process;
* Ian Brodie, former Chief of Staff to Prime Minister Stephen Harper;
* Ray Novak, Chief of Staff to Prime Minister Harper;
* Danielle Smith, Leader of the Wildrose Party of Alberta;
* Ezra Levant, *Sun* newspapers columnist and author of the bestselling books *Shakedown!* and *Ethical Oil*;
* Mark Milke, director of the Fraser Institute's Alberta Program and frequent columnist in the *Calgary Herald* and other newspapers;
* Rob Roach, director of research at the Canada West Foundation.

These and all our other students are the true legacy of the Calgary School. Though they share some common background through having studied with us, they are not a cabal or a coterie or a movement; they are individuals following their own paths. And I am sure they are mindful of Nietzsche's words: "You badly repay your teacher if you always remain the student."[30]

Endnotes

1   Paul Mitchinson, "Calgary Neo-Cons Hunt Controversy," *National Post* (July 22, 2000); John Ibbitson, "Educating Stephen," *Globe and Mail* (June 26, 2004); Marci McDonald, "The Man behind Stephen Harper," *The Walrus* (October, 2004), pp. 34–49; Peter Foster, "School for Paranoia: The Not-So-Scary School behind Stephen Harper," *National Post* (January 28, 2006); Frédéric Boily, ed., *Stephen Harper: De l'Ecole de Calgary au Parti conservateur: les nouveaux visages du conservatisme canadien* (Québec: Les Presses le l'Université Laval, 2007). Links to all the media articles (but not Boily's book) can be found at http://poli.ucalgary.ca/knopff/node/22.

2   Allan Kornberg, Thomas Flanagan, and George Watson, "The Goldwater Candidacy, Right-Wing Conservatism, and the 'Old Fashioned' Americans," *Australian Journal of Politics and History* 13 (1967), pp. 323–330; Barry Cooper and Allan Kornberg, "Procedural Changes in The Canadian House of Commons: Some Reflections," *Journal of Constitutional and Parliamentary Studies*, 2 (1968): 118.

3   Plato, *Laws*, 625.

4   Barry Cooper and Peter Emberley, eds., *Faith and Political Philosophy: The Correspondence between Leo Strauss and Eric Voegelin, 1934–1964* (Columbus, MO: University of Missouri Press, 2004).

5   Leo Strauss, *Die Religionskritik Spinozas* (Berlin: Akademie für die Wissenschaft des Judentums, 1930).

6   Lawrence Martin, *Harperland: The Politics of Control* (Toronto: Viking Canada, 2010), pp. 123–125.

7   David Jay Bercuson and Barry Cooper, *Deconfederation: Canada without Quebec* (Toronto: Key Porter, 1991).

8   David Jay Bercuson and Barry Cooper, *Derailed: The Betrayal of the National Dream* (Toronto: Key Porter, 2004).

9   Rainer Knopff and F.L. Morton, *Charter Politics* (Scarborough, ON: Nelson Canada, 1992): F.L. Morton and Rainer Knopff, *The Charter Revolution and the Court Party* (Peterborough, ON: Broadview Press, 2000). The latter book was a runner-up in the competition for the Donner Prize in 2001, the year that my own book *First Nations? Second Thoughts* won the first prize.

10 Rainer Knopff, *Human Rights and Social Technology* (Ottawa: Carleton University Press, 1989), with Thomas Flanagan.

11 Ezra Levant, *Shakedown! How Our Government is Undermining Democracy in the Name of Human Rights* (Toronto: McClelland & Stewart, 2009).

12 Thomas Flanagan, *Louis "David" Riel: "Prophet of the New World,"* 2nd ed. (Toronto: University of Toronto Press, 1996; first ed. 1979); *Riel and the Rebellion: 1885 Reconsidered,* 2nd ed. (Toronto: University of Toronto Press, 2000; first edition 1983): *The Collected Writings of Louis Riel*, with G.F.G. Stanley, Gilles Martel, Glen Campbell, Raymond Huel (Edmonton: University of Alberta Press, 1985).

13 Thomas Flanagan, *Métis Lands in Manitoba* (Calgary: University of Calgary Press, 1991); *Manitoba Métis Federation et al. v. Canada and Manitoba*, 2007 MBQB 293.

14 Barry Cooper, *Alexander Kennedy Isbister: A Respectable Critic of the Honourable Company* (Ottawa: Carleton University Press, 1988).

15 Barry Cooper, *It's the Regime, Stupid! A Report from the Cowboy West on Why Stephen Harper Matters* (Toronto: Key Porter, 2009), pp. 247–256.

16 http://www.cdfai.org.

17 Tom Flanagan, *Waiting for the Wave: The Reform Party and Preston Manning* (Toronto: Stoddart, 1996).

18 See the second edition, *Waiting for the Wave: The Reform Party and the Conservative Movement* (Montreal: McGill-Queen's University Press, 2009), pp. 201–216.

19 David J. Rovinsky, "The Ascendancy of Western Canada in Canadian Policymaking," *Policy Papers on the Americas*, Volume IX, Study 2 (February 16, 1998), http://csis.org/files/media/csis/pubs/1998_rovinsky.pdf.

20 Jeffrey Simpson, "That's not a machine gun in the violin case, it's a political manifesto," *Globe and Mail* (January 29, 1992), http://poli.ucalgary.ca/knopff/sites/poli.ucalgary.ca.knopff/files/MachineGunSimpson.pdf.

21 Stephen Harper and Tom Flanagan, "Our Benign Dictatorship," *The Next City* (January 1997), pp. 35–40, 54–57; "Conservative Politics in Canada: Past, Present, and Future," in William Gairdner, ed., *After Liberalism* (Toronto: Stoddart, 1998), pp. 168–92.

22 Tom Flanagan, *Harper's Team: Behind the Scenes in the Conservative Rise to Power,* 2nd ed. (Montreal: McGill-Queen's University Press, 2009; first edition 2007).

23 David Akin, "Harper, Ignatieff lay out election themes" (August 31, 2010), http://cnews.canoe.ca/CNEWS/Politics/2010/08/31/15199031.html.

24 Tom Flanagan, *First Nations? Second Thoughts,* 2nd ed. (Montreal: McGill-Queen's University Press, 2008; first edition 2000).

25 The Donner Canadian Prize for the best book of the year in Canadian Public Policy; and the Canadian Policy Science Association, Donald Smiley Prize, best book of the year in Canadian politics, both awarded 2001.

26 Tom Flanagan, Christopher Alcantara, and André Le Dressay, with a foreword by Manny Jules, *Beyond the Indian Act: Restoring Aboriginal Property Rights* (Montreal: McGill-Queen's University Press, 2010).

27 Flanagan et al., *Beyond the Indian Act,* pp. 142–46.

28 "An Open Letter to Ralph Klein," *National Post* (January 24, 2001).

29 Goethe, *Faust,* I, 1237.

30 *"Man vergilt einem Lehrer schlecht, wenn man immer nur der Schüler bleibt,"* Friedrich Nietzsche, *Also Sprach Zarathustra,* I, 22, 3, http://www.gutenberg.org/cache/epub/7205/pg7205.html.

Chapter Two

Of Homesteaders and Orangemen:

An Archeology of Western Canadian Political Identity

Richard Avramenko

When a book appears in one's mailbox, sent by the author himself, and that author is a prominent political theorist, one must pay attention to that book. Such was the appearance of *Suddenly There! Twenty Years of Killing Time Around Southern Alberta: 1985–2005* in my mailbox. The "book," if we can call it such, is a barely polished publication of Barry Cooper's hunting notes, with roughly drawn maps of sloughs and duck blinds on various homesteads around Alberta, ample pictures of dead fowl, dead deer, dead trucks, and quite living hunters. The title of the book, Cooper explains, comes of an insight from his hunting pal, Ted Morton, who, reflecting on the nature of the endeavor, said, "Suddenly There! That's what all hunting is about. Geese or deer, ducks or pheasant. There is nothing and then: suddenly there." That Cooper poached the expression is not surprising, because Morton's insight is an unselfconscious declaration of what lies at the heart of empirical political science. For Cooper, "empirical political science includes the analysis of consciousness by the consciousness of the analyst. *This* consciousness is always somebody's, and that somebody is engaged in a permanent effort at responsive openness to reality and reflective verification. It is hard to conceive of anything more empirical."[1] *Suddenly There!* is the story of the discovery of a particular consciousness. It is an anamnetic experiment that uncovers the symbols and experiences informing a new political consciousness. One could retitle the book— *Alberta: Suddenly There!*

Empirical political science, as Cooper points out, is not distinguished by the use of sophisticated quantitative models. Instead, "the meaning of *empeirikos* is that of a skill in discerning things that arise from practice."[2] At the heart of the word one finds the Greek *peras*, which means a limit, or boundary—the sort of boundary one discovers when, say, out walking around in farmers' fields with guns, shooting at things. It stands in contrast to *apeiros*, that which has not been experienced or cannot be experienced. The empirical political scientist, like the fisherman or hunter, learns about and expresses boundaries. In more technical terms, he has "the capacity of intellectual discrimination, or collecting and separating."[3] For Cooper, this capacity of separating and collecting allows him to conclude that the conventional categories employed to make sense of Canadian identity are inadequate for the Western Canadian experience. As Cooper puts it, "the political unit of Canada has no identity. It has several identities expressed in several regional and literary mythologies. What is particularly significant, at least for a westerner, is that the parochial myth of southern Ontario that gives genuine expression to a regional identity is expressed in the misleading language of a pan-Canadian identity."[4] Just as Alberta is Suddenly There, the empiricist discovers that the myth of Laurentian Canada is Suddenly Not There.

The phenomenological experience at the heart of *Suddenly There!* finds more conventional expression in *It's the Regime, Stupid!: A Report from the Cowboy West on Why Stephen Harper Matters*. In this book—which is another fine example of empirical political science—Cooper collects and separates the various "regimes" that constitute the patch-work world of Canada. "Regime," of course, is just another way to say "identity," which explains one of the central arguments of the book: "there are alternative identities west (and east) of the Laurentian centre."[5] For Cooper, the myth lying at the heart of the Canadian experience is that of "two founding peoples," Upper and Lower Canadians, or, Ontario and Quebec. In Ontario, this identity is bound up with a "garrison mentality." In Quebec, it is a "revolutionary consciousness" in which the virtuous French seek to triumph over the malicious and suppressive English.[6] The West, on the other hand, "is not a transplanted imaginative Ontario garrison." Instead, as we have seen from *Suddenly There!* and from the anamnetic experiment introducing *It's the Regime, Stupid!*, the West has its own story to tell.[7] For Cooper, this story is bound up with "resistance."

In what follows, I would like to push Cooper's empirical political science and continue collecting and separating the experiences, symbols, and myths that lie at the heart of Canadian political consciousness. Like Cooper, I would like to explore the disconnect between the narrative dominating discussions of Canadian identity and the political reality of the Western Canadian experience. The "two founding peoples" thesis, while suitable and quite possibly satisfying for Eastern Canadians,[8] fails Westerners not only because it is incongruous with their lived reality, but also because it is a continuous reminder of their status as second-class provinces. Simply put, the myth and symbols of Eastern Canada are an insult to Westerners. As the power of the Western provinces continues to increase vis-à-vis Eastern Canada, this insult will not stand. Unlike Cooper, however, I would like to posit something more declarative than "resistance." Resistance, after all, also lies at the heart of the two founding peoples myth: Upper and Lower Canada, with some help from a couple of colonies on the Atlantic, banded together to resist becoming American. The central aim of this essay is to unfurl a new narrative that sheds light on the more insidious core of the Laurentian myth and also puts a little more flesh on the barebones resistance myth. I have coined expressions for these distinct political identities in English-speaking Canada: in the West, The Homestead Consciousness, and in Laurentia, The Orangeman Consciousness.

The Upper Canadian Experience

In his *Democracy in America*, Alexis de Tocqueville posits what can neatly be called the "origins and identity thesis." The thesis implies that people have memories of their origins, but these memories are inert. People participate in political communities and cultural traditions, the origin of which they have never consciously considered. They have unselfconscious collective memories of things past.[9] Thus, to understand why a people thinks and acts as it does, one necessarily needs to look back to these points of departure. As Tocqueville puts it,

> Go back; look at the baby in his mother's arms; see how the outside world is first reflected in the still hazy mirror of his mind; consider the first examples that strike his attention; listen to the first words which awaken his dormant powers of thought; and finally take notice of the first struggles he has to endure. Only then will you understand the origin of the prejudices, habits, and passions which are to dominate his life. The whole man is there, if one may put it so, in the cradle.[10]

In Tocqueville's understanding, just as a great deal can be learned by looking at the individual's point of origin, the same is so when looking at the point of origin of a people. As he puts it, "Something analogous happens with nations. Peoples always bear some marks of their origin. Circumstances of birth and growth affect all the rest of their careers."[11] Thus, if it were possible to go back and look in the cradle of a nation, one could learn much about that people. As he says, "if we could go right back to the elements of societies and examine the very first records of their histories, I have no doubt that we should there find the first cause of their prejudices, habits, dominating passions, and all that comes to be called the national character."[12]

When Tocqueville looks into the American cradle, he sees two interrelated characteristics: a love of liberty, and a common religion. As he puts it, "The immigrants, or as they so well named themselves, the Pilgrims, belonged to that English sect whose austere principles had led them to be called Puritans. Puritanism was not just a religious doctrine; in many respects it shared the most absolute democratic and republican theories."[13] Now, why, in a discussion of the Eastern experience, should we care about the American point of origin? The reason is simple—from this stock Canada received one of its earliest waves of immigration. With the outbreak of the American Revolution, a substantial number of these Americans (an estimated 50,000), loyal to the British crown, arrived in Canada. Another wave followed at the end of the war—the Loyalists who had stayed to fight on the side of the British. Towns such as Belleville and Kingston—the first capital of the confederated Canada—were founded by these Loyalists, and in the rest of the colonies (including Quebec) they quickly became the political and economic elite. Thus, when we look into the cradle of the Canadian experience in Upper Canada, we espy American Puritans. We see a people who brought with them Puritanism, an abiding love of liberty, and an inherent dislike of Americans.

This love of liberty, however, must be qualified. The United Empire Loyalists, as they like to call themselves, did indeed leave the American colonies holding firm to the concept of freedom, especially the freedom to practice their religion. The people who remained in the American colonies—the revolutionaries who took up arms against the English—chose to fight against the encroachment of the crown on their liberty and property. In other words, the colonists who stayed in the American colonies held firm to the idea of freedom from the oppression of the crown. The refugees who arrived in Canada were loyal to King George, named their new towns after him (Kingston), and endured great hardships to hold on to their freedom to be part of the Empire. In short, the Upper Canadian experience is borne of American principles, but with these principles turned against America. In the Canadian cradle, one sees an anti-American, religiously fervent, pro-British child.

At the heart of Upper Canadian political consciousness, then, is Protestantism. In particular, it is of the Puritan and Loyalist brand of Protestantism. It is of the brand of Protestantism that openly and actively resists denominations not severe enough in their moral lives. But it is not only against impure variants of Protestantism. It holds itself over and against Catholicism (especially in Lower Canada) and, indubitably, the non-Christian native religions and Judaism. One might even go so far as to say the Puritans' love of freedom can be characterized as a freedom from contamination, a freedom from outside influences sullying their exercise in pure moral behaviour.

This freedom from impurities, it would seem, would best be served by some sort of insularization of the community, and this is precisely what Northrop Frye describes in his now famous "garrison mentality" thesis. When Frye peers into the Canadian cradle he sees

> small and isolated communities surrounded with a physical or psychological "frontier," separated from one another and from the American and British cultural sources: communities that provide all that their members have in the way of distinctly human values, and that are compelled to feel a great respect for the law and order that holds them together, yet confronted with a huge, unthinking, menacing, and formidable physical setting—such communities are bound to develop what we may provisionally call a *garrison mentality*.[14]

Frye's image is a very good one. A garrison is a military outpost. The word has its roots in the French "to defend." A garrison is a human construction designed to defend the distinctly defined community within from the dangers without.

Frye's description of the garrison, however, is not of the edifice itself—he is talking specifically about a mentality, a consciousness. Thus, the garrison is not merely corporeal. It also stands to defend against dangers within. As Frye puts it, "a garrison is a closely knit and beleaguered society, and *its moral and social values are unquestionable*. In a perilous enterprise one does not discuss causes or motives: one is either a fighter or a deserter."[15] The edifice gives shape to the community; but in a structural-symbolic way it defines the identity therein. Simply put, in a small and beleaguered community there is little room for dissent, never mind sedition. If a traitor opens the gates, the whole community is lost. The garrison is a military outpost and, as in all military establishments, the members must wear the same uniform. Likewise, in the garrison mentality, the members must wear a uniform mentality, lest the community be lost.

While one might object to this characterization, objections need not be too vociferous. One might regard such a circumstance as welcome, even comforting. In the garrison, one feels safe; one does not feel terror in the face of the actual, physical enemy. One is part of a community and, if not rooted in that deeply aristocratic way, one is in a world of familiarity, a world where one belongs, where one is welcome. In short, one feels at home in the garrison. In the world of the garrison, one is free to be part of the community. One is free to participate in the collective life—in the identity-providing and identity-protecting world. If there is any fear in the garrison, it is from the prospect of being locked out or excluded from the community. This point is not lost on Frye, who argues that "the real terror comes when the individual feels himself becoming an individual, pulling away from the group, losing the sense of driving power that the group gives him, aware of a conflict within himself far subtler than the struggle of morality against evil."[16]

Frye's construction of this garrison identity has had considerable currency in the discourse on Canadian identity. Margaret Atwood puts the symbol to good use when she characterizes the unifying theme in Canadian literature as survival.[17] The idea, however, also has its critics. Cooper, for instance, suggests that Frye's assessment is in the service of a particular interest. Specifically, it is serving the interest of extending or extrapolating this very local and particular expression of the Canadian experience to the whole country. As Cooper puts it, Frye's interest (as well as Atwood's) is to make "Canada, the imaginative experience centered in the Loyalist heartland, Canada the political reality."[18] The experience in this cradle is one of unity and both Atwood and Frye are saying the whole of Canada would be best served by emulating this model. It is, after all, a place where one feels at home, a place where one is sure of one's identity, a place where one feels safe, where one's moral and social values are unquestionable.

The problem with this model is that it is based on a structural-spatial identity. The garrison, like a Greek *polis*, derives its security and integrity not merely from its walls. Instead, it depends on a cohesive politics within; the structural stability of the political unit is almost entirely bound up with the structural-symbolic unity of the members therein. In other words, while a garrison requires political homogeneity within its walls, it also requires a homogeneous political consciousness. There must be a convergence of feelings and ideas within. In the cradle of Upper Canadian history there was indeed a convergence of feelings and ideas: anti-American, anti-Catholic, pro-British, and very Protestant. While Cooper, borrowing from Frye, calls these shared Upper Canadian feelings and ideas the garrison mentality, I would like to call this mentality, or consciousness, provisionally—the *Orangeman Consciousness*.

The Orangeman Consciousness

Invoking the Orange Order might meet with some resistance and consternation, but the symbol is appropriate, because even a quick glance into the Upper Canadian cradle reveals a babe wrapped in Orange swaddling. The Orange Order had its origin in Ireland in the seventeenth century. In 1688, the Catholic King of England, James II, was driven from the country by Protestant forces. He returned shortly after to Ireland (with the support of the (Catholic) French) where he was welcomed by the local Catholics. In 1690, William of Orange, the new Protestant King of England, brought his forces to Ireland to oust the Catholic King. William defeated the troops of James II on July 12, 1690 at the Battle of the Boyne and subsequently imposed Protestant rule and law on the country. The Orange tradition began thenceforth, with Irish Protestants celebrating their "delivery" from Catholic rule in Ireland by William. As Hereward Senior suggests, "To preserve the memory of the Protestant victory of King William, or what became, in effect, the 'Orange Tradition,' several Orange clubs were organized, usually taking the form of fraternal societies."[19] The clubs drew their membership from all levels of society, making it something of a democratic organization. Membership in the Orange Order dwindled through the 18th century until the rise of a popular Catholic movement, called the Defenders. This movement, Senior reports, "was directed against Protestant clergy and landlords in the south of Ireland and . . . threatened the position of the Protestant peasantry in the north. The threat of the 'Defenders' resulted in a revival of the Orange tradition, and a federated Orange society was organized in 1795 from which the present Canadian Orange movement springs."[20]

The movement had its greatest appeal in the rougher elements of society. The tradition of marching on July 12th was, ostensibly, to celebrate the 1690 victory of William of Orange, but, among the rank and file members, it was also an occasion to stir up some old-fashioned fun. As Senior writes, the peasant members of the Orange Order had "the tradition, or at least the habit of brawling at fairs, cock-fights and other public gatherings where opponents tended to divide along religious lines." Marching on July 12th provided a provocative and annual occasion to partake of these simple delights. The coarse and belligerent tenor of the movement can also be heard in their toast:

> To the glorious, pious and immortal memory of King William III,
> who saved us from rogues and roguery, slaves and slavery, knaves
> and knavery, from brass money and wooden shoes: and whoever
> denies this toast may he be slammed, crammed and jammed into
> the muzzle of the great gun of Athlone, and the gun fired into the
> Pope's belly, and the Pope into the devil's belly, and the devil into
> hell, and the door locked, and the key forever in an Orangeman's
> pocket.[21]

Coarse, belligerent, and anti-Catholic, the Orangemen held themselves up
as defenders of the Protestant faith, guardians of unquestionable moral and
social values.

This revival of the Orange Order in the late eighteenth century came
right in time for the century of emigration to the New World. The migra-
tion of Orangemen to North America, however, was asymmetrical. While
many Orangemen emigrated to America (there was a chapter in New York,
for example), American Republicanism did not accord well with
Orangeism. An Order honoring a British King simply did not fit in a country predicated on the ousting of that same monarchy. Canada, however, was
another matter. As Senior reports, "it was in British North America that
Orangeism found favourable ground, and none more favourable than the
province then called Upper Canada."[22] Strongholds of Orangeism were
established in Kingston, Perth, Brockville, Belleville, Cobourg,
Peterborough, and York (Toronto), to name a few. As Senior reports, "by
1830, Orangeism had taken root in Upper Canadian Society . . . . As a fraternal society, its future was assured because increasing waves of Irish
Protestant immigrants would find Orangemen willing and able to help
them obtain a place in the New World society. . . . Orangemen tended to
vote in favour of Protestant candidates."[23]

In general, Orangeism emerged as a major player in Canadian politics
and the color of Upper Canadian politics. Many of the important Protestant
politicians of the time, including the first Prime Minister, Sir John A.
MacDonald, were card-carrying Orangemen. In addition to Sir John A., the
third Prime Minister, Sir John Abbot, was an Orangeman. The fifth Prime
Minister, Sir MacKenzie Bowell, was not only an Orangeman, he was the
Grandmaster of the Orange Order of BNA, 1870–1878. In his survey of the
literature on Orangeism in Canada, Senior confirms the connection between
Orangeism, Protestantism, and Loyalism. Donald Creighton demonstrates a
union between the Orangemen and the United Empire Loyalist concerning

the constitutional societies.[24] Some historians go farther—not only were Upper Canadian politicians either personally involved in Orangeism or serving Orange interests, they brought a certain flavor of politicking with them. A.R. Lower, for example, "accuses the Orangemen of introducing a donnybrook atmosphere into Upper Canada elections."[25] Given their history of coarseness and belligerence, this is not at all surprising.

The Orangeman Consciousness is thus meant to symbolize a firm set of opinions beyond the we/they character of Frye's garrison mentality. The Orangeman Consciousness says something about who "we" is, and who "they" is. "We," inside the garrison, are Upper Canadians; "we" are Protestant, "we" celebrate the victory of Protestantism over Catholicism, "we" are monarchists, "we" are anti-American, and "we" are militant in protecting our feelings and ideas because, as Frye himself writes, our *moral and social values are unquestionable.* The view of the Orangeman towards the immigrants settling the West is summarized by the words of the Right Honorable Sir McKenzie Bowell, "The Galicians, they of the sheepskin coats, the filth and the vermin, do not make splendid material for the building of a great nation. One look at the disgusting creatures after they pass through over the CPR on their way West has caused many to marvel that beings bearing the human form could have sunk to such a bestial level."

The West and Resistance

The question to be asked here is this: has this Orangeman Consciousness, centred in the Orangeman towns along the St. Lawrence, spread to the rest of English Canada? Is this characterization of the Upper Canadian cradle mythopoetically adequate for the West? Cooper's position on this question is unambiguous: "Frye has said that the national sense of political unity is an east-west feeling centered upon the St. Lawrence. This, let us say flatly, is nonsense. There is no Laurentian feeling in British Columbia. The dim memories of such a feeling on the prairies are mostly hostile."[26] Cooper is correct. There is no east-west feeling that stretches *ab mari usque ad mare.* Frye, however, is correct that feelings exist on this axis, but the scope simply does not include the West. It is a sentiment pertaining to the regions of the two founding peoples, with the Maritimes an afterthought and the entire West unthought. It is precisely this sentiment that begot a maple leaf flag—a perfectly adequate symbol for a truncated view of Canada, but, since no sugar maples grow west of Ontario, without meaning in western Canada.

For the West to fit this mold, we would have to assume both some sort of cultural diffusion flowing from the Laurentian garrisons and that the Orangeman Consciousness could find fertile ground outside the Loyalist Heartland. This is precisely the sort of model Tocqueville witnessed in the American context. The Puritans, with their unifying idea, would land in New England. After a generation, they would start moving to the interior of the continent. The culture of the New England township would spread itself across the frontier. The pattern was always the same. The immigrants would land on the East coast and, before heading out west, absorb the political consciousness and practices of self-government so cherished in New England. Tocqueville refers to this process as "freedom's apprenticeship."[27]

When we look at the Canadian West, this model of cultural diffusion simply does not pertain. Immigration patterns did not follow this pattern for the West. Accordingly, an alternative imaginative project for Western identity must be established and there have been several efforts to do so. Cooper, for instance, claims that rather than the garrison mentality, the West, as part of its historical consciousness, has resistance. By way of example, he points to the events and experiences at the Red River Settlement, near present-day Winnipeg. For those unfamiliar with this story, which I assume is the case even for many Western Canadians, let me provide a brief account. The Red River Colony (also known as the Selkirk Settlement) was founded in 1811 by the Earl of Selkirk. The settlement was part of Selkirk's plan to have his company, the Hudson's Bay Company, outmaneuver its chief rival in the fur trade, the Montreal-based Northwest Company.

Selkirk arranged for small groups of Scottish immigrants to settle the colony, but the population was largely Métis, who were mostly French-speaking and Catholic. This attempt to create an agricultural colony was never particularly successful, but the offer of free land kept a steady stream of settlers arriving. The unprofitability of the colony, however, led the Hudson's Bay Company to cut its financial support and by the 1860s the Métis outnumbered the Scottish immigrants. After confederating in 1867, the new Canadian government bought what was called Rupert's Land—which is basically all of present day Western Canada—from the Hudson's Bay Company in 1869. Under the Prime Ministership of Sir John A. MacDonald, William McDougall was appointed governor of the new Canadian territory. This transfer of authority follows the familiar pattern of colonialism—a large territory, populated by indigenous peoples, living a non-European, non-Protestant, non-Orangeman lifestyle, is suddenly placed under the authority of a foreign power and told to conform to the mores and laws of the central colonial authority. In this case, the colonial authority consisted of the English-speaking Protestants from Upper Canada. In other words, the French-speaking, Catholic Métis suddenly found themselves under the authority of Orangemen.

Not surprisingly, this transfer of authority was not welcomed. McDougall, in his zeal to recreate the Red River Colony on the pattern of the Loyalist Heartland, prematurely sent land surveyors to parcel the land into the square township system used in Ontario.[28] The Métis, led by Louis Riel, had already established a provisional government and were negotiating with the Canadian government for the inclusion of Assiniboia as a province in the Confederation. The premature arrival of the surveyors, alongside numerous other objections, led to Riel's men preventing McDougall from entering the territory at the U.S. border.

At the same time, in this territory was a party of pro-Canadian Anglophones intent on resisting Riel's provisional government. Most notable of these was the Irish-born laborer Thomas Scott. Scott himself was a bit-player in the drama. He was described by Lord Dufferin as being from a decent Irish family, "but he himself seems to have been a violent and boisterous man such as are often found in the North of Ireland."[29] In addition to the violent men found in those parts, one also finds Orangemen. Scott was a "fervent Orangeman" and, not surprisingly, opposed the inclusion of a Métis-led province into Canada. After a series of quarrels and insults, Scott, along with 47 others, were arrested by the Métis and imprisoned in Fort Garry. In prison, as reports have it, Scott, typical of an Orangeman, continued his violent and boisterous ways in expressing his hatred of Métis, Catholics, and French. After a failed escape attempt, Scott was eventually convicted of treason and insubordination and sentenced to death. He was executed on March 4, 1870.

The execution of this vulgar and violent bully ought not to have changed the course of Canadian history, except for the fact that he was an Orangeman. Scott's execution became the rallying point for the fervent Orangemen in Toronto and, in general, in Upper Canada. His life, though brutish and unremarkable,

> became a *cause célèbre* after death. To a degree quite unconnect-
> ed with his own tragic fate, he came to symbolize one of the unre-
> solved problems of the new confederation. Was the Northwest to
> be the patrimony of Ontario or was its settlement to be a joint

venture of English and French Canadians? The more extreme reaction may be seen in a resolution of Toronto Orangemen carried by the *Globe* on 13 April 1870: "Whereas Brother Thomas Scott, a member of our Order was cruelly murdered by the enemies of our Queen, country and religion, therefore be it resolved that . . . we, the members of L.O.L. No. 404 call upon the Government to avenge his death, pledging ourselves to assist in rescuing Red River Territory from those who have turned it over to Popery, and bring to justice the murderers of our countrymen." Thomas Scott thus became a martyr in the cause of Ontario expansion westward.[30]

The Scott execution fanned the flames of anti-Catholicism and similar traits associated with Orangeism.

The Rebellion was quashed when the Canadian government sent a military expedition to the colony to establish federal authority. The expedition was successful, but so too was the Riel Rebellion of 1869—it eventually led to the creation of the province of Manitoba and the inclusion of several of Riel's key demands, such as protection for the Catholics and the creation of a separate (French-Catholic) school system. Riel, however, fled the settlement and went into exile in Montana. The story ends in 1885 when Riel, returning to what is now the Saskatchewan-Alberta border to represent Métis grievances, led another armed rebellion. After this "North West Rebellion," Riel was arrested, convicted of treason, and executed.

According to Cooper, this resistance and rebellion lies at the core of Western political consciousness. Whereas in the American experience, territories like California, Texas, and Oregon "had supplied pressure for annexation, Red River had resisted it."[31] In the cradle of the West, Cooper suggests, is resistance. As such, "the myth of Red River served the same purposes in the West as the myth of Loyalism did in Ontario. Even for immigrants from Canada the Loyalist myth proved unsatisfactory since it corresponded not at all to their Western experience. The myth of Red River, in contrast, could be adopted by all settlers."[32]

To base Western identity entirely on this myth, however, is problematic. First, the claim that the Riel Rebellion has descended into the collective consciousness of Westerners assumes at least a modicum of familiarity with the story, that somehow immigrants have had time to adopt, even by osmosis, this political consciousness. In other words, for this story to function as the defining myth of Western political consciousness, a pattern of immigration reflecting Tocqueville's cultural diffusion would be needed. Immigrants to the West, however, did not stop off in Winnipeg for a generation, or even a half a generation, before heading farther west. Just as they did not absorb the Orangeman Consciousness in Upper Canada (not that they would be capable of such a thing), it is doubtful that the consciousness of resistance and rebellion was carted in a wholesale way farther west. Even though the rebellion ranged as far west as the Alberta-Saskatchewan border, there was too much distance—temporal, spatial, and cultural—between the resistance and the settlers who arrived on the prairie.

Cooper himself points out that the era ended in 1885 with the completion of the trans-continental railroad. Gone were the days of Selkirk's West. Gone were the days of the Northwest Company and the Hudson's Bay Company. And the railroad allowed for the new immigrants to leapfrog this defining cultural event. The bulk of the old-world immigrants began arriving in the early part of the twentieth century, 35 years after the rebellion, and the typical immigration pattern was not conducive to absorbing this consciousness. Immigrants would typically alight in the east, board a train, and find themselves in a short time on the prairie hunting survey markers. The pattern of immigration completely bypassed Winnipeg, the place where the local consciousness is most decidedly defined by these events. Finally, even if there were time to absorb this consciousness, most of these newcomers spoke no English and had low levels of literacy, if any at all.

This is not to say that resistance plays no part in Western identity. On the contrary, it tells part of the story. The problem, however, is that the conflict at Red River was a continuation of the struggle between the two founding peoples—the French and English. It is a continuation of the narrative informing the thought of Frye, Atwood, and the Laurentian establishment. It is part of the narrative that begets the maple leaf flag as a sugary compromise between English and French, Protestants and Catholics. If we are to accept that resistance, as it descends from this event, is the basis of Western identity, then we must admit that the West has the same foundation as Quebecois identity today. The resistant in Selkirk was to Anglo-Protestant hegemony, to Orangemen and the Orangeman Consciousness. The resistance in Quebec today is to the same sort of hegemony, though it is now couched in different language. Resistance today in the West is to those "eastern bastards," as bumper stickers in the West indicate. Resistance is certainly part of Western political identity, but there is something more—something more distinctly Western.

The West and Horizons

As we survey further the thinking on this issue, a distinctly Western layer emerges. The suggestion as to its identity comes from two schools: literary critics and landscape geographers. The West is largely prairie and prairie life, like life in any other geographical setting, has a direct effect on thinking. The prairie is a vast and uninterrupted expanse. When one stands on a prairie, one sees 360 degrees of horizon. The sky appears enormous, the person standing on it—miniscule. This relationship between the individual and his landscape, according to the critics of Western Canadian literature, is a central feature influencing the character of the fiction. Laurence Ricou, for example, claims that landscape plays a pivotal role in the self-understanding of the people on the prairie. As he puts it, "What is noteworthy about Canadian prairie fiction is that the imagination so often starts with the same basic image to explore these questions. The landscape, and man's relation to it, is the concrete situation with which the prairie artist initiates his re-creation of the human experience."[33] Writers of prairie fiction—artists who unselfconsciously put to paper an encapsulation of their time, place, and culture—cannot help but to begin with the land. As Ricou later writes, "the reflection of the collective consciousness, or subconsciousness, in the repeated references to land in prairie fiction is constant, and convincing."[34]

How does this collective consciousness appear constantly and convincingly in Western Canadian literature? Another literary critic, Henry Kreisel, suggests that life on the prairie creates two ways of regarding the world. First, as intrepid homesteaders on the hostile prairie, people regard themselves as imperturbable forces, creatures challenging nature and, by virtue of their physical survival, triumphing. Yet, in the second place, the vastness of the prairie, the enormous forces it hurls at them willy-nilly, reminds them rapidly of their insignificance. As Kreisel puts it: "Man, the giant-conqueror, and man, the insignificant dwarf always threatened by defeat, from the two polarities of the state of mind produced by the sheer physical fact of the prairie."[35] In other words, the prairie constantly contrasts the finite (*peras*) and the infinite (*apeiros*). The image is of a solitary vertical figure jutting out of the vast horizontal world, and this contrast is constantly present, exerting its influence on human consciousness. This experience pertains not just to individuals, but to cities. The site of Calgary, for instance, rising majestically on the horizon as one approaches, is an experience unique to prairie life.

This connection between physical landscape, psychical landscape, and political landscape recurs in Western Prairie fiction. As Ricou puts it, "Prairie man raised above the surrounding land has an unobstructed view to the horizon. In a contemplative pose, eyes fixed on the distant horizon, he is often portrayed pondering the ultimate question of the nature of man and God."[36] The vastness of the prairie forces one to note the contrast between finite and infinite. Pondering this contrast impels the prairie person to think in different political terms, especially with regard to freedom. Ricou understands this well: "The uninterrupted view to the horizon gives the impression of uninterrupted personal freedom."[37] Simply put, the geography of the prairie alters the available horizons, and those altered horizons alter in turn the horizons of legitimacy and political authority.

In the West, when one looks to the horizon, one sees few boundaries. The boundaries defining political consciousness in Orangeman country simply do not pertain. When we speak of boundaries—or the lack of boundaries on the prairie—we are speaking, as Ricou has suggested, of a completely different way of regarding politics. This completely different way of regarding politics pertains to the central political issue of modern politics: freedom. Whereas in a garrison one is surrounded by walls and thus thinks freedom that comports with such man-made boundaries, prairie life perforce develops an understanding of liberty that comports with the physical landscape. Simply put, in the West—the world of homesteads, vast prairies, and hunters—liberty is necessarily thought of differently than in Upper Canada. One is free in a much different way in the West, where there are no natural (or artificial) impediments to one's horizons. In Laurentia, where the garrison, the severe religion, the proximity of others, the presence of danger, and maple trees are impediments to the horizon, one must think of liberty much differently.

The West and Liberty

In his famous essay, "Two Concepts of Liberty," Isaiah Berlin outlines two contrasting sorts of liberty. One is "negative liberty," the other, "positive liberty." Negative liberty, Berlin writes, involves the answer to the question "What is the area within which the subject—a person or group of persons—is or should be left to do or be what he is to do or be, without interference by other persons?"[38] This understanding of freedom forms the basis of classical liberalism, especially as endorsed by thinkers such as Thomas Hobbes, John Locke, Adam Smith, and John Stuart Mill. Of course, this view of liberty is more nuanced than absolute freedom, because there are things humans are never free to do, no matter the circumstance. The idea, however, is summarized nicely by Berlin: "there ought to exist a certain minimum area of personal freedom which must on no account be violated; for if it is overstepped, the individual will find himself in an area too narrow for even that minimum development of his natural faculties. . . . It follows that a frontier must be drawn between the area of private life and that of public authority."[39] Elsewhere Berlin calls this "the area of non-interference"[40] and this area is, when we think of negative liberty, sacrosanct.

Positive liberty involves the answer to the question "What, or who, is the source of control or interference that can determine someone to do, or be, this or that?"[41] The answer to this question is me: I am my own master. As Berlin puts it, people who think in terms of positive liberty would say, "I wish my life and decisions to depend on myself, not on external forces of whatever kind." There is, however, another element involved in this vision, and this is the idea of rationality and human will. Whereas negative freedom is based on the simple formulation of absence of external impediments, positive freedom narrows the issue to things uniquely human. With this understanding of liberty, one is likely to say: "I wish, above all, to be conscious of myself as a thinking, willing, active being, bearing responsibility for my choices and able to explain them by reference to my own ideas and purposes. I feel free to the degree that I believe this to be true, and enslaved to the degree that I am made to realise that it is not."[42] On the surface, there seems to be no great difference between the two liberties. With positive liberty, however, one needs to be free even of internal impediments. For example, one must be free even of internal forces, such as the passions. To be free, one needs to be free even of one's nature, especially those things regarded as sub-human.

If, for example, we are enslaved to our passions, which we share with animals, then we are not free. We are only free when our "dominant self," as Berlin puts it, is allowed to shine forth. The dominant self, Berlin argues,

> is then variously identified with reason, with my 'higher nature', with the self which calculates and aims at what will satisfy it in the long run, with my 'real', or 'ideal', or 'autonomous' self, or with my self 'at its best'; which is then contrasted with irrational impulse, uncontrolled desires, my 'lower nature, the pursuit of immediate pleasures, my 'empirical' or 'heteronomous' self, swept

by every gust of desire and passion, needing to be rigidly disciplined if it is ever to rise to the full height of its 'real' nature.[43]

Thus, if we are not acting in accordance with our so-called "higher nature," then we are not free. If we translate this formula into moral language, it sounds more familiar. If we are not behaving according to certain moral and social values, we are not free. If these moral and social values to which we must adhere to be free are the same as those of, say, the Christian moral world, then if we are not being good Christians, we are not free. And this is precisely what we are told in the Christian moral system: do not be a slave to your passions; master your passions; master the desires of the body.

This, of course, can be said of any moral system, so long as we claim that the values contained therein are "higher" or, if we want to be secular, we claim they are more "enlightened." Liberty in this sense means one must adhere to unquestionable moral and social values—whether they be Christian, Muslim, or communist—to be free. If they are "higher" values (they are, after all, in accordance with either reason or God or history), why would any free person not follow them? If the higher moral tenet is, for example, "love thy neighbor," a free person would naturally follow it. Failure to follow it would only indicate the incapacity to realize the real self. It indicates that one is not one's own master. As odd as the conclusion sounds, this is Berlin's point: positive liberals will argue that if one is not following unquestionably the "higher" moral and social values of the group, one is not free.

It is this higher moral tenet that lies at the core of positive freedom: love thy neighbor. What this means is that positive freedom is bound up with the idea of collectiveness, rather than individualism. As he puts it, for positive liberals,

> the real self may be conceived as something wider than the individual (as the term is normally understood), as the social 'whole' of which the individual is an element or aspect: a tribe, a race, a Church, a State, the great society of the living and the dead and the yet unborn. This entity is then identified as being the 'true' self which, by imposing its collective, or 'organic', single will upon its recalcitrant 'members', achieves its own, and therefore their, 'higher' freedom.[44]

If one adds "garrison" to this list of social wholes, one will discern the direction of the argument. When social wholes, be it tribe, race, or garrison, are used to justify a moral system, it opens the door to the "coercion of some men by others to raise them to a 'higher' level of freedom." This reasoning makes it "possible, and at times justifiable, to coerce men in the name of some goal (let us say, justice or public health) which they would, if they were more enlightened, themselves pursue, but do not, because they are blind, or ignorant or corrupt."[45]

Positive freedom is the sort of freedom that necessarily emerges from a beleaguered garrison. It characterizes the garrison mentality and, as Berlin describes it in its pathological form, is conterminous with the Orangeman Consciousness. The Orangemen thought themselves in possession of higher moral truths, both theologically (Protestantism) and politically (Loyalism). The Orangeman Consciousness embodies all that Berlin finds dangerous about positive liberty. Orangemen consider themselves to be adhering to higher moral truth. Orangemen, like Thomas Scott and Sir John A. MacDonald, see it as completely justifiable to coerce people to think about liberty in the same way as a white, Anglo-Saxon Protestant, for whom identity is formed around the homogeneous group in the garrison.

Negative freedom, on the other hand, characterizes the West. Whereas positive freedom fits the colonizer, negative freedom is the natural fit for the mind of the colonized. Negative liberty is the natural fit not only because of the physical landscape, but because many homesteaders were simply not of the Anglo-Protestant stock. Sons and grandsons of Anglican manses stayed in Orangeman country—in Kingston, Brockville, and the Danforth. Head west past the 100th meridian and one first finds the Métis Catholics and after that, a catalogue of other peoples seeking freedom from oppression, be it political or religious.

On the prairie one finds, for example, persecuted central Europeans: Mennonites and Hutterites. From Eastern Europe: the Doukhabors, Russians, and Ukrainians. From the Pale of Settlement came the Jews—all of whom left the old country in search of freedom from the oppression, freedom from the persecution, freedom from the violent bigotry that was the order of the day in Eastern Europe.[46]

There were, of course, other homesteaders who had neither lived in colonies nor stemmed from these religious groups. The point, however, is that immigration on the prairie was different from that of Upper Canada. In the Alberta cradle, one is as likely to find Kashubas, Avramenkos, Wolfsons, Sengauses, Waschuks, Gogols, Silbersteins, and Schneiders as Mathesons, MacDonalds, and Scotts in Upper Canada. There is good reason Albertans refer affectionately to Edmonton as Edmonchuk, and good reason for giant Orthodox Easter eggs outside towns like Vegreville. The immigrants in the West were recruited from the Pale of Settlement and beyond. These were not immigrants fleeing the United States so as to hold fast to their British roots. These were not Irish Orangemen coming to Canada because it was more hospitable to their Orangeism than the United States. These were peasants deliberately recruited from Eastern Europe under the immigration policies of the then Minister of Interior, Clifford Sifton. It was Sifton who saw the great economic potential of a developed agricultural base in the West and therefore opened immigration offices in Eastern Europe with the express intention of finding peoples both hardy and desperate enough to resettle on the harsh prairie. As he put it, the immigrants needed for the West were "stalwart peasants in sheep-skin coats, born on the soil, whose forefathers have been farmers for ten generations."[47]

The Homestead Consciousness
So what does this look into the cradle of Western identity bring to light? First and foremost, it reveals that a distinct set of circumstances lies at the heart of Western political identity. Rather than the two founding peoples, garrisons, Loyalists, and militant Protestants, one finds resistance, prairie horizons, and a love of negative liberty. In the West one finds what may provisionally be called the *Homestead Consciousness*. This consciousness, it must be recognized, is not merely a nuanced variation of the Orangeman consciousness. It is an altogether different way of thinking; consequently, it leads us to recognize a distinct society.

The Homestead Consciousness is a mature way of thinking that emerges from a cradle of oppression, be it religious oppression in the Austrian Empire, pogroms in Odessa, the colonial imposition of New England-style townships on the Red River Colony, or the federal imposition of "higher" moral codes, be they wrapped in terms of social justice, national health plans, or human rights commissions. The Homestead Consciousness is a way of thinking that accords with the landscape—with horizons of legitimacy and political authority based on the freedom, the self-reliance, and the rugged individualism both born of and necessary for the survival of a homesteader on the vast and unrelenting prairie. It is a way of thinking that asks only not to be impeded from pursuing one's own way of life; a way of thinking that cannot abide the imposition of values from abstract and illegitimate authority. It is the way of thinking that simply cannot abide uniform life in a garrison.

The gulf between the Orangeman Consciousness and the Homestead Consciousness is wide. The question to be asked is whether these entirely different modes of thinking can be reconciled. From the vantage of the Orangeman Consciousness, the answer would be rather simple: "As long as those peasants (the current word is 'redneck') in the West start thinking like us and recognize that our view of community is a) more rational, b) more enlightened, and consequently, c) more just and free, we will stop treating them like colonial subjects. There will be no reconciliation until they think like we do." The Orangeman Consciousness will therefore perpetuate the tradition begun with the deployment of beastly Orangeman to fight the Catholic Métis in Red River, and elevated to a refined level of xenophobia and anti-Semitism with the Nativist movement in the early twentieth century. It is also helpful to recall the words of Sir Mackenzie Bowell, the fifth Prime Minister of Canada: "The Galicians, they of the sheepskin coats, the filth and the vermin, do not make splendid material for the building of a great nation. One look at the disgusting creatures after they pass through over the CPR on their way West has caused many to marvel that beings bearing the human form could have sunk to such a bestial level." This prejudice continues to this day in anti-Alberta rhetoric.[48]

During the January 2006 federal election, the Ontario establishment wheeled out the infamous abortion doctor Henry Morgentaler, who claimed about the Alberta-led Conservative Party: "I don't trust the Conservative party and I don't think women in Canada or people who love women in this country should trust the Conservative party as far as abortion rights are concerned."[49] The Conservative Party, of course, was led by an Albertan, Stephen Harper. Abortion was not even an issue in the election, but the meaning is clear: Not only do these Albertans dwell on a lower moral plane, they are like Americans. During the same election, Bloc Quebecois leader Gilles Duceppe was less veiled in his anti-Alberta rhetoric, claiming that a vote for the Conservative party was to cede power to Calgary—it would be un-Canadian to vote for representation outside of the geopolitical sphere of the two founding peoples.[50] This is not to say that Quebeckers are also Orangeists. Canada, as a cultural and political entity, has always been defined by the quarrel between franco-Quebeckers and anglo-Ontarians. The rising power of the West, especially Alberta, threatens this discourse. Should this discourse break down, it will seriously undermine the "bargaining" power Quebec has vis-à-vis the Orangeist establishment in Upper Canada. Hence, pointing to the West, and Alberta in particular, as the enemy is de rigueur for Quebeckers as well. Hence, the

West is symbolized in Duceppe's ads in Quebec by a cowboy hat over the word "Calgary." Albertans, Quebeckers are being told, are outsiders, and, with their interest in oil, they are decidedly Texan Americans. Even then-Prime Minister Paul Martin invoked the anti-Alberta rhetoric during the campaign, suggesting the Alberta-led Conservatives had plans to create "two-tier healthcare," which everybody knows is code for "American." Anti-Albertanism, not surprisingly, is predicated on the same identity-giving premise the Loyalists and Orangemen brought to Upper Canada: anti-Americanism. Americans, after all, are gun-toting, money-grubbing, selfish, religious nuts, are they not? Just like those Albertans.

The fact that anti-Albertanism is regularly couched in anti-American language is hardly surprising. Broadly speaking, negative liberty is the order of the day in America. In fact, we could go so far as to say that, in the American cradle, there was something of a natural selection of the liberties. Those who ascribed to positive liberty packed their bags and left for Upper Canada in 1776. What remained was a tradition strongly imbued with liberty associated with the self-reliance, personal responsibility, and rugged individualism. In this sense, Alberta *is* like America. The immigrants who arrived on the prairie were the tired, the poor, the wretched, the huddled masses yearning to breathe free.

This anti-Albertanism represents more than a difference of opinion regarding policy. There is, one might argue, a sinister side to it, the same sinister side that emerged with the aforementioned Nativist movement. For example, when an Albertan visits Ottawa, she will invariably be asked if she has had the chance to make a trip through "loyalist country." These cultural descendants of Loyalists will insist on visits to all the Orangemen towns along the St. Lawrence, because there one finds "real towns," not the post-office-grain-elevator-Bank-of-Montreal embarrassments on the prairies. Here, unlike the shanty towns in the West, one can find architecture, history, beautiful (Protestant) churches, cottage industry artisans, and the sort. In the West, one finds only inauthentic experiences of Canada. The towns are dusty, dirty, and, one almost hears, *temporary* towns. One hears echoing in the background a history of aversion to the lowly *shtetl* and their inhabitants. Anti-Albertanism thus has this ring: they are dirty, *shtetl*-dwelling, money-grubbing, peasants who pose a grave threat to the sanctity of our self-enclosed higher moral reality.[51]

To conclude, if we want to inquire into Alberta's political self-understanding, we must do this vis-à-vis the so-called problem of Canadian identity. This problem, however, is framed only within the narrative of the

French-English/Catholic-Protestant conflict that ends long before the 100th meridian, where the great plains begin. The effort to construct a national identity based on problems descending from this conflict is inappropriate for the West. Albertans have an identity—an identity that might very well be symbolized by a cowboy hat. It is not an identity and tradition needing to be invented, nor one for which apology is needed. Whether Westerners buy into the identity imposed on them by the Loyalist-Orangeist establishment is an altogether different matter. Some Westerners do accept it. Some perforce reject it. But in the end, the Homestead Consciousness stands in firm opposition to the colonial arrogance and belligerence descending from the Orangeist tradition in Upper Canada. The stalwart peasants in sheep-skin coats, born on the soil, and whose forefathers have been farmers for ten generations have come into their own and are unlikely any longer to take lying down being belittled as provincials, having their natural resources appropriated, or being excluded from government. The West, in point of fact, is Suddenly There!

Endnotes

1   Barry Cooper, "Eric Voegelin, Empirical Political Scientist," in *The Restoration of Political Science and the Crisis of Modernity*, ed. Barry Cooper (Lewiston, NY: Edwin Mellen Press, 1989), p. 282.

2   *Ibid.*, p. 272.

3   *Ibid.*, p. 273. For further reflection on the relationship between hunting and philosophy, see my "Of Firemen, Sophists, and Hunter-Philosophers: Citizenship and Courage in Plato's *Laches*," *Polis*, vol. 24:2 (Fall 2007), 203–230.

4   Barry Cooper, "Weaving a Work," in *Canadian Political Philosophy: Contemporary Reflections*, eds. Ronald Beiner and Wayne Norman (Don Mills, ON: Oxford University Press, 2001), p. 380.

5   Barry Cooper, *It's the Regime, Stupid!: A Report from the Cowboy West on Why Stephen Harper Matters* (Toronto: Key Porter Books, 2009), 83.

6   Ibid., p. 77.

7   Ibid., p. 83.

8   For the purpose of this paper, Eastern Canada refers to the region of the St. Lawrence River Valley (aka, Laurentia), roughly from Toronto to Montreal. More generally, it will refer to these parts of Ontario and Quebec known before Confederation (1867) as Upper and Lower Canada. I reject the standard misnomer (and political arrogance) of referring to this region as "Central Canada." The center of Canada, after all, is a little east of Winnipeg.

9   The relationship between time, memory, and national identity has recently surfaced in political science, especially with regard to how memories are created or

manipulated for the sake of current political power-brokering. See for example, Eric Langenbacher "Changing Memory Regimes in Contemporary Germany?" *German Politics and Society* 21, no. 2 (2003): 46–68 and "Memory Regimes and Support for Democracy in Contemporary Germany," paper presented at the annual meeting of the American Political Science Association, Philadelphia, 2003; and Jan-Werner Mueller, *Memory and Power in Postwar Europe: Studies in the Presence of the Past* (Cambridge: Cambridge University Press, 2002).

10 Alexis de Tocqueville, *Democracy in America*, trans., George Lawrence (New York: Harper Perennial, 1969), 31.

11 Tocqueville, 31.

12 Tocqueville, 31–32.

13 Tocqueville, 36.

14 Northrop Frye, *The Bush Garden: Essays on the Canadian Imagination* (Toronto: Anansi, 1971), 225. Emphasis added.

15 Ibid., 226. Emphasis added.

16 Ibid., 226.

17 Margaret Atwood, *Survival* (Toronto, Anansi, 1972). Frye and Atwood, not surprisingly, hail from Toronto.

18 Barry Cooper, "Western Political Consciousness," in *Political Thought in Canada: Contemporary Perspectives*, Stephen Brooks (Toronto: Irwin Publishing, 1984), 214–215.

19 Hereward Senior, *Orangeism: The Canada Phase* (Toronto: McGraw-Hill Ryerson, 1972), 3.

20 Senior, 4.

21 As cited in Sir Jonah Barrington's *Personal Sketches of his Own Times* (New York, 1856), 156.

22 Senior, 7.

23 Senior, 12. For more see Cecil Houston and William Smyth, *The Sash Canada Wore: A Historical Geography of the Orange Order in Canada* (Toronto: University of Toronto Press, 1980).

24 Donald Creighton, *Dominion of the North* (Toronto: Macmillan, 1957). As cited in Senior, 14.

25 A.R. Lower, *Colony to Nation* (Toronto: Longmans, 1953). As cited in Senior, 13.

26 Cooper, "Western Political Consciousness," 215.

27 Tocqueville, 240.

28 This is the same system ballyhooed by Tocqueville as the essence of American (Puritan) democracy.

29 Quoted by J. E. Rea, "Thomas Scott," *Dictionary of Canadian Biography* (Ottawa: Library and Archives Canada, 2000). (http://www.biographi.ca/EN/ShowBio.asp?BioId=38817&query=).

30 Ibid. George Brown, the founder of *The Globe* (now *Globe and Mail* (Toronto)), was a well-known anti-Catholic.

31 Cooper, "Western Political Consciousness," 223.

32 Ibid., 225.

33 Laurence Ricou, *Vertical Man/Horizontal World* (Vancouver: University of British Columbia Press, 1973), xi.

34 Ibid., 5.
35 Henry Kreisel, "The Prairie: A State of Mind," in *Context of Canadian Criticism*, ed. Eli Mandel (Chicago: University of Chicago Press, 1971), 256.
36 Ricou, 7.
37 Ricou, 7.
38 Isaiah Berlin, "Two Concepts of Liberty" in *Liberty*, ed., Henry Hardy (Oxford: Oxford University Press, 2002), 169.
39 Berlin, 179.
40 Berlin, 173.
41 Berlin, 169.
42 Berlin, 178.
43 Berlin, 179.
44 Berlin, 179.
45 Berlin, 179.
46 The story of the Jews, most of whom were fleeing pogroms in the late nineteenth century and early in the twentieth, is especially interesting. Once arriving in Alberta, most of these Jewish-Russian immigrants lived on one of three farming colonies, organized by the Jewish Colonization Association, clustering around vacant homesteads near Trochu, Rumsey, and Montefiore. For more, see *The Land of Promise Experience in Southern Alberta* (The Jewish Historical Society of Southern Alberta, 1996), v.
47 Clifford Sifton, "The Immigrants Canada Wants," *Maclean's Magazine*, 1 (April, 1921) 16, 22-24. For an exhaustive account of the life and times of Clifford Sifton, see D.J. Hall, *Clifford Sifton: Volume One, The Young Napoleon, 1861–1900* (Vancouver: University of British Columbia Press, 1981) and *Clifford Sifton: Volume Two, A Lonely Eminence, 1901–1929* (Vancouver: University of British Columbia Press, 1985).
48 For more on the nativist movement in Canada, see Hall, *Clifford Sifton: Volume One*, 259–269; William H. Katerberg, "The Irony of Identity: An Essay on Nativism, Liberal Democracy, and Parochial Identities in Canada and the U.S." *American Quarterly*, 47:3 (September 1995): 493–524; James Watt, "Anti-Catholic Nativism in Canada: The Protestant Protective Association,", *Canadian Historical Review* (March, 1967): 45–58.
49 "Harper makes direct appeal for Quebec vote," as reported by CTV.ca News, January 16, 2006. (http://edmonton.ctv.ca/servlet/an/local/CTVNews/20060116/elxn_tory_campaign_060117?hub=CalgaryHome).
50 "Bloc pulls anti-Alberta card out of its arsenal," as reported by CanWest News Service, January 20, 2006. (http://www2.canada.com/national/features/decision-canada/story_05.html?id=21930c97-f780-46cd-b9fc-d95d05252cc0).
51 The specter of anti-Semitism appears in the case of Louis Riel, who changed his name to Louis "David" Riel and considered himself a prophet of a lost tribe of Israel. One wonders how much this "David" leant itself to the visceral Orangeist reaction to both Riel Rebellions. For more, see Thomas Flanagan, *Louis "David" Riel: "Prophet of the New World,"* (Toronto: University of Toronto Press, 1979), and Flanagan, *Riel and the Rebellion: 1885 Reconsidered* (Toronto: University of Toronto Press, 2000).

Chapter Three
Hunting for Cowboys

Rainer Knopff

Barry Cooper loves cowboys. His most recent book on Canadian politics—*It's the Regime, Stupid*—is subtitled "a Report from the Cowboy West."[1] The book begins with Barry accompanying his rancher friend Sandy Soutzo to a Medicine Hat cattle auction; it ends (leaving aside the "Postscript") with the two friends at a similar auction in 2008, this time in High River. Between these bookends—in a chapter asking "Cowboy Conservatives?"—Barry trashes C.B. Macpherson's *Democracy in Alberta* for neglecting "the economic activity whose existence is annually celebrated in the Calgary Stampede, the cattle industry."[2] Those familiar with Barry's life in Alberta—"the west of the West"[3]— know that he enjoys not only auctions, but also roundup and branding festivities. Barry clearly loves cowboys.

Barry also loves to hunt, not only in the metaphorical sense of stalking the truth, but also in the sense of producing game for the dinner table. Each fall he and several friends, including me and my sons, become enthusiastic locavores, stocking our freezers with locally produced organic meat. Barry has kept meticulous notes on our adventures afield over several decades, and has circulated them as a prized volume of reminiscences among his hunting buddies. A casual hunter would not go to such lengths. Barry clearly loves hunting.

In the southern Alberta context, these two loves of Barry's—cowboys and hunting—are complementary in some ways and at odds in others. This "essay"—and I borrow the term advisedly from Barry, who uses it often (including to characterize *It's the Regime, Stupid*)—explores these relationships and tensions. The conflicts between cowboys and hunters are particularly interesting because they replicate the broader political tensions Barry sees in the Canadian "regime" between the ethos of the "Cowboy West" and the conflicting "garrison" mentality of "Laurentian" (i.e., central) Canada. Simply put, too few Alberta hunters are imbued with the cowboy ethos, as Barry understands it. Like the Canadian regime as a whole, the Alberta regime has its own inner contradictions.

*   *   *   *   *

The place to begin is with another of Barry's friends, the now sadly departed Ralph Hedlin. In 1971, Ralph and his son Paul co-authored *Game Policy Needs in Alberta* on behalf of the Western Stock Growers' Association. The document explored a longstanding "conflict of interest" between hunters and ranchers, one that was "inevitable and irreconcilable" under existing game laws but that might be resolved to the mutual benefit of both sides with appropriate policy change.[4] The conflict stemmed from the "insistence of the modern Alberta hunter that game is 'free,'"[5] despite the fact that there are real "supply cost[s]"[6] for landowners, whose provision of game habitat often conflicts with their economic interest. Maintaining or improving the habitat on which game animals depend is an "economic disutility"[7] for the landowner whenever income can be produced through less habitat-friendly practices (e.g., grazing game cover or replacing it with crop production). In short, it often pays the landowner "to assault the game population on the habitat side."[8] This is obviously not in the hunter's interest.

Of course, the habitat that benefits the ranching economy—i.e., grassland for cattle grazing—also benefits some game species (such as grass-consuming elk), but this simply gives ranchers "a built-in incentive to minimize the number of [competing game] animals" on their land.[9] In such cases, the interests of ranchers and hunters might coincide to some extent, because hunters can help reduce the competing wildlife, especially with the cooperation of the relevant government authorities. This is precisely what has occurred for years in the Milk River Ridge area of southern Alberta, where a small, annual "pest control" elk hunt, targeted at cow elk, keeps the herd at a miniscule size of about 200 on a landscape that could support thousands of these animals. The Milk River Ridge is one of Barry's favored hunting grounds, but he does not hunt elk there; indeed, he rarely sees any. A few elk hunters benefit from such "pest control" hunts, but elk hunting as such suffers.

The Western Stock Growers' Association wanted to change the incentives that lead ranchers to reduce the supply of game and wildlife habitat. Ranchers, hunters, and the environment would all be better off, in their view, if game and habitat became benefits rather than costs for landowners. "At a minimum," argued the Hedlin report, the rancher's "cost of supplying game [must] be covered,"[10] but it would be even better to exceed this "minimum" and enable landowners—through access fees and the like—to realize a positive income from game and game habitat. Wherever such market incentives had been tried, the report maintained, game habitat, and thus the supply of game, had improved, to the ultimate benefit of not only hunters but also the environment. In short, the Stock Growers' Association—the "cowboys" on this issue—were making the case for "market environmentalism."

In promoting market environmentalism, Alberta's cowboys were fighting an uphill battle, and their most vociferous opponents were the very hunters who, the Hedlins claimed, would share in the policy's long-term benefits. The Hedlin report recognized and understood this opposition, underlining the extent to which frontier history had "burned deep in the consciousness" of hunters "that game was 'free.'" Existing law embodied this view by defining game as a public resource, something that no individual could own, and by lodging management of this resource primarily with the state (as representative of the public owners). As far as hunting was concerned, public management could legitimately ration access—e.g., through license fees, bag limits, and lottery draws for certain "tags"—but landowners had no right to charge fees for hunting access. Such fees were, and still are, legally prohibited in Alberta. It is ironic, from an environmental perspective, that landowners *can* charge energy companies for access to mineral resources, which are also publicly owned.[11] To realize similar, and more environmentally friendly, benefits from hunting access, the Stock Growers in the 1970s knew they had to overcome the strongly entrenched view that "game was free." They failed, suffering defeat at the hands of a hunting lobby for which "paid hunting"—i.e., payments by hunters to landowners—was anathema. It was the defeat of "market environmentalism" by an ethos that favors bureaucratic public control.

Which brings us back to Barry Cooper, who is no fan of bureaucracy. *It's the Regime, Stupid* is above all an extended critique of gratuitous bureaucracy. Excessive bureaucracy, says Barry, enervates citizenship, leads to dependency and corruption, and often undermines the very ends it purports to pursue. On the last point, for example, the Canadian Wheat Board (CWB) has not served the interests of western grain farmers by monopolizing the marketing of regulated grains. Evidence of the counterproductive effect of this misguided attempt at supply and price management is that "[i]n Ontario, which is not subject to CWB control,"—i.e., where the market, rather than bureaucracy, prevails—wheat production has increased by nearly 75 per cent [while] in the [bureaucratized] West it has declined by almost 40 per cent."[12] Barry does not romanticize markets, but he certainly prefers them to bureaucracies.[13]

Among other things, this means that Barry favours "market environmentalism" when it is feasible. Writing about Canada's national parks, he and Sylvia LeRoy conceded that "full-fledged privatization of national parks is probably not feasible nor perhaps even advisable," but nevertheless emphasized the "many market solutions that can be harnessed to the environmental cause."[14] Park user fees, for example, "can go a long way toward regulating use,"[15] and thus help balance the preservation and human enjoyment of wilderness. Concerned with "the dangers of public land management through bureaucratic regulation," LeRoy and Cooper pointed to "the obvious alternative [of instituting] a regime of stable property rights and positive incentives that make environmental protection an opportunity and a responsibility, not merely conformation to regulatory necessity."[16]

Preferring market mechanisms, including market environmentalism, to bureaucratic regulation is one of the features of the "cowboy vision"[17] Barry so admires. Not that cowboys are immune to the blandishments of government subsidy or bailout in times of economic hardship – such as during the BSE ("mad cow") crisis—but, comparatively speaking, the cowboy ethos promotes a greater degree of self-reliance than the survivalist "garrison-state" mentality that grew out of the historical experience of "Laurentian" Canada. In the cattle business, Barry reminds us, "the price at auction is the market price. No one quarrels with it or complains."[18]

Barry has not written about "user fees" for hunters, but it is a safe bet that he sees eye to eye with his old friend Ralph Hedlin on this issue—and also with his friend Ted Morton, who revived the Hedlin proposal in 2007. Ted joined the University of Calgary Political Science Department in 1981, the same year Barry arrived. He and Barry quickly became regular hunting partners (and both became part of the "Calgary School" discussed in Tom Flanagan's contribution to this volume). In 2004, Ted took leave from the university and won a Progressive Conservative seat in the provincial legislature. In 2006, he was appointed Minister of Sustainable Resource Development (SRD), a portfolio that included all matters related to hunting and fishing policy (some of us used to joke that no one was better suited to be "Minister of Hunting and Fishing"). Ted was also a friend of Ralph Hedlin, and had read the 1971 Stock Growers report. He thought the report had addressed real problems and that those problems were becoming more acute because of the evolution (or decline) of the cattle industry.

The Hedlin report explored how market-based mechanisms might induce ranchers to "supply" more game and game habitat. The result would have been a kind of income "diversification" for ranchers. There was no indication in the report, however, that such diversification might have helped secure the continued viability of ranching on the landscape. The report appeared to assume that cattle ranching was, in itself, a sustainable economic activity. This was no longer a safe assumption in the mid-2000s when Ted Morton became minister of SRD. By this time, the economic viability of cattle ranching in Alberta was in question. The BSE ("mad cow") crisis, escalating feed-grain prices, and the rise in the Canadian dollar were putting great pressure on already marginal ranching operations. Especially in recreationally attractive parts of southern Alberta, ranchers (few of whose children were inclined to take over such marginal operations) had strong incentives to sell off parts of their holdings, thus fragmenting the landscape in ways that often degrade wildlife habitat—and that certainly do not foster or benefit hunting.

Blaine Marr, a southern Alberta rancher, eloquently described the problem:

> [T]he sell off of prime ranchland and wildlife habitat along the eastern slopes of Alberta . . . has been going on for years, but has greatly increased after BSE collapsed the cattle market. The purchasers of this land are not ranchers, they are baby boomers retiring and eager to invest and develop. These ranches and the habitat they protect are disappearing forever, which causes shrinking hunting opportunities every year. Do not be surprised when hunters go back to their favourite ranch where they get access every year, that someone else will answer the door. This person will have no idea what they want, and may have no intention of ever allowing hunting.[19]

Some kinds of industrial diversification—e.g., selling access rights for energy development—could provide needed income diversification for some ranchers, and thus help resist the kind of fragmentation Marr describes, but such industrialization can also be ecologically costly.

If ranchers in the past had too few incentives to maintain game habitat, at least they helped maintain the kinds of extensive, non-industrialized open spaces that some wildlife needed. The persistence of such open spaces was now in doubt. The kind of hunting-based economic diversification favoured by the Hedlins had apparently helped stabilize the ranching economy in other jurisdictions. Could similar ecological benefits be realized in Alberta? Deciding to find out, Minister Morton appointed a Land and Wildlife Stewardship Working Group (LWSWG) to investigate and make recommendations. (Full disclosure: I served on that committee.)

Coming to essentially the same conclusions as had the Hedlins, the

LWSWG recommended a policy initiative entitled Open Spaces Alberta (OSA). This initiative had two components. The first, known as Hunting for Habitat (HFH), proposed giving large landowners an allocation of game tags that they could sell on the open market. Where similar models had been implemented—e.g., in Utah—ranchers had begun to derive as much as 25%-30% of their revenue stream from hunting.[20] Not only did this income diversification help stabilize their operations, but it entailed significant habitat improvements and increased game supply. Areas that had previously followed the same elk suppression model as we find on Alberta's Milk River Ridge saw elk herds increase from a few hundred to several thousand. To see if similar benefits could be realized in Alberta, the LWSWG proposed that a program along these lines be tested in Alberta's Wildlife Management Unit (WMU) 108, which includes the Milk River Ridge. A pilot project was also proposed for the adjacent WMU 300 to the west, which includes foothills and mountain rangeland of such majestic beauty, and hence recreational value, that it is subject to the kind of intense fragmentation pressure described above by Blaine Marr (Marr ranches in WMU 300).

The second OSA component, the Recreational Access Management Program (RAMP), offered participating landowners public assistance in managing hunter access to their properties and provided very modest financial compensation (at taxpayer expense) for the costs and inconveniences of such access. As an access management program with minimal financial compensation, RAMP was not expected to play a significant role in stabilizing land and improving habitat; those were the functions of the HFH proposal. RAMP was to be piloted along with HFH in the same two WMUs.

As in the 1970s, Alberta's "cowboys"—i.e., ranchers—were generally in favour of the economic incentives in the OSA proposal, while Alberta's hunting organizations passionately opposed any form of "paid hunting." The hunting lobby was particularly incensed by HFH, which involved direct payments by hunters to landowners. RAMP was somewhat less controversial because its financial compensation of landowners came from the general public rather than in the form of direct "user fees," but even RAMP was seen as an unacceptable form of "paid hunting" by many hunters.

Minister Morton accepted the LWSG's recommendations and proposed pilot studies of both HFH and RAMP in WMUs 108 and 300. Intense controversy about the program became an issue in the 2008 provincial election, however, leading Premier Ed Stelmach to kill the HFH pilot studies. The less controversial RAMP proposal survived, and three-year pilots began in 2009. These pilots were subsequently reduced to two years, and recession-induced budgetary constraints ended RAMP's financial compensation component after the first year.

The demise of the RAMP studies illustrates the weakness of relying on the general public purse for such programs. More importantly, the "free game" mindset of Alberta's hunters had once again defeated any direct "user fees" paid by hunters directly to private suppliers of game and game habitat. The result was the loss of an ecologically promising kind of economic diversification for ranches. At least for certain game animals in some areas, such as elk on the Milk River Ridge, the result was also the continued bureaucratic rationing of a limited supply of hunting opportunities. Here, as with Barry's Wheat Board example, we see the expansive and liberating potential of markets being constrained by perverse incentives and bureaucratic control.

If Alberta's hunting controversy has some parallels with the Wheat Board issue, it has even stronger ones with the perennial Canadian health care debate. Like game, health care is widely seen in Canada as a good that must be "free," at least in the sense that users should not directly pay providers. So strongly entrenched has this view been that Canada shares with Cuba and North Korea the dubious distinction of being the only countries whose citizens generally cannot purchase private insurance for care covered by the public system. Here, too, the result is bureaucratic rationing of procedures and long waiting lists.

The health care and hunting debates are parallel also in the intolerance for middle-ground approaches exhibited by the critics of market incentives. For those critics, the health-care choice is one between US-style privatization and the existing Canadian/(North Korean, Cuban) model. They see no sustainable middle ground. Any step out onto the "slippery slope" of private provision threatens to send us careening all the way "down" to the American model.

For opponents of "paid hunting," Texas and Europe play the bogeyman role occupied by the United States in the health care debate. In these jurisdictions, hunting opportunities are entirely a function of private markets, and the so-called "public hunter" is unknown. The "public hunter"—someone who pays the government for a license and perhaps a draw "tag," but who otherwise hunts "for free"—plays the role of the patient accessing "free" health care in publicly funded systems. As in the health-care debate, every move to "paid hunting" allegedly puts us on the slippery slope to complete privatization—and to the utter demise of the public hunter.

But not all slopes are slippery and many stable middle-ground systems exist. With respect to health care, most western democracies—Britain, Australia, Germany, Switzerland, and France are just a few prominent examples—occupy a middle ground in which paid access to a private system co-exists well with a public system. These systems out-perform Canada's on many outcome measures, and do so at lower cost to the taxpayer. Among other things, they are not nearly as plagued by long waiting lists on the public side. They represent the kind of "third way" (neither American nor Cuban) that former Alberta Premier Ralph Klein once proposed as a health care approach for Alberta.

Similarly, not all jurisdictions that allow "paid hunting" end up with the Texas model. Utah, for example, requires landowners who sell allocated tags on the open market to provide comparable opportunities to "public hunters." In this context, ranchers no longer seek to suppress elk but allow this now valuable animal to multiply (much as MRI machines tend to multiply in response to private incentives). True, Utah's "public hunters" get only partial access to the expanding elk herd, but their access is much better than it was when the state pursued the kind of "pest-control" hunts that still exist on Alberta's Milk River Ridge. As already noted, moreover, the economic diversification provided to Utah's ranchers helps maintain the kinds of open spaces desired by many environmentalists. Nor are there any signs of Utah sliding down a slope that ends in Texas. As with health care, so with game management: stable mixed systems exist and produce better outcomes than their wholly public (and fully bureaucratized) alternatives. The HFH proposal in Alberta, which explicitly eschewed the Texas model, was an adaptation of Utah's mixed system. It proposed the same kind of "third way" with respect to game management that Premier Klein had suggested with respect to health care.

Both "third way" proposals failed. The health care version failed, to a considerable extent, because of federalism. True, there was strong opposition to privatization within Alberta itself, but to this was added the weight of the "Ottawa-led PR campaign about the importance of health care to the definition of Canadianess."[21] For Barry, this "propaganda campaign … convey[ed] the message that Canadians are defined by the government-funded services they consume, especially medical services."[22] Even though health care falls within provincial jurisdiction, moreover, the government funds come in part through transfer payments from Ottawa. This means that Ottawa can punish provincial moves toward what Barry considers "sensible privatization"[23] by withdrawing transfer payments. That is precisely what Ottawa threatened in response to Klein's "third way" in health care.

There was no similar federal contribution to the failure of the "third way" in game management. In both the early 1970s and again in the late 2000s, the cowboy approach was defeated entirely by a domestic Alberta hunting lobby devoted to the shibboleth of "free game." Alberta may be the heart of the "cowboy west," but some Albertans dissent from the cowboy ethos on at least some issues. The dissenters, moreover, are sometimes powerful enough to win the day, even without "Laurentian" allies.

*　　*　　*　　*　　*

I end this essay where Barry ends his, at the 2008 High River cattle auction he attended with Sandy Soutzo. At that auction, Sandy told Barry that 90 percent of cow-calf operators were over sixty. "He found this demographic fact troubling," reports Barry. "What lay ahead? Could the industry continue?"[24] A good question! The cowboy ethos can, of course, outlast cowboys themselves, just as the "garrison" mentality of Laurentian Canada persists even though the original "garrisons" are now museums. Still, it would be sad if actual cowboys continued to decline in the "cowboy west."

"The young guys," Sandy told Barry, "just aren't interested. They think it's just too hard." For many ranches, the hardship is surely explained in part by the economically marginal nature of the operation. Diversification would help, bringing in new revenue streams to make it worthwhile for "the young guys" to stay on the land and keep it whole rather than selling it off piecemeal in the manner reported by Blaine Marr. A hunting economy based on some degree of "user fees"—an economy in which sportsmen hunt "for" (i.e. "on behalf of") cowboys—has contributed to this kind of beneficial diversification in other jurisdictions. To date, Alberta's hunters have refused to "hunt *for* cowboys" in this sense. This refusal may hasten the future Sandy Soutzo worries about, a future in which "hunting for cowboys" (as in seeking to find any) will become increasingly difficult.

Endnotes

1   *It's the Regime, Stupid: A Report from the Cowboy West on Why Stephen Harper Matters* (Toronto: Key Porter, 2009).
2   Ibid., 114.
3   Ibid., 113.
4   J. Paul Hedlin & Ralph Hedlin, *Game Policy Needs in Alberta* (Toronto: Hedlin, Menzies, and Associates, Limited, 1971), 8.

5   Ibid., 4.
6   Ibid., 5.
7   Ibid., 6.
8   Ibid., 5.
9   Ibid.
10 Ibid., 41.
11 See Curtis Eaton, Allan Ingelson and Rainer Knopff, "Property Rights Regimes to Optimize Natural Resource Use—Future CBM Development and Sustainability," *Natural Resources Journal*, 45:2 (2007).
12 *It's the Regime, Stupid*, 135.
13 Ibid., 162.
14 Sylvia LeRoy and Barry Cooper, "Off Limits: How Radical Environmentalists are Stealing Canada's National Parks," Public Policy Sources, vol. 45, A Fraser Institute Occasional Paper (2000), 49. (http://www.fraserinstitute.org/publicationdisplay.aspx?id=13264&terms=national+parks)
15 Ibid., 49.
16 Ibid., 50.
17 *It's the Regime, Stupid*, 127.
18 Ibid., 11.
19 Blaine Marr, "A Landowner's View of Open Spaces Alberta," *The Pincher Creek Echo*, April 11, 2008. (http://www.pinchercreekecho.com/ArticleDisplay.aspx?archive=true&e=1961240).
20 N. Haynes McCoy, D. Reiter and J. Briem. 2003. *Utah's Cooperative Wildlife Management Unit Program: A Survey of Landowners, Operators and Landowner/Operators* (Logan, UT: CWMU Association and Jack H. Berryman Institute Rangeland Resources Department, Utah State University, 2003)
21 *It's the Regime, Stupid*, 180.
22 Ibid., 181.
23 Ibid.
24 Ibid., 242.

Chapter Four

Teaching Public Law

Janet Ajzenstat

In the 1990s, I taught public law in the Department of Political Science at McMaster University. It was the golden age: the Canadian Charter of Rights and Freedoms was barely ten years old and the superior courts were still establishing rules of interpretation.[1]

I used the "Calgary perspective," developing evidence to suggest that Canadian courts were assuming an unprecedented role in the determination of public policy, and asking whether in some cases the policy in question would have been better left to Parliament. The Calgary perspective has this supremely excellent feature: it facilitates even-handed treatment of hotly contested political issues. As Stanley Fish might say, it enables the instructor to "academize" classroom disputes.[2] I would let discussion about a policy's merits run for a time: the pros and cons of legalizing abortion, the famous issues in criminal law pitting public safety against the rights of the accused, the "fairness" of Canada's refugee determination process; but sooner or later, usually sooner, we would get down to business. How did the judges reach their conclusions? Was the policy or statute radically changed? And then, the central query: should legislators be empowered to respond?

The class was officially limited to 50 students but was always oversubscribed. I thought of myself as a success and began to think of developing a graduate program; my ambitions were growing.

Then Came a Year of Interruption

I was persuaded to participate in a project to collect and publish the debates on colonial union in the British North American legislatures. It began with William Gairdner's suggestion that "we" (an unspecified "we") publish and comment on the Province of Canada debates from 1865. Before long the team emerged: Gairdner, Ajzenstat, Ian Gentles, Paul Romney, and as researcher-in-the-field, Jeffry McNairn. At an early meeting, we decided to expand the project to include British Columbia, the Red River settlement, the Maritime Provinces, and Newfoundland. I think that I was the first to suggest the inclusion of the West, prompted by memories of Barry Cooper's tirades against the scholars who assume without second thought that the formative events of Canadian history occurred in Upper and Lower Canada and points east. As the scope of our undertaking became evident, I arranged to take a sabbatical.

A year and some months later, my head was buzzing with new ideas.[3] I was not yet ready to tell the full story of Confederation in class; I would leave that for the anticipated graduate program. But I had acquired a new appreciation of Confederation's roots in the tradition of British constitutionalism from the seventeenth century. I would have to recast my lectures. And I was looking forward to it. Who says that research and teaching are incompatible?

From Day One the Course Went Wrong

My old notes, recall, required me to ask whether public policy should be determined by the courts as well as, or in preference to, the legislatures. Now, fired by study of John Locke, Blackstone, A.V. Dicey, and the thundering rhetoric of the Confederation debates, I wished to ask whether legislatures, that is, legislatures run on the Westminster lines, play a role in securing rights. I had difficulty making myself comprehensible.

In *The Canadian Founding, John Locke and Parliament,* I tell the following story. To mark the twentieth anniversary of the Charter of Rights and Freedoms, Irwin Cotler, then Canada's justice minister, argued that the 1982 bill had initiated a "revolution of law in this country as grand in its way as Pasteur's revolution in health care." Before the Charter, he said: "Canada had a history of state-sanctioned institutionalized discrimination. . . . The judicial emphasis was with the powers of government, rather than the limitations of the exercise of power. There was a preoccupation with legal federalism. Although there was an implied bill of rights, there was no constitutional protection of law."[4]

Cotler's depiction of Canada before the Charter perfectly captures the view of some, perhaps many, Canadians still today: from Confederation, we had been at the mercy of legislators careless of individual rights; we had endured "state-sanctioned discrimination." With the introduction of the Charter the courts had means to protect us.

The Founding Debates Project had uncovered a sharply different picture, one that pointed to parliamentary debate as the principal guarantee of individual rights. The common law as formulated and interpreted by courts plays a role, but the principal and original guarantee of rights lies with Parliament.

How Was I to Convey This Idea?

In vain I appealed to the early chapters of F.L. Morton's *Law, Politics, and the Judicial Process*, in which Voltaire, Montesquieu, and other European eminences are shown arguing that the parliamentary system contributed as much as the common law to England's vaunted rights tradition.[5] The invocation of European philosophers did not resonate. As for the suggestion that Canada's Parliament today is a guarantee, students found the idea incomprehensible, if not risible. The professor had said it; the assertion had to be given at least passing attention, but it was, surely, highly improbable. That was the general feeling.

I assigned the *Alberta Press Case* (1938), in which Chief Justice Duff struggles with the idea that parliaments ensure freedom of political speech. Duff relies on the clause in the preamble to the British North America Act (1867), which reads: "Whereas the provinces of Canada, Nova Scotia and New Brunswick have expressed their Desire to be federally united into One Dominion under the Crown of the United Kingdom of Great Britain, and Ireland, with a Constitution similar in principle to that of the United Kingdom. . . ." Having thus ascribed constitutional status to the Parliament of Canada, he continues: "The statute [the B.N.A. Act] contemplates a parliament working under the influence of public opinion and public discussion. . . . There can be no controversy that such institutions derive their efficacy from the free public discussion of affairs, from criticism and answer, and counter-criticism, from the freest and fullest analysis of and examination from every point of view of political proposals."[6]

It is a glorious passage, marred by the assertion that "there can be no controversy." Clearly there was controversy, and Duff knew it. He succeeds in suggesting that there is a connection of sorts between parliamentary government and freedom of speech; he leaves us with the idea that free speech facilitates parliamentary government. But he notably does not show us how or that parliaments guarantee free speech. My students did not fail to note that the offensive statute, the Alberta Press Bill, had been passed by a British-style legislature. They applauded Duff for rejecting the statute, but did not accept his over-all contention. To a man or woman, they remained convinced that rights are better secured where some prior tradition of law, such as a constitutional bill of rights, limits legislative powers.

I could hear them thinking: "Is she really trying to tell us that legislative debate promotes rights? It can't be true; rights aren't something you take sides on; rights are rights; they're something about which everyone agrees and should agree."

"We should have 'trained' people in charge," some of the bold students would say. By "trained people," they meant lawyers. In vain I would point out that there were always lawyers in Parliament and in the departments and agencies of government. They were offended by the jostling of parties for office. They did not like political acrimony. "Why can't they all get along?" "That's a very good question," I would reply. "We're rational beings; when the facts are before us, why don't we agree more often?" Again, I could hear them thinking: "It's because some people are stupid."

"We have the Court," they would say. I would remind them that the courts are often divided on an issue. Statutes and constitutions must be interpreted and interpreters may differ. In vain!

In that unfortunate year after my sabbatical, my first thought was that I was looking at the collapse of liberal democracy. My second and more seasoned reflection was that the students were not voicing a new attitude, but an *old* one, indeed, a *perennial* one. The Charter had given it a new gloss but what I was seeing in the law-class auditorium was a version of a debate older than the idea of parliamentary government or codified rights.

The students were looking for surety. They wanted government by good people. It is not an un-admirable desire! In a former age they would have asked for government by the wise, or the virtuous. (In our challenged times, a limp phrase like "trained leaders" was the best they could manage.)

My sabbatical had borne in on me that the overriding conclusion of British political thought from, let us say, the time of John Locke, has been that the search for wise and virtuous leaders results in oligarchy at best, or more likely, tyranny. Leo Strauss famously ascribes this argument to Plato. (The *Republic* appears to recommend rule by the wise, but the prescription has cruel and self-contradictory, indeed ridiculous consequences. Hence Strauss's conclusion: Plato intended us to read the *Republic* as a dystopia.) We could look elsewhere for such a doctrine among the ancients. We might find it in the story of Republican Rome's fall. In Allan Bloom's classes at the University of Toronto, I was taught to look for it in Machiavelli's *Prince*.

The argument against the rule of the wise takes the form of a concrete and practicable principle of government with the development of parliamentary institutions in England and in the Netherlands in the early years of the seventeenth century. It is nowhere better expounded than in Locke's

Second Treatise of Government (1690). I do not say that England was well governed from early in the seventeenth century; of course not; a century of war and struggle ensued. Tradition dates parliamentary government from 1688. And even then, it was decades before it was well established. Nevertheless, the argument for parliamentary government as security for individual rights was abroad throughout the century, contested and yet ever more appealing.

It has two elements: the good constitution will guarantee the contestation of political leaders for office at more or less regular, and more or less frequent intervals, thus ensuring that those who are denied office, or ousted from it, have good reason to accept a political reverse, or in other words, have insufficient reason to resort to violence and every hope that by adhering to constitutional rules they will be returned to power. That is the first element. The second is related. There is no unchallengeable list of substantive policies to which leaders may appeal.

My students were uncomfortable with the idea of perpetual disagreement on policy; they wanted to discover, or be told about, *the* overriding Canadian way of life, the substantive issues on which all Canadians agree and should agree. There was surely more to the Canadian political way of life, surely more to love about this country, than parliamentary institutions and an exhaustive distribution of legislative powers between levels of government.

I needed a well-defined argument, a memorable way to put the case for continuing contestation in parliament, perpetual dissent, noise, even—dare I say it?—incivility. I did not have one. Two years later, Ontario's early-retirement policy caught up with me. The law class was disbanded. I turned to other projects.

When, quite recently, Christopher Alcantara at Wilfrid Laurier University asked me to attend a session of his graduate seminar on Canadian politics, I jumped at the chance. I thought of facing ten to fifteen good students, none of them known to me, and like a gift out of thin air the argument I had been searching for appeared in my thoughts in the form of an image.

I would ask the students to image a snapshot of the Canadian Parliament in session at any time in our history from 1867. Unless taken at a very unusual moment in Canada's past, the picture will show what to all appearances is an oligarchic regime. (So I proposed to argue.) Government leaders are trying to ram through their program with the support of a more or less docile majority or coalition. The opposition sulks across the way, its arguments and objections tolerated, recorded, indeed "honoured," but more or less ignored.

"Now suppose you take in a movie camera," I imagined myself saying. "Keep it running for ten or twelve years. I suggest that you will see a depiction of Parliament as a true deliberative institution." I did not get a chance to run the full exercise. Professor Alcantara's students got the point immediately. If I were speaking to a big class I would ask the students to pick the span of years. Let the ones with a historical bent show off. You might suggest that, in addition to changes of party in office, they look for instances in which parties pass ideas back and forth. (Think of free trade policies, or arguments for curbing the deficit.)

In the parliamentary regime, deliberation is open to all shades of opinion, and when the vote on a particular topic is taken, every vote has the same weight. Moreover, and most important, parliamentary decisions are not final. Laws can be modified or repealed. Debate continues in the extra-parliamentary arena. Majorities erode; new majorities form; minorities join coalitions, or swell to majority proportions. The parliamentary form of government will often seem imperfect; it will never satisfy the impatient. Yet it is difficult to think of a system that yields a more inclusive governing institution. It is difficult to think of one that does more to keep before the public initially unpopular contentions and policies.

The courts purport to be final arbiters, putting an end to political dispute and contestation, setting us straight, getting things right. (Hence their appeal for anxious students.) A court may reverse a judicial decision, but the reversal suggests that the previous decision had been an error; judicial reversals convey the perhaps unfortunate idea that courts are imperfect. Legislatures rejoice in reversals; a parliament that reverses a legislative decision is acting in the best traditions of the institution, revealing its strengths.

In the Westminster tradition, this non-finality feature goes by a curious name: parliamentary sovereignty. One session of parliament cannot bind subsequent sessions. On this principle, or doctrine, or practice, call it what you will, hangs the idea, argued repeatedly in the Confederation debates, that parliaments secure our freedoms.

The Canadian Founders on Rights

To repeat: what I found in the study of the legislative debates on Confederation was the contention, fully and understandably developed, that the parliamentary regime secures individual rights. (I say, "fully and understandably," but the fact is that on my return to class I was not yet in a position to lecture on the subject.)

The usual view of John A. Macdonald presents him as a high-handed party advocate and oligarch. But in the debates on colonial union in the Province of Canada, he speaks as a proponent of popular sovereignty, an equalitarian, and a defender of parliamentary free speech. Here is his exposition of rights security in the parliamentary regime. He is describing the general government of the proposed federation—the institution that will come to be known as the Parliament of Canada:

> We will enjoy here that which is the great test of constitutional freedom—we will have the rights of the minority respected. In all countries the rights of the majority take care of themselves, but it is only in countries like England, enjoying constitutional liberty, and safe from the tyranny of a single despot or of an unbridled democracy, that the rights of minorities are regarded.[7]

By "rights of the minorities" Macdonald did not mean—or did not mean exclusively—ethnic or religious minorities. He was referring to the view of the opposition parties and groups in the colonial assemblies, upper chambers, and in the population at large. Parliamentary government secures a country against oligarchy; the majority party governs, but cannot suppress dissent. Dissenting arguments must be heard; they are recorded and published. And so the deliberative process continues, fluid, flexible, enabling the best possible security for rights; not the best absolutely, it may be, but the best possible.

"It is only in countries like England . . . that rights of minorities are regarded." It is an idea to conjure with.

The prevailing tradition among the social scientists and historians of this country holds that the Canadian Fathers made no proposals to secure British North American liberties. Donald Creighton, sometimes thought of as Canada's master historian, says of the Fathers: "They were mid-Victorian British colonials who had grown up in a political system which they valued, and which they had not the slightest intention of trying to change by revolution. For them the favourite myths of the Enlightenment did not possess even a quaintly antiquarian interest. . . . [They] . . . would have been sceptical about both the utility and the validity of abstract notions such as the social contract and inalienable rights of man."[8] Creighton's influence has been profound.

In a short paper I can only hint at the wealth of arguments at

Confederation in support of parliamentary government as surety for rights. Not all the speakers were as moderate in tone as Macdonald. But all, almost without exception, were informed about arguments originating in the seventeenth century and they did their best to write into our constitution the elements of parliamentary government, thus ensuring to British North Americans the fundamental British liberties.

The Fathers of Confederation are the thirty-three men who drafted Canada's constitution at the Quebec Conference of 1864. Once drafted, the scheme was referred to the colonial parliaments for ratification. The rule was simple; without a parliamentary "yea" vote for union, a colony would not be admitted. The debates between the Fathers (most of them on the front benches) and the legislative back-benchers, are our best source of the Fathers' intentions and a good source of British North American opinion. We may call the Fathers and the ratifying legislators collectively, *founders.*[9]

What the founders meant by "rights" is today perhaps better captured by the term, "civil liberties." Civil liberties describe limits on the government's interference and to that extent mark out the area of individual freedom and responsibility. They are thinking of the right to life, liberty and property—to use Locke's formulation—and freedom from arbitrary arrest or detention, freedom of speech and thought, and freedom of worship. The founders had always in mind freedom from oppression by authority, even—or especially—democratically elected authority.

There were differences among them and, unsurprisingly, given the centrality they accorded individual freedoms, one difference predominated, becoming in fact the central theme of the process that gave birth to Canada. Some of the founders were content to argue that individual rights would be preserved in the proposed union under the twin protections of parliamentary government and federalism. But others, among them the most vociferous opponents of Confederation, believed that union would impair the colonists' rights, and that the new country would be a poorer bulwark against tyranny and authoritarianism than the colonies it would subsume.

A mistake of signal importance—one still widely accepted in academe—is the idea that Confederation pitted Tories against Liberals, with the Tories favouring union and the Liberals opposing. Thus it is sometimes said that Canada is a "Tory party invention," a country made by John A. and his colleagues. The facts prove otherwise, as Christopher Moore argues persuasively.[10] When the time came to draft the union constitution, each colony was at pains to ensure that both the government party and the opposition party or parties were represented. Confederation was not a matter for expression of ideological and partisan interests. All were convinced that the national legislature they were designing should allow the contestation of political parties for office; all knew that parliaments should welcome the admission of ideologies and arguments on a footing of equality. They knew that to assign constitutional priority to one ideology—to assume a preference for Toryism, for example—would have the effect of entrenching oligarchy.

In the ratifying debates in the provincial parliaments, the crucial division was not between the Liberal and Tory parties, but between those favouring the federation of the colonies and those opposing. And on the issue of federation there were Liberals and Tories (and independents) on both sides. The great question was this: would Confederation undermine the colonists' rights? Those favouring Confederation (we may call them Confederates) argued that there would be no diminution of liberty under the new constitution, because it would entrench the familiar features of parliamentary government that secure it; to wit, the right of political dissent in the legislature and the general population.

The opponents of Confederation (the anti-Confederates) were not convinced. They agreed that parliamentary government secures liberty. But the Quebec Resolutions proposed to harness parliamentary institutions to American-style federalism. The colonists would be obliged to obey two levels of government.

The typical anti-Confederate argument took this form: we in New Brunswick (let us say) do very well with our provincial legislature. All domestic matters are settled by our own government after due deliberation. All matters can be reviewed and amended. We are free to argue for repeal of unsatisfactory political measures, and to vote out an unsatisfactory government. But if Confederation wins the day, some matters affecting New Brunswickers will be settled by a national legislature, in which New Brunswickers will be in a minority. We may have to live with laws that we cannot countenance and that—most important—we cannot see any prospect of changing. We will be giving up our present, perfect freedom to live by laws of our own making.

Confederates like George Brown said repeatedly that the federation's general government would legislate only on general matters, that is, on matters affecting equally every individual in the federation as a whole. Matters affecting particular regions, or particular traditions and religions, would fall to the provinces. Thus, issues affecting New Brunswickers as New Brunswickers would never come before the union government. On this point George Brown and George-Etienne Cartier agreed. Matters dear to French Canadians as French Canadians would not be subjected to debate in the Parliament of Canada—a legislature sure to be dominated by English-Canadians. Reading the debates today, it is apparent that the founders were thinking in terms of what would come to be called "water-tight compartments."

Let me amplify the idea that in the decade before Confederation most of Britain's North American colonies or provinces (the terms were used interchangeably) had come to enjoy considerable political independence.

In 1848, or shortly thereafter, the Province of Canada, the Maritime Provinces, and Newfoundland had won "responsible government," the constitutional principle or practice requiring the government of the day to maintain the confidence of the majority of representatives in the parliament's elective chamber. Why the British government granted this measure is to me something of a mystery.[11] Lord Durham had recommended it and the colonial constitutionalists had ardently campaigned for it; it is correct to speak of a colonial "struggle for responsible government." I understand that much. But the fact is that with the adoption of "responsible government," each province or colony came to resemble a self-governing unitary state. Nominally, they were still British dependencies, but for all practical purposes—on domestic matters, certainly—Britain's powers of interference were severely curtailed. To repeat: the colonies had the character of small sovereign nations. And they were stiff with pride: they boasted of their parliamentary institutions and their ability to secure their people's freedoms.

Listen to Stewart Campbell in Nova Scotia: "I am a free man. I claim the rights and attributes of a free man, speaking in the presence of a British free assembly. I have the right to criticize the judgment they [the Confederates] formed and an equal right to give expression to my own." William Lawrence, another Nova Scotian, boasted: "We are a free people, prosperous beyond doubt, advancing cautiously in wealth. . . . Under the British Constitution we have far more freedom than any other people on the face of the earth." More freedom than any other people on the face of the earth![12]

Newfoundland's George Hogsett made a similar contention: "We have here a constitution for which the people nobly fought, and which was reluctantly wrung from the British government. We had the right of taxing ourselves, or legislating for ourselves, and were we then . . . to give up all the rights we possess, rights which, if properly worked and administered, would secure us all the advantages and prosperity a people can want or require?"[13]

At Confederation, then, the question was this: would a province's population suffer a diminution of rights and freedoms? The advocates of Confederation had to prove to the satisfaction of the anti-Confederates that the union of the colonies and the constitutional division of legislative powers contemplated at the Quebec Conference would not impair the freedoms to which British North Americans had become accustomed.

Consent of the Governed

On 15 February 1865, Legislative Councilor David Christie said in the Province of Canada debates on the Quebec Resolutions:

> . . . life, liberty and the pursuit of happiness are the unalienable rights of man, and . . . to secure these rights, government are instituted among men, deriving their just powers from the consent of the governed. This is the secret strength of the British Constitution, and without a full and free recognition of it no government can be strong and permanent.[14]

The secret strength of the *British* Constitution? Did the parliamentary reporter slip up? Did Christie really describe the British Constitution in the famous words of the American Declaration of Independence? But there was no mistake in reporting. Speeches in the Province of Canada debates were prepared for publication; legislators had the opportunity to revise. Not everyone crashed into the deliberations with Christie's flamboyance, but all knew they were participating in a momentous decision. They were proud of what they said and they wanted to leave an accurate record.

Let me sum up Christie's statement in more sober language. He was arguing that British North Americans no less than citizens of the United States were beneficiaries of the seventeenth-century natural-law argument for the equality of man. British North Americans, like their neighbours to the south, were John Locke's heirs. Most participants in the Confederation debates agreed with Christie on this matter. Not a few thought that British institutions offered a superior guarantee. In the Province of Canada debates, John A. Macdonald argued that the constitution of the United States was "one of the most skillful works which human intelligence ever created . . . one of the most perfect organizations that ever governed a free people." Of course, he and Cartier and George Brown had thought of a few improvements!

Christie claimed as part of the British heritage the two most notable features of the political tradition that originated in the seventeenth century: the "unalienable rights of man," and the principle of popular sovereignty, which he defined, borrowing Jefferson's language, as the requirement that governments derive their just powers from the consent of the governed. As Jefferson's formulation indicates, the propositions are intimately related.

In *Constitutional Odyssey*, Peter Russell asserts that the Fathers of Confederation regarded popular sovereignty as a "dreadful heresy." He writes: "[At] Canada's founding its people were not sovereign and there was not even a sense that a constituent sovereign people would have to be invented." On this subject Russell is wrong. He did not have the documents before him. He was betrayed by the failure of two generations of scholars to consult and discuss our founding debates. We were all betrayed.[15]

Locke's formulation runs as follows: "For no government can have a right to obedience from a people who have not freely consented to it." In the Canadian Legislative Assembly, James O'Halloran said: "the people are the only rightful source of all political power." In the Nova Scotia Assembly, William Lawrence said, "the principle which lies at the foundation of our constitution is that which declares the people to be the source of political power." In 1870, in the Legislative Council of British Columbia, which was considering whether to join Confederation, E.G. Alston stated: "I am not disposed to regret the occurrence of the difficulties in Red River, for it will teach the Canadian government, and all governments, that though you may buy and sell territories, you cannot transfer the human beings therein, like so many serfs and chattels, to a fresh allegiance with impunity; that the consent of the people must be first obtained; and that though the soil may be sold, the soul is free."

"The soil may be sold, the soul is free." Is that a grand statement? Yes! Is it a Lockean statement? Yes!

Think again about Christie holding forth on the rights of man. What was the occasion? Was the Parliament of the Province of Canada merely passing the time of day, discussing in an offhand way the union document that had been drawn up at Quebec City the previous fall? No; as early as 1858, the matter of obtaining "the people's consent" to the union of the colonies had been discussed among colonial leaders and with the British Colonial Office. At that time, it had been decided that the principle of popular consent would be satisfied by a majority vote in favour of union in each colonial parliament.[16]

In due course (1864), the colonial elites met at Quebec to draft the union document; they were then required to return to their provincial parliaments to put the necessary ratifying resolution. No province could be yanked into Confederation without that yea vote. But in each province, as soon as the ratifying resolution was tabled, fierce debates broke out. Not all members could be persuaded that a parliamentary vote would suffice. In every province, there were some—and in Nova Scotia many—who held out for ratification by referendum, that is, by household vote. Space does not permit me to discuss the fascinating quarrels in those provincial parliaments. The important point is that all participating were convinced that the Lockean principle should be followed: "the people" had to be consulted. To repeat: the quarrels were about *how* to consult them.

The idea that there was no provision for consulting the population in the making of the Canadian Constitution muddles Canadian thinking to an intolerable degree. The acknowledgement that legitimate government rests on the consent of the governed is described as a feature of the American constitution, but not the Canadian! Our scholars have been left without a way of thinking coherently about the seventeenth-century's natural rights tradition in connection with parliamentary government.

Law Class: Reprise: What is to be Done?

In the first weeks of the law class, many students exhibited a naïve libertarianism. They regarded legislatures as a threat to individual freedom. Parliament's rules and regulations invade the private sphere; the courts draw the line and thus protect us. That was the mantra. As the year continued and they mastered Charter decisions from the 1980s, their views shifted. Many became enthusiastic about the Charter, not as a protection against legislative fiat, but as a means to embrace new "rights,"—gay rights, for example—or more generally, the rights of the disadvantaged in society, rights of entitlement, we may say.

This is the place to admit that I was never completely successful at "academizing" discussions in the law class. It might be argued that I was not successful at all. The students who liked the Supreme Court's decisions on the abortion issue, or the refugee determination rules, etc., argued more or less wholeheartedly for giving the courts the last word on policy. Is the Supreme Court involved in determining policy? Yes, they would say, and a good thing too. Our endlessly acrimonious legislators are too far behind the times and too absorbed in their own political careers. The courts usually reach the right decision, and are in the best position to protect it from interfering political interests.

Students who disliked the Court's opinions (pro-life students, let us say; or students who thought that refugee applicants take unfair advantage of Canada's rules) faced a dilemma. They sometimes argued for judicial self-restraint. But at bottom they were no more comfortable than their classroom peers with the idea that legislative deliberation anchors rights. They were no more comfortable with the idea of *Parliament.*

All or almost all were guided by their interest in the policy outcome and their native sense of what is "fair." Many of them were in the law class because they hoped to become lawyers or to go into a law-related field. Not a few had taken courses in women's rights, or the rights of "disadvantaged" citizens. They were good-hearted women and men.

Whether they inclined to a libertarian perspective, or embraced a complete agenda of progressive rights, few were prepared to think well of the parliamentary regime. Some had read John Locke's arguments about the "social contract," "property," and the "state of nature." None, to my knowledge, were familiar with the Locke who defends parliamentary institutions. None were in position to understand poor Justice Duff. And some, as I have suggested, were drifting toward the idea that we should turn our attention to the means needed to elect superior individuals to our governing institutions.

All were to one degree or another persuaded of two things: there is little in Canadian political history to boast about. And there are few reasons to think parliamentary institutions admirable.

What is to be done? I have no idea.

Endnotes

1   We read the abbreviated accounts of Supreme Court decisions in Peter H. Russell, Rainer Knopff, and Ted Morton, *Federalism and the Charter, Leading Constitutional Decisions* (Ottawa: Carleton University Press, 1989), and for general background, F.L. Morton, *Law, Politics and the Judicial Process in Canada* (Calgary: University of Calgary Press, 1992), and Rainer Knopff and F.L. Morton, *Charter Politics* (Scarborough, Ont: Nelson Canada, 1992).

2   Stanley Fish, *There's No Such Thing as Free Speech and a Good Thing Too* (Oxford: Oxford University Press, 1994).

3   We published excerpts from the legislative debates in the seven British North American jurisdictions: British Columbia, the Red River Settlement, the Province

of Canada, Nova Scotia, New Brunswick, Prince Edward Island, and Newfoundland. Janet Ajzenstat, Paul Romney, Ian Gentles, and William D. Gairdner, eds., *Canada's Founding Debates* (Toronto: Stoddart, 1999). The University of Toronto Press reissued it in 2003; the University of Laval brought out the French edition under the direction of Stéphane Kelly and Guy LaForest in 2004.

4   Janet Ajzenstat, *The Canadian Founding, John Locke and Parliament* (Montreal & Kingston: McGill-Queen's University Press, 2007), 49.

5   Morton, *Law, Politics and the Judicial Process*, 1–19. He also includes an excellent essay on the rule of law in the Canadian Constitution, and reproduces Justice Rand's famous opinion in *Roncarelli v. Duplessis*.

6   For the abbreviated version of Duff's decision read by my students, see, Russell, Knopff and Morton, *Federalism and The Charter*, pp. 291–298. It is unfortunate that Duff referred readers to the Constitution's preamble and only to the preamble. Scholars have often contended, perhaps following Duff, that the Constitution Act (1867) contains no concrete prescription for the principle of responsible government. Thus Peter Russell argues: "The constitution drafters saw no need to spell out the vital democratic principle that government be directed by ministers who have the confidence of the elected branch of the legislature . . . . The only hint of responsible government in the final constitutional text is the reference in the preamble to the BNA Act to a 'Constitution similar in Principle to that of the united Kingdom'" (*Constitutional Odyssey, Can Canadians Become a Sovereign People?* (Toronto: University of Toronto Press, 1992), 26). But Russell is wrong. A careful reading of the Act, with special attention to sections 53 and 54, shows that the constitutional elements necessary for the practice we call "responsible government" are all present and correct. It is true that the term itself—"responsible government"—is not used. I would argue that it was not employed because in the nineteenth century "responsible government" could be taken to describe a number of systems, including American-style republicanism. Janet Ajzenstat, *The Once and Future Canadian Democracy, An Essay in Political Thought* (Montreal & Kingston: McGill-Queen's University Press), 63–67.

7   John A. Macdonald, in the Canadian Legislative Assembly, 6 February, 1865. Cited in *Canada's Founding Debates* (hereafter CFD), 206.

8   Donald Creighton, *The Road to Confederation: The Emergence of Canada, 1863–1867* (Toronto: Macmillan, 1964), 142–143. Peter H. Russell asserts his agreement with Creighton on this point in *Constitutional Odyssey*, 10–11.

9   The description of the founders in these pages reproduces the argument of *The Canadian Founding, John Locke and Parliament*. It owes much as well to a short essay written for the Macdonald–Laurier Institute and published on their web site in the fall of 2010 (Ajzenstat, "Confederation and Individual Liberty," November 2010 (http://www.macdonaldlaurier.ca/files/pdf/ConfederationLiberty.pdf)). I gratefully acknowledge the editorial assistance of Brian Lee Crowley and John Robson.

10   See Christopher Moore, *1867, How the Fathers Made a Deal* (Toronto: McLelland & Stewart, 1997), ix.

11   For a recent and persuasive account of the struggle for responsible government see

John Ralston Saul, *Louis-Hippolyte LaFontaine and Robert Baldwin* (Toronto: Penguin Group, 2010).

12 Stewart Campbell, Nova Scotia House of Assembly, 17 March, 1866 (CFD, 371); William Lawrence, Nova Scotia House of Assembly, 17 April, 1866 (CFD, 384).

13 George Hogsett, Nova Scotia House of Assembly, 23 February, 1869 (CFD, 98).

14 David Christie, Province of Canada, Legislative Council, 15 February, 1865 (CFD, 191).

15 Russell, *Constitutional Odyssey*, 33.

16 See G.P. Browne, *Documents on the Confederation of British North America, Edited and with an Introduction by G.P. Browne* (Montreal & Kingston: McGill-Queen's University Press), 2009; Section A: The Reaction of the Colonial Office to the Canadian Initiative of 1858. For this new edition, Janet Ajzenstat has supplied a second Introduction.

Chapter Five

Spiritual Disorder and Terrorism:

On Barry Cooper's *New Political Religions*

Michael Franz

Barry Cooper's *New Political Religions, or an Analysis of Modern Terrorism* is one of the most important achievements of North American political science in recent years.[1] In a relatively slim volume running to fewer than 200 pages, Cooper has made impressive headway toward at least four significant objectives:

* Illuminating the motivating inner core of terrorist action, principally by employing Eric Voegelin's analysis of pneumopathology;
* Extending Voegelin's analysis of ideologically motivated political activism from modern mass movements to the rather different phenomena associated with small cell terrorist organizations;
* Distinguishing those elements of Islamist terrorism that are peculiarly Islamic from those that are common to spiritually disordered activism per se;
* Analyzing the motivating wellsprings of modern terrorism in a manner suggesting implications for both political policy and counterterrorist tactics.

In my view, Cooper has authored the single most penetrating analysis of religiously motivated terrorism yet published, far surpassing some of the most widely read works on the subject in terms of discernment, theoretical precision, and practical applicability. At the same time, he has broken new theoretical ground by showing that modern terrorism can be brought within the set of political phenomena made intelligible by Voegelin's pathbreaking analysis of spiritual disorder.

I'm quick to acknowledge my admiration for the book, but my larger purpose is to assess it with the seriousness that it merits, which requires questioning its questionable aspects while also pointing to its impressive strengths. My analysis is structured by reference to six (somewhat overlapping) questions: How effectively does the book address its target audience?

To what extent are we encountering something new when confronting contemporary, religiously inspired terrorism? To what degree is Islamist terrorism traceable to elements inherent to Islam? To what extent is Islamic extremism attributable to so-called "root cause" conditions of life on the ground in the Islamic world? How convincing is Cooper's diagnosis of contemporary terrorism as a spiritually disordered political religion? What are the most important ways in which Cooper's approach augments leading understandings of terrorism?

How effectively does the book address its audience?

Cooper isn't explicit about his intended audience, but it seems easy enough to infer that the book was written principally for scholars of terrorism who might benefit from the theoretical perspective that it provides. I suspect that Cooper also wrote for theoretically trained readers who aren't conversant with the current literature on terrorism, but in any case, his prime objective seems to have been to enrich the literature on terrorism (and the attendant debates on counterterrorism) by showing the explanatory power of a diagnostic perspective informed by concepts such as spiritual disorder and political religion.

If that was indeed Cooper's principal intention, it was certainly well advised. Political theorists who do not follow the academic literature on terrorism might be surprised to find that the average level of philosophical and theological sophistication evinced in it is quite low by almost any standard, and this is true even for a surprisingly high percentage of those writers who deem themselves capable of offering specialized studies of religiously inspired terrorism. Moreover, the literature shows no discernible indications of influence from Voegelin's studies in the history of political pneumopathology (nor, for that matter, of scholars engaged in related researches such as Waldemar Gurian, Franz Borkenau, Nikolai Berdyaev or Raymond Aron). Needless to say, an attempt on Cooper's part to augment this literature (which has significant impact on policy as well as scholarship) was an entirely worthwhile enterprise.[2] And yet, while this was a laudable undertaking, I wonder if the book was as successful as it might have been.

On the one hand, Cooper has evidently taken pains to become conversant in the general literature on terrorism, and to acquaint himself not only with the general approaches of leading writers, but also with a wide array of operational details associated with terrorism and counterterrorism. (His concluding chapter on "Counternetwar" is particularly impressive in this regard.) The book is admirably free of the particular strain of condescension one sometimes sees when political philosophers address those engaged in narrower, more technical studies. If Cooper was intent upon leavening this literature by drawing upon his background in philosophical matters and Voegelin's analysis of spiritual disorder, he did not attempt to do so without rolling up his sleeves and learning what he might learn from those whom he might teach.

On the other hand, Cooper sometimes presupposes in his readers what I think he should be teaching. Although I can cite several examples, I should limit my discussion to two instances that will serve to illustrate the point and address a third in a note.[3] In the course of Cooper's second chapter (which develops critical concepts for his analysis), he offers a strikingly powerful account of the inherent futility of terrorist violence and of its propensity to become continuous or perpetual despite this very futility. Drawing upon Hannah Arendt's distinction between properly political action and actions of the human as *homo faber*, Cooper succeeds in showing that terrorist violence is a mode of fabrication. Regarding fabrication as understood by Arendt, Cooper observes that,

> First, fabrication is inherently violent. Making something consists in working upon material that has already been removed from nature. This removal can be effected only by violence "as by killing a life in cutting down a tree to provide wood." Second, the work of making something is always guided by a model or pattern that precedes the thing made, the work after which it is constructed. The "idea" is prior to the material thing. Third, "the process of making is itself entirely determined by the categories of means and end." The process ends with the product, and the product, the end, justifies the means. So far as the instrumental use of violence is concerned, the table justifies the violence done to the tree that turns it into material at hand.[4]

The ensuing section becomes increasingly intricate and demanding philosophically, with Cooper introducing (in a rather off-handed manner) a couple of paradoxes and bringing both Lessing and Kant into play. In doing so while making a point of profound importance, he consigns much of his audience to the sidelines, effectively addressing only those already initiated into the philosophical mysteries.

Briefly to indicate Cooper's profound point and to show how he conveys it, we can consider the following section:

> [T]errorism is a mode of fabrication, the application of violence to human material in order to create a desired product. But because human beings have the capacity to begin, to initiate what never has been before, to act and to reveal in their actions a new meaning and a new story, there is no product. As a result, every so-called product is temporary and, in the context of violent making, nothing more than the pretext for further violence.[5]

Immediately following this passage, Cooper notes—in a transitional sentence introducing a new issue—that the mode of consciousness seeking to treat human beings in the mode of fabrication makes a "categorical error." That observation is exactly correct and very important, in my view, but quite unlikely to be grasped by readers lacking relatively extensive theoretical training (who might well not understand the nature of a categorical error *per se*, much less what this particular categorical error may be). Cooper's important and badly under-appreciated point is likely to fall upon deaf ears, partly because the allusions to Arendt's thought are left as mere allusions, and partly because the unspoken premises enabling Cooper to diagnose a "categorical error" are left largely unspoken.

To treat them explicitly, I believe that Cooper's conclusion depends upon the following points:

* The terrorist uses violence both to frighten a recalcitrant populace into accepting his demands and also to fabricate a perfect future from the materials of the degraded present.
* Fabrication presupposes material that is malleable, lacking individuation, agency, or a given nature that would resist alteration; however, humans are endowed by nature with each of these characteristics.
* Moreover, the given nature of human beings is "crooked timber," to use Kant's term, and hence categorically unsuited to the fabrication of any "straight" or perfect future.
* Hence all terrorist attempts to alter human beings or their mode of association are fated to failure.
* This will prove to be no mere failure, but rather one of a terribly persistent sort, since terrorists who are resolved to wring something straight out of material that is immutably crooked must continue their futile attempts endlessly.

Again, I believe that each of these points is entirely valid and of the highest significance. Yet, many of the readers whom Cooper might wish to influence are unlikely to grasp them based upon his presentation. They are clear enough for those who have worked through the classic problems of philosophical anthropology, or who have engaged in theoretically guided historical analysis of analogous ideological attempts to construct a "master race" or "socialist man." But for the average student of international affairs or security studies they may well remain opaque.

In my opinion this example points to a take-it-or-leave-it character that appears at various points in the book, a character that bespeaks something like "argumentative impatience," or the offering of mere assertions for points that really require argumentation and evidence.

A second example can be seen in Cooper's repeated assertions that terrorists are not only engaged in futile, morally illegitimate acts, but also that they are well aware of the futility and moral illegitimacy of their actions. Despite the frequency with which this assertion appears, Cooper offers very little in the way of argumentation or evidence for it. The point is far from inconsequential, as it seems to be a necessary condition for validating a central proposition of the book (perhaps *the* central proposition), namely, that certain terrorists are spiritually diseased.

We can view the centrality of the proposition from two different angles. In practical terms, Cooper needs the point that terrorists are aware of the futility of their actions, because it supports the diagnosis that they are spiritually diseased against the alternative possibility that they are merely misguided in tactical or strategic matters. And, in ethical terms, Cooper needs the point that terrorists are aware of the moral illegitimacy of their actions, because his pneumopathology thesis holds that they are not merely morally obtuse but "morally insane." To cite a couple of instances:

> The curious twilight form of existence, where members of a terrorist group both know and refuse to acknowledge what they know perfectly well, is enacted by both leaders and followers.[6]

> The reality that terrorists carefully avoid facing is that killing the innocent is inherently illegitimate. Moreover, terrorists are sufficiently aware of this truth or of this ethical reality that they go to great efforts to deny it.[7]

Passages that assert this basic point—or which are premised upon it—can be found at many points in the book, but these two examples will suffice for present purposes, as they touch upon the related but distinct issues of terrorist self-awareness regarding tactical and ethical matters.

It is clear that the structure of Cooper's argument requires this basic point in its tactical and ethical aspects, but not clear that he substantiates it adequately for those unprepared to accept it on its face. When noting the pneumopathological tendencies of specific individuals, Cooper sometimes indicates that they seem otherwise intelligent and competent, as if to suggest that when they engage in violent but futile action or incitement, they *must* know better. But this is not terribly satisfying. History offers an abundance of cases in which generally successful people fall prey to particular strategic blind spots, or in which more-or-less upstanding characters slip into ignominy due to a single strain of moral incapacity. Similarly, Cooper sometimes seems to presume that certain patterns of action can be taken to *imply* that agents are aware of the futility of what they are doing, as when terrorists engage in an action that will purportedly install them as leaders of a new order—but do so while taking care to avoid detection by police from the old order. Again, this is not terribly satisfying, as we know that inconsistencies and hedging of various sorts are quite common among ordinary people, and that activists of various stripes can be actuated by extremely robust self-confidence while also being stalked continually by self-doubt.

Cooper tries to make a dramatic point—that terrorists are engaged in murderous but pointlessly ineffective acts while knowing full well that the acts are pointless—yet his arguments and evidence seem insufficiently substantial to support it. He may be convinced that these terrorists know better in their heart of hearts, and that their actions in the presence of such knowledge constitute a type of spiritual disorder. And he may have convinced me of this as well. But the business of diagnosing spiritual disorders in others on the basis of written accounts is an inherently dubious one for most general readers in terrorist studies, both because it deals with spiritual matters and also because it does so in a judgmental manner inconsistent with the tolerant ethos of the academy. Skepticism (or even dismissiveness) comes with the territory for a writer like Cooper who is importing theoretical exotica into the conventional field of terrorism studies, and I think the book would have been more effective if he had worked more patiently to persuade readers who require some persuading if they are to follow his line of analysis.

To what degree are we dealing with something new when confronting contemporary, religiously inspired terrorism?

This question is taken up fairly frequently in contemporary treatments of terrorism, but in almost every instance the time frame is much narrower than what Cooper is prepared to consider. Similarly, current accounts almost always treat terrorism itself in a much narrower way, with a primary emphasis on tactics and techniques, whereas Cooper is willing to consider underlying motivations in a way that opens many more possible lines of continuity to movements from the past.

For example, Russell Howard understands "New Terrorism" in contradistinction to the politically motivated, commando-style terrorism of the Baader-Meinhof gang or of Abu Nidal of the Fatah National Council. "New Terrorism" is associated with Osama bin Laden and al Qaeda, and is said to be novel in at least six ways: it is more violent; better financed; undertaken by terrorists who are transnational and dissociated from particular states; who are better trained in the arts of war and the black arts; whose organizations are more difficult to penetrate; and who possibly have access to weapons of mass destruction.[8] Cooper is likewise interested in distinguishing between what he terms "traditional" and "modern" terrorists, and between the politically motivated terrorists of the 1970s and the religiously motivated ones of the early twenty-first century. However, since Cooper is prepared to move beyond *what* terrorists do to consider *why* they do it, his time frame in considering precursors extends back to include the Thugs, Assassins and Zealots of prior centuries, and permits him to note that "contemporary religious terrorists have followed a pattern remarkably close to that initially made by several spiritual movements of the late medieval and Christian West."[9]

Cooper's book shows that he is well aware of current conventions for distinguishing "new" terrorists from those of earlier periods, but also that he is not entirely persuaded of the adequacy of these conventions. He is prepared to follow them as far as they go, as in the case of Bruce Hoffman's analysis,[10] but seems to suggest that they do not go far enough due to an insufficiently inclusive methodology. Thus, following a summary of Hoffman's distinctions, Cooper contends that "an arguably more adequate way to understand the logic of religious terrorism is to consider it as a second reality."[11] From this perspective, Cooper seems less impressed than his more conventional counterparts with the purportedly novel aspects of so-called "new terrorism." For example, conventional analysts tend to regard "traditional" terrorists as having been more concerned with terrorism as a performance for a public audience other than the victims themselves; they wanted "a lot of people watching and a lot of people listening and not a lot of people dead,"[12] whereas the terrorists of September 11, 2001, clearly wanted a lot of people dead. However, utilizing the perspective and conceptual tools he draws from Voegelin and Arendt, Cooper notes that traditional and "new" terrorism both involve performance aspects. Traditional terrorists were typically performing for a television audience, and "new" terrorists perform for this audience as well; "the difference is that the performance of the religiously motivated terrorist is conducted on an imaginative 'cosmic' stage, a stage with an imaginary world-transcendent dimension, as well as upon the mundane stage of the commonsense world, the world of the first reality."[13]

On balance, Cooper's unconventional approach to terrorism seems to leave him relatively underwhelmed by the purportedly novel aspects of "new terrorism," and more inclined to find fundamental continuities not only with terrorists of earlier decades, but with ideologists and religious sectarians of earlier centuries. Thus, Cooper writes,

> The change from what we have loosely called traditional terrorist acts, the propaganda of the deed where the object is to terrify a large number of onlookers by killing a few, to the suicidal mass murders of September 11, 2001, clearly indicates a change in operational style. But only the style has changed. The substance remains: a pneumopathological consciousness projects a second reality and acts murderously within first reality by killing a lot of otherwise innocent people.[14]

There is not much doubt that Cooper regards the killings perpetrated by ideological activists and medieval sectarians as likewise having been undertaken within closely comparable second realities, however immanentist they may *formally* have been in ideological cases or however apocalyptic in sectarian ones. Yet Cooper is not unprepared to acknowledge certain aspects of contemporary terrorism as notably different from prior forms, so it makes sense to ask: What—if anything—does he regard as significantly new in contemporary terrorism? Are the changes witnessed within terrorism in recent decades substantial or merely stylistic? Does Cooper see spiritually significant differences or merely formal ones distinguishing contemporary terrorist acts from the range of acts that were undertaken in the service of ideological or totalitarian movements? What—if any—are the important differences between religiously motivated terrorists of the present day and radical sectarians of prior eras? All of these are important questions, and though Cooper's analysis raises them, it does not resolve them.

To what degree is Islamist terrorism traceable to elements of Islam?
Cooper addresses several historical and doctrinal issues that bear on this
question, yet he does not analyze it in a sustained manner.

At certain points, Cooper *seems* to offer a relatively straightforward
assessment of the issue, as when he writes: "To put the matter plainly: contemporary Islamists have more in common with members of the Kach
Party in Israel or the Christian Identity movement in Idaho than they do
with the broad traditions of Islam."[15] Clear as that may seem at first blush,
the "more in common" in this sense doesn't quite imply that Islamists have
nothing in common with the broad traditions of Islam. Similarly, Cooper
observes that,

> With respect to Islam, understood in as wide a sense as possible,
> we should not expect consistency between the pious traditional
> Muslim who seeks in his or her religion only to learn how to live
> in accord with God's will, and the fanatic who is clear that he
> knows God's will and that God's will demands that he attack the
> Great Satan by flying airplanes into buildings or by other murder-
> ous deeds.[16]

This is almost unexceptionable, and yet one can still wonder whether a traditional Muslim seeking to live in accord with God's will might not have
different propensities than a traditional Christian or Jew—due to the doctrinal peculiarities of the three religious traditions and the different pragmatic histories of the societies and religious communities formed by them.

In fact, Cooper seems prepared to acknowledge such differences and
peculiarities, at least in general terms, and also to acknowledge that they
lead to differing propensities in political life—again, in general terms. For
example (and a single example should suffice as backing for a restatement
of the question), Cooper observes that,

> The most obvious characteristic of the early history of the Islamic
> community was its political success. Unlike Christianity, which
> penetrated an already existing political order, imperial Rome,
> Islam combined temporal and spiritual activity in a single act of
> imperial-religious founding. . . .The victories of the Prophet were
> understood to be the victories of God. . . . [B]ecause Christianity
> was not concerned initially with founding a political order. . .
> [w]hen Christians have acceded to seats of power, this has not typ-
> ically been regarded as proof of the truth of Christianity, and the

end of any particular earthly city—the sack of Rome in 410 by
Alaric, for example—has not typically been understood as a reli-
gious catastrophe so much as a political disaster. . . . Not so with
Islam.[17]

As Cooper goes on to show, there was a very different resonance within
Islam when the Mongols destroyed Baghdad and killed the last Abbasid
Caliph in 1258. Although the response of the Islamic world was multi-
dimensional (involving greater emphasis on a more mystical, less immanentist interpretation of Islam as well as efforts to convert the conquerors),
and though it shared some elements also seen in Jewish and Christian history (such as a stress on a recovery of the original purity of the founding
period), the Islamic response also included an emphasis on jihad. Cooper
connects this with the writings of Taqi al-Din ibn Taymiyya and the origins
of the ideology of "salafism" or "jihadist salafism," which in turn he identifies as "an important constituent element in the spiritual complex of the
terrorist attack of September 11, 2001."[18]

Jihadist salafism is, of course, but one (polluted) stream running out
of Islam, which has also given rise to sublime manifestations. We should
also note—as Cooper does—that Jewish and Christian history show disordered streams as well. However, these caveats do not drain the force from
the question: to what degree is Islamist terrorism traceable to elements of
Islam? Are its core elements spiritually destabilizing? Are they destabilizing to a greater degree than those of the Jewish or Christian traditions?
Certain analysts have been willing—imprudently or not—to speak
straightforwardly regarding core frictions, as when Samuel Huntington
writes: "The underlying problem for the West is not Islamic fundamentalism. It is Islam, a different civilization whose people are convinced of the
superiority of their culture and are obsessed with the inferiority of their
power."[19] We can use similar terms to ask the pressing question: What proportion of the problem of Islamic fundamentalism should we ascribe to
Islam?

What proportion of the problem of Islamic fundamentalism should we ascribe to the so-called "root cause" conditions of life on the ground in the Islamic world?

Cooper displays a keen awareness and appreciation for the problems confronted by young men whose days are spent on the "hot, filthy, ugly, and
chaotic streets of Cairo or Damascus."[20] His account of the tensions and

frustrations of pragmatic existence confronted by potential extremists is thoughtful, detailed, and, at times, even empathetic. And yet, when engaged in the theoretical work of diagnosing the consciousness of violent extremists, Cooper's account can also seem quite dismissive of the importance of factors such as poverty and unemployment. Noting the "categorical limitation of all 'root cause' arguments," Cooper writes:

> There are no "root causes" because every grievance, whether political or personal, is specific. Moreover, the use of terrorism to address a grievance is bound to make matters worse, not better, because if it is successful, and a particular grievance is indeed addressed, the result will be to encourage someone else, with an entirely different grievance, to use terrorism in a quite different context . . . .As Paul Bremmer, former counterterrorism coordinator for the State Department, said: "There's no point in addressing the so-called root causes of bin Laden's despair with us. We are the root causes of his terrorism. He doesn't like America. He doesn't like our society. He doesn't like what we stand for. He doesn't like our values. And short of the United States going out of existence, there's no way to deal with the root cause of his terrorism."[21]

A passage such as this seems quite direct and final, but it doesn't quite settle the issue that I wish to pursue. The passage says more about the unworkability of fighting terrorism by means of ameliorating "root cause" grievances than it does about how such grievances actually figure in the dynamics of consciousness of the budding terrorist. In this sense, Cooper seems prepared to accord them some importance, though there are limits to this. That is, Cooper recognizes a powerful stimulus toward extremism in the tension arising from the discrepancy between, on one hand, a young man's convictions regarding the spiritual superiority of Islam over the West and, on the other hand, his distress regarding his personal poverty and powerlessness relative to his Western counterparts. In this sense, so-called "root cause" problems should be taken seriously. However, when theoretically considering the etiology of actual instances of terrorist murder or pneumopathological consciousness, Cooper seems inclined to stress that so-called "root cause" problems do not operate as either sufficient or necessary conditions. We can see that they are not *sufficient* conditions because millions of individuals suffer from poverty and unemployment in the Islamic world but do not murder innocents or lapse into pneumopathological fantasies of attaining paradise thereby. And we can see that so-called "root cause" problems do not operate as *necessary* conditions for terrorism, because plenty of actual terrorists simply do not suffer from them. Cooper notes that this is true of the wealthy and privileged bin Laden himself, and also of the September 2001 terrorists, who "were not young, poor, ill-educated, or psychologically damaged . . . ."[22]

Yet, looking at the full sentence from which this last quote was drawn, it appears that we cannot quite dismiss "root cause" problems as irrelevant: "Moreover, the profile of the September 2001 terrorists was much different than the typical Hamas recruit: they were not young, poor, ill-educated, or psychologically damaged, as so many of their predecessors seemed to be."[23] So, we must ask: how important are the degraded day-to-day conditions of life for understanding those Hamas recruits? Are "root cause" problems important for understanding the motivations of rank-and-file terrorists, but not their commanders or the ideologists who inspire them? Allowing that "root cause" problems don't stand scrutiny as necessary conditions when viewed in the context of an aggregated population, are they nevertheless necessary conditions within the consciousness of an individual pneumopath? That is, are they not necessary to produce the tension of consciousness giving rise to pneumopathology, with its dissonance between the conviction of Islam's spiritual superiority and its political and economic inferiority? Finally, to restate the broad question, what proportion of the problem of Islamic fundamentalism should we ascribe to the so-called "root cause" conditions of life in the Islamic world?

How convincing is Cooper's case that modern terrorism is a spiritually disordered political religion?

In light of the historical and contemporary evidence, one cannot offer an entirely straightforward answer to this question. It is clear that Cooper succeeds impressively in showing that Voegelin's diagnostic approach can be quite illuminating with regard to the thought and activity of *certain* terrorists and terrorist organizations. More specifically, evidence indicates that some terrorists arrogate to themselves a status as members of "an Elect," one that is engaged in apocalyptic or epochal, world-transforming action. Believing that they are surpassingly enlightened and pure, they bestow upon themselves a violent mission of purification in the service of some divine power, or some perfected future state that they prophesize. Operating in the everyday "first reality," but on the basis of a mission stemming from an imaginary "second reality," they refuse to apperceive the facts that their murderous actions are pragmatically futile as well as morally depraved. As such, they exhibit patterns of consciousness and activity that are essentially equivalent to those exhibited by the earlier communist and fascist ideologues whom Voegelin diagnosed so penetratingly.

Despite Cooper's efforts at explication and application, it is just as clear that Voegelin's diagnoses have very little pertinence with regard to the activities of other terrorists. In most cases of this sort, the lack of pertinence has nothing to do with any shortcoming in the diagnoses offered by Cooper and Voegelin, but everything to do with the sheer absence of spiritual content—ordered, disordered or otherwise—in the activities of the terrorists. In some instances, terrorism is simply a tactically useful mode of combat in the course of a mundane power grab, and a spiritual analysis of it would be akin to the proverbial effort to wring blood from a turnip. In some cases, the terrorist does not arrogate to himself any sort of transcendent status or historical mission. Rather, he does what he does merely to make a living, or out of a fascination with guns, or to impress women, or to exact retribution for a slain compatriot in the midst of an essentially tribal conflict.

To sharpen the point, some terrorist organizations and creeds bear the marks of political religions, whereas others are so spiritually obtuse—so flat-lined in spiritual terms—that "political religion" is simply unwarranted as a descriptor. All terrorism is pathological, but not all terrorism is pneumopathological. That being the case, those who are interested in the applicability of Voegelin's and Cooper's mode of analysis to contemporary terrorism would do well to consider capable historical accounts of recent terrorist activity to help determine just how large pneumopathology looms and just how energetically one should argue for the usefulness of the mode of analysis that diagnoses and explicates it.

Among the leading accounts that can serve this purpose, those offered by Jessica Stern and Mark Juergensmeyer are particularly valuable,[24] but the recent work of the historian Michael Burleigh provides the most illuminating point of reference for assessing Cooper's approach to terrorism. Burleigh's work is important not only because it is extensive in scope and meticulous in detail, but also because it is "capable" in the sense that Burleigh is well informed theoretically regarding the phenomenon of political religions. As noted above, most writers on terrorism are not well equipped conceptually or theoretically for addressing the phenomenon on the level of its spiritual motivations. Burleigh is a conspicuous exception, and one who is—at least potentially—an especially valuable touchstone on multiple grounds: He is thoroughly versed in the history of spiritual undercurrents in political modernity, a thoroughgoing advocate of "political religion" as a conceptual category, and an explicit admirer of Voegelin's analyses of spiritually disordered movements.

Burleigh's recent work shows a keen awareness that the political convulsions of the past 75 years are an upwelling from currents flowing from at least as deep as the Enlightenment. Burleigh made his reputation initially as a historian of the Nazi era in Germany, writing five books that culminated in the award-winning, *The Third Reich: A New History*.[25] Interestingly, admirably, and in a way reminiscent of Voegelin, Burleigh shifted his research program dramatically just as his work became widely heralded. In 2005, he published *Earthly Powers*, which he describes as "an exploration of the politics of religion, and the religion of politics, in Europe from the Enlightenment to the Great War." This was followed by a second, "entirely free-standing" volume, published in 2007, entitled *Sacred Causes*, a book that follows on *Earthly Powers* by linking "these themes to the totalitarian political religions and beyond."[26]

The subtitle of *Sacred Causes* is *The Clash of Religion and Politics, from the Great War to the War on Terror*. The span treated by the two books preceding *Blood and Rage* runs from 1789 to 2001, or from "The Terror" to The War on Terror," and the principal category employed in these works is political religion. Consequently, when Burleigh sharpened his focus directly upon terrorism in 2009's *Blood and Rage*, one might reasonably have anticipated that he would treat contemporary terrorist organizations predominantly (or at least fairly frequently) as political religions. But he did not.

Blood and Rage shows that those who seek understanding of terrorism suffer no shortage of cases to study. In less than 20 years in Italy alone, between 1969 and 1987, "there were some 14,591 terrorist attacks; 1,182 people were wounded and 419 killed, the worst year being 1979 when there were 125 fatalities. One hundred and ninety-three of these deaths were caused by neo-Fascist terrorists...143 were attributable to the extreme left, and 63 to Middle Eastern terrorist groups operating in Italy."[27] Of these various numbers, it isn't really the body count that shocks the reader in the post-9/11 world, but rather the sheer number of incidents. And that number of 14,591 only covers a relatively brief span in Italy, omitting the many thousands of incidents perpetrated by groups like ETA in Spain, the Red Army Faction in Germany, or the Provisional IRA in Ireland.

What is most bracing about Burleigh's account as a point of reference for Cooper's work is how frequently he finds merely mundane personal motivations underlying terrorist violence. Burleigh's book seems to suggest that many, many more terrorists acted as they did—and became who they were—not because of spiritual agitation or any sort of "second reality" apocalypticism, but rather because of "first reality" processes involving motivations and attractions that were thoroughly prosaic. In Italy, for example, he suggests that student leftists were gradually hardened by violent encounters with riot police, shifting from protest signs to slings to firearms, and then becoming entranced by the aesthetic and sexual appeal of guns. He quotes an Italian Red Brigades terrorist who notes that:

> Arms have a fascination of their own, it is a fascination that makes you feel in some way more . . . more virile . . . this sensation of feeling stronger, more manly . . . I found myself . . . showing them to women to try to impress them . . . and then it seemed somehow more noble to use arms instead of, I don't know, fighting with one's fists let's say.[28]

Pecuniary interests were also involved in cases like that of Patrizio Peci, head of the Turin Red Brigades, who was initially recruited by being given a factory job that exceeded his former earnings as a waiter, plus 200,000 lire per month as a logistician as well as free accommodations, utility bills, clothing, equipment, and an annual holiday on a property owned by the organization. The deal was so sweet that his girlfriend threatened to kill herself if she could not join too, though she seems to have had multiple grounds for envy, since Burleigh writes that,

> Peci liked guns, reaching out for his .38 Special on the bedside table first thing each morning. "It gave me a feeling of power and security. It was my good friend. I was more jealous towards it than towards a woman."[29]

In Burleigh's telling, the story of how most Provisional IRA terrorists took to killing requires little more in the way of conceptual equipment than one can find in the everyday toolkit of psychologists and sociologists. Humiliating manhandling by British soldiers is cited, along with the enraging effects of discriminatory arrest and unjust detention. Individuals didn't need to experience brutality or discrimination directly, as televised beatings of northern Catholics were enough to excite tribal sympathies and render southern Republicans militant even though they resided many miles away from the violence. From the perspective of the terrorist's self-understanding and also in his external interpretation, Burleigh's account is decidedly this-worldly, with very little evidence of spiritual engagement:

> The decision to embark on a career of politicised violence was invariably construed by PIRA members as something forced upon an individual, in this case by state or sectarian violence against the community that he (or she) was defending, rather than a personal choice that could also reflect a no less keen desire to experience the thrill of clandestine activity within a secret organisation that bestowed status on its members. Status within the PIRA partly derived from belonging to an ultra-republican family already, not least because this brought automatic trust. If the terrorist came from a republican family living in a republican area . . . then his adoption of the gun and bomb was both socially sanctioned and morally justified.[30]

At other points in *Blood and Rage*, Burleigh accords motivational significance to simple *esprit de corps* within militant organizations, impulses of hatred and revenge in the midst of ongoing struggles, and "habituation" to violence.[31]

Likewise, when treating "jihadi-salafist" terrorists, his explanatory account is seamlessly aligned in standard sociological terms with his accounts of European terrorists. For example, he contends that young Palestinians in Gaza were drawn to the Islamic Congress or Hamas by comparison to the PLO, because these groups were suited to a generational rebellion against the social hierarchy and the politics of the older generation.[32] He also accords importance to the coddling treatment of male children within Muslim households as "little princes" who subsequently "go off the rails" frequently, turning to violence "as an outlet for pervasive sexual repression in their communities."[33] Membership in radical Islamist groups is also ascribe to a desire for atonement for lives of crime. Writing of Islamist gangs in European prisons, Burleigh observes that they:

> . . . [P]rovide security and solidarity to new prisoners and a coordinated response, up to riot and mutiny, when one of them is confronted by a prison officer. Many of them are bitter and disillusioned, prey for Islamist recruiters operating either among fellow inmates or as social workers and chaplains. Poorly educated, these men are like empty vessels for jihadist recruiters who can peddle them any version of Islam they wish provided it is implacable

enough and promises personal redemption through focusing their aggression on the host society.[34]

Here as elsewhere, Burleigh accords no importance to anything like a genuinely spiritual revolt against the limitations of worldly existence. Tellingly, he does not distinguish between leaders and functionaries in this regard, and does not even raise the question of whether the jihadist recruiters who are doing the pouring of implacable Islam into the "empty vessel" prisoners might themselves be motivated by a disordered spirituality. Indeed, disordered spirituality—by contrast to dysfunctional personality or social dislocation—is simply absent from Burleigh's account at every organizational level from mere functionaries like Richard Reid up to leaders such as Khalid Sheikh Mohammed or Osama Bin Laden.

So, how convincing is Cooper's diagnosis of contemporary terrorism as a spiritually disordered political religion? Not very convincing, in my view, in one specific sense: Cooper tends to address contemporary terrorism as an essentially uniform bloc rather than a highly variegated cluster of actions undertaken for purposes that differ not just by degree—but in kind. Indeed, Cooper sometimes makes generalizations so sweeping that he compares terrorism as a vast bloc with other vast blocs in a way that must seem quite cavalier to readers inclined toward case-by-case analyses, as in the following passage:

> In the chapters that follow, we shall see the elements that came together in the totalitarian regimes of the twentieth century reconstituted in a recognizably similar ideological context that surrounds contemporary terrorism. Moreover, it seems clear that contemporary religious terrorists have followed a pattern remarkably close to that initially made by several spiritual movements of the late medieval and Christian West.[35]

To be clear, I am not suggesting that Cooper is simply mistaken or even careless when drawing such parallels. What I am suggesting is that his analysis looks much more valuable as a *suggestive line of interpretation* than as a *rigorous psycho-spiritual diagnosis*.

What are the most important ways in which Cooper's approach augments leading understandings of terrorism?

A reading of the range of cases considered in a book like Burleigh's *Blood and Rage* might lead others to join me in concluding that Cooper's book adds up to something less—or at least something other—than a rigorous diagnosis. However, such a reading might also leave readers thirsting for an analysis like Cooper's to offer some interpretive depth as leavening for Burleigh's rather flatly descriptive account. This comparison is worth pursuing here (even at the risk of making Burleigh's book loom a little too large in a review essay on Cooper's text) as it can illuminate the distinctive virtues of Cooper's approach.

Viewed as a whole, *Blood and Rage* is a conventional historical narrative, and Burleigh is content to offer descriptive accounts of people and events, rather than diagnostic analyses of underlying spiritual disorders. There is nothing improper about that, and it would be silly to fault a historian for writing descriptively as a historian rather than analytically as a political theorist or a spiritual psychologist. However, the mode in which Burleigh elects to address terrorists and their organizations poses an issue of importance because, when addressing totalitarian movements, he treated them consistently as political religions rooted in a disordered spirituality. Indeed, his chapter on "The Totalitarian Political Religions" in *Sacred Causes* is an extraordinary analysis of disordered spirituality, one that can be regarded on a quality level roughly comparable to anything ever written about fascists or communists by the likes of Voegelin, Aron, Gurian, or Henri de Lubac. That Burleigh has broken from this mode when turning to terrorists compels us to ask: Should we follow him in discarding the concepts of political religion and disordered spirituality when considering terrorism? Or should we regard this as a lamentable move that prevents Burleigh from penetrating to the deeper wellsprings of terrorist activity in the way that Cooper's analysis can?

I lean strongly toward the second of these options. Burleigh's treatment of terrorism tends to be flatly descriptive rather than penetratingly analytical, partly because he fails to develop content-rich diagnostic concepts (as Cooper does) and because he chooses to address neither the self-understanding of terrorists nor the writings that guide their thought and activity (as Cooper also does).

Burleigh's primary concept for categorizing the problem with terrorists is "*moral insanity*." It appears occasionally throughout the book (and in earlier books), and is first employed on the second page, where Burleigh describes terrorists as "morally insane, without being clinically psychotic."[36] Burleigh is correct, in my view, to employ this concept and to employ it in contradistinction to clinical insanity. "Moral insanity" is not only appropriate, but importantly helpful, though, in the final analysis, it is a merely descriptive term rather than an analytical concept. Backing up a bit, we can see the appropriateness and helpfulness of the notion of "moral insanity" by considering the case of a man like Mohamed Atta, leader of the 19 hijackers involved in the 9/11 attacks, which cannot be understood adequately by reference to conventional notions of "ignorance" or "immorality" or "insanity." Far from being an ignorant man or a foolish pawn who was manipulated by commanders more clever than himself, Atta was a bright, reasonably well-educated student of architecture, and was quite effective in his role as an operational planner and commander. And far from being "immoral" in the ordinary sense, Atta was an intensely religious man who conceived of himself as a willing martyr for a cause that he regarded with an almost superhuman moral seriousness. Atta's effectiveness and intelligence, as well as the strength and seriousness of his convictions, place him outside of what we mean when terming someone "insane." No pill prescribed by a psychiatrist would have cured his affliction. That affliction, however, is no less real simply because it eludes conventional psychiatric diagnosis or therapy. A man who regards the killing of thousands of innocent non-combatants as a sacred act pleasing to God is most definitely afflicted, and afflicted with a very grave condition. We cannot term it "insanity" in the standard clinical sense, though we may indeed need to understand it as some sort of "moral insanity."

However, associating Mohamed Atta with moral insanity is a *categorical description* of his condition, not an *analytical diagnosis* of it. The categorical description of moral insanity is not useless, since it highlights an important distinction between a moral/spiritual condition on one hand, and a psychotic condition on the other. Nevertheless, it remains a mere categorical description, just as "clinically insane" is a categorical description and not a psychiatric diagnosis. A psychiatrist who authorized the commitment of an individual to an institution on vague grounds of being "clinically insane" would be drummed out of his profession—unless he could back it up with a specific diagnosis of a condition such as manic-depressive disorder or paranoid schizophrenia. Interestingly, Cooper also employs the term, "moral insanity" in *New Political Religions*, yet he backs it up with specific diagnostic concepts such as pneumopathology, scotosis, second reality, and the refusal to apperceive reality,[37] for which he provides precise, detailed descriptions. Cooper's analysis could conceivably be wrong, but it is much more robust, because it is built upon specific, content-laden concepts of analysis that are in turn built upon a theory of consciousness. Burleigh's analysis is not an analysis at all, properly speaking, but rather a narrative description, due to the fact that it is built on a categorical term lacking in specific content.[38]

A second reason why Burleigh's treatment of terrorism is, by comparison to Cooper's, flatly descriptive rather than penetratingly analytical is because he chooses to not to address the self-understanding of terrorists as expressed in their writings. He is explicit about this on the first page of *Blood and Rage*:

> This book focuses on life histories and actions rather than the theories which validate them, roughly in accord with St. Matthew's precept, "By their fruits shall ye know them." This is not because I am dismissive of ideas and ideology—quite the contrary—but because these seem a relatively neglected part of the picture. Ideology is like a detonator that enables a pre-existing chemical mix to explode. Terrorists make choices all along their journey, and it is these I am most interested in.[39]

Underlying this passage, I see an unspoken premise to the effect that the actions or "fruits" of terrorists interpret themselves. That is a premise that I do not share. Burleigh isn't contending that terrorist actions don't require interpretation when he cites, "By their fruits shall ye know them." Rather, he implies that we can "know" terrorists, or interpret them as actors, by considering their specific actions and choices rather than the words they speak or the ideologies they heed. This I would deny.

To be clear, I would agree that we can *judge* terrorists in moral terms on the basis of their actions and choices, but that is not the same as *understanding* the consciousness in which they undertake these actions, for which we need access to the words they speak and the ideologies to which they pay heed. The actions of terrorists cry out for condemnation, but they also cry out for understanding. Of these two, understanding is by far the more difficult, requiring a detailed knowledge of what terrorists have done and of what they have written about what they elected to do, and a developed spiritual psychology for interpreting their words and deeds. Of these three elements, Burleigh provides the first but neither the second nor the third—which are precisely the elements concerning which Cooper excels.

Pursuing this point toward its conclusion, we might ask what Burleigh means by the analogy that, "Ideology is like a detonator that enables a pre-existing chemical mix to explode." Based on *Blood and Rage*, one could only conclude that the "pre-existing mix" consists of ignorance, poverty, humiliation and generational revolt, which are then "weaponized" and detonated through the agency of ideology. However, cities like Cairo and Damascus are home to millions of individuals who are relatively unlearned and poor, who chafe under the domination of an older generation, and who feel humiliated by their powerlessness by comparison to modern Israel and the West. Despite the fact that the atmosphere in these places is thick with jihadi-salafist ideology (alongside more mainstream Islam), relatively few individuals succumb to extremism—much less to terrorist violence.[40] Consequently, the really pressing question is: What makes some individuals prone to accept an ideology that can, in turn, fanaticize them and actuate specific violence from sources of discontent that are general and latent in the broader population? This is not a question that can be answered by a historical narrative describing the actions of terrorists. It is a question that can be answered only by reference to a spiritual psychology built upon a theory of consciousness—such as the one that Cooper has taken the lead in providing.

In closing, I would pick up on this last sentence to emphasize that Cooper has truly taken the lead among analysts of terrorism in showing the way toward an adequate understanding of religiously inspired terrorism's motivational wellsprings. His *New Political Religions* pursues the deepest, most difficult problems associated with terrorism, and provides the most penetrating conceptual tools as well as the most illuminating analytical approach currently available. The actions of terrorists pose a wide array of troubling problems for policymakers and counterterrorism operatives, but for scholars seeking an understanding of the interior consciousness of the terrorist, the most troublesome question is this: How can a terrorist believe that killing innocent non-combatants is an act that is pleasing in the eyes of God? Barry Cooper's *New Political Religions* is the only scholarly work yet to address that question successfully, which distinguishes it as one of the most important achievements of North American political science in a generation.

Endnotes

1   Barry Cooper, *New Political Religions, or An Analysis of Modern Terrorism* (Columbia: University of Missouri Press, 2004).

2   Although the primary source of the perspective Cooper wishes to introduce to terrorism studies is the work of Voegelin, that is not the only source. Hannah Arendt's work is also an important tributary.

3   In the course of his illuminating treatment of the Islamist firebrand. Sayyid Qutb, Cooper doesn't seem to utilize fully an opportunity to impress upon his audience

a point of the highest theoretical and practical importance. Toward the end of his account of Qutb, Cooper writes:

> The basic structure of Qutb's position is, in short, a conventional ideological conceit: the experience of revolution is supposed to bring about a new reality that exists only in the imagination of the revolutionary. To use the conceptual terminology introduced above in chapter 2, the pneumopathological nature of the animating emotions would not be obvious until the damage was done. It may be, therefore, that preemptive violence, which has its own risks and consequences, is the only way to extinguish the pathos of Qutb's murderous eschatological heroism. (Cooper, *New Political Religions*, 127)

This is a point of potentially explosive importance for readers who are unversed in the history and analysis of spiritual disorder, yet Cooper does not explain it in a way that could show its full force to the uninitiated. The key point within the point is one first made by Voegelin in his analysis of Karl Marx in his *History of Political Ideas*. Voegelin noted that Marx's anticipation of a future free from conflict and scarcity bears a clear resemblance to the anticipations of medieval millenarians, but with one exceedingly important difference that makes Marx far more dangerous than any radical sectarian reformer. Medieval millenarians sought, first, to change hearts and only then to change the world. By means of their preaching, they sought to surround themselves with an "Elect," a circle of purified persons whose changed hearts would in turn permit them to transform the world and bring it to its final phase. Conversely, because Marx's "historical materialism" holds that "consciousness does not determine life, but life determines consciousness," he depends upon the life experiences involved in revolutionary activity itself to accomplish the metanoia that will bring "socialist man" and the final phase of history into existence. In pragmatic terms, the crucial difference between these related disorders is easy to understand. Human nature being what it is, the *metanoia* never actually arises in either case. Medieval millenarians generally came to bad ends and were malign forces in the world, but they did relatively little damage; lacking an "Elect" of any special purity or effectiveness, their transformational projects fell flat when hitting the hard wall of worldly reality. By contrast, Marx's project could only become evident *after* revolutions failed to produce socialist men free of self-interest, and hence millions died as a result of his eschatological activism. The implication for policy is obvious once this core idea is unpacked a bit, and Cooper is quite right to note that preemptive violence against violent extremists of the ilk of Qutb must be considered. My only critical point here is that the idea was not unpacked in a way permitting it or its implications to be grasped adequately by many readers.

4   Cooper, *New Political Religions,* 38. The source for the quotation within this excerpt appears to be Hannah Arendt, *The Human Condition* (Chicago: University of Chicago Press, 1958), 153ff.
5   Cooper, *New Political Religions*, 39.
6   *Ibid,* 26.

7   *Ibid.*, 40.

8   Russell D. Howard and Margaret J. Nencheck, "The New Terrorism," in *Terrorism and Counterterrorism: Understanding the New Security Environment* (4th ed., New York: McGraw-Hill, 2011, 142–164), 143–144.

9   Cooper, *New Political Religions*, 14.

10   *Ibid.*, 55–56.

11   *Ibid.*, 56.

12   This oft-quoted remark is attributed to Brian Jenkins and quoted in Cooper, *New Political Religions*, 31.

13   *Ibid.*, 56.

14   *Ibid.*, 50.

15   *Ibid.*, 14.

16   *Ibid.*, 74.

17   *Ibid.*, 78–79.

18   *Ibid.*, 96.

19   Samuel P. Huntington, *The Clash of Civilizations and the Remaking of World Order* (New York: Simon & Schuster, 1996; Touchstone Books paperback edition, 1997), 217–218.

20   Cooper, *New Political Religions*, 19.

21   *Ibid.*, 23–24.

22   *Ibid.*, 154.

23   *Ibid.*

24   See Jessica Stern, *Terror in the Name of God: Why Religious Militants Kill* (New York: Ecco, 2003) and Mark Juergensmeyer, *Terror in the Mind of God: The Global Rise of Religious Violence* (Berkeley: University of California Press, 3rd Edition, 2003).

25   Michael Burleigh, *The Third Reich: A New History* (New York: Hill and Wang, 2000).

26   Michael Burleigh, *Earthly Powers: The Clash of Religion and Politics in Europe, from the French Revolution to the Great War* (London: HarperCollins, 2005); *Sacred Causes: The Clash of Religion and Politics, from the Great War to the War on Terrorism* (New York: HarperCollins, 2007).

27   Michael Burleigh, *Blood and Rage: A Cultural History of Terrorism* (London: HarperPress, 2008) 191.

28   *Ibid.*, 194. The quotation appears exactly as abbreviated by Burleigh in the text.

29   *Ibid.*, 215.

30   *Ibid.*, 313–314.

31   *Ibid.*, 61.

32   *Ibid.*, 386.

33   *Ibid.*, 441.

34   *Ibid.*, 441–442.

35   Cooper, *New Political Religions*, 14.

36   Burleigh, *Blood and Rage*, Preface, x.

37   Cooper, *New Political Religions*, 41–47.

38   As an aside, it might be noted that Burleigh does not cite Cooper's *New Political Religions* in *Blood and Rage*, nor do his references to Voegelin in other books

make it clear that he has read much other than the early German-language works. I am not in a position to say what Burleigh has or has not read, but note this parenthetically to imply a question about the conceptual shortcomings of *Blood and Rage.*

39   Burleigh, *Blood and Rage*, Preface, ix–x.

40   The comparative question of Islam's propensity for sprouting extremist offshoots relative to other religions is an exceedingly complicated one that cannot be taken up in earnest within the confines of this essay. It should be noted, however, that Burleigh has relatively little to say about it, and among the few points that he does make, the following is particularly unsettling: "Since Islamist terrorism is a deviant outgrowth of a religion, much attention needs to be paid to the terms on which that religion is permitted to function in non-Muslim societies" (483). Even when we allow for the historical facts that the founder of Islam was a warrior as well as a prophet, and that the divine and the political are not as rigorously distinguished as in Christianity and Judaism, and that the pragmatic victories of early Muslim armies were regarded as proof of the truth of the creed, thereby intermingling matters of faith with the occupation of worldly territory, I still believe it is inaccurate to flatly state that Islamist terrorism is a deviant outgrowth of Islam. On the contrary, instrumental terrorist violence against innocents—as well as adherence to a distorted creed that sanctifies such violence—are outgrowths of a personal disorder at the level of the spirit. Historical peculiarities of Islam are not irrelevant to the phenomenon as it exists in Muslim lands, but neither are they the *core* of the problem. Cooper's handling of this complex of problems is far more nuanced and precise than Burleigh's.

Chapter Six

Thinking with Technology

Leah Bradshaw

In his contribution to *Canadian Political Philosophy*, Barry Cooper describes his work as a kind of "braiding" that has "combined analysis of the major questions in the history of political thought, especially classical political philosophy, with the immediate questions of the day."[1] Cooper has spent a lifetime engaged in the practices of empirical political science, whether those evolve on the deepest matters of philosophy and modernity, or whether they focus upon present concerns of Canadians and Albertans, ranchers and hunters, journalists and pundits. One of the truly remarkable things about Cooper's work is the fact that he sees these disparate concerns as one "braid." We live in the world, we are of the present, and we approach the most visceral things (hunting down a goose) and the least visceral of things (philosophical thinking) with a unified embodied presence. What Cooper means by *empirical* political science owes much to Eric Voegelin, as Cooper has acknowledged in an early work on *The Restoration of Political Science and The Crisis of Modernity*. There, Cooper wrote that "empirical political science, as Eric Voegelin has shown, includes not only the skills of Aristotelian fishermen and hunters, it includes as well the development of textual analysis into well-founded insights concerning their meaning. Most importantly, empirical political science includes the analysis of consciousness by the consciousness of the analyst."[2] Empirical political science, for Voegelin and Cooper, begins with thinking about my own thinking, and trying to understand how it is that I situate myself in the world.

Cooper's (and Voegelin's) depiction of *empirical* political science is not a widely accepted one in the discipline of political science. For most political scientists, there is a great gulf between what they identify as *empirical* investigators (those who measure and quantify patterns in the natural and political world) and *theoretical* investigators (those who make up patterns in their minds and then seek to impose them on the world). In this dyad, the so-called empiricists bracket out consciousness as a superfluous category, and the so-called theorists hold that what is true is what exists in their minds, regardless of the stubborn resistance of reality.

Hannah Arendt (someone else whom Cooper acknowledges as having had a profound influence on his thinking)[3], is extremely good at explaining the consequences of the split between *empiricism* and *theory*, as that split has characterized much of modern political discourse, and as it has had a powerful and destructive impact in the world. To see *empirical* investigation as the cataloguing and classification of matter, is actually to organize experience according to valuations of what one can make and manipulate into being. The person who thinks that he or she is undertaking a "neutral" investigation is in fact someone who is making the world in a particular way. As Arendt says, "the use of the experiment for the purpose of knowledge was already the consequence of the conviction that one can only know what [man] has made himself, for this conviction meant that one might learn about those things man did not make by figuring out and imitating the processes by which they had come into being . . . The experiment repeats the natural process as though man himself were to make nature's objects."[4] A good example of what Arendt is talking about can be found in the hugely popular canons of contemporary bio-ethics. If you set about trying to find brain patterns that will "explain" certain forms of mental illness (like schizophrenia, bipolar disorder), you will inevitably discover those patterns that will then corroborate your hypothesis. The patterns arrived at through "empirical investigation" become more real than the suffering human being.

In contrast, the person who sees himself or herself as a *non-empiricist* is likely to be an ideologue, not a philosopher: "An ideology is quite literally what its name indicates: it is the logic of an idea . . . to an ideology, history does not appear in the light of an idea (which would imply that history is seen *sub specie* of some ideal eternity which itself is beyond historical motion) but as something which can be calculated by it."[5] The ideologue is different from the "empiricist" in that he thinks he can make a world by deducing patterns that are more systematic and more logical than the apparent incoherence of ordinary life, but his impact upon the world is similar to the alleged empiricist, because he attempts to remake the world according to a human construct. As Arendt remarks, "the danger in exchanging the necessary insecurity of philosophical thought for the total explanation of an ideology is . . . exchanging the freedom inherent in man's capacity to think for the strait jacket of logic with which man can force himself almost as violently as he is forced by some outside power."[6] Arendt's example of the power of ideological thinking is of course the horrifying experience of Nazi Germany which "proceeded to drive ideological implications into extremes of logical consistency: a 'dying' class consisted of people condemned to death; races that are 'unfit to live' were to be exterminated."[7]

To be clear about what we are discussing: Barry Cooper claims that empirical political science is the bringing together of common sense observation upon and participation in the world, the reliance upon great texts for a better understanding of the reality we inhabit, and a reflection upon one's own consciousness as it participates in reality. To return to Cooper's metaphor, these different modes of engagement are "braided" together in such a manner that none of the strains can be separated out in a discrete way. To attempt to separate the strands would be to corrupt our sense of reality. Hannah Arendt analyzes exactly what happens when the braid is separated into discrete strands. World and consciousness are bifurcated. Differing camps settle in on either side of the split. The self-proclaimed empiricists attest that reality can be uncovered through careful experiment and identification of meaningful patterns in natural and historical phenomena. The self-proclaimed theorists (ideologues) proclaim that the world is up for manipulation by the power of ideas to transform and remake in accordance with a logical plan. The empiricists think they can dispense with thinking, and the theorists think they can dispense with given reality. Both are lacking the kind of reflection upon consciousness that Cooper identifies as the ground central to true political science.

In the remainder of the paper I want to sketch out briefly how we got here, that is, how we got into this stand-off between crude empiricism and ideology, say something about how deeply embedded we now are in this bifurcated sensibility, and finally offer some thoughts about the prospects of engaging in what Cooper regards as a true political science.

In his book, *Action into Nature*, Cooper emphasizes the modern "turn" in consciousness occasioned by Galileo's discoveries. "The event that paradigmatically began the modern age of scientific cosmology was Galileo's act of looking at the sky with the aid of a telescope."[8] As Cooper notes, Galileo's discovery was an *event*, not merely a thought, and the instrument that he employed to look at the heavens fundamentally challenged the way that human beings know things through the immediacy of the senses: "Truth, apparently, was what our instruments served up to our senses. Pure senses, in other words, could be adjusted or modified by instruments to apprehend what otherwise would have remained unknown and beyond them."[9] Galileo's discoveries, and the instruments he used to make them, challenged not simply the physical configuration of the cosmos as it was known to human beings, but the hierarchy between thinking and acting that had informed consciousness throughout the Western tradition: "Contemplation, properly speaking, aimed at the apprehension of substance and meaning: it relied, as Democritus said, on trusting sense experience to reveal phenomenal truths. Galileo's act threw all that into question . . . Indeed, the entire meaning of theory changed from that of a reasonably connected series of truths that had been given directly to the senses and that was directed at accounting for the reality of substance, to become a scientific 'working hypothesis.'"[10]

Cooper's preoccupation with Galileo as the benchmark for the change in consciousness that marks modernity is one that he shares with Hannah Arendt. Like Cooper, Arendt emphasizes that the revolution ushered in by Galileo is in many ways more significant than the one begun by Copernicus, or even the Protestant Reformation, precisely because Galileo, through his invention, "put within the grasp of an earth-bound creature and its body-bound senses what had seemed forever beyond his reach."[11] Once it is possible to make things that alter our perception of the world and consciousness, then it seems that that which is available to us through the fabrication of hypotheses and instruments is more real than what we can know with the mere senses.

The method of Galileo and his successors requires that one stand apart from nature, rather than participate in it. This may seem to be a simple point, but as Arendt points out, the shift in perspective—standing over and above nature, so as to measure, quantify and manipulate it—is of such magnitude that "one may doubt whether prior to the modern age anything like science existed at all."[12] For the "pure scientist" in the modern world, the method is revelatory, that is, it yields certain knowledge about phenomena that could not be accessed in any other way. Yet, there is no comfort in this certainty, for one can always imagine that if one just had better tools, more research grants, or greater sample fields, one's knowledge would be overturned for a higher knowledge. In fact, the succession is infinite and human anxiety is heightened by the scientific "revolution." In Arendt's words: "the world of the experiment seems always capable of becoming a man made reality, and this, while it may increase man's power of making and acting, even of creating a world . . . unfortunately puts man back once more into the prison of his own mind, into the limitations of patterns he himself created."[13] One of the more intelligent reactions to the scientific predilection is Descartes's anti-science. If the human mind is capable of devising ways of looking at reality that are fundamentally challenging to the sense perception understanding of the world, and further, capable of inventing instruments that can transform nature in accordance with a plan or a pattern, then, Descartes proclaims, really the human mind is independent and supreme. Descartes is the original ideologue, trusting neither in his senses nor in the material substance of the world, but only in the "prison of his own mind." The way out of that prison for Descartes is the affirmation of doubt itself: "Whatever may be the state of reality and of truth as they are given to the senses and to reason, 'nobody can doubt of his doubt and remain uncertain whether he doubts or does not doubt.' The famous *cogito ergo sum* ('I think, hence I am') did not spring for Descartes from any self-certainty of thought as such . . . but was a mere generalization of a *dubito ergo sum*."[14] As Martin Heidegger noted, the "more extensively and the more effectually the world stands at man's disposal as conquered . . . the more importunately does the *subjectum* rise up, and all the more importantly too, do observation of and teaching about the world change into a doctrine of man, into anthropology." [15]

Neither the self-proclaimed empiricist, always on the quest for better methods, better patterns and keener instruments that he is convinced will give him a deeper knowledge of the true structure of reality, nor the reactive ideologue who resists this quest by asserting that his own mind is the origin of all meaning, is a very happy person in the modern firmament. Heidegger characterizes the modern mood as one of "anxiety." We turn to Heidegger here because, although he has an analysis of modern science and its counter-revolution in humanist subjectivity that is similar to Cooper's and Arendt's, Heidegger believes that that we are trapped within the consciousness that we have ushered in. The Copernican revolution, for Heidegger, is an inescapable one.

Heidegger speaks extensively about *technology*, but really, for him technology is indistinguishable from modern science.[16] As he writes, "the essence of technology is by no means anything technological."[17] Rather, it is a "way of revealing."[18] The revelatory element of technology is embedded in the origins of modern science, specifically physics. Modern science "pursues and entraps nature as a calculable coherence of forces."[19] The essence of modern technology, according to Heidegger, lies in its "enframing" character, which it owes to physics and to the reorientation of our intellectual bearings from that which *is* (eternity) to that which *becomes* through our own creation. A technological world is one propelled by scientific method, in which everything is positioned as a "standing reserve," waiting to be harnessed and exploited by human ingenuity. Heidegger is persuaded that the world we have made through the application of scientific method, and the transformation of matter itself through the instruments of our own creation, have resulted in a new mode of *being*. We are enframed by this modern apocalypse. If there is any "truth" to be uncovered in the modern world, it is a truth that will reveal itself through technology: "The name 'standing reserve' assumes the rank of an inclusive rubric. It designates nothing less than the way in which everything presences that is wrought upon by the revealing that challenges. Whatever stands by in the sense of standing reserve no longer stands over against us as object."[20]

Heidegger's notoriously cryptic depiction of the interweaving of science and technology is one embraced by both Hannah Arendt and Barry Cooper. Arendt draws a clear distinction between pre-modern and modern mathematics. Plato regarded mathematics as one of the highest forms of knowledge, subordinate only to philosophy, and that was because "mathematics was the proper introduction to that sky of ideas where no mere images (*eidola*) and shadows, no perishable matter, could any longer interfere with the appearing of eternal being."[21] Mathematics in the classical understanding reaches beyond appearances, toward something eternal, but it does not ensnare the eternal. In fact, because mathematical understanding is limited by its practice in a finite human being who has entered into the cosmos and did not create it, mathematics requires the higher speculative understanding of philosophy so that it will not overstep its boundaries.[22] We do not hold, in the modern world, that mathematics ought to be restrained by philosophy. This hubristic rejection of the hierarchy between philosophy and science is what Arendt terms the embrace of "universal" over "natural" science: "Only we, and we only for hardly more than a few decades, have come to live in a world thoroughly determined by science and technology whose objective truth and practical know-how are derived from cosmic and universal, as distinguished from terrestrial and 'natural' laws, and in which knowledge acquired by selecting a point of reference outside the earth is applied to earthly nature and human artifice."[23]

Cooper maps out a succinct four-fold characterization of "technological consciousness": 1. There is "no reason to respect nature. Being without purpose or final cause, it sanctions nothing." 2. Spontaneous divine and human intervention is impossible under technology, because science is interested in uncovering processes and patterns, not in welcoming unfathomable acts or miracles. 3. Paradoxically, "notwithstanding the metaphysical impossibility of the miraculousness of human initiation, human being is nevertheless the only source of will." 4. The paramouncy of will is clouded by the productivity that is yielded by the technological "turn."[24]

It might be helpful here to point to some examples of what Heidegger, Arendt and Cooper are talking about. The "enframing" characteristic of technology is such that it is difficult (Heidegger would say impossible) to think outside the reality that we have constituted for ourselves. If you can figure out how to break down atoms in such a way as to create new forms of energy that do not exist in nature, and if that new energy makes it possible to increase wealth, comfort and productivity, and you are living inside the actual benefits of that technology, how can you claim that what we have made is not *real?* The fabricated reality no longer appears to me as a consequence of an act of human will, but merely as a given: the way things are. On what grounds would one doubt the "revealing" capacity of technology? Nuclear power plants actually do generate energy. Cell phones do work.

Enframing characteristics of technology may be particularly prescient in the new communications technologies.[25] Whereas some may see these as liberating people for an ever expansive capacity to relate to others, regardless of time or space, thoughtful spectators of the communications revolution are cautious about making claims for enhanced individual freedom. Graham Longford warns that in an age of digital technology, "the Internet and the World Wide Web regulate and *govern* users, enabling and cultivating certain conduct, activities and forms of life while simultaneously constraining and neutralizing others."[26]

Jodi Dean examines what she calls "technoculture," the vast proliferation of information engines that supposedly give us greater command and knowledge of the choices we make, and finds quite the opposite effect. Dean's fear, consistent with the Heideggerian mood of "anxiety," is that "network communications gives many of us the sense of being forever behind, or forever lacking what everyone else has. The promise of information gives us the sense of always being uninformed, unsure, never quite sure that what we think we know hasn't been proven otherwise and that were we diligent enough, we might have discovered our error. Our fears, then, are linked to an overwhelming doubt that can never be resolved. And this brings with it the risk that our desires to know may become desires for relief."[27] Zadie Smith, commenting on the phenomenon of "Facebook" (a recent technological innovation in which almost every undergraduate student participates), worries that her idea of personhood is "nostalgic, irrational, inaccurate." Smith cites Facebook's founder, Mark Zuckerberg, from his own Facebook page, on which Zuckerberg identifies his principal interests: "minimalism, revolutions and eliminating desire." The last interest may be the most telling, and corroborates what Jodi Dean says about the anxiety induced by "technoculture." Technological enframing may actually have the effect of disparaging desire, especially if one considers Socrates' definition of *eros* as the longing for that which can never be attained. To *desire* is to be needy, not efficient and competent. Smith writes: "When a human being becomes a set of data on a website like Facebook, he or she is reduced. Everything shrinks. Individual character. Friendships. Language. Sensibility. In a way it's a transcendent experience: we lose our bodies, our messy feelings, our desires, our fears. It reminds me that those of us who turn in disgust from what we consider an overinflated liberal-bourgeois sense of self should be careful what we wish for: our denuded network selves don't look more free, they just look more owned."[28]

Is technology in all its manifestations *enframing*, or is it not? Tom Darby writes about the "new justice" of the modern world and its intrinsic relation to technology. There *are* standards, Darby says, by which we judge speech and action in the modern context, but the standards are technological ones. "Efficiency, the end (=purpose =completeness) of the projection of technology constitutes the boundaries of technology." Technology is "self-referential," "autonomous" and "progressively sovereign." There are no standards outside technology that we can realistically enlist to halt its progress.[29] Yet we hear lament in the words of many of the authors considered in this essay. They speak of science and technology with a critical voice, and that voice has to be accounted for.

Here, we return to our opening thoughts from Barry Cooper on "empirical political science," with its threefold characteristics of the skill of "Aristotelian fishermen and hunters," textual analysis into "well-founded insights," and "analysis of consciousness by the consciousness of the analyst." Empirical political science, on these terms, is decidedly non-scientific and non-technological. It requires attention to engagement with the natural world, the discipline of learning from the great philosophers of the past, and an honest introspection into one's own thinking. Importantly, any one of the three practices associated with "empirical political science" requires an openness to a ground of knowing that can not be converted into what Heidegger calls a "standing reserve" (material at the ready to be converted into technological innovation). Let's take them one by one and look at the possibilities within each for resisting the enframing tentacles of technology.

The metaphor (drawn from Aristotle) of "hunters and fishermen" is intended to impress upon us the significance of sense experience. "In the

Nicomachean Ethics," Cooper writes, "Aristotle advised us to pay attention to the undemonstrated sayings and opinions of experienced people, because experience has given them an eye to see things aright."[30] There is a skill that is derived from practice. We may be skeptical about what sorts of opinions are yielded by the users of cell-phones and Facebook junkies, who, after all, may have long experience in the kinds of activities in which they are immersed. But it is still possible to choose (to a certain extent) what one experiences, and the kind of knowledge one hopes to cultivate from that experience. Matthew Crawford completed a Ph.D. in political theory at the University of Chicago, got himself a well-paying position in a think tank in Washington, and then threw off his professional career to open up a motorcycle repair shop. The man can write as well as repair machines, and in his book, *Shop Class as Soul Craft: An Inquiry Into the Value of Work*, Crawford makes a powerful case for the possibility of resisting scientism and technology through the practice of a skilled trade: "The physical circumstances of the jobs performed by carpenters, plumbers, and auto mechanics vary too much for them to be executed by idiots; they require circumspection and adaptability. One feels like a man, not a cog in a machine. The trades are a natural home for anyone who would live by his own powers, free not only of deadening abstraction, but also of the insidious hopes and rising insecurities that seem to be endemic in our current economic life."[31] Learning a trade means learning from a "flesh and blood person" whom one emulates. As one becomes more skilled, more experienced, in one's tasks, "something about the world is coming into clearer view." Crawford tells us that "the sense that your judgments are becoming truer is part of the experience of being fully engaged in what you are doing."[32] The competent tradesman is someone who participates in an *order of being* in which there are standards toward which he strives, not an infinite regression of technological possibility. As he becomes more skilled at what he does, he becomes more confident as a human being, less afraid, less anxious. For Crawford, the resistance to technology is possible, and it is most probably in good work. He advises seeking out "the cracks where individual agency and the love of knowledge can be realized today, in one's own life."[33] If we think with Crawford, then stage one of "empirical political science" is possible, even if it requires what Crawford himself calls a "contrarian streak" to the ethos of the technological society.

Stage two of "empirical political science" entails paying attention to the great texts of the Western tradition. Cooper closes his book, *Action Into Nature*, with citations from the Bible, the Kohelet and Anaximander. All the citations evoke what Cooper calls "unavoidable truths of the cosmos." These are truths about the coming into being and passing away of each and every human being, the unknowable ground of being into which each and every human being is inserted, and the necessity that all things should perish. The citation from Anaximander reads: "The origin of all things is the Boundless [*apeiron*]. . . it is necessary that things should perish into that from which they were born; for they pay one another penalty [*dike*] for their injustice [*adikia*] according to the decree [*taxis*] of time."

Cooper chose to end his book with meditations on mortality from some of the great texts in the Western tradition. This was a wise choice. Thinking about dying, as Socrates says, is the beginning of philosophy. But we might also combat technology by turning to the great thinkers of the past for their thoughts on justice and what we are fitted for in this world. Human beings, Aristotle said, are defined by their capacity for reason, and by their natural home in political communities. "That man is much more a political animal than any kind of bee or any herd animal is clear. For . . . nature does nothing in vain; and man alone among the animals has speech. . . Speech serves to reveal the advantageous and the harmful, and hence also the just and the unjust. For it is peculiar to man as compared to the other animals that he alone has a perception of good and bad and just and unjust and other things [of this sort]; and partnership in these things is what makes a household and a city."[34] It is not easy in the modern world to understand what Aristotle is claiming. To be a reasoning and speaking being is inherently connected to the capacity to distinguish between the good and the bad. To fulfill one's purpose as a human being is to live among others, in a political community, in which one builds a partnership for the sake of a good life. In an age of "globalization," fluidity of borders and identity, and the celebration of individual autonomy, all facilitated by rapid communications and ease of movement, Aristotle's recommendations for a good life sound antiquated. It requires attention to his texts and, through that attention, an immersion in another way of thinking that opens up the possibility of a different kind of world. By reading Aristotle, it is possible to recover a sense of what is lost in a technological society.

Here are some of the things I have learned from Aristotle. The purpose of a human life is to pursue happiness, and happiness is bound up with reasonableness and virtue. Happiness is not a state, but an activity, and it requires some exploration of what we are fitted for (not just what pleasures us). We are fitted for contemplation of the highest and most divine things (this is where thinking about death is paramount), and we are equally fitted for specifically human action in—among others—family and community, in which we are called upon to exercise not just our intellectual capacities, but our moral characters. The moral virtues of courage, moderation, generosity, and justice cannot be pursued to the exclusion of the intellectual virtues or of thinking about what is beyond our temporal existence.

Reading is a route to independence in, and from, a technological society. Though Eric Voegelin may have emphasized the classic texts as revelatory "tools" for us to recover something of what it is to be a human being in a scientific/technological society, I am not dissuaded that there are many contemporary writers (mostly of fiction) who can help us equally well. Reading good books is an opening to the experience of others, perhaps with a better understanding of things, that is recorded carefully and at length in a narrative that requires sustained concentration (something that technological information does not require). Elsewhere, I have written about the "therapeutic" benefits of reading, "opening oneself to the best accounts one can find that map the terrain of the modern world." I have suggested there that "it is safe to say that a person who reads authors like Alice Munroe and Jonathan Franzen is not likely to spend his or her money buying a kidney from a destitute person in a developing country, in order to forestall their death, just because it is possible to do that. Such a person is less likely to see every human relation as one of opposition, with winners and losers in a struggle of the will. Such a person is less likely to believe in the perfectibility of either himself or the world."[35] George Steiner, the great contemporary literary critic, remarked that "no man can read fully, can answer to the aesthetic, whose 'nerve and blood' are at peace in skeptical rationality, are now at home in immanence and verification." A good reader, as Steiner says, is one who reads "as if"—as if *poesis* were a permanent possibility.[36]

Finally, we consider the third axis of "empirical political science" identified by Cooper: "the analysis of consciousness by the consciousness of the analyst." This means that I have to have the capacity to think about my thinking—what anchors it and what threatens it. I turn to Hannah Arendt for what I find to be the best explanation of the "two-level" account of consciousness. Where do we go when we think? How do we put order in the phenomena before us, and how can we be sure that the order we assign to things is a good one? Presumably, human beings have always had the capacity to think, but Hannah Arendt says that it has not always been the case that we human beings have had the responsibility to reflect upon consciousness. The "consciousness of consciousness" she dates from the time of ancient Greece in which "the Olympian gods were laid low by philosophy."[37] With the inception of philosophy, "it is important to note," writes Arendt, "that the immortal and divine part within man does not exist unless it is actualized and focused on the divine outside; in other words, the *object* of our thoughts bestows immortality on thinking itself. The object is invariably the everlasting, what was and is and will be, and therefore cannot be otherwise than it is, and cannot *not* be."[38] One cannot think about *nothing*.

Thinking philosophically for Arendt *is* the two-fold process of consciousness that she describes as a "silent dialogue." She looks to Socrates for what she describes as the "two-in-one" of the inner dialogue that I have with myself, when I retreat from the business of the world and I examine my own thoughts. "Without consciousness", Arendt proclaims, "in the sense of self-awareness, thinking would not be possible."[39]

The two-in-one inner dialogue is the prerequisite for moral action in the world, though in itself it furnishes no moral prescriptions. The person who cannot go home with himself and be at harmony with himself in the dialogue he has with himself is a person who is incapable of conscience. Importantly, for me, Arendt insists that this inner dialogue, while philosophical, is not a specialized kind of knowledge intended only for the learned and the few: "Thinking in its non-cognitive, non-specialized sense as a natural need of human life, the actualization of the difference given in consciousness, is not a prerogative of the few but an ever-present faculty in everybody."[40] The inability to think in these terms may be prevalent among the "scientists, scholars and other specialists in mental enterprises" and, if we believe Matthew Crawford, we may be far more likely to find thinking among the plumbers and motorcycle repairmen. A life *without thinking* on Arendt's terms is quite possible, but it is a life that fails to fulfill its essence. "Unthinking men are like sleepwalkers."[41]

In conclusion, I would say that empirical political science, as that science is defended by Barry Cooper, is indeed possible in the contemporary scientific, technological climate. But it is a hard road, and it is a road that resists the *Zeitgeist*. Efficiency, productivity, goal-orientation, values choices, and technological literacy are the conventional goods held out to the young. I am a university professor and a mother, and this is the advice that I give to the young. Learn to make and fix things. Matthew Crawford recommends turning one's attention to carpentry and cars, but I think cooking may easily substitute in this universe of activity. One can learn a lot from making one's own food (Cooper would probably add: from killing it, too). Secondly, if you are privileged enough to have leisure, read good books. I have a citation taped to my refrigerator from James Baldwin: "You think your pains and heartbreaks are unprecedented in the history of the world, but then you read. It was books that taught me that the things that tormented me were the very things that connected me with all the people who were alive, or who have ever been alive." Last, think about where you go when you think. As Hannah Arendt says, "do not contradict yourself." Know that justice is stronger than injustice, because injustice cannot be thought, except as the absence of justice.

Endnotes

1   Barry Cooper, "Weaving a Work," Ronald Beiner and Wayne Norman, eds., *Canadian Political Philosophy* (Oxford and New York: Oxford University Press, 2001), 383.

2   Barry Cooper, *The Restoration of Political Science and the Crisis of Modernity* (Lewiston/Lampeter/Queenston, NY: Edwin Mellen Press, 1989), 282.

3   In "Weaving a Work," Cooper identifies Eric Voegelin, Leo Strauss and Hannah Arendt as the three people who have guided his investigations of political thought (albeit with an emphasis upon Voegelin) 383.

4   Hannah Arendt, *The Human Condition* (Chicago and London: University of Chicago Press, 1968), 295.

5   Hannah Arendt, *The Origins of Totalitarianism* (San Diego, New York and London: Harcourt Brace and World, 1975, 1st edition 1948), 469.

6   Arendt, *The Origins of Totalitarianism*, 470.

7   Arendt, *The Origins of Totalitarianism*, 471.

8   Barry Cooper, *Action Into Nature* (Notre Dame and London: University of Notre Dame Press, 1991), 35.

9   Cooper, *Action Into Nature*, 35-36.

10 Cooper, *Action Into Nature*, 37.

11 Arendt, *The Human Condition*, 260.

12 Arendt, *The Human Condition*, 264.

13 Arendt, *The Human Condition*, 288.

14 Arendt, *The Human Condition*, 279.

15 Martin Heidegger, "The Age of the World Picture," *The Question Concerning Technology and Other Essays*, trans. William Lovitt (New York, San Francisco and London: Harper Colophon Books, 1977), 133.

16 I think this is also true for Cooper. Cooper cites Voegelin in impressing upon us that "the consequences of natural science and technology are not the results of brilliant insights by scientists and technicians but have resulted from the account of the structure of phenomena as objective, which permits the introduction of human agency into the natural causal chain." *Action into Nature*, 191.

17 Heidegger, *Question Concerning Technology*, 4.

18 Heidegger, *Question Concerning Technology*, 12.

19 Heidegger, *Question Concerning Technology*, 21.

20   Heidegger, *Question Concerning Technology*, 17.
21   Arendt, *The Human Condition*, 266.
22   Plato may well have been aware of the dangers of a mathematics that is detached from philosophy. In an exchange with Glaucon (Book VII) Socrates warns of the dangers of employing geometry to advance actions, when it does not grasp the "limiting" conditions of philosophy. Men of action may think that geometry is all about "'squaring,' 'applying,' 'adding' and everything of the sort," whereas the real purpose of geometry is "for the sake of knowing what is always, and not at all for what is at any time coming into being and passing away." (Plato, *Republic*, trans. Allan Bloom (New York, 1968) 526-527.)
23   Arendt, *The Human Condition*, 268.
24   Cooper, *Action into Nature*, 45.
25   Indeed, Cooper says that "one of the conclusions I drew from the study of 'posthistorical' life in the technological society was that entertainment and the media, especially TV, were central agencies of control." Cooper undertook an in-depth study of the Canadian Broadcasting Corporation (Cooper, "Weaving a Work," 381; Cooper, *Sins of Omission: Shaping the News at CBC TV* (Toronto: University of Toronto Press, 1994).)
26   Graham Longford, "Pedagogies of Digital Citizenship," *Techne: Research in Philosophy and Technology: Special Issue on Education and Citizenship in the Digital Age* (Vol 1:9, Fall, 2005): 68.
27   Jodi Dean, *Publicity's Secret: How Technoculture Capitalizes on Democracy* (Ithaca and London: Cornell University Press, 2002) 148.
28   Zadie Smith, "Generation Why," *The New York Review of Books* (November 25, 2010).
29   Tom Darby, "On Globalization, Technology and The New Justice," David Tabachnick and Toivo Koivukoski, eds., *Globalization, Technology and Philosophy* (Albany, NY: State University of New York Press, 2004) 66–67.
30   Cooper, *Restoration of Political Science*, 272.
31   Matthew Crawford, *Shop Class as Soul Craft: An Inquiry into the Value of Work* (New York: Penguin Books, 2009) 53.
32   Crawford, *Shop Class*, 207.
33   Crawford, *Shop Class*, 210.
34   Aristotle, *The Politics*, trans. Carnes Lord (Chicago and London: University of Chicago Press, 1984), 1253a10–20.
35   Leah Bradshaw, "Technology and Political Education," *Techne: Research in Philosophy and Technology* (Vol. 1:9, Fall, 2005), 24–25.
36   George Steiner, *Real Presences* (Chicago: University of Chicago Press, 1989), 229.
37   Hannah Arendt, *Thinking: Volume One of The Life of the Mind* (New York and London: Harcourt Brace and Jovanovich, 1971), 135.
38   Arendt, *Thinking*, 136.
39   Arendt, *Thinking*, 187.
40   Arendt, *Thinking*, 191.
41   Arendt, *Thinking*, 189.

Chapter Seven

Precarious Restorations:

Religious Life in the Contemporary World

Peter Emberley

If nothing else, what world events since 9/11 have made evident is that religion is not going to vanish just because intellectuals have declared that God is dead. Nor has the ploy of rendering religion impotent by making it merely a private matter, so that it does not play out in the common world, led to widespread departure from churches, temples, and synagogues. And equating religion with aesthetics, moralism, or a civic religion has failed to be enduring. Life, as Oscar Wilde once said, is rarely pure and never simple.

Before I advance any further, I would like to frame my comments on the religious life in the contemporary world, by explaining the meaning of the words I am using. "Religion" comes from the Latin word *religio,* which means to bind. I understand this in various ways—the soul binding itself to the numinous, individuals binding themselves to the beliefs and practices understood to trigger openness to the numinous, and the binding of the community to itself, as witness to the divine. As for the second term, "world"—with its emphasis on what is seen, heard, and debated by all, and, in its proximity in meaning to civic, signifying citizen, with its cognates civil, civility, civilize and civilization—I take this to mean the forms of belonging, association and solidarity which make us a people, and not isolated autonomous beings, cut off from the mutual affection, connections of interest, and maturing that comprise our common life.

To speak of religion and the world implies both a coming together and a separation of these phenomena. Not only may the contact between them be the source of mutual reciprocity and benefit, it is also the source of dangerous temptations. Anything more or less than a gossamer contact between them risks issuing in political overreaching and spiritual compromise, or political mediocrity and mystification. To speak of religion as concerning itself with the numinous, or the transcendent, is to speak of an ultimacy over which no monopoly should be tolerated, and the use of which in realizing the absolute in the here and now can only portend the gravest dangers to the human artifice. The political task, then, is how to sustain responsiveness to the transcendent, and, at the same time, prevent its translation into a project to achieve an immanent perfection, or universal conflagration.

Across this country there is a renaissance of religious devotion, conviction, and organization. Some of this renaissance is a desperate cry of abandonment and alienation in a world that has become frightening and unfamiliar. Some of it is a wisdom that has come from age, tribulation, and discernment, and that now sees in obedience, gratitude, waiting and anticipating—rather than endless striving and negating—a way of being human, of participating in a more contoured reality. Much of it entails a recollection of what was historically sacrificed in the modern experiment of making the immanent world the substitute for the divine. Whatever its source, the new inflection is no longer confined to private life, or within social fellowships in civil society. It has become a public voice, and it is pressing for change in the terms and reasonings of our public conversation. If we design ourselves after the gods we pray to, we cannot afford to neglect this new political pressure, nor the gods that our neighbours worship.

The restoration of religion is, as we are all anxiously aware, a worldwide phenomenon. While many versions of it baldly cover what is in fact garden-variety envy, fear and intolerance, if not the raw will-to-dominate used to justify the extinction of those who are strangers, there is here, too, a statement of resistance to pursuing the seductive experiment of the West, which was to abandon the desire for republics of virtue and to substitute satisfaction in the imminent world for escape in the transcendent. For us, the present recovery of religious enthusiasm has to be received with mixed sentiments—we can comprehend that there is a dissatisfied remainder left after the modern experiment with personal and social satisfaction, and factoring out of the desire for the absolute, but we have also endured a century of cataclysmic violence and hatred, almost beyond human scale, that employed religious symbols to exploit and amplify the otherwise healthy competition and tension between religious communities. Our hopes lie in the possibility that religious revival will leaven the world with subtle discernment, patience and charity, but our historical experience counsels an antidote of skepticism and prudence that we do not find in sufficient abundance to take us through the difficult shoals of late-western modernity.

The recrudescence of religion, both domestically and internationally, can only be met with surprise and perplexity. For five centuries, the process that some call secularization or dis-enchantment has been the hallmark of the modern West. For many decades, indeed centuries, in our universities, at the cutting edge of intellectual life, in the arts, at the centre of our common civilizational destiny, and in our public conversation, there has resided an antipathy and opposition to religion, even if short-lived ersatz religions have often filled the vacuum. The most significant historical events of the last five centuries have involved the evacuation or substantive revision of key foundations of the Judeo-Christian tradition. The Protestant Reformation, while attempting to re-spiritualize Western life, shifted Christianity from a religion of philosophical signification to one of pious intention. The scientific revolution removed the study of cosmic design and purpose from the ambit of human reason. The deism and theism and of the sixteenth and seventeenth centuries either made God equivalent to the rational network of the cosmos, or banished him beyond the needs of humans. The romantic movements of the eighteenth century made God equivalent to feelings of plenitude or absence, thus risking an equation of such feelings to the creative power of the human mind. The Marxist, Freudian and Nietzschean deconstructions of religion have reduced it further to a human construction for maintaining solidarity and collective norms and ideals, or as a balm to deformed life, or as a form of organized cowardice in face of the meaninglessness of existence. This history is the dynamic of modern Western civilization; as the influence of the West has expanded, it has become the dynamic of world civilization, triggering repetitions of our history throughout the non-Western world. That dynamic (which incorporates not only the material and organizational achievements of the West, but more importantly, interpretations of what it is to be human in the voices of philosophy, poetry and history) has had the hallmark of disseminating the transcendental vision of the true, the good and the beautiful as it migrated from Plato to Augustine to Kant to Nietzsche, and has made any authoritative, true restoration difficult to conceive. We will, instead, be the de-conditioned beings, stripped of the predicates of existence that once ordered and dignified our individual and collective lives. Our most ardent project, now, is to be liberated from necessity, and the limits it imposes. Bereft of moderation or even an understanding of its purpose, and lives of greed and moderation, we are left to being permitted to do anything. Our institutions and their correlating political practices have conveniently fallen fully into line, even though they needed to be nudged.

To this constraint on religious revival has also to be added a second: the implications of living at a time when the unfolding of a global, technological society, not only worldwide, but down to the smallest capillaries of society and life, is progressively insinuating a narrow set of technical imperatives into all spheres of human activity, and yet posing as a total solution to the question of human order. What had once emanated from independent realms of the household, political association, civil society, the professions, the world of art, the religious community, and the university—each with its own diverse means and ends emerging from separate purposes and goals (or, as Oakeshott writes, "voices")—is ever more an ecumenic organization, requiring total conformity to the technical intention, which is the most efficient coordination of all means and ends through systematization and optimalization, as Jacques Ellul, in his book *The Technological Society*, has elaborated for us. Regardless of where we are in the globe, or how we are differentiated by gender, experience, custom or belief, we are urged to pull for greater efficiency and adapt our differences to the overall technical objective. This trajectory, which progressively has displaced other forms through which our universality and wholeness could be pursued, is increasingly the paramount collective activity through which our desire for perfection or the absolute is being expressed publicly. Its flabby ecumenism may be a poor substitute for the eternal, but it seduces us with its easy invitation to say with John Lennon "You may say I'm a dreamer, But I'm not the only one, I hope someday you'll join us, And the world will live as one."

What is cunning about this historical dynamic is that the closing down of the range of options coincides with the appearance of a profusion of difference and expansion of creative freedom. Our televisions, bookstores, cinemas, museums, music, architecture and even churches offer up a menu of apparently endless possibility—of desire, adventure, and hope. But, in depending heavily on the new technologies, and the logic inherent to them, not to say the metaphysical principles that they have unreflectively inherited from the modern era, and finding themselves both emancipated from older restraining ways of being, while constrained by new rules of engagement, these new technologies generate a multiplicity, rather than a genuine plurality, of human opportunities. Under its aegis, we are all different, but different in all the same way.

In the very act of justifying their utility or reason for being, they inscribe the logic of the technological system within themselves (instrumentality, reductionism, efficiency). For example, when religion empties out its primal elements—of tribulation, alienation, sacrifice, transgression and terror—in favour of techniques of self-fulfillment and social cohesion—it insinuates the sameness of technological subjectivity, desire, rationality and pleasure in its core. Older ways of being which spoke to our capacity to transcend our bodies and wager for more, such as the heroic life, or the renunciant or sacrificing life, are abandoned as one might discard dysfunctional relics. In a world that gratifies every whim and deems the pursuit of such consumption as a recognition of the authenticity of the self, not to say an entitlement, no language of restraint can survive, leaving only the expectation of a life of perpetually gratified wishes.

Technology has, of course, produced ersatz environments in which the passion for honour, the desire for immortality, or love of wholeness can be experimented upon—which one sees in the recently emerging recovery of legend, myth and epic fantasy in film and computer simulations—and these simulacra may appear as safer environments for playing out potent desires - but when there is neither real risk nor redemption in these activities, they are quickly discarded, leaving passions dissatisfied and looking for satisfaction elsewhere. Technological modernity is, after the first glow, decadent and boring.

It is no wonder that young men, in particular, are recruited into movements that trade on danger and honour, for they are looking to play for true stakes in life, even when they eventually find those movements promising far more than they deliver. What modern terrorism is teaching us is that in a world where there is no risk, no courage, nothing absolute at stake, and where global technology offers merely a simulacrum of the absolute in somnolent labour and consumption, men will play—play to the death—for stakes that are perceived to be truly absolute. Humans live by myths - myths which project a great canvas of adventure, danger, risk and redemption - but when the tensions of those myths are translated into mere social antagonism, or rival socio-economic platforms, to be replaced by various regimes of safety administered by technocrats - whether they are moving goods and services, or administering global rights emptied of the prospect of spiritual renewal, the desire for risking "all" finds no object worthy of its passion.[1] It is desire and disobedience, risk and horror, transgression and death, that trigger religious myth—that canvas on which human longing is etched. The gamble of usurping religion by technology—by a false eternal, if you will—has contributed greatly to the heightened tensions we are seeing discharged around us, and risks compromising the true object of our spiritual needs.

These dangers are significantly heightened by two other features of our globalized cosmopolitanism. The first is the inflation of our needs and wants, which has stirred a global waspishness, a greedy desire, manifest in everything from the stockpiling urged on us by box stores to the gratuitous power of today's automobile, from on-command choice of 400+ television channels to electronic devices crammed with a surfeit of converging technologies and the promise of infinite possibilities, from global tourism to eco-challenges. All are emanations of an immoderation that must inevitably empty out the mutual affection, connections of interest, and maturing that our far less glamourous, but nonetheless common, life is intended to provide. We are like leaky jars, to use an image from Plato, which, as we are being filled up, keep emptying, leaving us increasingly pained by absence. This condition contributes to our envy, quarrelsomeness, and lust for power. The non-finality of our desire, played out on the terrain of the here and now, gives us the love of dominion, not only over others, but even over reality itself. It is as if sating ourselves with the surrogates within our control, we can possess the eternal. Rage is the natural form that this dream takes. Rules and regulations, to the point of surfeit, can be legislated to stem the tide, but, as Rousseau points out, an individual experiencing resistance assumes an intention against himself, and naturally rebels to the point of violence. At this point, the world becomes a never-ending site of conflict, possessed of the attitude that whatever impedes expansion is an undue limitation.

The second characteristic is succinctly captured in the CBC's new mantra, "nothing stays the same, not for a day, not for an hour, not for a minute," joining every other broadcaster in jolting us lockstep into the apocalyptic mood of our times, often—as is the case with CTV, FOX and CNN—accompanied by doric music, prompting a mood of frantic anticipation, imminent danger and, more ominously, of armies on the march. At some level, to be sure, it is important that we are reminded of the perfidy, vice and sins of omission committed by others like us, if only to recall how susceptible we are to them. And there is something salutary in being aware of the earth's proneness to disaster, the vulnerability of our food, water and air to contamination, and the thin barrier of convention protecting us from barbarism. But the immediacy of the message, and the urgency with which we are induced to react, has also brought what Marshall McLuhan warned would occur as we moved into the neo-primitivism of the communications age where, as he says, "terror is the normal state ... for in it everything affects everything all the time."[2] Were our perceived reality entirely limited to this virtual reality that seems to amuse us so seductively, our lives would be a continuous self-overcoming animated by dreams of great emancipations, such as the hope that we may yet become wholly unconditioned beings, free again to live a life of pure potentiality, like a child's life of wishes, animated by purposiveness without purpose. But this is precisely what the constant technological upgrades in our lives aim at, captivating us by the simulacrum of progress, when in fact, we are—as Benjamin Barber points out—"just amusing ourselves to death" while the real civilizational tasks of reparation, restoration and renewal are neglected.

Year after year, the stakes are raised as new heights of re-making the conditions of reality are undertaken, be it through recombinant DNA engineering, or the search for a new planetary home, or the desire to isolate, once and for all, the death-gene—the ultimate act of magic, which, were it to happen, would wholly actualize our hope of escape from the conditions of reality. Though it lies in our future, it is already feeding hopes of a great overcoming, towards a future that would no longer necessitate the restraint and moral discipline that were understood to enable the higher capabilities such as *noesis* and contemplation, and which, since Parmenides, were the hallmark of human excellence and the anodyne of the fear of our death. Whether by word or force, used in our times as magic, we *will* re-constitute the conditions of our existence, so that the daily work of cultivating our gardens and renewing order become unnecessary. Instead, by ordering our lives through calculative rationality and volatile desire alone, our unbound passions have brought us to the seductive task of pursuing a false eternal of cosmic mastery (an error that both Plato and Augustine encountered in their times and consummately diagnosed as a psycho-pathology). With audacity, this has become our civilizational enterprise, which cannot be completed until all otherness is mastered and re-made in our own image, legislating our all-too-human foibles and enthusiasms to all of existence. Whether it was boredom with established truths, or rancour from being excluded from the booty that has become available since the sixteenth century, or a civilizational miscalculation that took us down this path of increasing immoderation and the eclipse of older ordering principles, this is our fate, and it is lived each day in our restlessness, vibrating like jigger bugs, and nurturing a stock-piling of undifferentiated "stuff, living a child's life of wishes."

Perched on precarious rubble from the collapse of classical rationalism, we anticipate a further great over-coming. This keeps us perched, animated like those jigger-bugs on a hot wire, with anticipation of the next big thing, and, as the twentieth century has demonstrated, it has made us susceptible to final solutions. Our dangerous play with ultimacy and the continuous rising of stakes has taken us to the point that ordinary political tools, such as promising and forgiveness, seem to be irrelevant, given the scale of events that the twentieth century has unleashed. Older ways of thought may no longer be available to us, except perhaps, in personal ways, or in epicurean gardens. One of the great casualties of our time is the growing disappearance of leisure under the pressure of "busy-ness," but without leisure we cut ourselves off from the reflective life that provides us with those salutary "yes, buts" that prevent us being enthralled by the immediate, and by ill-considered enthusiasms, such as those that Aristophanes depicts in his play "Birds," dreams to which the twentieth century still is susceptible and willing to entertain. In our finitude, we seem unable to shake our dangerous play with ultimacy and final solutions. We are continually seduced by the hope of radical deliverance and ultimacy. The phenomena all coalesce in their apocalpyticism, in their great fervour for a tremendous self-overcoming.

The result of our dangerous play with apocalpytic symbolism is that it must inevitably produce the unhealthy cry that "only a god can save us." There may be a great error in dichotomizing is and ought, for there always *is* a desire for perfection, and the courageous, organized control of contingencies reinforces modest religious hopes that leaven our everyday lives, rather than sowing dreams of radical salvation. The problem with apocalypticism is that it ignores the day in, day out, struggles for order and reason, and their accompanying small pieties. It allows garden-variety frustrations and disappointments to be used as justification for violence and terror. It sows the violence that turns against the basic facilities and processes required for a country to function, not to say thwarts the basic decency, tinged by nobility, that human society requires. But that is not our present state: increasingly many of us live hopelessly empty existences that are nothing more than a swirl of undifferentiated happenings, where nearly all is indulged. Even more, they are elevated by being protected by rights and good intentions, which in reality have largely been colonized by the micromanaging and moralizing sadists of today's vast bureaucracies. So fearful are we to return to our patrimony, and so unable are we to re-collect earlier principles of order that had acknowledged a heterogeneity of souls and human goods, let alone the autochthonous traditions and ways of being, such as one may still find, in Alberta or Quebec, and Nova Scotia and that until quite recently resisted central Canada's sirenic call to the homogenizing vision of Canada.

But how could things be different when the CBC's moniker, noted above, ensures our lockstep embrace with the empire of nihilistic technology that has no remembrance of principles of order pre-dating Machiavelli? Denying both divine reality and common sense, we have been thrown back on relying only on the human will: should we be surprised that our national broadcaster sees fit to vaunt that it will be the purveyor of the most volatile passions: "greed, envy, things we desire, more immediate"? This same media source conflates the "it" with Mark Kelly's "it's personal," which reinforces the dangerous tendency in modern society that watchers will refrain from identifying with the public world, but find fulfillment in the deep chasms of human private subjectivity. When not even the national broadcaster can cultivate a measure of continence and dignity, it cannot be surprising that we have come to live in a world filled with rage, presumption, and excessive forbearance, loosely held together by a rootless cosmopolitanism, and the soft values of tolerance, forgiveness and charity. Having jettisoned all limits and radicalized the key aspects of Christianity, we are left bereft of any impediment to the nonsense that threatens our existence, if not our ultimate survival. But then, clinging to survival has become the only "value" remaining, even if in its bare facticity it does not hold up any bar beyond comfortable self-preservation and a frail residue of the heroic Hegelian dialectic of recognition that was the civilization's "engine" in the form of resisting "dissing" one another.

Embarked on this trajectory, it was inevitable that the revolt against the last man would ensue with the forceful and shameless democracy in which everyone sees himself an overman, a maker of his own values. It is a veritable return to the Piraeus and to Thrasymachus and all the chthonic forces that required the abdication of moderation, proportionality, and justice. The Götterdämmerung we unleashed on ourselves is now a global phenomenon that is embraced worldwide (even by those who cheerfully accept the supervised normalcy of everyday life) and held together by the fear of mutually assured destruction and the glut of consumption that helps us to forget how dire our situation really is. Even our theologies—and perhaps especially those—and philosophies are increasingly impotent to address our disorders, if even to recognize them. Too few are those beautiful souls who see deracination as a deprival. We are rather like the Platonic philosopher who had to adopt the Stoic withdrawal from public life, cultivate the garden of his own soul, and allow barbarism to dissipate, if it will:

> like someone who takes refuge under a little wall from a storm of
> dust or hail driven by the wind, the philosopher—seeing others

filled with lawlessness—is satisfied if he can somehow lead his
present life free from injustice and impious acts and depart from it
with good hope, blameless and content.[3]

But is this really the best we can hope for? Is it perhaps an error to emphasize the philosophical deconstruction of religion alone? The Western tradition, after all, is composed of both Hebraism and Hellenism, worshipful
obedience and the desire to know. Perhaps it would be sound, in our confused and immoderate times, to tilt towards "Hebraism" and attend to the
lively world of orthopraxy.

An antidote to the despair that "only a god can save us" in the meltdown of metaphysics is recollecting the organized work of dozens of religious groups, or citizens with religious beliefs, comprising the lively
diverse networks of civil society, on the travesties of human smuggling, the
trade of human organs, child prostitution, third-world poverty, and the
needs of strangers who have suffered natural disasters. Apocalyptic longings for a big change risks sapping individuals from their vocation of getting on with the less dramatic, incremental steps of human organization.

The third and final constraint on the re-emergence of religion within
our public life is the deep, insurmountable, divisions within the Academy.
These are summarized with great succinctness by Alasdair MacIntyre, in
his book *Three Rival Versions of Moral Inquiry*, whose argument is that the
academic community is torn into three incommensurable camps: i) the
encyclopedists, who continue the enlightenment project of empirical fact-
finding; ii) the genealogists, who, derived from Nietzsche's anti-founda-
tionalism, deny both the objectivity of the facts and the universality of
method; and iii) the rational craft-tradition that MacIntyre equates with
Thomism. The problem is that the three orientations speak past one another, as if in parallel universes. Since none can generate criteria upon which
the others would agree, there is no orthodoxy that consolidates radically
disparate points of view. It has led, MacIntyre writes, to an "inability to
unite conviction and rational justification," and an "inability to arrive at
agreed rationally justifiable conclusions," despite his own preference for
Thomism.

To illustrate the conundrum MacIntyre identifies, consider debates
that pit evolution and natural selection against intelligent design. Thomists
follow a method based on an objective system of metaphysics erected on
the idea of nature created by divine intelligence, whose purposes and ends
constitute a vast network to be explored by reason and will. Empiricists

pursue a method dependent on the human senses, which generates evidence of purposiveness without overarching purpose. Genealogists look to language and grammar, and the political influences that underwrite them, for the source of uncritically accepted assumptions about the given-reality of words and things. They hold that no intelligent design naturally exists, even decrying the Darwinian explanation of natural selection, because it still suffers from an excess of intelligent design. No method, evidence, or conclusion is more compelling than another; the consequence is that, in an era of recombinant DNA engineering and the genome project, universities are impotent to speak authoritatively about what ought to be done. There is, however, something important at stake here. Either we are human beings who have a unique destiny that calls us to build a human community dedicated to promoting what is the best achievable in us, or we are accidental inhabitants of a purposeless universe, held together by nothing more than arbitrary conventions that demand conformity for the sake of co-existence, which the vicious will breach whenever opportunity allows.

I began this paper by pointing to the gap between large parts of the intellectual community and ordinary Canadians. Those latter Canadians live with the reality of technological society, the heated-up social atmosphere, anxiety and fear, and the violence of the dispossessed. When they turn to traditional means of deliverance, they discover that everything is essentially contested. The impasse in which the intellectual world has mired itself might end in a new synthesis, but at this point it can give scant support or guidance to regular religious believers.

We are the beings, as Aristotle writes, that desire to know. To not-know, but to act resolutely, has given us the legacy of some of the darkest moments of Western history. We stand at an awkward moment, though not for the first time. Already in the seventeenth century, Blaise Pascal, commenting on modern man's fate to know what modern science has revealed—that we know too much to deny, but too little to be sure—realized that, faced with the dread that arises when we confront "the eternal silence of these infinite spaces" of the universe, we are left to wager blindly on the existence of God. It is a wager we must reckon, which, if we win, we win everything, if we lose, we lose nothing, and thus inclines us to wager that God is.

Here we have the modern dilemma in its rawest forms. Cut off from cosmological or metaphysical certainty, unable to extend our absolute trust to authorities whose discernment is vouched to be superior to our own, and yet unwilling to throw and disperse ourselves in the desiccate worlds of industry, material self-interest and science, we opt pragmatically, through imagination or an act of will, to bracket out the causes of our doubt and adopt religious possibilities which, while no longer known to be true, nonetheless conform to an aesthetic of our choice. It is a choice burdened with absolute gravity and that we hope will generate real-world results.

We see too much to deny and too little to be sure . . . and yet, at the same time—we may be at a moment where there is the greatest urgency in remembering this—a vast part of our political heritage is indebted, not merely historically, but metaphysically as well, to ideas that have their source in our religious traditions. The idea that we are a people, held together by more than our material interests and pragmatic negotiations, is of Greek if not earlier origin; that we should see our fellowship across time as a history, as God's special providence, and informed by cross-genera-tional moral obligations, is indebted to Jewish tradition, to the unique understanding of man's covenant with God and the sacredness of human reproduction that binds the generations together. That we should think of humans as unique individuals in whom the margin of indeterminacy and spontaneity in existence allows for liberty and individuality, is indebted to the Christian grasp of the human will. That same insight also provided us with an understanding of the experience of willing freely to live by a high-er law, such as that given in mercy, forgiveness, and charity, even when jus-tice and reason seem to be trumped. The idea that our labour and vocations are less burdens of existence than a special providence, that our steward-ship of the environment is another facet of our unimpeachable obligations to life, issues from the same source. That we would make a cornerstone of society the centrality of tolerance and mutual respect is inconceivable without the religious promise of an eternal life where we may see God "face to face;" that we still need to legally proscribe discrimination and hatred testifies that we are still seeing as through a glass darkly. That we see our charitable obligations as loving others more than they deserve is mortgaged to the idea of expiatory sacrifice, a self-emptying in order to be, a giving back as a way of participating in reality. The idea that while the claims of perfection are on us, we must simultaneously acknowledge the intractability of the world to immanent self-perfection, so that our human-ity does not suffer, means, too, that practices such as institutionalizing and limiting authority, allowing but regulating private property, and warring against those unjustly transgressing against us, are to be begrudged, but tolerated. Politically, socially, economically, our beliefs concerning our rights and duties cascade out of a tradition of religious insight and discernment, and they are metaphysically indebted to it. These political institutions and practices, it needs to be said often and loudly, are evidence against the claim, made by the enemies of the West, that our lives are godless. But equally—even if our enemies were right about the West's separation of Church and State such division arose not out of godlessness, but from a prudent assessment that the love of the numinous should be channeled through our moral and political lives, partly to protect the artifice of politics and mostly to ensure that our experience of the numinous be allowed to thrive uncompromised by political interests. Paradoxically, we need religion, in its reach to transcendence, so that we do not perish of religion excessively hopeful of a perfection in the here and now. The issue of our time is for how long our healthy political and moral practices can persist in the absence of a philosophical or theological backdrop.

My opinion is, "not long." I referred above to the waspishness of our expanding greedy desire. No one can deny the steady deterioration of civil society and, most importantly, the manners, social etiquette, and public forms of social intercourse. I am making no brief for these mediating practices in and of themselves, but they have served in the past as buffers between individuals of different gender, class, race, political viewpoint, and personal ebullience. Today, our contacts with one another in daily intercourse, on the public stage, and in international contact are increasingly punctuated by mutual provocation and mutual anxiety. In this dare-all attitude of celebrating and maximizing danger and risk, virtually no one gives way, and often tensions ramp up in vast disproportion to the actual importance of what is at stake. We are rarely any longer citizens, but lonely monads, or quanta of power within tribes, who confront every encounter increasingly as a zero-sum game, and in rage. We are losing the sense of playful irony on the surface in favour of a corrosive irony that limits itself to exposing dark subterranean desires and transgressions. The disappearance of manners and self-control is a bellwether of the breakdowns of the future, disorders that have to include the observations of Hannah Arendt on the event of throwing the satellite Sputnik into space. That event created a new Archimedean point (now of the cosmos) and all the man-made technologies upon which it rests, as a substitute for the political actor whose enacting produced events in the political realm that renewed the world, and for which we had compensatory practices—such as promising and forgiving—that limited the rippled effects of our actions. Our widening sense is that we are not at home in the world, but rather that we must situate ourselves as if we stand at a point in the cosmos, and thereby, like one who has one eye to the zenith and the other to the ground, see and understand nothing of the middle realm—the political and ethical phenomena—that must be addressed first to prevent blindness. Consequently, we lack discrimination for the range of phenomena in which our being is enacted and addressed.

Today's renascence of religion is also bringing a renewed appreciation that the causes for our agitated and rageful states may not reside in the world, but in our disordered and unmoored inner being. In resistance to the dare-all attitude of celebrating and maximizing danger and risk, we may be seeing a recovery of the notion that "giving way," while not a good in itself, is a means of obtaining more, indeed the greatest things, the things that are the only cure for the worldly itch, whether that itch be sex, money, power, or, generally, emptiness. The new openness to the religious life allows us to acknowledge that greedy desire impairs the true function of the human soul. The objection to the surfeit of rageful acts around us is not a moralistic one. It is predicated, instead, on the idea that contempt for convention is ugly, that ugliness is an impediment to the fulfilment of what is properly human, and that in the face of the transcendent, "giving way" is primarily a discipline for turning to the eternal. The beautiful is, as it were, an invitation for the divine to break through the human condition's horizon of immanence, through our desires and passions, and reveal itself. It offers a spiritual therapy that releases us from the world's diversions and distractions. It releases us of the burden of seeking the realization of the absolute in the here and now. It involves irony—not the irony of needy self-love, but an irony of generosity, an irony that speaks to an aspiration that transcends the dark mechanics of desire and passion, however much we have depended on it, politically and morally, from Augustine to Nietzsche, in deference to the unregenerate passions and desires of our being.

But what realistic possibility is there for shifting modernity to such a restoration? The Platonic-Aristotelian philosophical formulation is available only through an act of will, or perhaps in select "epicurean" gardens, which, however, cannot re-direct the ways of the world. We cannot, as Arendt writes, jump over our own shadows. (One is reminded of the short-termed influence of Leo Strauss on the Reaganites that finally came to nothing.)

So, which tools and phenomena are still available to us in the wake of the deconstruction of the Western history of political philosophy? The task is made all the more sensitive in the critique of Christianity and laying on it partial responsibility for the distemper of our times, because the deconstruction of Christianity can only lead to the collapse of a house of cards, taking with it cherished desires, hopes, opportunities, and much that is humane in our lives, comprising what many moderns would consider essential to their social well-being. We wish to again aim high, but the times cannot favour a restoration of classical thought.

So, rather like Rousseau in his Machiavellianism, one has to adopt pernicious principles if only to tame them. With considerable reluctance and irresolute commitment, it seems that one must use the tools of modernity, even those of post-modernity, to restore something of the Greek-Christian legacy: this is what Nietzsche understood (and perhaps also Strauss), even if the risks are great and moderation is temporarily sacrificed. Older options will not work, but will merely recycle the same dilemma of our times *ad infinitum*. However much we are drawn to the ancients and to Christian writers, we are ineluctably corrupted by the radical historicism of our times. It is our destiny to have to work with the cards that have been dealt to us, for there is no "turning around" for us and our dangerous play with ultimacy. We can only push forward in the hopes that using the corrosive tools of our times might open up unknown possibilities of restoration.

We can be tempted to avail ourselves of a glimmer of possibility residing in a dark, subterranean corner of current intellectual life. The thinkers who may offer a means of restoration, paradoxically, emanate from Nietzsche's announcement of the death of God. The God who is dead, however, is the God of philosophical signification, expressible by His presence in creation, history, and the Word, leaving open the possibility of a God not defined by our desire for salvation or truth. This God is wholly other, not restricted to an economy of guilt and retribution, condemnation and indictment, sorrow and remorse. This is a God whose unseen gaze unsettles and haunts us, and who is the source of numinous astonishment or dread, accompanied by a fear that even our presence might defile Him, thus undercutting our self-serving wish for redemption from contingency, complication, and impurity. This is a God who requires a hazarding of ourselves, an emptying out of ourselves into a self-absence that draws us out into openness. The nothingness of this God does not demand guilt for our transgressions, or accommodation to our true ordained nature, but requires instead a discernment of the *unheimlich*, or "uncanny," to use Heidegger's felicitous term. To be that which we are entails avoiding the triggers of the everyday world that reinforce our safe commonness in everyday life and that generate how we gauge our needs for God. The requirement of self-absence must preserve the numinous mystery of Being as Other beyond our reach.

In *The Gift of Death*, Jacques Derrida appeals to the sacrifice Abraham makes of Isaac, describing it as an anguished "trial of undecidability." There exists here an anguish that comes from having no banisters of support, especially others and their communal needs, and no eternal justification. The God Derrida invokes is a god beyond the categories of presence, a singular Other who, much like Rudolf Otto's *mysterium tremendum*, is experienced as numinous dread, or who, like Karl Barth's God, is one whose word, being absolute, no human words can be adequate to represent. Here, in trembling, Derrida writes, is the gift of infinite love: "We fear and tremble before the inaccessible secret of a God who decides for us although we remain responsible, that is, free to decide, to work, to assume our life and our death."[4] Abraham's dark and paradoxical responsibility to God, a responsibility that departs by exceeding those ethical demands of society that are based on the rational validation of a general principle, puts the burden of the numinous on the singularity of the choice Abraham must make and opens to a future that is unknown and incapable of being anticipated. To see in the renunciation of one's own fear and desires an inexplicable wish of God is one's death by an act of sacrifice before God that opens to the experience of an infinite love. We are asked to maintain openness and capacity for response before the Other, which translates into the impossible demand that in every act we are responsible for all and for everything.

I am about to distort what Derrida writes, for it is evident that Derrida is not alluding to a transcendent Deity, but to the invisibility and secrecy of one's own otherness or, as he says, "what I call God in me." His "gestures," however, may still provide us with some indication of how believers seeking to be *en courant* with contemporary theology might nuance their spiritual discernment with a different inflection (allowing even a subversion of all that precedes it). Though Derrida's reflections may seem a religion without religion, and—it goes without saying—without church, it can make a legitimate claim to being recognized under the vaguer category of spirituality. The postmodern God emerging here speaks of a destiny requiring a renunciation of all that one desires on earth, and of letting be to be seized. This God, who loves more the absence than what is present, speaks to a love of great longing, and not possession. It is a God who withdraws behind all names and all bargaining, and yet does not condone a mysticism separated from clarifying reflection. Such a God still speaks to the beautiful—not perhaps the classical beauty of balance and proportion, but the kind of beauty that Edmund Burke had described as "sublime," a state of astonishment in the soul, in which all its motions are suspended, with some degree of horror. This God will take us on for our grief, not our skill in conforming to Him. This God breaks what John Caputo, in his recent book on Derrida, calls the "mad economy" of the kingdom of God, where "relationships no longer depend on investments and assured returns, but upon ledgers that are wiped clean and books that no longer need to be balanced."[5] This God, to be sure, stretches almost to breaking the gossamer contact with us, of which I spoke at the beginning of this essay. But His absence, and the humility He demands, while risking an inversion into vainglorious poverty and contempt for the unregenerate, may also disperse the dark mechanics of desire and recognition that infect our togetherness with others, sowing instead hope and renewal.

Such mechanics are analyzed with rigorous clarity in the writings of Rene Girard. In his works, *The Scapegoat* and *Violence and the Sacred*, Girard describes human desire not as benignly original and spontaneous, but as always mediated by the desire of another and always conflictual.[6] There is no mythic time before competition and political constraint, nothing romantic about the origins of society. Desire, he says, is essentially mimetic—we see another enjoying what they desire, and we desire their desire, not because what they desire is objectively good for us, but because they desire it. In fact, we become so obsessed with our rivals, that we lose sight of the objects for which we compete and begin to focus angrily on one another. Now each just wants to prevent the other from obtaining the object they desire, desiring only the prestige that comes from victory over the other. Rivals, formerly different, become mirror images of each other, returning tit-for-tat endlessly. The more intense their mimetic rivalry, the more prone retaliating others are to join in on one side or the other, with an increasing number of individuals polarizing against fewer and fewer enemies, creating an environment of acute danger and anxiety. Then, at the apparent height of the contagion of mimetic rivalry, when a society is teetering on the brink of destroying itself, the mimetic contagion suddenly focuses on one person, whose guilt and responsibility for the social violence is universally acknowledged. Scape-goating extinguishes their rivalry. The death is a catharsis, triggering memory of the sense of community that generated the violence, and restoring peace and order. More importantly, the scapegoat is a catalyst to a purging of the dark mechanic of desire.

The lesson to be learned from the scapegoat mechanism, for Girard, is not sociological (namely, that individuals must renounce mimetic desire, thus ensuring social unity), but metaphysical. In the classic locus of the scapegoat mechanism, namely Christianity, the god who sacrifices himself to end the mimetic violence becomes the victim who forgives, evidencing the miracle of transcendent love emerging from immanent collective violence.

It speaks, too, of a redemptive power born in guilt that gives to choice the ability to refuse mimetic rivalry and instead embrace love. The turnaround is so dramatic and awesome because, where the scapegoat is worshiped as a god is born the hope that it lies within human possibility to be like the god who gives himself freely. While such a god will seem remote from a world enmeshed in mimetic desire, it holds up a model in the sacrificing Christ for a more scrupulous attention to cathartic purification. It affirms what many ordinary individuals have learned in the school of hard knocks: that out of brokenness and despair, indeed at the very bottom, where anguish de-creates our worldly being, may open up the absence that is God, and the bond across distance, which as Simone Weil writes, triumphs over infinite separation.

Bin Laden's demonization of America and the West is a classic illustration of the scapegoat mechanism. The myth he promulgated of the persecution of Islam by the West was a bid to achieve Islamic solidarity around his own traditionalist Islam, a pan-Islamic world order as an alternative to globalization. It suffered from the same wrong-headedness to which zealous partisans of globalization are prone: channeling the absolute into politics. We have suffered—and most likely will suffer again at the hands of his heirs—from Bin Laden's exploitation of garden-variety disappointments and envy to trigger the scapegoat mechanism of "9/11." But what he did not count on, in his bid to provoke an all-out cultural war, was that the use of the scapegoat mechanism also aroused an outpouring in America and elsewhere of charity, compassion and, as hard as it is to believe, forgiveness, which muted and even stayed the natural response of revenge. We have been reminded that it lies within human power to purge the desire for revenge, resentment, greed, and narrow calculation, even though it requires a harrowing event of ritualistic sacrifice to expose the mimetic mechanism.

Derrida's and Girard's thoughts on our religious longing sear to the point where the soul glistens, where both the poverty and audacity of our being is brutally exposed. The scenario of a life lived at its rawest moment, where even reason coils up against itself and is cancelled out, must be repeated over and over to thwart the recrudescence of atavistic longings.

Here everyday life is depleted of its drama and potentialities, and life stands as if at the Götterdämmerung, the turbulent chaos of the gods' twilight, where all compromises, concessions, and prudent ironies are disdained and abandoned, and where—as in the thought of Kierkegaard and Barth—the burden of proof comes to rest on the moment of decision. Their demand on us entails navigating a terrain in the soul with great heights and but also fearsome abysses. For those of us of more timid spirit, it may also be right to ask what the fall-out is of discarding prudent reserve and irony, and of allowing no concession to the fallenness of the world. It turns away from the idea that the human vocation is to gradually heighten simple existence into a living drama. It demands more than prudent conciliation and consensus building, more than the repair of the artifices and institutions that were historically designed to preempt apocalyptic ruptures and leaps. As it has seeped out from the *École Normale Superieure,* it has, perhaps even contrary to intentions, ramped up a lust for apocalyptic transformations of the world. That is to say that one of its legacies is the desire to use force as if it were magic, especially evident in the perhaps too hasty rescinding of the virtue of prudence and of the political safeguards traditionally designed to hold powerful passions in check and to harness the errant love of the unconditioned.

Equally audible in the present world dialogue are dissenting voices with arguments that have found receptive ears that resist the allure of the continental trend towards decisionism and its apocalyptic message. One of these dissenting voices is theologian George Weigel, whose book, *The Cube and the Cathedral: Europe, America and Politics Without God*, was prompted by two bellwether warning signs: the glaring omission of any reference to Christian culture in the newly-drafted EU constitution, and the population meltdown in Europe, where not a single country is maintaining population replacement, a signal perhaps of resignation and abandoned hope of a human future. Appealing to Christopher Dawson's *Christianity and European Culture*, he argues that so foundational is Christianity to tolerance, civility, democracy, pluralism, human rights, the dignity of the human person, limited and constitutional government, the principle of consent, and transcendent standards of justice that hold the state accountable, that the gradual inanition of Christianity omens a serious political crisis in the future of Europe. The proof test, Weigel challenges, may be how Europe responds with tolerance and civility to Muslim immigration, and how Muslims themselves develop an Islamic case for tolerance, civility and pluralism. The difficulty, Weigel notes, is that European cultural pluralism was underwritten by the idea of a Trinitarian god, and the Christian doctrine of God's ongoing creative action in history. Weigel's point is that the exclusion of Europe's Christian heritage from Europe's public life threatens those moral commitments that define European democracy and preserve it from excessive compromise. Without the painstaking audit of historical Christian Europe's endowment, no prognosis of Europe's future and the repairs it must undertake can be prudently attempted.

A parallel argument is made in a new wave of books by, or on, Isaiah Berlin, particularly in response to the emergence of the statehood of former East European nations. Like Weigel, Berlin refused to embrace totalizing accounts of history and politics, a refusal that was intended as a rejoinder to the potentially apocalpytic decisionism of continental thought. Berlin's cautious skepticism, which entailed eschewing universal laws and focusing instead on the complexity and heterogeneity of human experience, is exhibited in particular in his resistance to reducing a plurality of values to a single master-value and in his sensitivity to the protean character of human experience. One element of Berlin's writings is the heavier focus on the practice of the Romans—the reliance on administration, rules, institutions, and the accompanying emphasis on practical wisdom, and public speech—in opposition to the Greeks' metaphysical impulse, or later totalizing accounts grounded on universal laws, destined histories, and ultimate harmonies. In the Roman legacy, he saw a culture more likely to protect human rights, promote the common good, defend legitimate pluralism, and give an account of the diversity of moral commitments that make democracy possible. Here, theorizing politics involves a positive appreciation for human complexity and variety, an awareness of a world of separate and distinct goods, unrealizable in their totality and incapable of reconciliation.

However the contest between French thinkers like Girard and Derrida and Anglo-American thinkers like Weigel and Berlin will play themselves out within the new era of religious exploration, there is—finally—one other glimmer of hope for the restoration of religion in our culture, one that may be residing much closer to home. Surveying our domestic politics and the trajectory upon which the world seems to be headed will lead some to predict a future of escalating conflict, a zero-sum game played out through warring beliefs, and the inevitability of clashing civilizations. But others may see thousands, tens of thousands, of ordinary individuals engaged in simple devotional pieties. Here, in what I will identify as orthopraxy (or, correct practice), to be understood in contradistinction to orthodoxy and its dependence on the predicative logic of metaphysics, resides an option that MacIntyre fails to acknowledge in his catalogue of intellectual paradigms.

What I have observed with initial hesitation, but growing attention, is the re-emergence of devotional and ritual practices such as the Jesus Prayer ("Lord Jesus Christ, Son of God, have mercy upon me, a sinner") and the rosary, the Marian movement, pledges of chastity and voluntary simplicity, reverence of icons and chanting, reverence for the earth of one's ancestors and spiritual labyrinths, conforming to kosher laws, living lightly, or the practice of mindfulness. These are not intended to be measured up against the true, but they nonetheless give deep meaning to the ordinary routines of life. Here, simple existence is transformed into living drama. The fact that these practices are performed with playful irony, and not with a solemnity appropriate to the burden of truth, has made them inter-denominational, ecumenical and leisurely. In these movements, popular sentiments, such as those whimsically expressed by Antoine de Saint-Exupery ("Perfection is reached, not when there is nothing more to add, but when there is nothing more to take away"), dovetail with the proposals of speculative thinkers like Simone Weil, who writes of our need to decreate, through practices of self-retraction and self-renunciation, that part of us that is mired in the mechanics of necessity. One example is her proposed experiment: "A method of purification: to pray to God, not only in secret as far as men are concerned, but with the thought that God does not exist."[7] One sees here a discipline, a strength, which resists the temptations of greedy desire and decadence.

In Western history, whenever consensus on the dominant orthodoxy broke down—say during the fourth century BCE, or the fourth to the ninth century, or the sixteenth century—Western society reverted to orthopraxy, in such forms as the schools of the Cynics, Skeptics, or Epicureans, the monastic movements, the Jansenists, or thinkers such as Montaigne and Pascal. These were interludes, a stepping out from the push of the past and the pull of the future, times of reassessment and load-shedding of doctrinal dogmatism. In our own time, which bears affinity to these watersheds, it is quite likely that Western institutions, emasculated by centuries of reform, will have to turn for support to Africa, South America, the Caribbean, and Asia, to former colonies where the original well-springs of religious life have survived much longer than in the West. The forms through which religious longing is explored in orthopraxy are measured not in their truth, but in a practical payout or, in the words of Matthew, "by their fruits you shall know them." These movements have, moreover, a counterpart in the intellectual world, for when one looks on the borders of the three factions MacIntyre identifies, one finds neo-Thomists of the *nouvelle theologie*, neo-Foucauldians, and hermeneutical/constructivist positivists, all three of whom—incidentally—are much closer to ordinary religious believers, who by nature are bricoleurs, randomly picking up bits of this and that, like birds building a nest, or using the abandoned nests of other birds, weaving forms of sanctification into the contours of everyday life.

What I find suggestive here is the potential of spiritual discernment, which unites creative intuition and insight with disciplining practices. They testify to a commitment to resist the seductive temptations that empower the earthly body, in favour of practices rarefying the spiritual body. They may be the focus of rebuilding human community, even or especially if the togetherness being explored is played out against the backdrop of the many forms of brokenness in society around us—in violence, addiction, abandonment, humiliation, and fear. Here, clutching at the straw of hope drawn out of hopelessness, is attendance to the contingency that not even globalized technology can subdue, and whose universality may remind us of our capacity for transcendence. Here too, incidentally, one may find nuanced and wide-ranging commentary on the spiritual disciplines, a favourite of mine being Josef Pieper's important reflections on festivity, play, the appreciation of beauty in art and nature, and leisure, among many other modalities of everyday life. If the modern age has rendered it impossible to resort to a transcendence on which we are to confer the signification of philosophical truth, it has not precluded a transcendence signified by pious intention; Pieper's labours have found much in the rituals of everyday life.

My defense of orthopraxy is, of course, not unproblematic. The retreat from dogmatic truths to orthopraxy, and a tolerant liberal commitment to playfulness, is not without dangers, especially when we extend such tolerance beyond our own borders to a tense world gripped by religious diversity. We are being asked to recognize religious practices, justified by beliefs that are integral to another community's divine economy. The events of the last four years have taught us that we cannot tolerate epicurean gardens that can easily become threats to human survival. But rather than hardened objection, and demand for conformity to Western ways, the West has an opportunity of guiding a process that recapitulates its own protracted transition from the pre-modern to the modern. One advantage of the West's two millennia of experimenting and improvising with possibilities in our religious traditions is that we have acquired subtle ways of avoiding the fallacy of misplaced concreteness, while fully satisfying the requirements of religious duty. Our religious traditions also exhibit an extraordinary capacity to preserve by reforming, as traditional ways were grafted onto the emerging modern economies, polities, and ideas of liberty. Our error, in relation to a non-West that resists or hesitates in absorbing Western ways, is failing to generate holding patterns that sustain traditional restraint while opening out the real achievements of Western modernity—in justice, equal opportunity and constitutionalism, as well as government by representation—and harnessing our expectations to evolving communities like Ismaili Muslims, Shaktas Hindus, and Mahayana Buddhists, among others, not to say avoiding derailments such as the counter-Reformation.

In conclusion, we stand at a crossroads, with two redemptive possibilities shedding a faint light on our hopes for renewal. But where hope lies, there is almost always also danger. Not surprisingly, the two most obvious candidates for the redemptive possibilities to which I have alluded, Evangelical Christianity and Islam—where canonically-mandated strict adherence to practices coincides with the appeal to a radical transcendence—are also the fastest growing religious communities in the world. They have pitted themselves against one another and are demanding a choice: you are either for us, or against us. Quite simply, each says the other is wrong. There is also a fateful confluence here, in the resemblance they have to one another in emptying out what has for a long time been understood as the "political"—a tradition of compromise, conciliation, and plurality. There is a divine simplicity here that does not allow for politics: one is trembling before God, the other is cleaving to right practice, but neither counsels debate. They share the belief that the holy book is not allowed to be interpreted, that it is to be understood literally, not allegorically. Both offer simple unproblematic rules on how to live. There is a danger that each is tempted to act on the premise, "You can never change my mind, because this is it. It doesn't matter if the country or the world blows apart, this is the way it has to be."

This approach empties out politics. It denies debate, discussion and compromise. It is apolitical, and hence—not surprisingly—it supports direct referendum and recall. They are both saying, "what I do, I want you to do." Their attraction is obvious, when the alternative is the wishy-washy liberalism and socialism that says "let's all hold hands, sit in a circle, and come to a consensus." In the world of Evangelicals and the Taliban, everyone is invited to conform to the ruling principles, not to discuss, debate and interpret. Both communities can be seen as a healthy purgative, but since they are a purgative and extreme, they will, like a pendulum, have to return to a centre, because the simplicity of the answer cannot hold.

Judaism has survived for three millennia because it is interpretive, with a strong intellectual tradition that gives its people a great sense of history and belonging, well-situated within the Western tradition. It has avoided the radical hope that simple practices and beliefs will purge the decadence and corruption of the modern world. The same may be said of the Roman Catholic church, whose equivocations, as in its deferred apology for complicity in the Holocaust, or its recent withdrawal of an apology for the Crusades, seem to suggest a policy of bending as the political winds blow, and may explain why some evangelicals have said to me "but you're not Christian, you're Catholic." Such bending in fact evinces commitment to a tradition of interpretation and practical wisdom. Whether this middle ground between polarities can be restored, or whether we are in a protracted historical period of warring factions deeply mistrustful to the point of hatred of one another, which is monopolizing much of the tension in the world, are matters which I do not know how to answer.

I will conclude that though they may be the greatest threat to the modern liberal consensus, they may also be the source of restoration of a moral ballast that that consensus has lost. What unites these two protagonists is their opposition to the orgy of modern hedonistic consumption and to the fateful will to use technology to remake human nature. Which is only to say, that in their temperance on these matters, they remind us of the danger of the project to make the immanent world a substitute for transcendence. Both of them evoke a transcendence, comprehensible in humanistic terms, that is allowing history to continue to unfold, and that permits the self-questioning that has been the hallmark of Western life, despite some extravagant claims, in certain academic circles, that we are at the end of history.

Endnotes

1   See Clinton Curle, *Humanité: John Humphrey's Alternative Account of Human Rights* (Toronto: University of Toronto Press, 2008), who examines the spiritual roots of the first draft of the United Nations Declaration of Human Rights.

2   Marshall McLuhan, *The Gutenberg Galaxy* (Toronto: University of Toronto Press, 1962), 32.

3   Plato, *Republic*, 496d–e.
4   Jacques Derrida, *The Gift of Death*, David Wills, trans. (Chicago: University of Chicago Press, 1995), 56.
5   John Caputo, *Prayer and Tears of Jacques Derrida: Religion Without Religion* (Bloomington, IN: Indiana University Press, 1997).
6   Rene Girard, *The Scapegoat*, Y. Freccero, trans. (Baltimore: Johns Hopkins University Press, 1986) and *Violence and the Sacred* (New York: Continuum, 2005).
7   Simone Weil, *Gravity and Grace*, Arthur Wills, trans. (Lincoln: University of Nebraska Press, 1952), 66.

Chapter Eight

Tracking the Good in Plato's *Republic*:

The Literary and Dialogic Form of the Sun, Line,

and Cave Imagery

Zdravko Planinc

There is something comic about Socrates speaking dramatically. At an awkward moment in the *Republic*, when the discussion of justice seems to have lost its way and Socrates and Glaucon are fumbling in the dark, Socrates breaks the silence in a tragic voice and announces: "Here! Here! (ἰοὺ ἰού) Glaucon. Maybe we've come upon a track (ἴχνος)." He then balances the mood somewhat self-consciously by pointing out that they have both been "most ridiculous (καταγελαστότατοι)" to miss it (432d).[1] Hunting for justice is serious business; but mistakes made along the way— when they don't cost lives—can be amusing. Now, Glaucon is a hunting enthusiast: always "most courageous in everything" (357a), he breeds hunting dogs and fighting cocks (459a), and has proven himself in battle, at least to the satisfaction of his *erastes* (368a). However, this is a different sort of hunting—a hunting with words, a dialogue, a dialectical ascent. For all his eagerness, Glaucon lacks experience and makes mistakes. In the bush, he would not confuse tracks for the animal itself: a track is an absence, a static sign of a living, breathing animal that has moved on. In the bush, he would not confuse one animal's tracks for another's. In conversation, however, Glaucon becomes confused more often than he will admit. Although the "track" of justice is not justice itself, when it is all a matter of words, it seems to him that it is. Although the "track" of justice is not "the track of the good (τὸ τοῦ ἀγαθοῦ ἴχνος, 462a)," the difference seems inconsequential in the heat of the pursuit. Glaucon has a good deal to learn. Throughout the long night's discussion recounted in the *Republic*, Socrates is more than patient in showing Glaucon what he needs to know if he is to become as skillful in philosophy and political rule as he wishes to be. But Socrates has his doubts. At a later point in the dialogue, he explicitly admonishes Glaucon that those who are "uneducated and without experience in truth (ἀπαιδεύτους καὶ ἀληθείας ἀπείρους)" will never be proper stewards of a city (519bc). Before getting to that point, however, there is still tracking to do, and Socrates worries that while they are searching out the way, Glaucon's tendency to indulge in the speculative thinking he takes for philosophy will make him the more laughable of the two of them. He worries not only that Glaucon's misreading of the signs might lead them astray. More worrisome is the thought of what Glaucon might do if he were to come across the animal itself.

Much of the discussion in the *Republic* is spent tracking justice. Tracking the good takes another route: the "longer way around (μακροτέρα . . . περίοδος)" toward the "most beautiful look at things (κάλλιστα αὐτὰ κατιδεῖν, 504b)." Midway through the *Republic*, Socrates judges that it might be the right time for his conversation with Glaucon and Adeimantus to take the "longer way." He sets out hopefully, as always; but his confidence in their ability to follow is quickly disappointed.

To this point in the dialogue, the evening's discussion had overcome false starts, premature conclusions, misleading digressions, and dubious assumptions that would lead it into dead ends; and now Socrates finally considers it possible to paint, in words, a fair "image of a man (ἀνδρείκελον), taking hints from what Homer called the god-like (θεοειδές) and the image of god (θεοείκελον, 501b) in human beings," the image of a man who would himself be a fine "painter of regimes (πολιτεῶν ζωγράφος, 501c)." Earlier in the evening, when Glaucon and Adeimantus had first intervened to insist that Socrates defend justice properly against the strongest possible account of the superiority of injustice and provide a philosophic antistrophe to the strophe of sophistry and tyranny, Socrates began by suggesting a correspondence between justice in a soul and justice in a city, and the lengthy, meandering, and faltering building of a city in speech got underway. Now, when Socrates gathers himself to set out on the "longer way" with Glaucon and Adeimantus, he seems willing to begin again, wiping the slate of the previous discussion clean of as many blemishes and imperfections as possible. All that seems to remain of it is an understanding of philosophers as the most just human beings, whom Socrates now "dares" to say should be established as the "most perfect (ἀκριβεστάτους, 503b)" guardians, leaving open the question of how such "painters of regimes" themselves might wipe clean the slate of the city in speech. Before that question can be addressed, it remains to determine how philosophers demonstrate the "god-like" in human beings. Justice is not enough; the end (τέλος) of the greatest study (μεγίστου . . . μαθήματος) most befitting them is the most complete and perfect thing, the measure (μέτρον) of all things (504cd). Although Adeimantus is initially surprised to be reminded that there is "something greater than justice" (504d), he and his brother readily consent when Socrates says that the good is "what every soul pursues, . . . for the sake of which it does everything" (505e), and therefore that "the idea of the good is the greatest study (ἡ τοῦ ἀγαθοῦ ἰδέα μέγιστον μάθημα, 505a)." Adeimantus and Glaucon both seem eager to join Socrates in setting out on the track of the good. But their first steps are badly mistaken.

Adeimantus interrupts Socrates to ask if the good is pleasure (ἡδονήν) or knowledge (ἐπιστήμην) or some other such thing (506b), just moments after Socrates had stated explicitly that he accepted neither the opinion of the many that the good is pleasure (ἡδονή) nor the opinion of the more refined that it is prudence (φρόνησις, 505b). Socrates' reply is overtly ironic: "What a man! It's been plain all along that other people's opinions wouldn't be enough for you" (506b). The assumption that pleasure is among the highest things has clouded the discussion from its beginnings. When Glaucon and Adeimantus first intervened to prompt Socrates to a proper defense of justice, they began by asking him if justice is the sort of good chosen for its own sake, or for its consequences, or for both. Socrates had answered quite clearly that justice is the sort of good chosen both for itself and for its consequences, the most beautiful one. However, Glaucon and Adeimantus both insisted that he speak of justice in itself, without consequences, abstract and static—and the only examples they knew of this form of good were joy and pleasure (χαίρειν καὶ ἡδοναὶ) (357b–358a). Instead of showing himself capable of setting out on the new beginning Socrates proposes, Adeimantus slips back into conventional errors. To make matters worse, he attempts to deflect his embarrassment at Socrates' criticism by insisting that Socrates give an account of the good as a conviction or dogma (δόγματα, 506b), a supposition (οἰόμενον) or an opinion (δόξας), and he must be reminded that even true opinion without knowledge is like a blind man traveling the right way (ὁδὸν ὀρθῶς, 506c): the end of the longer way cannot be reached by luck. Glaucon comes to his brother's defense. He chastises Socrates for hesitating and insists: "go through the good, as you went through justice, moderation and the rest" (506d). Embarrassment upon embarrassment. Earlier in the evening, when the discussion had turned to sketching a pattern of the virtues to match the order of the city in speech, Socrates spoke out with uncharacteristic impatience: "Know well, Glaucon," he said, "in my opinion we'll never get an accurate grasp of the matter with the methods (μεθόδων) we're now using in the argument. There is another longer and harder way (μακροτέρα καὶ πλείων ὁδὸς) leading to it" (435cd). But Glaucon insisted on having it his way then. And he now insists that Socrates use the same impossible method for the longer way itself. It is no wonder that Socrates declines, claiming not to be up to it: "let's leave aside for the time being what the good itself is (αὐτὸ μὲν τί ποτ᾽ ἐστὶ τἀγαθὸν ἐάσωμεν τὸ νῦν εἶναι, 506de)," he says. Instead, he offers to describe what seems to be a "child of the good and its likeness (ἔκγονός τε τοῦ ἀγαθοῦ φαίνεται καὶ ὁμοιότατος, 506e)."

To this point in the *Republic*, there has been a rough symmetry and proportion to the attention Socrates has given to Adeimantus and Glaucon. When Plato's brothers falter and raise their objections to Socrates' way of proceeding, they speak together, almost as one person —an unusually dramatic moment after an evening spent exchanging the role of interlocutor in a stately manner. And from this point on, Socrates speaks almost exclusively with Glaucon. Adeimantus does participate briefly in the later discussion of types of unjust regimes and souls (548d–576b), but he could easily have avoided it by resisting the temptation to tease his brother for having a victory-loving and honour-loving (φιλονικίαι καὶ φιλοτιμίαι) timocratic soul (548cd). Throughout the *Republic*, Socrates' relation to Glaucon is an odd combination of concern and critique, initially engaged but giving way to increasingly noticeable exasperation. Indeed, this characteristic of the dialogue seems entirely consistent with the sketch of their relation given by Xenophon. In the *Memorabilia*, Xenophon writes: "Glaucon . . . was attempting to become a demagogue and had his heart set on leadership in the polis, though he was less than twenty years old; and none of his friends or relations could stop him, though he would get himself dragged from the platform and make himself ridiculous (καταγέλαστον). Only Socrates, who concerned himself with him for the sake of Charmides . . . and Plato, could stop him" (3.6.1). In the brief conversations between them that Xenophon composes, Socrates' final words of advice to Glaucon are: "Watch that your daring ambition doesn't lead to a fall! Don't you see how risky it is to say or do what you don't understand?" (3.6.16). Much of the drama of the *Republic* is an elaboration of these remarks: Charmides would join Critias to become one of the Thirty Tyrants; both would be killed when the regime was overthrown; Polemarchus would be killed in opposing the Thirty; and although we know nothing certain about Glaucon's later life, he seems neither to have yielded to the temptation of tyranny nor to have demonstrated much courage in resisting it. In the *Republic*, Socrates shows Glaucon, who is young and full of high ideals, the dangerous consequences of being half-hearted in pursuing them. And he does so, for the most part, with tolerance and charm. When Glaucon's apparently rigorous ways first led the dialogue's search for an understanding of justice into a thicket of confusion, Socrates graciously shared the responsibility in saying that they had both been "most ridiculous," stumbling around blindly in the dark (432c–e). And when Glaucon again insists on the same methods for the account of the longer way, Socrates is again gracious. But his patience does not last.

The passages of the *Republic* that follow Socrates' decision to postpone setting out on the "longer way" with Glaucon and Adeimantus are possibly the most interpreted and discussed passages in all of Plato's dialogues: Socrates' account of the "sun," the "line," and the "cave," in the almost inescapable, pseudo-technical jargon of scholars. They are often thought to be the key to unlocking Plato's metaphysics and political theory: the *Short Course* to the "longer way," as it were. A catalogue of the many and various understandings of the sun, line, and cave would be a history of Platonism itself. I have no desire to attempt one. However, if some comment is unavoidable, I might say that the history of the interpretation of these pages of the *Republic* strikes me as the revenge of Adeimantus and Glaucon: they are read the way Adeimantus prefers to read a text in order to derive an understanding of philosophy that Glaucon would accept. Whether or not interpreters find such an understanding of metaphysics and political theory generally agreeable is another matter, as is all the quibbling about whether or not the metaphysics and the political theory are consistent: the shared project of determining, or I should say constructing, the foundations of Platonism from these passages remains unquestioned throughout. The entire account of the sun, line, and cave is given a false concreteness, misplaced from the vivid imagery Socrates uses; it is pondered as if it were a puzzling object made of words that can be solved by being made to reveal the clearer set of words it is intended to allegorize; the first step of most of the intricate solutions proposed is the assumption that the allegory of the whole is a function of an internal relation of the parts; and more particularly, a summary reading of the divided line is used to decode the sun and the cave as allegories. It is all an Adeimantean reduction of philosophy to dogma, conviction, and opinion using Glauconian methods—methods that will never work, as Socrates tells Glaucon.

What is lacking in all such readings is a sufficient recognition that everything said in these passages is said in conversation. Socrates' account of the sun, the line, and the cave is not an encrypted form of the "longer way." It is, rather, a conversation in which Socrates attempts to show Glaucon and, indirectly, Adeimantus, the dangers—both intellectual and political—that might befall them if they were to abandon their resolve to follow him to the end of the "greatest study" at this late point in the evening's discussion. What is also lacking in reductive readings is a sufficient recognition that this conversation is a conversation recounted in a work of literature. To state it most simply and controversially: Plato's philosophy is poetry; and the dialogues are written in such a way as to escape being trapped in the "old quarrel between philosophy and poetry" (607a), a stand-off that was centuries-old even in Socrates' time. The dialogues are written to be read as literature; however, no work of literature addresses literate readers without also addressing other works of literature. I have argued at length elsewhere that Plato has used the *Odyssey* systematically in the composition of the dialogues. The *Odyssey* is not the only source-text he uses—several of Aristophanes' comedies are also used in the *Republic*, for example—but the *Odyssey* is by far the most important for an understanding of Plato's project. And Plato may not have used it in the composition of all the dialogues, but its traces are evident in the most significant ones.[2] His intent in refiguring the *Odyssey*, again to put it simply, is to present Socrates as the greatest hero of Greece. Socrates is a new Odysseus, Athens is his Ithaca; and the episodes of Socrates' life—his diverse encounters with sophists and philosophers, young men and compatriots—take on the aspect of dramatic events in Odysseus's wanderings and homecoming. It has always been a difficulty to determine the relation of Plato's dialogues. Computer analyses of grammatical usages have proved to be as unable to solve it as biographical and historical speculation or impressionistic thematic groupings of the texts. However, if the events described in many of the dialogues parallel episodes in the *Odyssey*, the poem serves as a template. One need only consider the manner in which Plato refigured the poem and distributed its parts across the dialogues to gain an insight into his understanding of their relation, no matter when they were written. Now, if all this is anywhere close to being right, it would follow that an interpretation of the scene in which Socrates is disappointed in the inability or unwillingness of Adeimantus and Glaucon to set out on the "longer way" would be illuminated by a comparison of the source-text used in its composition. And that is what this paper will attempt to accomplish. It will analyze the dialogic and dramatic aspects of these passages of the *Republic* by comparing them to the passages in Book 12 of the *Odyssey* describing the Thrinakian debacle in which all of Odysseus's few remaining companions are killed by Zeus for slaughtering the sacred cattle of Helios. There will also be some comic relief. But first, a summary of Homer's story.

Odysseus learns about Thrinakia from Teiresias (11.100–115) and Kirke (12.127–141). They both tell him that his ship will be destroyed and his companions will die if any harm comes to the cattle and sheep of Helios, and that his own homecoming will be hard. Beyond that warning, however, they tell him different, though complementary things. From Teiresias, the only soul in Hades with intelligence or mind (νόος, 10.494), he learns that he must contain his own spirit and the spirits of his companions (αἴ κ᾽ἐθέλῃς σὸν θυμὸν ἐρυκακέειν καὶ ἑταίρων, 11.105) if the herds are to be left unharmed, and that Helios sees and overhears all things (ὃς πάντ᾽ ἐφορᾷ καὶ πάντ᾽ ἐπακούει, 11.109). From Kirke, he learns more about the herds: they are uniquely immortal, neither dying nor giving birth (γόνος δ᾽ οὐ γίγνεται αὐτῶν, οὐδέ ποτε φθινύθουσι, 12.130–1); their number approximates the number of days and nights in a year; and they are tended by goddesses born to Neaira and Helios himself. When Odysseus and his companions eventually approach Thrinakia, he strongly advises them to avoid the island (νῆσον ἀλεύασθαι, 12.274), to pass it by and row the ship onward, claiming that Teiresias and Kirke both advised him to do so; but he gives no reasons for the warning (12.271–6). Eurylochos, speaking with the support of the crew, protests. "You are a hard man, Odysseus," he says; "your force is greater (σχέτλιός εἰς, Ὀδυσεῦ: περί τοι μένος, οὐδέ τι γυῖα κάμνεις,12.279)." He and the crew want to stop and rest, to have a hearty dinner and a good night's sleep, before continuing. Odysseus must consent: "I am only one man," he replies; "you force me to it (ἦ μάλα δή με βιάζετε μοῦνον ἐόντα, 12.297)." However, Odysseus immediately requires his companions to swear an oath that they will leave the herds unharmed (12.298–301). And shortly after they land on the island, at an assembly called for the purpose, Odysseus explains both that the herds belong to Helios and that the god sees and overhears all things (12.320–3). After he speaks, his companions' proud spirits consent (ἐπεπείθετο θυμὸς ἀγήνωρ, 12.324). All is well. And all remains well for the month they are kept on the island by bad weather, until Odysseus removes himself to pray to the Olympian gods for advice and, in his absence, Eurylochos gives the crew bad advice (κακῆς . . . βουλῆς, 12.339). No longer satisfied with Kirke's supplies of grain and wine (12.327), supplemented by local fish and fowl (12.332), Eurylochos counsels them to sacrifice some of Helios's cattle for their meals, in the full knowledge that Helios might not be appeased with a promise of a temple dedicated to him on their return to Ithaka. Even though they are aware that it might lead to their deaths, the rest of the crew give their assent (ἐπὶ δ' ἤνεον ἄλλοι ἑταῖροι, 12.352). The consequences of the transgression are immediate. Odysseus learns much later, from Kalypso who herself hears it from Hermes, that one of the goddesses tending the herds reports it to her father, and Helios then protests to "Father Zeus" (Ζεῦ πάτερ, 12.377) and the council of the Olympian gods, asking for a fitting atonement (ἐπιεικέ' ἀμοιβήν, 12.382). Helios says he took delight in the herds whenever he ascended into the starry heaven (οὐρανὸν ἀστερόεντα) and whenever he turned back from heaven to earth (ἂψ ἐπὶ γαῖαν ἀπ' οὐρανόθεν προτραποίμην, 12.380–1). If the guilty are not punished, Helios threatens to "go down to Hades and shine his light on the dead" (δύσομαι εἰς Ἀίδαο καὶ ἐν νεκύεσσι φαείνω, 12.383). Zeus prevents the inversion of the order of the cosmos—of day and night, life and death—by agreeing to the demands. The crew, in the meanwhile, see omens (τέραα, 12.394) of their fate sent by the gods: "the skins crawled, and the meat that was stuck on the spits bellowed, both roast and raw, and the noise was like the lowing of cattle (εἷρπον μὲν ῥινοί, κρέα δ' ἀμφ' ὀβελοῖσι μεμύκει, ὀπταλέα τε καὶ ὠμά, βοῶν δ' ὣς γίγνετο φωνή, 12.395–6)." When they leave Thrinakia, Zeus destroys the ship. All the men are drowned, sent to Hades. Only Odysseus survives by lashing the keel and mast together and enduring until he eventually reaches Kalypso's island.

In the *Republic*, the scene of Odysseus urging his crew to bypass Thrinakia becomes the scene of Socrates attempting to take the "longer way around;" and Glaucon takes the role of Eurylochos in leading the resistance of the small crew of interlocutors. Unlike the *Odyssey*, however, in the *Republic* no one dies. The terrible ordeals and life-and-death struggles of Odysseus and his crew become episodes in a conversation in which matters of utmost importance are discussed seriously; the conversation moves toward greater understanding; and the life-and-death consequences follow another day. Socrates is a new Odysseus, but an Odysseus who speaks from greater knowledge and experience, better able to anticipate dangers to himself and others because he has lived through them all before. In the *Republic*, Plato goes so far as to suggest that Socrates is Odysseus reincarnate. The dialogue concludes with a story in which a man named Er returns from the dead and tells what he saw: the judgment of souls in the afterlife, the way in which they choose new lives, and the manner of their rebirth by travel through the cosmos along the axis mundi. The gods allow Er to see only one such event. On that day, Odysseus's soul is the last to choose a new life. Having overcome its last vice, the love of honour (φιλο-τιμία), it rejoices to find the life of a man who "minds his own business" (620c). In other words, a wiser Odysseus chooses the just life that Socrates lives. Socrates is thus a more "god-like" and daimonic Odysseus. Where Odysseus could speak from the knowledge of what he had learned from Teiresias and Kirke to warn his crew, and from the greater knowledge of what he had learned from Hermes and Kalypso when he recounted the events for the Phaiakians, as Odysseus reincarnate, Socrates himself becomes the daimonic intermediary for Glaucon and Adeimantus, speaking from memory of the greatest possible range of experience. One need not accept the reincarnation symbolism at face value to appreciate Socrates' ability to foresee possible hazards in an interlocutor's casual words, thoughts or gestures and to respect his great efforts to show them how they might avert the loss of their homecoming. In the *Odyssey*, Odysseus cannot prevent the death of Eurylochos and the crew; he does not know enough about the dangers to persuade them not to rest at Thrinakia. In the *Republic*, Socrates patiently explains all the dangers to Glaucon and repeatedly offers to assist his escape.

At Thrinakia, Odysseus's homecoming is still distant. He has difficult things yet to live through before he becomes the man, knowledgeable in the many cities and minds of men (πολλῶν δ' ἀνθρώπων ἴδεν ἄστεα καὶ νόον ἔγνω, 1.3), who inspires the poet's song: not only his confinement on Kalypso's island, during which he has time to reflect on his failings and the deaths of his companions, but also the trial of his second sailing to the land of the Phaiakians and the many troubles that await him on Ithaka before he can sleep in his own bed. In contrast, Socrates' homecoming, the end of the "longer way," is something he has already attained, an understanding that is always already present in him; however, in the conversation reported in the *Republic*, it is also much farther off. His homecoming will not be successful unless he can show Glaucon and Adeimantus the upward way to an understanding of justice in the cities and minds of men that they so courageously set out to find. Coming to a proper understanding of politics and philosophy requires them to undertake the greatest study, to approach the most perfect thing, the good itself, and to learn its consequence for justice, both in the soul and in existing cities. When Socrates judges it the right time to set out on the "longer way" with them, he attempts to forestall the worst. He speaks as if it only remained to paint the Homeric image of a god-like man who is himself a painter of regimes; he speaks as if he were Odysseus in the court of the Phaiakians, and even as if he were Odysseus home again with the wisdom necessary to rule justly and transform Ithaka into something resembling the Phaiakian court. In other words, he speaks as if Thrinakia had already been bypassed, his companions had been saved, and the confinement on Kalypso's island had been unnecessary. But Glaucon and Adeimantus rebel. When Eurylochos and the rest of Odysseus's crew mutiny at Thrinakia, they first insist on rest; but Odysseus knows that the hidden danger is that they could subsequently insist on slaughtering the immortal herds of Helios and be punished by the gods with death. When Glaucon and Adeimantus mutiny, refusing to press on further in dialogue, they first insist on rest; they demand that Socrates provide an account of the good as a dogma, supposition, or opinion, something needing no further reflective ascent; and they imagine the good as something like joy or pleasure, desired in itself, without consequence, abstract and static. Glaucon makes the hidden danger explicit when he demands a methodical account of the good, done his way: first, derived from a fixed premise, and then, an explanation of its usefulness. In the *Odyssey*, the crew loses its homecoming by resting and cutting up immortal things. In the *Republic*, Glaucon takes on the role of Eurylochos and risks losing his homecoming by insisting on the stasis of opinion, premise or hypothesis, from which only diairetic cutting follows; he refuses dialectical ascent and insists on descent instead. Socrates has no alternative but to explain the dire consequences.

The sun, the line, the cave: Plato's Odysseus first describes Thrinakia for his Eurylochos and warns him to go beyond it; then he tells him about the temptation to slaughter the cattle, and about the inverted order of the world men would bring upon themselves if they compelled Helios to take light to Hades; but he also tells him the way to escape.

When Socrates begins by saying he will leave aside an account of the good itself, there is disappointment evident in his voice. However, he does not quite keep his word. He patiently describes the sun as the offspring of the good to Glaucon, but in such manner as to suggest what Glaucon would prefer not to hear. Plato has Socrates' account refigure Odysseus's description of Thrinakia for his crew, giving a more complete explanation of its order and the way in which mortals should honour it: in proper contemplation, recognizing the need to move beyond. Helios is a god, and is explicitly said to be so by Socrates (508a); and the filial relation of the sun to the distant good itself is derived from the relation of Helios to his "Father Zeus (Ζεῦ πάτερ, 12.377)." Helios is a god who sees and overhears all things, in other words, a god who implicitly knows all things. Socrates begins his account by briefly mentioning the human experiences of seeing and hearing and their slightly different ways of enabling us to know things; however, given that hearing raises the question of the relation between the structures of language and the nature of things, Socrates concentrates on vision. There is a human ability or capacity to see; and there is an attribute, characteristic or quality of visibility to things. Similarly, there is a human capacity to intellect or know; and there is a quality of intelligibility to things. Socrates neither elaborates on an epistemological relation between seeing and knowing nor suggests a metaphysics or an ontology; he only notes the similarity, recognized commonsensically in speech in the verb εἶδον. Insofar as his imagery is suggestive of a fuller account, it is conspicuously opposed to the premises of modern philosophy, and even to modern assumptions about the premises of Platonism, in its insistence that the relation between intellection and intelligibility is not unmediated in the same way that the relation between vision and visibility is not unmediated. What is more, Plato has Socrates use vividly Homeric imagery to express this: vision and visibility are "yoked together" by a yoke that is more honourable than those yoking other teams (συζεύξεων τιμιωτέρῳ ζυγῷ ἐζύγησαν, 507e–8a). The yoke in the realm of the visible is light. The comparable yoke in the realm of the intelligible can be called both knowledge (ἐπιστήμη) and truth (ἀλήθεια, 508e). Light is the sun's illumination of the visible realm, and the way in which the sun itself is visible to the eye; knowledge and truth is the good's illumination of the intelligible realm, and the idea of the good is the way in which the good itself is intelligible, or visible, to the mind. The visible and the intelligible realms together do not constitute all that is, any more than the visibility and intelligibility of any thing together exhaust its nature, existence or being. The sun and the good, therefore, as causes of light and truth, are the rulers of their respective realms, but they are also beyond them. If the cattle of Helios can be said to be yoked, then Socrates' account is an explanation of how his crew should honour them. They are immortal, neither giving birth nor dying; and their immortality is evident to the eyes, but more so to the mind. They are to be left unharmed and only contemplated, both in themselves and in their relation to Helios and Zeus. However, the visible and intelligible attributes of their immortality are not equivalent to their immortality itself, for that is very much in their flesh, their nature and existence. The continuum of the degrees of immortality extends far beyond them to the highest divinities; and mortals must honour every divinity in the most fitting way, properly recognizing the nature of its immortality.

Socrates' account is given not only to suggest something about the order of the visible and intelligible realms; it is given more to indicate the dangers of contemplation. When Odysseus approaches Thrinakia, he is aware that the island holds two dangers: the temptation to rest and not continue on the homeward voyage; and the temptation to slaughter the cattle. Contemplation that does not dishonour the gods does not, in itself, represent a danger. However, Thrinakia represents the temptation to the improper practice of contemplation, a temptation that might initially seem benign, but which has disastrous consequences. In Socrates' account, there are several sorts of blindness described. Mistaking the realm of becoming—that which comes into being and passes away—for the realm of being is a common sort of blindness in the soul (ψυχῆς, 508d); in the symbolism of the *Odyssey*, it would be comparable to imagining an ordinary cow as one of Helios's cattle, mistaking the mortal for the immortal. A more treacherous sort of blindness occurs when the eye looks directly at the sun. In describing the visible realm, Socrates says that the eye is the "most sun-formed (ἡλιοειδέστατόν, 508b)" sense organ, a characteristic, he oddly continues, that might lead to the assumption that sight and the sun are identical. The sort of blindness suggested by this remark is not physical, and the implication is made explicit in his parallel account of the intelligible realm. Light and sight are "sun-formed (ἡλιοειδῆ)," but to hold them to be the sun is wrong; so too knowledge and truth are "good-formed (ἀγαθοειδῆ)," but to hold either or them to be the good is wrong (509a). And to complete the parallelism where Socrates does not explicitly: the intellect might be the most good-formed part of the soul, but this characteristic should not lead to the assumption that the mind and the good are identical. The most treacherous sort of blindness mistakes an activity of the mind for an activity of the soul, of the whole person, and imagines that intelligibility and existence are identical. Contemplation, improperly practiced, leads one to imagine oneself a god.

Glaucon hears the description, but he does not hear the warning. He says Socrates is describing such an "impossible beauty (ἀμήχανον κάλλος, 509a)" that he can only imagine the good itself to be "pleasure (ἡδονὴν, 509a)." Pleasure is a sort of good enjoyed for itself alone, without consequence; to imagine it as the highest thing is a projection of the mind's enjoyment of itself. Socrates immediately insists on showing the gods the proper respect: εὐφήμει (509a), he says, an exclamation that could be translated, "use words of good omen or none at all." He sees that Glaucon has surrendered to the Thrinakian temptation and immediately reminds him of what he has forgotten about the sun and the good. The sun not only provides the visibility of things, but also their "generation, growth and nourishment, though it is not itself generation (γένεσιν καὶ αὔξην καὶ τροφήν, οὐ γένεσιν αὐτὸν ὄντα, 509b)." And the good not only provides the intelligibility of things, but also their "existence and being (τὸ εἶναί τε καὶ τὴν οὐσίαν, 509b)," though "the good is not being, but is beyond being, exceeding it in dignity and power (οὐκ οὐσίας ὄντος τοῦ ἀγαθοῦ ἀλλ᾽ ἔτι ἐπέκεινα τῆς οὐσίας πρεσβείᾳ καὶ δυνάμει ὑπερέχοντος, 509b)." Socrates reminds Glaucon that contemplating the visibility and intelligibility of things is not the same as understanding the nature and existence of things, and that the ultimate origin or cause of all things deserves the greatest honour. In the symbolism of the *Odyssey*, Socrates would have Glaucon swear an oath that on Thrinakia he will not be tempted by the immortal herds and will honour Helios and Zeus in all he does. Resting on Thrinakia might be unavoidable, but Glaucon's next words show how quickly the danger arises.

Glaucon summarily dismisses Socrates' invocation of the good beyond being as "daimonic hyperbole (δαιμονίας ὑπερβολῆς, 509c)," even conventionally swearing by Apollo, god of the visible and the intelligible, to affirm his unwillingness to go any further. He insists that they must stop and rest on Thrinakia. At this point in the *Republic*, Plato breaks the narrative dramatically by having Socrates comment explicitly on the conversation he is recounting. The exasperation is unmistakable in Socrates' remark, made the following day, that Glaucon's dismissal was "very ridiculous (μάλα γελοίως, 509c)." In the moment, however, Socrates does not lose his patience. Instead, he chides Glaucon: "You are to blame for compelling me to tell my opinions about it (σὺ γάρ . . . αἴτιος, ἀναγκάζων τὰ ἐμοὶ δοκοῦντα περὶ αὐτοῦ λέγειν, 509c)." Socrates consents, as did Odysseus, even echoing the resignation in Odysseus's reply to Eurylochos's unfounded protests: "I am only one man, . . . you force me to it (ἦ μάλα δή με βιάζετε μοῦνον ἐόντα, 12.297)."

Socrates tries another tack. He realizes that, if the conversation with Glaucon is to continue, he will have to "leave out a great deal" (509c)—or seem to do so—and allow Glaucon to imagine that things are going his way. He limits the discussion to a consideration of the visible and intelligible realms alone, acknowledging the sovereigns (βασιλεύειν, 509d) of the two realms formally, but leaving them out. In the *Odyssey*, in the absence of Helios and Zeus, the temptation to slaughter the cattle is overwhelming for Eurylochos; and despite his conventional pieties, he suffers from a sophisticated sort of blindness: after having mistaken mortal for immortal, he mistakes immortal for mortal. Similarly in the *Republic*, in the absence of the sun and the good, and of the illumination they provide in light and truth, the temptation to cut up reality will similarly be overwhelming for Glaucon. Socrates allows it free rein immediately, and even insists on it—but only in speech, where its consequences can be more readily attenuated. With a bad pun and a profession that he is not "playing the sophist (σοφίζεσθαι, 509d)" to distract attention from the fact that what follows is a diagnosis of the origins of the worst excesses of sophistry in seeming intellectual rigour, Socrates limits the discussion to visibility and intelligibility—to what the eye and the mind perceive—precluding any possibility of understanding the nature and existence of things.

The first cut is deep: the cut between visibility and intelligibility, on the one hand, and the nature and order of things, on the other; the cut between the surface of things, evident to the eye and the mind, and their essence or reality. This is the cut that skins the sacred cattle of Helios. Then, there is the oddly compelling image of a line of finite length, the illusory concreteness of which allows Glaucon both to imagine that the visible and intelligible realms together add up to whole of reality and to indulge himself in the false precision of diairetic cutting. The line is first cut into two segments; then each segment is cut again; and the discussion of the segment corresponding to the visible realm suggests that further cuts are possible by categories of objects included in that class. Socrates begins and ends this discussion by referring explicitly to line segments (τμήματα, 509d, 511d), allowing Glaucon—and countless scholarly interpreters of these passages—to assume a continuity in the categorical distinctions between the line segments in his account. However, the conversation itself moves up the line, as it were, from the strongly visual character of the segmented line, to the geometric figure one can abstract from the image, to matters beyond geometry. The separate line segments are drawn together by proportion. After being cut apart, they move toward one another like the parts of one of the slaughtered cattle of Helios, struggling to reconstitute its living and immortal form. And the segments are illuminated from beyond as well; although the sun and the good were ostensibly banished from consideration, the proportion of the line divisions is not a measure intrinsic to number, as it initially seems, but rather is itself measured by the degree to which the objects corresponding to the segments themselves participate in clarity and truth (ὥσπερ ἐφ᾽ οἷς ἐστιν ἀληθείας μετέχει, οὕτω ταῦτα σαφηνείας ἡγησάμενος μετέχειν, 511e)—in other words, by the degree to which they are illuminated by the light of the sun and the good. Without light, diairesis is blind; and Glaucon should know that cows are not butchered according to mathematical proportion, but rather at the joints (cf. *Phaedrus* 265e).

What turns Glaucon in the right direction, though, and briefly overcomes his resistance to anything beyond the Apollonian, is a rhetorical device. Half-way through his account, Socrates introduces a cut that is not a clean cut, a diairetic distinction the second part of which is opposed to diairetic cutting: the distinction between the "habit of geometers (τὴν τῶν γεωμετρικῶν . . . ἕξιν, 511d)" and dialectic. Geometric thinking and dialectic are two orientations, not to different objects, but rather to the same objects: images (εἰκόσιν) and hypotheses (ὑποθέσεων, 510b). They are, in other words, two possible orientations of the soul (ψυχὴ, 510b, 511a; cf. 511d), and not only of the mind, toward the visible and intelligible realms together as well as toward the reality that underlies them—the reality the soul "sees" through the eyes and the intellect. Given that they are activities of the soul largely focused in the intellect, however, Socrates concentrates his account on hypotheses, without explaining how hypotheses are derived, and opposes the two orientations with directional terms: geometric thinking moves from hypotheses "to an end (ἐπὶ τελευτήν)" whereas dialectic moves from them "to a beginning that is free from hypotheses (τὸ ἐπ᾽ ἀρχὴν ἀνυπόθετον, 510b)." He also describes each as a "method" or "way" (μέθοδον, 510b,c). It would be misleading to oppose them too strictly and claim that geometric thinking descends and dialectic ascends or that geometric thinking is practical and dialectic is theoretical. Their difference is the same as the difference between the "longer and harder way" Socrates would travel to its end and the ways Glaucon tends to prefer, the ways that threaten to ruin everything (435cd). Dialectic ascends, but it also descends; and geometric thinking descends, often mistakenly or inappropriately, but it also has its own form of illusory ascent. Insofar as geometry, as a discipline, is both axiomatic and a method of deriving proofs from axioms, accepting hypotheses uncritically and "descending" from them is unproblematic. But insofar as this form of thinking can be habitual, it can also be manifest in domains of theory and practice in which it is entirely out of place and destructive. Geometry and all comparable sciences have affinities to the technical arts, if not to the acquisition of the moral virtues, but no similarities at all to the intellectual virtues. However, it is the habit of geometric thinkers to project the form of such knowledge into all realms, and consequently to imagine that the dialectical ascent foundational to the pursuit of wisdom and prudence is an aspiration to the mastery of the highest axioms, and furthermore to imagine that life itself can be lived as theory applied on the model on technique. Axioms and derivation, hypotheses and application, stasis and cutting – in other words, it is the Thrinakian temptation.

In contrast, Socrates says somewhat enigmatically, dialectic takes hypotheses as "steppingstones and springboards (ἐπιβάσεις τε καὶ ὁρμάς)" and uses them to ascend to "what is without hypothesis at the beginning of all (τοῦ ἀνυποθέτου ἐπὶ τὴν τοῦ παντὸς ἀρχήν, 511b)." Insofar as this is an activity of the soul in the intelligible realm, the dialectical ascent above hypotheses is followed by a descent through "ideas themselves, from ideas to ideas, and ending in ideas (εἴδεσιν αὐτοῖς δι' αὐτῶν εἰς αὐτά, καὶ τελευτᾷ εἰς εἴδη, 511c)." The highest idea, the idea of the good, is the beginning of the descent in this realm; however, it is not thereby the highest thing. Ultimately, when the "beginning of all" has been attained, the descent in the intelligible realm "depends on that which depends on this beginning (ἀψάμενος αὐτῆς, πάλιν αὖ ἐχόμενος τῶν ἐκείνης ἐχομένων, 511b)." Plato has Socrates describe dialectic in a manner that refigures, in formal terms, the account Odysseus heard from Hermes and Kalypso of Helios's delight in contemplating his immortal herds as he ascended into the heavens and turned back again to earth. The soul ascends toward, and descends from the idea of the good in the intelligible realm as the sun ascends and descends in the visible realm, contemplating unchanging things and leaving them unharmed; and beyond the highest visible and intelligible things there is the "beginning of all:" Father Zeus, the good itself, the measure of all things, however the god prefers to be called.

Socrates intends his account not only to show Glaucon how to contemplate the herds of Helios properly, resisting the temptation to skin and butcher them; he also intends it to instill a sense in him that there is something beyond proper contemplation as well. His Apollonian imagery is a mask for more of his daimonic hyperbole. For the moment, Glaucon finds it charming.

In the *Odyssey*, the punishment for slaughtering Helios's cattle is death. Eurylochos and the crew are sent to Hades and lose their homecoming; and Odysseus is given time to reflect on his failings on Kalypso's island. The punishments avert the overturning of the cosmic order threatened by Helios. Had the crew remained alive and unpunished, he would have gone down to Hades to shine his light on the dead (12.383); the living, in other words, would have become the spiritually dead. Beyond this suggestive implication, however, the more overtly political consequences of succumbing to the Thrinakian temptation are not developed in the *Odyssey*. The incidents through which Odysseus learns of the minds and the cities of men are often distinct, and the Thrinakian episode is not an explicitly political lesson for him. The deaths of Odysseus's crewmen have an important symbolic function when they are the consequence of, or represent failings that he must overcome in himself. The deaths at Thrinakia might be said to occur as a consequence of a failure in leadership and a failure to recognize and honour the highest mysteries beyond conventional pieties; but they are not deaths that result from Odysseus's inability to master his honour-loving and victory-loving. The episode with the most significant political importance for Odysseus is the confrontation with the Cyclops Polyphemos. Insofar as the *Odyssey* can be read as a work of political philosophy, it shows Odysseus learning of the cities of men through encountering the worst in the Cyclops and the best in the Phaiakians, and then being faced with the challenge of how to rule Ithaka justly on his return. In his absence, the politics of Ithaka has tended toward the worst; the leader of the rival suitors, Antinous, is a man of Cyclopean brutality. In overcoming the suitors, however, Odysseus must struggle to overcome the Cyclopean elements in his own soul if his rule is to bring Ithaka closer to the regime of the Phaiakians. In the *Odyssey*, the constant, underlying political problem is brutality: men cannibalizing one another in the slaughter of warfare and civil strife, men devouring one another's substance in political rule. Brutality is not associated with high-mindedness. In the *Republic*, it is. The base injustices of war and domination remain a constant, of course, as do their thumotic roots in the desire for recognition and power; but the political argument of the *Republic* originates in the opposition of Glaucon and Adeimantus to Thrasymachus's defense of the most extreme sort of injustice, and in support of this opposition Socrates gives an account of the relation of sophistry and tyranny that he develops to include a consideration of the relation of all forms of high-mindedness and brutality.

After his momentary success in showing Glaucon the philosophic consequences of his resistance to undertaking the "longer way," Socrates turns to an explanation of the political consequences. The imagery of Socrates' account of the cave, the ascents possible from it, and the willingness or unwillingness of its denizens to escape or return to it, is strikingly vivid, but the narrative is both sketchy and complex. Plato bases it, in part, on the *Odyssey's* image of Helios shining his light in Hades; however, the cave is not a Hades: its prisoners are the living, and the spiritual death they suffer is not an unavoidable destiny. Plato also bases Socrates' imagery, in part, on the *Odyssey's* account of the Cyclops's cave; however, Polyphemos himself does not appear: the prisoners collectively seem to bring their condition upon themselves. To be free of it, each must overcome not only the Cyclopean element in his soul but, more importantly, the various ways in which he experiences the Thrinakian temptation—directly if tempted to rule, and indirectly if ruled. Insofar as there is an order to the disorder of the cave, it is ruled by human beings who suffer from the treacherous sort of blindness that results from identifying their knowledge with the good. Each of them considers himself Helios, a god-like source of illumination for all the mindless dead around him. He does not leave the world of the living to illuminate Hades, but rather makes the world dark around himself and attempts to draw the living into it. When there are enough of the spiritually blind to hold predominance in a society, they transform the human community into a Cyclopean cave. They are indistinguishably sophists and tyrants, the antitheses of philosopher-kings. Glaucon must surely be opposed to everything represented in Socrates' account of the cave, for he had demanded that Socrates give an account of justice antithetical to Thrasymachus's sophistic defence of the injustice of the tyrant. There is a challenge to Glaucon, then, in Socrates' presentation of the cave as an image of the political consequences of his resistance to undertaking the "longer way." Glaucon's refusal to press on further in dialogue with Socrates might seem motivated by weariness, or a temporary confusion, and his preference for geometric thinking over dialectic might seem a benign sort of intellectual idleness, but these failings are far from harmless. A man with a habit for geometric thinking is not a sophist; he is instead a man who cannot tell the difference between a sophist and a philosopher, and who, if he were compelled to choose, would almost certainly consider the sophist to be the better intellectual. The ways of geometric thinking and sophistry are the same; and applied sophistry is tyranny. The Thrinakian temptation in thought is a fascination with axioms and derivation, hypotheses and application, stasis and cutting. In politics, these things become dogma, arbitrary decree, and force. The worst brutality thereby comes from high-mindedness.

To understand everything suggested in Socrates' gnomic account of the cave would require going very far afield. The *Republic* is not a self-contained, autonomous work. It points beyond itself, not only substantively, but also textually; and not only to Homer and other source-texts, but also to Plato's other dialogues. Speaking generally, the ascending and descending ways of the *Republic* are paths that lead elsewhere, and the map it provides is sketchy and unclear. Sometimes the way up and the way down seem to be the same. Plato has Glaucon speak prophetically when he says that sorting out all this out is the work of a lifetime (450b), if not a journey of a thousand years (621d). The ascent of the "longer way" is begun in the *Republic*, the direction to take is shown, but where is an account of reaching its end given? Similarly, Socrates' description of the philosophic and political consequences of resisting the "longer way" and yielding to the Thrinakian temptation begins a descent, but where is an account of its ominous end given? The strikingly sinister imagery of Socrates' description of the cave might be enough to cause Glaucon some concern; however, there is much more to be said about the worst that can happen, and it is not said in the *Republic*. To discover how and where it is developed at length would require following the track of the Cyclops through Plato's dialogues; and that, in turn, would require first learning more about his habits through an analysis of the importance of the Cyclops episode in both the mythology and the politics of the *Odyssey*. It must suffice for the moment to notice that, in the *Republic*, Plato's analysis of the possible political consequences of the relation of geometrical thinking to sophistry is expressed in an unusual image. If a man identifies himself with Helios and makes the world a Hades around himself, he finds himself reduced to keeping a fire and running a shadow-puppet theater. A man holding puppets in his hands is not as terrifyingly powerful as he might imagine himself, neither lord over all the dead nor Polyphemos preparing to eat two of Odysseus's companions. There is something funny going on here. I do not mean the joke that scholars unwittingly play on themselves when they interpret Plato's critique of sophistic attempts to recreate the world artificially in the cave as evidence of a Platonic two-worlds metaphysic hidden in the dialogues. I mean instead a joke being made by Plato at someone's expense. And perhaps more than one person's expense. Insofar as the cave is an account of education, Socrates says suggestively that education is not like putting sight into blind eyes, as "the professions of some people (ἐπαγγελλόμενοί) proclaim it to be" (518bc; cf. *Prot.* 319a, *Gorg.* 447c, *Euthyd.* 273d). Insofar as the cave is not an allegory to be decoded, and rather part of an ongoing conversation, the joke is on

Glaucon. To appreciate it properly, in the sense in which it is made, we must put aside the examination of Plato's use of the *Odyssey* as a source-text and turn to Aristophanes.

First, a brief recapitulation: When Socrates attempts to set out on the "longer way," putting aside the difficulties of the night's discussion and beginning again from the philosopher-king, the rebellion of Glaucon and Adeimantus compels an answer from him. Where he would ascend, they insist on stasis and descent. His account of the sun, the line, and the cave shows them the dangers for philosophy and politics implicit in their objections; and if it does not entirely overcome their resistance, it does hold their attention. Through its striking imagery, Socrates attempts to find some dialogic common ground. Instead of ascending on the "longer way," he descends and attempts to persuade them, to make them less stubborn and more open to the possibility of the ascent. In response, Glaucon seems willing to carry on. He is always courageous, always willing to risk saying or doing something he doesn't understand (*Memorabilia* 3.6.16). Socrates finds enough reason to continue the discussion with him, but he has doubts about the likelihood of being able to guide Glaucon's enthusiasm past the obstacles of his "very ridiculous (μάλα γελοίως)" objections (509c). He puts Glaucon somewhat at ease, as he had previously in their conversation (432c–e), by sharing responsibility for the confusion, but in a back-handed way. They are on common ground and are both laughably blind, he says, one from coming from light into darkness and the other from coming from darkness into light; and though two such blind men might laugh at each other's blindness, and be ridiculous (καταγέλαστος) for doing so, the laughter of the former would be slightly less ridiculous to an intelligent man (518ab). But what direction should their amicable discussion now take? In the *Odyssey*, the Thrinakian episode ends with the deaths of the entire crew and Odysseus's long confinement on Kalypso's island. In the *Republic*, Socrates hoped to avoid a similar fate; the gambit of his assumption that his companions would follow along with his discussion of the philosopher-king taking the "longer way" was an attempt to bring them directly to the land of the Phaiakians *en route* to a safe homecoming. If Glaucon is now convinced of the dangers of the Thrinakian temptation, if his soul has been "turn[ed] around from a night-like day to true day (περιαγωγὴ ἐκ νυκτερινῆς τινος ἡμέρας εἰς ἀληθινήν, 521c)," then the turning-around should be evident even in the first steps of the ascending path of a proper philosophic education. Consequently, Socrates raises the topic of what subjects the guardians of the city in speech should study. If

Glaucon is not convinced, if he is still tempted by the stasis of abstract speculation, imagining that it transports him "to the Isles of the Blessed while still alive (ἐν μακάρων νήσοις ζῶντες, 519c)," the discussion will go nowhere; or rather, it will be fated to some equivalent of confinement on Kalypso's island, praying to be set free by a daimonic intermediary. As it happens, for all his heroic efforts, Glaucon does not do well when put to the test. The results are comic, not tragic. But Socrates cannot escape the trap of Glaucon's limitations. He must end the night in Glaucon's city in speech, with guardians who are only as philosophical as Glaucon imagines them to be, all of them unable to complete the ascent to the good itself. He ends the night, in other words, in Kalypso's polis—the *kallipolis*, as he names Glaucon's beautiful city (527bc).

At some point the guardians must take up dialectic. Before then there are studies in various subjects—number and calculation, plane and solid geometry, astronomy and music—that Socrates describes as a "prelude to the song itself (προοίμιά . . . αὐτοῦ τοῦ νόμου, 531d)." Each of these subjects can be studied as a given discipline; each has its axioms or established hypotheses and its deductions and applications. In other words, each can lead the soul downwards from hypotheses. However, each can also spark curiosity, speculation and dialectical inquiry—the ascent of the soul from hypotheses. The guardians of the city in speech, as they were left in the discussion, are not quite philosophers, but they are warriors. Which way will these studies lead them? and to what consequence? But more importantly, which way will the discussion of these studies lead Glaucon? Socrates takes him through a consideration of the several studies, one after another, before discussing dialectic explicitly again. In each case, he suggests how a study might turn the soul upward. In each case, Glaucon finds a way of understanding it that turns the soul downward. What is more, in each case he does so while trying his best to imitate Socrates. It is all quite amusing, this comedy of errors in which Glaucon earnestly attempts to show that he understands all these things, and the teasing Glaucon gets from Socrates for being unable to break the habit of geometric thinking is pleasantly understated. Nevertheless, Glaucon ends up looking ridiculous again.

When Socrates initiates the new discussion, he mentions that there are certain things in experience that "by nature lead to intellection (τῶν πρὸς τὴν νόησιν ἀγόντων φύσει, 523a);" some things sensed, for example, "do not summon the intellect to the activity of investigation (οὐ παρακαλοῦν-τα τὴν νόησιν εἰς ἐπίσκεψιν, 523ab)," and some do. Glaucon is confident that he knows which do not. He applies the schema of the divided line in a doctrinal way—a way not unknown to scholars of Platonism—and identifies such things as far-off appearances and shadow-paintings (ἐσκια-γραφημένα). That is not my meaning, says Socrates. Look at your fingers, Glaucon. Are they thick or thin, big or small, relative to one another or in themselves? But even when Socrates explains that behind such speculation there is "number and calculation (ἀριθμόν τε καὶ λογισμόν, 522c)," questions of the one and the two, Glaucon admits he "can't conceive (οὐ συν-νοῶ)" whether reflections on "number and the one (ἀριθμός τε καὶ τὸ ἕν, 524d)" take the intellect up or down. About geometry, he is more certain: it is useful for the business of war (526d). But when Socrates reminds him that there is more to it than that, Glaucon hastens to agree so enthusiastically that he goes to the absurd extreme of identifying geometry and philosophy: "geometrical knowing is of what is always (τοῦ γὰρ ἀεὶ ὄντος ἡ γεωμετρικὴ γνῶσίς ἐστιν)," he says, and it directs the soul upward "to the greatest extent possible" (527b). Then it must be studied by the guardians "in your beautiful city (ἐν τῇ καλλιπόλει σοι, 527c)," Socrates replies. How well does Glaucon know his geometry? And how good is he in a real battle? When the discussion moves on to astronomy, he suffers an embarrassing rout. Once again, Glaucon rushes to explain its practical applications, even in warfare; and once again, Socrates finds him "amusing (ἡδὺς, 527d)" for doing so. But worse, the enthusiast has made a mistake in his geometry and must "retreat a way (ἄναγε τοίνυν . . . εἰς τοὐπίσω, 528a):" from plane geometry, Glaucon should not have advanced to astronomy, the study of solids in motion, before considering solid geometry itself. To save face after Socrates' reproaches, Glaucon makes a point of announcing that he will attempt to praise astronomy in Socrates' way: "astronomy compels the soul to see what's above," he says, "and leads it there away from the things here" (528e–9a). Wrong again. For philosophy, it's precisely the opposite, Socrates reiterates, this time with slightly less patience: "gaping up (ἄνω κεχηνώς, 529b)" with the eyes is looking down with the soul. When the discussion turns to music and harmony, Glaucon is more cautious, waiting to take a cue from Socrates' own remarks before speaking up in imitation of him. Socrates mentions the Pythagoreans in comparing those whose ears seek out number in music to the astronomers whose eyes properly seek it out in observing the motions of heavenly bodies, and Glaucon immediately criticizes them: how "ridiculous (γελοίως, 531a)" they are, putting their ears before intelligence. A well-intentioned effort, but still misdirected. Socrates explains that the Pythagoreans he has in mind are not torturers of strings who look for the minutest measurement of sounds; they are, rather, philosophers who reflect on number in experience properly but "don't ascend to problems (οὐκ εἰς προβλήματα ἀνίασιν, 531c)."

Poor Glaucon. The laughs are on him. And the jokes are old too. They are all taken from Aristophanes' *Clouds*. Plato is having fun with his dear brother by casting him in the role of Strepsiades, Socrates' distressed and incompetent pupil. He is also having fun with Aristophanes by refining the presentation of sophistry in the *Clouds*. Plato agrees entirely with Aristophanes' critique, as far as it goes—except for its implication of Socrates. But sophistry, for Plato, does not originate in stupidity or vulgarity, or not only in them; it also originates in the high-mindedness mistaken for philosophy by the many, and is therefore all the more dangerous. He is at pains to account for this genealogy in the *Republic*, even to the point of using Glaucon as a comic foil to demonstrate the relationship of intellectual recklessness and imprudent political ambition. There must have been some pleasure for Plato in having Glaucon imitate Strepsiades while imagining that he is imitating Socrates, but we cannot speculate about the personal reasons. However, a comparison of the texts does allow us to appreciate something of the pleasure for Plato in topping Aristophanes by having Socrates play his role from the *Clouds* properly, this time with more experience in Method Acting.

A quick sketch of Strepsiades' screw-ups along the way to learning the "mysteries (μυστήρια, *Clouds* 143)" of the Thinking Shop (φροντιστήριον, 94) will show the extent to which Plato draws from the *Clouds* for the discussion of the higher education in the *Republic*. The beginning is not auspicious for Strepsiades. He causes one of Socrates' thoughts to "miscarry" (φροντίδ᾽ ἐξήμβλωκας ἐξηυρημένην, 137) by banging on the door. The student who answers it is quite willing to give examples of what sorts of things are studied there. The simplest involve number and calculation. The first story Strepsiades hears is of Socrates cleverly measuring the distance a flea can jump . . . in flea feet—a calculation of ratio or proportion (144154). When Strepsiades himself becomes Socrates' student—the worst ever, he says—the first examination he is given also concerns measures and rhythms. Socrates asks him to distinguish between two rhythms, the enoplian and the "digital (δάκτυλον, 651);" Strepsiades does not consider the meter, or the number, but rather looks down at his own fingers and makes an obscene joke or two. There is also geometry and astronomy. During his introductory tour of the school, Strepsiades sees instruments of measurement. When a set is said to be for geometry, Strepsiades asks,

"What's that useful for? (τοῦτ᾽ οὖν τί ἐστι χρήσιμον;, 202)." The obvious reply—"measuring the earth (γῆν ἀναμετρῆσαι)"—makes him think of the very practical business of surveying land allotments. When the student explains its higher purposes and shows him a map of the world, the hint of the relation between plane geometry, solid geometry and astronomy is entirely lost on him (206). Not that there are no embarrassments about the manner in which astronomy is studied at the school. Strepsiades learns that Socrates himself was once "gaping up (ἄνω κεχηνότος, 172 = *Republic* 529b)" at the night sky to investigate the revolutions of the moon and had a lizard shit on him. The students do worse: while they are bent over trying to discover what is under the earth, their asses are said to look upward and study astronomy independently (193–195)—a rare instance of looking down while looking up in several possible ways simultaneously. The study of music at the school is not much better. Apparently, Socrates is one of those who puts ears before intelligence, even torturing them to measure the minutest of sounds, because it is said that he once listened to gnats farting to determine if that is how they sing (156–165). Aristophanes' Socrates might not be much of a music theorist. He is, however, an excellent dialectician. When the chorus of clouds is singing its *parode* off-stage, Socrates eulogies them for Strepsiades: "they bestow on us intelligence (γνώμην) and discourse (διάλεξιν) and understanding (νοῦν);" however, they also bestow "circumlocution (περίλεξιν) and hoaxing (κροῦσιν) and power (κατάληψιν)" (317–318). They are an opening to the upward way, but they can also be interpreted in a manner that refuses the upward way. How does Strepsiades understand them? He becomes excited by Socrates' description and says his soul now longs to "chop logic (λεπτολογεῖν, 320; cf. 1496)" and "meet argument with counter-argument (λόγῳ ἀντιλογῆσαι, 321; cf. 901, 1037, 1040)." And logic-chopping, the art of being "negative and contradictory (ἐξαρνητικὸς κἀντιλογικός, 1172–73)," is what Plato calls eristic (*Republic* 454a), the diairetic excess of the worst, most victory-loving sort of sophistry.

When Socrates turns from the arts of the "prelude"—number, geometry, astronomy, harmony—to describe dialectic, "the song itself (αὐτοῦ τοῦ νόμου, 531d)," the "longer way" the soul takes in ascending toward the good itself, it is as if Glaucon hears nothing at all. Instead of following the music of Socrates' words (532a–d), Glaucon just waits until Socrates is finished and then asks for dialectic to be analyzed with the methods he understands and prefers: "tell what the character of the power of dialectic is; and then into exactly what forms it is divided; and finally what are its ways (λέγε οὖν τίς ὁ τρόπος τῆς τοῦ διαλέγεσθαι δυνάμεως, καὶ κατὰ ποῖα δὴ εἴδη διέστηκεν, καὶ τίνες αὖ ὁδοί, 532de)." The downward path is easier, and Glaucon has had enough. He asks Socrates to "bring them to a place of rest on the road and to the end of the journey (ἀφικομένῳ ὥσπερ ὁδοῦ ἀνάπαυλα ἂν εἴη καὶ τέλος τῆς πορείας, 532e)." If Socrates had hoped his evocative description of dialectic might finally lead Glaucon past the Thrinakian temptation, Glaucon's response disheartens him: "you'll no longer be able to follow further, dear Glaucon (οὐκέτ᾽, . . . ὦ φίλε Γλαύκων, οἷός τ᾽ ἔσῃ ἀκολουθεῖν, 533a)," he replies.

Dear Glaucon, ridiculous in both tragic and comic modes. Socrates keeps talking with him, though. He has enough experience of "the tragedy and comedy of life (τῇ τοῦ βίου . . . τραγῳδίᾳ καὶ κωμῳδίᾳ, Philebus 50b)" to know that life itself is "pitiful, laughable and strange (ἐλεινήν . . . καὶ γελοίαν καὶ θαυμασίαν, 620a)." Patience and tolerance are necessary. If Glaucon persists in his ways, no matter. It is only a conversation, and there are other things to discuss that might interest him more.

Endnotes

1   The Perseus Digital Library (Classics Department, Tufts University) has been used for the Greek texts of the *Odyssey*, the *Clouds*, and the *Republic* (http://www.perseus.tufts.edu/hopper/). In translating and paraphrasing Homer, Aristophanes, and Plato, I have relied on Alan Sommerstein's *Clouds* (Warminster: Aris and Phillips, 1982), Richmond Lattimore's *Odyssey* (New York: Harper and Row, 1967), and Allan Bloom's *Republic* (New York: Basic Books, 1968).

2   Zdravko Planinc: *Plato's Political Philosophy: Prudence in the Republic and the Laws* (Columbia: University of Missouri Press, 1991), 277–285 especially; *Plato through Homer: Poetry and Philosophy in the Cosmological Dialogues* (Columbia: University of Missouri Press, 2003); "Ascending with Socrates: Plato's Use of Homeric Imagery in the *Symposium*," *Interpretation* 31/3 (2004), 325–350; "Experiències equivalents de simbolització en Plató i Homer," translated by Bernat Torres, *L'Anuari de la Societat Catalana de Filosofia* 19 (2008), 133–139; "Aristophanic Themes in Plato's Republic: A Post-Voegelinian Reading," paper presented to the Eric Voegelin Society at the meetings of the American Political Science Association (Toronto, 2009). My work builds on the work of Barry Cooper, "'A Lump Bred Up in Darknesse': Two Tellurian Themes of the *Republic*," in *Politics, Philosophy, Writing: Plato's Art of Caring for Souls*, Z. Planinc, ed. (Columbia: University of Missouri Press, 2001), 80–121.

Chapter Nine

The Timeliness of Political Philosophy—

Reflecting on the Legacy of Voegelin and Strauss

Jürgen Gebhardt

I

A reflection on the legacy of Voegelin and Strauss must start from the following general questions: What is political philosophy? Why should the political scientist commit himself to it? The "hard-nosed" practitioner may think such questions irrelevant, although he might be willing to go so far as to accept *some* political theory as long as it remains an ancillary subfield within a strict social science understanding of politics. This position was recently maintained by Andrew Rehfeld. In his view, all modes of political theorizing that do not live up to the basic methodological presumptions of "science"[1] should be expelled from the discipline. This so-called "empirical political science," and the diatribe against political philosophy, evokes a sense of déjà-vu.

Years ago, the scholarly enterprise upon which Eric Voegelin and Leo Strauss embarked ran into the same self-contained and self-complacent "empirical" political science that was impervious to a critical examination of the intellectual foundations upon which the ideational and institutional givens of everyday politics are based.[2] Nevertheless, in 1953 Voegelin believed he saw the emergence of just such a political theory: It "has assumed a wide variety of forms according to the variety of conditions that occasion the inquiry. It has at present the general character of movements from different starting points converging toward a common goal rather than of final achievement."[3] In Voegelin's view, Leo Strauss was one of those working toward this "common goal."

In the following reflections on their quest for a theoretically grounded political philosophy, I am not going to offer one more detailed exploration of the theoretical positions of both thinkers and try to stake out the areas of agreement and disagreement between them. The initiated are well aware of the differences, and there is no need to repeat them in a summary fashion for those yet to become acquainted with them. It suffices to advert to the nuanced judgment of Barry Cooper and his coeditor Peter Emberley, who published the Voegelin-Strauss correspondence, thus paving the way for any serious comparative study of these thinkers: Their "apparent disagreement in terminology and details . . . can be seen as a difference in focus rather than of substance. . . . It would be inappropriate to build upon this difference in emphasis an interpretation of doctrinal divergence. Indeed, doctrinalization of thinking is precisely what each attempted to prevent. And this is, for us, the legacy that this correspondence leaves behind."[4]

Insofar as the correspondence points to a "cooperative exegesis of political reality,"[5] it might deepen our understanding of this enterprise to glance at the larger intellectual context and to delineate the larger sphere of theoretical discourse in which Voegelin and Strauss took part—and, I should like to add, in which thinkers like Michael Oakeshott, Hannah Arendt, and Bertrand de Jouvenal also took part. I do not intend to speak of identical theories. These thinkers differ widely in their respective approaches to human affairs, last but not least due to their differing life experiences and intellectual backgrounds. But I would argue that they share a pluri-morphic modality of the understanding of politics that is based on the classical paradigm of a *"peri ta anthropina philosophia."* They are engaged in a science of politics that addresses the questions of the modern human being in terms of the perennial issues of the human condition.

My approach implies that—at least in retrospect—we can discern the development of a multifaceted intellectual enterprise in the post-World War II period. I argue that the salient and common feature of this enterprise is the insight into what is substantial and important in human affairs. These thinkers share not just the principle of critically exploring the political phenomena of the West's twentieth-century crisis, they also subject key elements of modernity to philosophical scrutiny.

What comes into view here is a political science that transcends the intellectual limits of the prevalent modes of political, social, and philosophical theory. In opposition to the conventional tenets of the discipline at that time and the positivism of its basic assumptions, these thinkers—including Hannah Arendt—expressly referred to their enterprise as "political philosophy." Then (and now) political theory and political philosophy were thought of as mere sub-divisions of political science. For this reason, from the very beginning, academic political science conferred upon these thinkers the status of intellectual extraterritoriality. Ignoring the seminal works of Voegelin, Strauss or Arendt, the Anglophone political science establishment engaged in a heated discussion on the "decline of political theory' and proclaimed the "death of political philosophy" in the early fifties.[6] David Easton diagnosed a flight from "scientific reason" as evidenced, among other things, by the turn to "traditionalism."[7] Years later, John G. Gunnell still complained about "the intrusion of ideas promulgated by the German émigrés of the 1930s" being formed "in the context of German philosophy and the practical experience of totalitarianism." In his opinion "many of these individuals represented a position and orientation that threatened some of the basic premises of American political science and political theory."[8]

II

As already stated, Voegelin spoke of a movement toward a re-theoretization of political science, and this movement crystallized in the symbolic form of political philosophy. It started out as the reflective, that is to say, discursive response to the challenge of the crises that befell major parts of the world and that swept away much of what, up to that time, had been considered to be among the certainties of modern civilization. In the last analysis, it was a crisis that threatened to destroy our humanity. But this response also opposed those who viewed the crisis as signaling the essence or fulfillment of modernity. After all, philosophers like Martin Heidegger and Jean-Paul Sartre, the jurist Carl Schmitt, and the political scientist Harold Laski, just to name a few, had hoped and spoken for a historically perfected modernity, even at the expense of all ethical standards of civilization.

What in retrospect looks like a growing community of kindred minds in fact began as a handful of individuals who had distanced themselves from the reigning intellectual climate of opinion in order to re-establish theoretically the true meaning of the human condition. In this sense, I maintain that political philosophy does not merely critically address the crises of modernity, but is a modern intellectual enterprise itself.

With reference to Vico's *New Science*, Voegelin once remarked that "the term *modernity* has no absolute connotation." It was his view that the dominant modern political ideas themselves may in fact have to be considered "old," because they do not take the measure of the historico-political conditions of contemporary human existence. It is these conditions that a truly modern political science must be able to recognize.[9] Thus, I contend that political philosophy articulates itself as a modern discourse. It reflects on modernity within modernity and therefore represents a self-reflecting modernity. Voegelin and Strauss do not revolt against modernity, as one sympathetic observer put it, but instead try to awaken modernity to cognitive self-illumination. For this reason, we may indeed speak of the "timeliness" of political philosophy.

III

At first glance, it might appear petty to point to the semantic evidence that "political philosophy"—considered to be a comprehensive science of politics, Aristotle's architectonic master science—is a modern notion. But Strauss reminds us that "terminology is of paramount importance . . . one is under the obligation to pay the utmost attention to any term which one reads, or which one uses in one's presentation."[10] Voegelin similarly wrestled his entire scholarly life with the problem of finding the appropriate theoretical language. In the end, he formulated a quite radical position: "The symbols of the past ... cannot be used unquestioned as analytical concepts in our present historical situation." They must be reexamined "and this reexamination extends to our common language of 'philosophy,' 'being,' 'theology,' 'religion,' 'myth,' 'reason,' 'revelation' and so forth; a considerable upheaval in the conventional use of these symbols is to be expected."[11] Voegelin did not complete this re-examination himself. Without commenting on it further here, I want to call attention to this important and still unresolved issue of modern political philosophizing.

Strauss relates political philosophy to the tradition rooted in "classical political philosophy." He maintains that, originally, political science was identified with political philosophy and the writings of Plato and Aristotle; it is these writings that document the historical genesis of political science. This is a claim with which Voegelin could agree, and he would certainly not see it as a mere "historical statement." We all know that "philosophia politike" appears only once in the classical corpus;[12] most of antiquity spoke of practical science, or of practical philosophy devoted to the "political," the "ethical," and the "economic."[13] This tri-partition of practical philosophy marked Greek and Latin discourse and was transmitted by Boethius, Cassiodorus, and Isidore of Seville to the pre-Aristotelian tradition of the Middle Ages, as is evident in the famous Didascalicon of Hugo of St. Victor.[14]

According to Bertilloni, this tripartite division of practical philosophy was reduced to a purely formal scheme devoid of any theoretical content. Therefore, he characterizes this "philosophia practica" as "completely depolitized. It therefore acts without the tripartite system." Only in the course of the reception of Aristotle did this scheme of practical philosophy undergo a theoretical systematization in which the central traits of the original Aristotelian paradigm were restored: "That is to say, the difference between the connections that define the position of the individual in each of the three parts of the *philosophia practica*, the logico-ontological primacy of the *politica* over the *ethica* and over the *oeconomica* and the orientation of the ends of these latter two toward the *politica*."[15]

It should suffice here to point to the most exemplary case, that of Thomas Aquinas. In his commentary on Aristotle's *Nicomachean Ethics* the practical sciences fall within the domain of "*philosophia moralis,*" which is divided into "*monastica*" (i.e. individual), "*oeconomica,*" and "*politica*"—the original theoretical meaning of the Aristotelian "*episteme politike.*" It entails the supreme end of human affairs and determines the ultimate end of human life. As far as Aristotle is concerned, it is the most important and the truly architectonic science, and all other practical sciences are subordinated to political science.[16] This restitution of the "*scientia civilis sive politica*" to its dignity as the most important (*principalissima*) of the practical sciences by Thomas and other scholastic commentators on Aristotle rarely uses the term "political philosophy." Outside of this literature and in post-scholastic thought the term does not seem to appear during the Middle Ages.

This is in striking contrast to Islamic and (following suit) Judaic medieval thought: In Alfarabi's reconstruction of Plato and Aristotle, the term "political philosophy" figures prominently.[17] His *Enumeration of the Sciences* and the *Book of Religion* link political science to "political philosophy." "To operate perfectly, the royal craft requires knowledge of that political science which is part of philosophy, as well as knowledge of theoretical philosophy which, according to the *Enumeration of the Sciences*, constitutes the rest of philosophy—it *requires* knowledge of all philosophy." Without probing into the details of Alfarabi's semantics, it suffices to follow Mahdi's expert judgment: "This explicit extension of the domain of political science beyond Aristotelian ethics and politics to encompass a political cosmology and theology, a political psychology, and a political physiology was unheard of before Alfarabi."[18] This understanding of political philosophy became the starting point for Strauss's reconstruction of a modernized notion of political philosophy. As far as I can see on the basis of the semantic evidence, the term "political philosophy" gained only occasional currency in continental Europe in the late eighteenth and early nineteenth century. This change took place in the course of the growth of interdisciplinary specializations. It referred to a branch of philosophy that addresses the sphere of politics proper, as distinguished from philosophy in general and the other specifically philosophical disciplines. The *Encyclopedie* defines political philosophy as that part of philosophy "that teaches men to conduct themselves with caution, either as the head of state or the head of a family."[19] Antonio Rosmini, who published a *Filosofia de la Politica* (1837/39), provided an Italian example.[20] Here again, "*filosofia politica*" was conceived to be a special science that explores the ultimate reasons of the art of governing and whose goal is the realization of the final end of a truly civic community.

In contrast to these examples, the term "political philosophy" was unknown in nineteenth-century Germany. The traditional terms "*praktische Philosophie*" or "*moralische-praktische Wissenschaft*" or more contemporary terms like "*Rechtsphilosophie,*" "*Staatsphilosophie,*" "*Staatswissenschaft,* or "*Staatslehre*" were used instead. In eighteenth century Britain, a sub-disciplinary concept of political philosophy was in use that carried over into nineteenth-century Anglophone scholarship.[21] Here a more comprehensive vision of "political philosophy" developed within the context of "the continuing vitality of the idea of political science."[22]More than anywhere else, "the pervasive common experience of a certain kind of classical education" was a "crucial element in accounting for the nature and appeal of a science of politics". "The hypnotic, unshakeable spell cast by Aristotle's *Politics* is . . . clearly readable on the face" of the literature that set out to create a science of politics.[23] Thus, in 1843, Henry Broughan "produced a massive two-volume treatise on *Political Philosophy* covering everything from the fundamental principles of government, through a comparative account of existing forms, to the rights and duties of citizens and the functions of the states."[24] In the course of the academic institutionalization of the various conceptions of the political and social sciences "political philosophy" appeared on the curricular agenda. Examples may be found in the "moral science tripos" and the "history tripos" at Cambridge in the later nineteenth century, soon to be replaced by the term "political theory."[25] What remained, however, was a more or less canonized series of authoritative texts, extending from Plato and Aristotle to modern political thinkers, that went under the name of "history of political thought."

We may sum up our findings concerning Anglophone intellectual discourse by saying that the notion of political philosophy was more common there than elsewhere, albeit marked by a rather unspecific meaning. It suffered under the weight of an increasingly restricted concept of politics that "ceased to be the comprehensive category under which all that pertained to men's common life was to be assembled."[26]

This short, and quite preliminary, excursion into the history of the concept, tends to substantiate the previously formulated thesis that a comprehensive conceptualization of "political philosophy" as postulated by Strauss and Voegelin played no prominent role in Western intellectual discourse. But the rich symbolic complex of the Western understanding of the perennial issues of the human predicament was a living intellectual force in Strauss's and Voegelin's reconstruction of political science as a political philosophy that faces the challenges of the modern era.

IV

In his critique of the Cambridge School of Political Science (1924), Michael Oakeshott provided the crucial link between the sketch of the development of the concept in British academic literature and a coherent, epistemologically reasoned explication of the meaning of political philosophy. Oakeshott avers that "Political Science and Political Philosophy either mean the same thing or the term science has, in this connection, no valuable meaning at all." The true view of political science defines it as "moral science" and it is "more properly named Political Philosophy than anything else."[27] A closer look at Oakeshott's understanding of political philosophy confirms Eric S. Kos's judgment that it is "not unlike Strauss' Platonic understanding of political philosophy"[28]; and, I would add, it is not unlike Voegelin's either.

Strauss and Voegelin came to Plato and Aristotle in their quest for a philosophical grounding of their differently connoted hermeneutic studies. In their early years, they both adhered to a German vocabulary, even though their paths toward an understanding of the philosophical nature of the political differed—this notwithstanding the biographical fact that each profoundly experienced the intellectual and cultural crisis at the onset of totalitarianism. For Strauss, the starting point was the vexing question of the condition of modern Judaism, the Jewish question as he called it. In his scholarly *Philosophie und Gesetz* (1935) he concluded: "The criticism of the present, the criticism of modern rationalism as the critique of modern sophistry is the necessary beginning, the constant escort, and the unmistakable characteristic of the search for truth which is possible in our time."[29]

The reorientation implied in Strauss's turn to pre-modern rationalism began with a reopening of the quarrel between the moderns and the

ancients, viewed against the background of the "Jewish problem." He discovered the potential for philosophy in the true sense of the word, i.e.,
Platonic philosophy, in medieval Jewish and Islamic philosophy. This
insight was related to his reading of Maimonides, and following suit,
Alfarabi, who for Strauss became the supreme example of the "true
Platonist." As early as 1936 he called Alfarabi the "outstanding mind who
laid the foundation for the later developments and marked their boundaries
insofar as he made the rejuvenation of the Platonic-Aristotelian philosophy—philosophy per se—his duty".[30]

From this vantage point "political science" became identified with "*la
philosophie practique ou politique.*"[31] What Strauss intimated here was
subsequently developed in his mature work: a political philosophy that was
nourished on the spiritual and intellectual potential of classical, that is to
say, Hellenic political philosophy as he had discussed it in a brief lecture
on Maimonides and Cohen (1931). The truth of Socratic questioning
dawned on him as he examined Cohen's interpretation of Plato and
Aristotle: "To philosophize Socratically is to formulate the question . . .
concerning the Good, i.e., what exactly is the Good? Raising the question
of the Idea of the Good, that and that alone is Socratic philosophizing. . . .
The Socratic question regarding the right way to live includes the question
of the right way to live in community, or the right way to live together in
pursuit of the true state. Socratic questioning is essentially political."[32]
This theme is the ground bass of Strauss' political philosophy and his
understanding of the "political philosopher."

The Straussian agenda, as noted above, was intrinsically tied to the
Jewish question, since this is "the most manifest symbol of the human
problem as a social and political problem."[33] He wrote: "I believe I can say
without any exaggeration that since a very early time the main theme of my
reflections has been what is called the Jewish Question." And he offered
the following rare glimpse into the anamnetic depth of his philosophical
existence. As a young boy in his father's house, he met Russian refugees
who had fled a pogrom. To Strauss, who lived peacefully in a safe and well-
ordered social setting, a pogrom seemed something completely impossible.
"Nevertheless this story . . . made a deep impression on me which I have
not forgotten until the present day. It was an unforgettable moment. I
sensed in that moment that it could happen here."[34] This is in accord with
his disapproval of the assimilated Jew: "Why should we, who have a heroic past behind and within us, which is not second to any other group anywhere on earth, deny or forget that past?"[35]

Even though the utmost caution is called for here, in this connection I might be permitted to refer to Voegelin's "anamnetic" experiments, the purpose of which is to "recall those experiences that have opened sources of excitement from which issue the urge for further philosophical reflection."[36] As far as I know, Strauss never published such a self-reflecting meditation aimed at recapturing formative experiences, but this story seems to point to one such experience. Be that as it may, the Jewish question put the political-theological predicament on his agenda of political philosophy, the irresolvable tension between the truth of philosophy and the truth of the Bible, which turned out to be the bone of contention in his encounter with Voegelin.

The background to Voegelin's thought, the young America-experienced Austrian academic, was formed in an intense intellectual exchange within a fairly closed community of scholars. His existential Weberianism reflected on the German predicament of living in a disenchanted world. In contrast to Western societies, German conditions compelled political theory to reflect on the ethical and metaphysical presuppositions of social science. In Germany "(S)ouls are not connected . . . by the kind of firm faith in community values that would protect the instruments of human action from paralysis by the intellect. Instead, each individual is thoroughly exposed to the insecurity that is bound to follow the destruction that includes even this final innermost and unquestionable certitude. Among us (Germans), each individual bears the responsibility for the maxims of his actions in the community." Only "science serves self-reflection and the cognition of the factual contextual whole that our agency must intimate if it is to be responsible."[37]

This scholarly effort requires an "existential philosopher" who "lets the beam of his spirit glide over the world; he lets its meaning shine forth as the means to illuminate his own existence and—if not in order to understand his own meaning in the world—then at least to recognize his place in it."[38] This passage from 1930 anticipates Voegelin's understanding of the "meaning of science as a truthful account of the structure of reality, as the theoretical orientation of man in his world" that he articulated in the *New Science of Politics*.[39]

While still at work on the Weberian project of a comprehensive system of *"Staatslehre"* (theory of the state) based on the results of modern philosophy, Voegelin was confronted with the predicament of an insecure and spiritually unstable society succumbing to National Socialism. This event engendered his break with Weberianism and led to his theoretical reorientation.

On the political level, he moved closer to Christian authoritarianism, since it alone stood for the defense of Austrian independence. On the philosophical plane, he studied Hellenic, Jewish-Arabic, and Christian ideas intensely, and fitted them into his fresh understanding of the meaning of the Aristotelian "theory" of politics: "The question of what is the essence of science can be answered . . . only by a reference to man's specific orientation to *theoria,* to *contemplatio.* In this we follow Aristotle's opinion that *theoria* is the faculty of the *theiotaton* in a human being, [the presence] of the spirit." Thus, theory accomplished what Weber's latitudinarian value-neutral science had to forgo: passing judgment. "By means of its essential openness toward the world, theory can help us prevent the demonizing closure of a communal 'world.' It directs our gaze to the diversity of co-existing communities and can thereby prevent us from raising the value of our own community into an absolute, it directs our gaze through the scaled order of being from nature to God and thereby keeps us from divinizing a lower realm of being."[40]

In contrast to Weber's position, Voegelin notes the conflict between scholarly contemplation and the world of power politics. The theorist's withdrawal from social and political entanglements makes him the contemplative observer and analyst of the world of becoming, reflecting on its origins, causes, and forms, in order to reflect on its "where-from," its "how," and its "why." Theory passes scientific and philosophical judgments on the realm of the political and thus challenges its self-assertiveness. For this reason, in any political community, the contemplating theorist's existence is precarious if he practices the vocation of the scholar: "All thinking about the state is latent high treason."[41] Writing under the precarious conditions of 1937 he observed: "Every political community that has at the same time developed a scientific culture is faced with the problem of protecting its organization of loyalties from knowledge. There is no general rule for a solution. Nevertheless, one could say that sciences that do not deal with matters that are taboo, which is to say, with matters of importance to the organization of loyalties, in general have more space to maneuver . . . while the historical, political science, and social sciences always find themselves in a delicate situation." With reference to Plato's Second Letter, he concludes: "Wise men have therefore drawn the conclusion that many things should be said only within a small circle and certain things said to no one at all."[42] And again in a draft of the Introduction to his *History of Political Ideas* (1939) he reiterates: "We may safely assume that the most important results of political theory never have, and never will, become known except to the more or less happy few."[43]

We find the same theme in Strauss in his distinction between the philosopher's esoteric and exoteric teachings as he unveiled it in his research on medieval Jewish and Islamic thinkers. There he writes: "[P]hilosophy and science must remain the preserve of a small minority, and philosophers or scientists must respect the opinions on which society rests.... [T]his state of things creates a tension between the requirements of social science (knowledge of the truth and teaching of the truth) and the requirements of society (wholehearted acceptance of the principles of society)."[44]

There are three interrelated problems to the philosophical life that is devoted to self-reflexive contemplation. First, the above-discussed question of the socially conditioned personal situation of the thinker. Second, the meditative spirituality of the free and independent thought that advances experientially to the ends of existential illumination. These are the historically universal characteristics of persons engaged in the business of critical questioning. The third aspect, however, refers to the particular modality of practicing the art of philosophizing as it emerges in the effort to understand modernity in terms of philosophical reflection. It is scholarship, but in terms of political philosophy. Its practitioners, like Strauss, Voegelin, or Oakeshott, examine hermeneutically the responses offered in the course of humanity's search for truth in order to reconstruct a science of human existence in society and history that, as Voegelin phrased it, "presents itself with the claim of critical cognizance of order."[45] The "esoteric" part concerns the vocation of the scholar who works "in *Freiheit und Einsamkeit*" as defined by Humboldt. But there is no doubt that Voegelin's and Strauss's commitment to hermeneutic scholarship did in fact induce them to convey their knowledge and insights to the larger audience of those who were willing to share their insights.

At a later date, Voegelin stated that it was the duty of the political philosopher to undertake a critical analysis of reality according to the state of science "for his own sake as a man and to make the results [of science] accessible to his fellowman."[46] Strauss was more restrictive: "the esoteric teaching discloses itself only to the very careful and well trained reader after long and concentrated study."[47] This is a caveat that brings to the fore the intellectual hardships of the true scholarly study of philosophy to which especially the young philosopher must submit. But there is more to it. Esotericism follows from the true meaning of philosophy, i.e., that we cannot be philosophers, we can only try to philosophize. Philosophizing is not an esoteric activity, but it takes the hermeneutic form of listening to the conversations between the great philosophers or, more generally, the great thinkers in the history of humankind.[48]

Playing on the Platonic allegory, Strauss consistently maintained that "today we are in a second, much deeper cave than the fortunate ignorant persons with which Socrates was concerned. . . . We need history first of all to reach the cave from which Socrates can lead us to the light."[49] Today the scholar prepares the way for philosophy and, we may assume, in making the young listen to the voices of the past, he addresses the larger audience of those who desire to leave the second cave.

V

There is agreement between Strauss and Voegelin that the modern political philosopher is the scholar who opens us to the task of philosophical contemplation. In their notion of scholarship, Gadamer remarked, Voegelin and Strauss "remained attached to the German understanding of science."[50] Their scholarship is informed by the shared principles of modern hermeneutics that constitute German "*Geisteswissenschaft.*" In an age of intellectual and political crisis, whatever separated Strauss and Voegelin (taking their Heideggerian and Weberian prehistory, respectively, into account), they agreed on the philosophical importance of historical reflection in order regain a sense of the fundamental issues of human existence.

Voegelin spoke explicitly of the "*Geisteswissenschaft* of Politics" that—contrary to traditional hermeneutics—focuses on the political as the hallmark of human existence. Political philosophy turns to classic political science, not in order to dogmatically reanimate ideas of the past, but to restore political science to the dignity of the science of human existence in history and society.[51] As Strauss wrote: "An adequate understanding of the principles, as elaborated by the classics, may be the indispensable starting point for an adequate analysis . . . of present day society in its peculiar character, and for wise application, to be achieved by us, of these principles to our tasks."[52] In a letter to Strauss Voegelin joined his "critique of the attitude that believes that it understands a thinker better than the thinker understood himself," and shared his "insistence that the object of historical analysis is to recreate the meaning intended by the author."[53]

Strauss was convinced of the self-evidence of his hermeneutic approach and claimed a "textual immanentism" that understands the thought of the past exactly as it understood itself, prior to subsequent interpretation.[54] Voegelin would assent to this position, but he would also insist that the meaning of the sources has to be explicated discursively in rational analysis and that these hermeneutic principles have to be applied within the wider interpretive frame of a discursive inquiry into the nature of man in his historical development.[55]

Insofar as the project of "political philosophy" is a hermeneutically based reconstruction of a political science of order, it seems reasonable to suggest that, in effect, Strauss converted his textual analyses into a comprehensive interpretation of the meaning of the historical course of Western thought and the ensuing cultural crisis of modernity, as did Voegelin in his critical *History of Political Ideas* in which he retraced the making of modern Gnosticism.[56]

VI

Both thinkers express the horizon of the philosophical quest in similar terms but, under closer scrutiny, their views differ in some crucial aspects.

To Strauss, philosophy is a striving for the eternal whole, for the knowledge of God, the world, and man—or rather the quest for knowledge of the nature of things: nature in its totality is "the whole."[57] This modality of questioning expresses the ultimate purpose of philosophizing. Discovered once in classical philosophy, it remains the last and decisive word in the matter, and its complex symbolism requires no further exegesis.

Voegelin conceives the "comprehensive reality of God, world and society" to be the primary experience of cosmic reality. It is the primordial community of being in relation to which humans understand and define their humanity in terms of experiences of transcendence. Thus, human beings articulate their own nature in a differentiating historical process that brings forth the ongoing unfolding of human self-understanding; in the world-historical phenomenon of axial time, it has gained global dimensions.

From this Voegelinian vantage point, the classical philosopher and the revelatory phenomenon of Israel and Christianity mark spiritual turning points in the process of man's struggle to understand his humanity. For this reason, Voegelin originally placed his philosophical inquiry within the orbit of the historical development of human self-understanding that emerged in classical philosophy and Christianity. However, as Voegelin later argued, irrespective of the philosophical relevance of the Western manifestation of a genuine philosophy of order and history, the theorist must also acknowledge the geographical extent and the historical depth of the pluralist process of spiritual irruptions, all of which articulate the nature of the human being.

For Voegelin, the global nature of this process raised the question of whether societies outside the Western evocation of the idea of a universal humankind, that is "the non-Mediterranean Africa, and Europe, the Far East and the Americas," could be excluded from the universality of the human search for humanity and order.[58] Voegelin introduced the philosophical term "universal humanity" in order to denote this pluri-morphic articulation of humanity. Strauss wanted to restrict the philosophical questioning for the transcendent "whole" to the classics; Voegelin conceived the question as a constant in history. It expressed itself in equivalent experiences and symbolizations engendered by the primary tensional structure of existence in the in-between of perfection and imperfection, truth and untruth, life and death, and order and disorder.

Voegelin's later reorientation toward the ecumenic vision of universal humanity took place after Strauss's death. Nevertheless, it is clear why Strauss harbored deep doubts about Voegelin's notion of a philosophical science of order. While they agreed that, to the extent that science concerns itself with the human world, it must be a philosophical science, they disagreed on what constitutes the substance and form of this science, and on how it was to be reconstituted in the face of the contemporary crisis.

Voegelin's form of hermeneutics was determined by the interplay between the cognitive exploration of historical phenomena, based on the one hand on the advancement of the historical and social disciplines that are revealed in the multiple modes of human self-explication, and, on the other, on the reflective analysis of human existence with the intention of deciphering "empirically the patterns of meaning as they reveal themselves in the self-interpretation of persons and societies in history."[59]

For Strauss, this interpretive approach in terms of a philosophy of order and history smacked of historicism, for the truth of classical philosophy is principally "ahistorical." Thus, he insisted on the uniqueness of the classical search for the truth of the whole: it alone can lay claim to being "universally human." In Strauss's view, Voegelin systematically blurred the distinction between reason and revelation by describing them as expressions of equivalent experiences of transcendence. According to Strauss, the faith upon which Judaism and Christianity are based differs from knowledge in that faith does not represent a universal truth.

Throughout his life, Strauss recurred to the irresolvable conflict between philosophical knowledge and biblical faith. "No justifiable purpose is served by obscuring this contradiction, by the postulating of the tertium from there."[60] Strauss would only grant "that both Socrates and the prophets are concerned with justice or righteousness, with the perfectly just society which, as such, would be free of all evils. To this extent Socrates' figuring out the best social order and the prophet's vision of the messianic age are in agreement." But prophets predict the coming of a messianic age, while Socrates merely holds that the perfect society is possible.[61] Strauss does not grant that these symbolisms, Greek thought and biblical faith, merged into the constituent symbolism of European society. To do so would be to harmonize two opposite visions of order and thus create the tertium postulated by Voegelin in his "new science of politics." Where Voegelin attempted to fuse the theory of politics with the theory of history and thus synthesize the realms of philosophy and revelation, Strauss confined philosophical knowledge to the classical mode of questioning and pitted it against revelation.

A closer look at Strauss' understanding of biblical faith reveals that he defines revelation in terms of a self-contained compact body of texts. "Faith in revelation necessarily issues in preaching or proclaiming the message of revelation and therefore ultimately in a teaching."[62] Strauss never subjected this canonized corpus of writings to a historically informed critical analysis: in other words he accepted the dogma of biblical orthodoxy. For this reason, he assumed that Voegelin accepted Christian dogma: "In case you did this we would easily come to an understanding. Because my distinction between revelation and human knowledge to which you object is in harmony with Catholic teaching. But I do not believe that you accept the Catholic teaching. Here a considerable difficulty could result, from your getting rid of the principle of tradition . . . but Catholicism is most consistent in this respect."[63]

This misunderstanding is significant. First, Strauss did (and probably could) not know that Voegelin had never been a practicing Christian, just as Strauss had never been a practicing Jew. Second, Strauss's criticism of Voegelin's theoretical position raises a problem that had troubled others, too. Strauss denied that one could speak of the "religious foundations of classical philosophy." Reading the *New Science* (Voegelin's most "Christian" book), he complained that Voegelin prioritized revelatory knowledge at the expense of true philosophical knowledge. He believed that in doing so, Voegelin based his new science of politics on revelation, and thus turned from political philosophy to political theology, something to be expected of a believer in Christian dogma.

Voegelin attempted to dispel these suspicions concerning the theological and metaphysical "premises" of his study. More clearly than in his letters to Strauss, he explained to Thomas Cook that political science is faced with the fact that experiences of transcendence are constituent elements in social order. "The question whether anybody is an agnostic, or religiously inclined, or whether he is both at the same time . . . has, in my opinion, nothing to (do) whatsoever with theoretical issues. . . . A theory of politics, therefore, must take cognizance of these facts and interpret them on their own terms . . . . As a critical scientist I have to accept these facts of order, whatever my personal opinion about them should be."[64]

At first sight, the theological-political problem (a Straussian concept) seems to figure prominently in some way in the work of all political philosophers, but certainly more so in the thinking of Strauss and Voegelin. But again the difference is striking. With Voegelin, there never was a personal argument with his Christian upbringing or the teaching of the church. The problem that went under the term of "revelation" was always dealt with in terms of the anthropological evidence of human spirituality. In contrast, Strauss's scholarly work was bound up from the beginning with the claims of "revelation" as articulated in Jewish orthodoxy and with his own personal doubts, his lack of faith. Krüger has suggested that the young scholar could not believe (glauben), "and [had] to search for a possibility to live without faith (Glauben)."[65] To Strauss, this meant that one has to choose either the ancient, the Socratic-Platonic possibility, or the modern possibility, the Enlightenment; this choice conditions the nature of one's response to existence in the "second cave."

The solution for Strauss was to return to the Socratic-Platonic philosophy that is to be recognized as the only authentic philosophy because it allows for a life without faith. Krüger's critical response illuminates the Straussian problem: "It is philosophically wrong, to start from the question of one's own life and faith. . . . You orient yourself—albeit negatively—by the revelatory religion (Offenbarungsreligion)."[66] Viewed from this vantage point, an atheistic understanding of Socratic-Platonic philosophy was a necessary step, since it first liberated one from the "factual domination of Christ over the post-ancient humankind" in the form of an "a-Christian philosophy."[67] Second, it laid bare the genuine meaning of revelatory religion grounded on the orthodox reading of the Bible and demonstrated that philosophy (more precisely: political philosophy) and revelation represent two mutually exclusive codes of life and thought. According to Strauss, they are not mere historical paradigms of the human quest for truth and the right life, but are also in themselves legitimated by the fact that neither can refute the other.

In effect, these theses preserve the identity of the Christian, the Muslim, and, last but not least, the Jew. Philosophy, however, transcends this antagonism of codes in that it lives up to the task of "explaining" revelation, as Heinrich Meier, in his nuanced interpretation of "Reason and Revelation," has at least tentatively shown.

Here Strauss pondered "'the task of the philosopher' [and] what a philosophical explanation would have to achieve," and thus underscored "the weight that he accords the explanation of faith and revelation within the confrontation between philosophy and revelation. If the explanation were sufficient philosophy would demonstrate its superiority not only in the demonstrations of its limits of what is possible. Philosophy would prove at the same time to be the judge of the articulation of revelation in human reality."[68]

This tentative "explanation" is briefly alluded to in a passage in which Strauss explained to Voegelin "that the *theioi nomoi* is the common ground of the Bible and philosophy—humanly speaking." And he added: "it is the problem of the multitude of *theioi nomoi* that leads to the diametrically opposed solutions of the Bible on the one hand and philosophy on the other."[69]

In principle, this "political" recourse to the evolution of revelation and philosophy was not too far from Voegelin's notion of the "pneumatic" and "noetic" spiritual breakthrough, and the attendant vision of human order and community in Athens and Israel. "It need not be denied to the philosopher, "Meier interpreted Strauss, "to understand what is at stake when the prophet asserts for himself the experience of the call" as Moses, Paul, or Mohammad have done. "Even this experience . . . he can integrate in the comprehensive movement of reflection in which he takes up what he is not, what is opposed to him and is able to call him into question."[70]

However, this begs the question of why Strauss argued against Voegelin's position that the task of the philosopher-scholar is, on the one hand, to penetrate to the common ground of Moses, Paul and Mohammad, and on the other, to Plato and Aristotle; and this within a theoretical and historical reflection on the whole range of ordering experiences that are symbolized in varying models of "paradigmatic humanity." In this way modern political philosophy would be able to discern the "universal-human" character of the manifold spiritual irruptions and move beyond "the tradition-sanctioned distinction between faith and knowledge."[71]

Ultimately the problem of "belief" and "unbelief" appeared to have been pivotal to Strauss's hermeneutic argument with Voegelin about the "religiousness" of Platonic philosophizing, and more fundamentally to the interrelation of experiences of transcendence and philosophy.

In this regard, the differences in Voegelin's and Strauss's readings of the Parable of the Cave are important. To Voegelin, it describes the turning around, caused by the vision of the Agathon forming the soul through an experience of transcendence, and thus opening it to the ground of truth and knowledge. Whenever Strauss refers to the Parable, he refrains from a closer analysis and merely remarks that "it is only through the perception of the good on the part of the properly equipped human beings that the good city can come into being and subsist for a while."[72]

Where Voegelin envisions a breakthrough to transcendence, Strauss contents himself with the philosopher's apperception of the "truth of the whole" and restricts the Platonic and Aristotelian "theology" to the political realm of the city and the necessary function of the gods to safeguard the laws of the community.[73] In this he has been guided by Alfarabi and Maimonides, who insisted on the bifurcation of the prophet and the philosopher, of faith and reason, and thus confirmed Strauss in his a-theistic interpretation of Platonic political philosophy, and in particular of the Socratic question.

In an early inquiry into Xenophon, he came to the conclusion that "it would be an overstatement to say that philosophy was compatible with Athens: Socrates was executed for not believing in the gods of Athens, in the gods of the city. By considering and reconsidering this fact, we grasp the ultimate reason why political life and philosophy even if compatible for all practicable purposes, are incompatible in the last analysis: political life, if taken seriously, means belief in the gods of the city, and philosophy is the denial of the gods of the city."[74] The question "*quid sit deus*" was never far from Strauss's mind and, in the search for an answer that his hermeneutics denied him, he untiringly returned to Plato's Socrates and to the Socrates of Aristophanes and of Xenophon.[75]

Voegelin moved beyond the dichotomy of reason and revelation and centered the inquiry of the political philosopher on the existential predicament of human existence that is marked by the experience of order and disorder. As it emerged in Voegelin's later studies, the crucial point was that the human being deals with a variety of symbolizations that are evoked by experiences of transcendence and translated into modalities of political agency. It is these that structure the process of history in its global breadth and temporal depth. From his point of view, Voegelin could grant the societal function of normative representations like the gods of the city or any other community in history—civil theologies or religions that sustain the existence of political culture. So Voegelin admits the dictum "'there are no gods, but we must believe in them.' . . . . (T)he gods are the symbols by which transcendence is articulated."[76] But symbolisms may become opaque and void of meaning in the process of the historically open quest for truth. Thus: "The historical scene becomes littered with dead gods."[77]

Thomas L. Pangle quotes from Voegelin's *The Ecumenic Age*: "(T)here is no 'time' in which 'history' happens"—there is only history, that mysteriously fecund 'ground of being' that exhibits a single 'constancy,'" that "of a process that leaves a trail of *equivalent* symbols in time and space." Pangle concludes: "The nature of the hoped for restoration of the existential tension articulated by mythic symbolism is therefore far from clear. Will it necessarily be Christian? Quid sit deus?"[78] Indeed, the process of human self-reflection and self-actualization reveals the ongoing and open-ended struggle for the logos of human order that is the substance of political philosophy. Perhaps Strauss would have appreciated, or at least tolerated, Voegelin's explicit insistence that reflection on the drama of the human condition in time and space takes place within the confines of a philosophy of the political: "The philosopher is not a prophet. The truth as pronounced by the prophet is as valid for him as for any other man; but when the philosopher himself pronounces on the truth of existence, he is not permitted to use the symbols of Revelation, or, for that matter, of Myth. He is in the realm of reason; and in the noetic domain the drama of history is not enacted by the dramatis personae of a Jeremiah."[79]

VII

What Strauss called esoteric insights into the trans-political quest for truth ties in with the fundamental understanding of the contemplative life that transcends the dimension of political life. Voegelin also considered the contemplative life and the life of political action to be mutually dependent manifestations of human nature. Their co-existence is of necessity marked by tension and conflict. A human community cannot exist without the practical achievement of community-formation, but if the community were to suppress the theoretical mode of life, it would also destroy the potential of substantive reason. Strauss's classicism discussed the same problem in terms of the conflict between philosophy and the City. He pointed out that the works of the classical political philosophers are "an attempt to supply a political justification for philosophy by showing that the well-being of the political community depends decisively on the study of philosophy."[80] But political philosophy is in principle ambivalent toward the powers that be since it demands a critical distance to societal power-games. Notwithstanding this reservation, Voegelin and Strauss—both émigrés who were well received in the United States—acknowledged the mental and historical constituents of civility in Western democracy. For the purpose of political education in post-World War II Germany, Strauss applauded Voegelin's exposition of the idea of civil government, its theory, and constitutional practice.[81]

The views of Strauss and Voegelin basically converge in this respect: on the one hand the philosopher-scholar acts as a critical and creative authority, and as the guardian who transmits the standards and principles of order to society by means of persuasion and education; on the other hand he is devoted to the existential search for truth as it is revealed in man's quest for humanity. This search transcends the contingencies of the life-world and reaches out to the whole of human experience, with the intention of bringing it within the purview of discursive understanding, but without forcing it into the straitjacket of a closed system, or into the service of civil theology.

The foregoing considerations on the legacy of Voegelin and Strauss illustrate the essential meaning of "political philosophy" as a modern response to the perennial issues of the human predicament. Why should a political scientist commit himself to political philosophy? Because its theoretical reflection comes to grips with the challenge to apperceive and to understand the political as it has emerged in modernity.

Voegelin and Strauss are paradigmatic figures of political philosophy whose specific agendas may differ, but who both argue from a vision of humanity that has the potential to master the crisis and to rebuild a civil, and therefore a truly human, order for the time being. They never envisioned a blueprint, or a utopia for eternity. Political scientists, of whatever persuasion, should be able to understand the importance and dignity of this task. In this respect, political scientists, aware of the ever-present predicament of human order in history, may act as the guardians of civilization. For this reason, Strauss's and Voegelin's works should not be piously repeated, but the spirit of the works should serve as the source of inspiration for new and keener intellectual explorations of the political.

Endnotes

1   Andrew Rehfeld, "Offensive Political Theory," *Perspectives on Politics*, June 2010, 8(2): 465–86. See also Martyn P. Thomson, "Political Theory in the USA: Some Reflections," *Politisches Denken*, Jahrbuch 2010, Gerhart von Volker et al., eds. (Berlin: Duncker und Humblot, 2010), 107–125.

2   See, Jürgen Gebhardt, "The Vocation of the Scholar," *International and Interdisciplinary Perspectives on Eric Voegelin*, Stephen A. Mcknight and G. L. Price, eds. (Columbia, MO: University of Missouri Press, 1997), 10–34; Jürgen Gebhardt, "Leo Strauss: The Quest For Truth in Times of Perplexity," *Hannah Arendt and Leo Strauss*, P. Graf Kielmannsegg et al., eds. (Cambridge: Cambridge University Press, 1995), 81–104.

3   Eric Voegelin, "The Oxford Political Philosophers," *Published Essays, 1953–1965, Collected Works of Eric Voegelin,* vol. 11, Ellis Sandoz, ed. (Columbia, MO: University of Missouri Press, 2000), 15–46, 27.

4   Peter Emberley and Barry Cooper, "Introduction," *Faith and Political Philosophy: The Correspondence Between Leo Strauss and Eric Voegelin, 1934–1964*, P. Emberley and B. Cooper, eds. (University Park, PA: Penn State University Press, 1993), xxv.

5   Ibid., xi.

6   Alfred Cobban, "The Decline of Political Theory," *Political Science Quarterly*, September 1953: 335; Petri Koikkalainen, "Peter Laslett and the Contested Concept of Political Philosophy," *History of Political Thought* 20(2), Summer 2009: 336–59.

7   David Easton, *The Political System* (New York: Alfred A. Knopf, 1953), 17.

8   John G. Gunnell, *Between Philosophy and Politics: The Alienation of Political Theory* (Amherst: University of Massachusetts Press, 1986), 13–14.

9   Eric Voegelin, *Revolution and the New Science, History of Political Ideas VI, Collected Works*, vol. 24, Barry Cooper, ed. (Columbia, MO: University of Missouri Press, 1998), 146.

10 Leo Strauss, "How to Begin to Study Medieval Philosophy," *The Rebirth of Classical Political Rationalism* (Chicago: University of Chicago Press, 1989), 207–226, 220.

11 Eric Voegelin, *What is History? and Other Late Unpublished Writings, Collected Works* vol. 28, Thomas Hollweck and Paul Caringella, eds. (Columbia, MO: University of Missouri Press, 1990), 230.

12 Aristotle, *Politics* 1282b20.

13 E.g., Diogenes Laertius, *Lives and Opinions of Eminent Philosophers*, R. D. Hicks, trans., Loeb Classical Library (Cambridge: Harvard University Press, 1950), vol. I, V,28, 474. As far as I can see, to date there is no comprehensive study of the semantic concept of "political philosophy."

14 Cf. F. Bertilloni, "Les schemes de la *philosophia practica* anterieurs a 1265: Leur vocabulaire concernant la *Politique* leur role dans la reception de la *Politique* d'Aristotle," *L'Elaboration du Vocabulaire Philosophique au Moyen Age*, J. Hamesse and C. Steel, eds. (Turhout: Brepols Publishers, 2000), 171–202, 176–81; Hugo of St. Victor, *Didascalicon* II, 19.

15 "C'est–a-dire la difference entre les liens qui definissent la situation de l'individu en chacun des trios parties de la *philosophia practica*, le primat logico-ontologique de la *politica* sur l'*ethica* et sur l'*oeconomica* et l'orientation des fins de ces dernieres vers la *politica*" (Bolletini, "Philosophia practica," 183). Translated by editors.

16 *Corpus Thomisticum, Sententia libri Ethicorum*, liber I, lectio 2, 1–3; see *Commentary on Aristotle's Nicomachean Ethics* (South Bend: Dumb Ox Books, 1993), 9–10.

17 Alfarabi, *The Political Writings*, Charles Butterworth, ed. (Ithaca, NY: Cornell University Press, 2001), 78 and passim.

18 Mahdi Muhsin, *Alfarabi and the Foundation of Islamic Political Philosophy* (Chicago: University of Chicago Press, 2001), 120, 122.

19 M. Diderot and M. D'Alembert, *Encyclopedie*, Nouvelle Edition, vol. 26 (Geneva: Pellet, 1778), 553. Translated by editors.

20 Recent edition: Antonio Rosmini, *Filosofia della Politica*, Sergio Cotta, ed. (Milan: Rusconi, 1985).

21 William Paley, *Principles of Moral and Political Philosophy* (London: R. Faulder, 1785).

22 Stefan Collini, Donald Winch, John Burrow, *The Noble Science of Politics* (Cambridge: Cambridge University Press, 1983), 11.

23 Ibid., 375–76.

24 Ibid., 57.

25 Ibid., 347–50.

26 Ibid., 374.

27 Michael Oakeshott, *What Is History? and Other Essays*, Luke O'Sullivan, ed. (Exeter: Imprint Academic, 2004), 50, 56; compare Oakeshott's exposition of political philosophy in Michael Oakeshott, *Religion, Politics and the Moral Life*, Timothy Fuller, ed. (New Haven, CT: Yale University Press, 1993), 226–27.

28 Eric S. Kos, *Michael Oakeshott, the Ancient Greeks & the Philosophical Study of Politics* (Exeter: Imprint Academic, 2007), 131.

29 Leo Strauss, *Philosophie und Gesetz—Frühe Schriften, Gesammelte Schiften*, band 2, ed., Heinrich Maier (Stuttgart: J.B. Metzler, 1997), 9–10.

30 Leo Strauss, "Eine vermißte Schrift Farabis," *Gesammelte Schriften*, band 2, 176.

31 Leo Strauss, "Quelque remarques sur la science politique de Maimonide et de Farabi," *Gesammelte Schriften, Band 2*, 132–33. See his marginalia referring to the Platonic and Aristotelian division of practical science ("Farabi's Plato," *Louis Ginzberg: Jubilee Volume on the Occasion of his Seventieth Birthday*, (New York, The American Academy for Jewish research, 1945), 357–93); Leo Strauss, "How Farabi Read Plato's Laws," *What Is Political Philosophy?* (Glencoe, IL: Free Press of Glencoe, 1959), 134–54.

32 Leo Strauss, "Cohen und Maimuni," *Gesammelte Schiften*, band 2, 411–12.

33 Leo Strauss, *Spinoza's Critique of Religion* (New York: Schocken Books, 1965), 6.

34 Leo Strauss, "Why We Remain Jews: Can Jewish Faith and History Still Speak to Us?" in *Leo Strauss: Political Philosopher and Jewish Thinker*, Kenneth Deutsch and Walter Nicgorski eds. (Lanham, Md.: Rowman & Littlefield, 1994), 44.

35 Leo Strauss, "Progress or Return," *The Rebirth of Classical Political Rationalism*, Thomas L. Pangle, ed. (Chicago: University of Chicago Press, 1989), 232.

36 Eric Voegelin, *Anamnesis: On The Theory of History and Politics, Collected Works of Eric Voegelin*, vol. 6, David Walsh, ed. (Columbia, MO: University of Missouri Press, 2002), 84.

37 Eric Voegelin, "Max Weber", *Published Essays, 1929–1933, Collected Works of Eric Voegelin*, vol. 8, Thomas Heilke and John von Heyking, eds. (Columbia, MO: University of Missouri Press, 2003), 133–34.

38 Ibid., 133–34.

39 Eric Voegelin, *The New Science of Politics*, in *Modernity Without Restraint: The Political Religions; The New Science of Politics; and Science, Politics, and Gnosticism, Collected Works of Eric Voegelin*, vol. 5, Manfred Henningsen, ed. (Columbia, MO: University of Missouri Press, 2000), 91.

40 Eric Voegelin, "Popular Education, Science, and Politics," *Published Essays, 1934–1939, Collected Works of Eric Voegelin*, vol. 9, Thomas W. Heilke, ed. (Columbia, MO: University of Missouri Press 2001), 90.

41 Eric Voegelin, unpublished Fragment on Max Weber (ca. 1936), quoted in Jürgen Gebhardt, "Introduction," *Selected Correspondence 1924–1949, Collected Works of Eric Voegelin*, vol. 29, Jürgen Gebhardt, ed. (Columbia, MO: University of Missouri Press, 2009), 30–31.

42 Eric Voegelin, "Was dürfen die Menschen wissen?" (1937) ("What May People be Allowed to Know?"), *Published Essays, 1934–1939, Collected Works of Eric Voegelin*, vol. 9, 119.

43 Eric Voegelin, "Introduction to the 'History of Political Ideas," *Hellenism, Rome, and Early Christianity, History of Political Ideas I, Collected Works of Eric Voegelin*, vol. 19, Athanasios Moulakis, ed. (Columbia, MO: University of Missouri Press, 1997), Appendix A, 233. See Voegelin's response to Max Mintz's critique of this position (*Selected Correspondence 1924–1949*), 244–45.

44 Leo Strauss, "On a Forgotten Kind of Writing," *What is Political Philosophy?* (Glencoe, IL: The Free Press of Glencoe, 1959), 222.

45 Voegelin, *Anamnesis*, 342.

46 Eric Voegelin, *Israel and Revelation, Order and History I, Collected Works of Eric Voegelin*, vol. 14, Maurice P. Hogan, ed. (Columbia, MO: University of Missouri Press, 2001), 24.

47 Strauss, "Forgotten Kind of Writing," 222.

48 Leo Strauss, "What is Liberal Education?", *Liberalism: Ancient and Modern* (New York: Basic Books, 1968), 7.

49 Leo Strauss, "Besprechung von Julius Ebbinghaus, Über die Fortschritte der Metaphysik" (1931), *Gesammelte Schiften*, band 2, 437–39, 439.

50 Hans-Georg Gadamer, "Philosophizing in Opposition: Strauss and Voegelin on Communication and Science," *Faith and Political Philosophy*, 249–59, 249.

51 Eric Voegelin, *New Science of Politics*, 89.

52 Leo Strauss, "Political Philosophy and the Crisis of Our Time," *The Postbehavioral Era: Perspectives on Politics*, G.J. Graham and G.W. Carey, eds. (New York: Davis McKay Company, 1972), 217–242, 229.

53　Voegelin to Strauss, March 12, 1949, *Selected Correspondence, 1924–1949, Collected Works of Eric Voegelin*, vol. 29, 609.

54　See Norbert Altwicker, "Vorwort" in Leo Strauss, *Die Religionskritik Spinozas als Grundlage seiner Bibelwissenschaft* (Darmstadt: Wissenschaftliche Buchgesellschaft, 1981), x–xi.

55　Voegelin to Heilman, August 22, 1956, *Selected Correspondence 1950–1984, Collected Works of Eric Voegelin*, vol. 30, Thomas Hollweck, ed. (Columbia, MO: University of Missouri Press, 2007), 293.

56　Unfortunately there is still no theoretically and methodologically informed study of the modern hermeneutic scholarship of Voegelin, Strauss, and of Arendt and Oakeshott.

57　Leo Strauss, "What is Political Philosophy?", *What is Political Philosophy?*, 11.

58　Eric Voegelin, *The Ecumenic Age, Order and History* IV, *Collected Works of Eric Voegelin*, vol. 17, Michael Franz, ed. (Columbia, MO: University of Missouri Press, 2000), 376.

59　Eric Voegelin, *The Ecumenic Age, Order and History* IV, 106.

60　Strauss to Voegelin, March 25, 1951, *Faith and Political Philosophy*, 78.

61　Leo Strauss, "Jerusalem and Athens—Some Preliminary Reflections," *Studies in Platonic Political Philosophy*, (Chicago: Chicago University Press, 1983), 171.

62　Leo Strauss, "Reason and Revelation," in Heinrich Meier, *Leo Strauss and the Theologico-Political Problem* (Cambridge: Cambridge University Press, 2007), 141–180, 141, see 148–149.

63　Strauss to Voegelin, June 4, 1951, *Faith and Political Philosophy*, 89.

64　Voegelin to Cook, December 30, 1953, *Selected Correspondence 1950 – 1984*, 187–188.

65　Strauss to Krüger, December 27, 1932, *Hobbes' politische Wissenschaft und zugehörige Schriften – Briefe, Gesammelte Schriften*, band 3, Heinrich Maier, ed. (Stuttgart: J.B. Metzler, 2008), 414,420.

66　Krüger to Strauss, December 29, 1932 *Gesammelte Schriften*, band 3, 424.

67　Strauss to Krüger, draft of a letter, December 27, 1932, *Gesammelte Schriften*, band 3, 415, 416.

68　Meier, *Strauss and the Theologico-Political Problem*, 32.

69　Strauss to Voegelin, February 25, 1951, *Faith and Political Philosophy*, 78.

70　Meier, *Strauss and the Theologico-Political Problem*, 43.

71　Strauss to Voegelin, June 4, 1951, *Faith and Political Philosophy*, 89.

72　Leo Strauss, *The City of Man* (Chicago: Rand McNally, 1964), 119.

73　Leo Strauss, *The Argument and the Action of Plato's Laws* (Chicago: University of Chicago Press, 1975), 156, 182–183.

74　Leo Strauss, "The Spirit of Sparta or the Taste of Xenophon," *Social Research*, 6, 1939: 502–536, 532.

75　Leo Strauss, *Socrates and Aristophanes*, (New York: Basic Books, 1966); Leo Strauss, *Xenophon's Socratic Discourse* (South Bend, IN: St. Augustine's Press, 1998); Leo Strauss, *Xenophon's Socrates* (South Bend, IN: St. Augustine's Press, 1998).

76　Voegelin to Robert Heilman, December 30, 1958, *Selected Correspondence, 1950–1984*, 371.

77 Eric Voegelin, *In Search of Order, Order and History* V, *Collected Works of Eric Voegelin*, vol. 18, Ellis Sandoz, ed. (Columbia, MO: University of Missouri Press, 2000), 84.

78 Thomas L. Pangle, "Leo Strauss and Eric Voegelin on the Meaning of Modernity," Paper Prepared for delivery at the 2010 Annual Meeting of the American Political Science Association, September 2–5, 2010, 3.

79 Voegelin, *What is History? and Other Late Unpublished Writings, Collected Works* vol. 28, 50. An interesting case of misreading the theoretical intentions of either thinker is John J. Ranieri, *Disturbing Revelation: Leo Strauss and Eric Voegelin and the Bible* (Columbia, MO: University of Missouri Press, 2009). In Ranieri's view their critique of biblical teaching is unconvincing because it is conducted "from the perspective of classical political philosophy" and, so Rainieri argues, it is conducted on the "basis of a highly idealized abstraction... in the sense of a set of ideas lacking institutional embodiment in the present" (231). Whatever that may mean?

80 Leo Strauss, "On classical Political Philosophy," *What is Political Philosophy?*, 93.

81 Eric Voegelin, "Democracy in the New Europe," *Published Essays, 1953–1965, Collected Works of Eric Voegelin*, vol. 11, 65. See Strauss to Voegelin, February 11, 1960, *Faith and Political Philosophy*, 103–104: "I do not have to tell you why it would be very good if it were made accessible to American political scientists." See also Catherine and Michael Zuckert, *The Truth about Leo Strauss: Political Philosophy and American Democracy* (Chicago: University of Chicago Press, 2006), 78–79 and passim.

Chapter Ten

A Probing of Consciousness

Jene M. Porter

In his essay, "Eric Voegelin, Empirical Political Scientist," Professor Barry Cooper presents three meanings that Voegelin, following Aristotle, gives to the concept of experience that is so fundamental to empiricism. The first meaning is "the undemonstrated sayings and opinions of experienced people," who, Cooper goes on to say, have developed the eye to see things aright and have an "openness to phenomena." The second meaning is related to the fact that the very premises of science are "established by experience"; therefore, experience generates "criteria for selection or exclusion of phenomena within a science." The third meaning, found in Aristotle's *Posterior Analytics* (100a 3ff), is that perception leads to memories, and memories of the same phenomena constitute an experience that comes to "rest in the soul." The third dimension to experience brings us to the analysis of consciousness. Since experience presumes consciousness, "empirical political science includes the analysis of consciousness by the consciousness of the analyst."[1]

Defining empiricism, as Voegelin wished to do, through the foundational category of experience presents, at first glance, a host of difficulties. There is an eerie mirror-image resemblance to the very positivism that Voegelin wants to replace in that experience appears to function in an explanation the same way that sense data did for positivism. In short, there is a structural similarity between the two epistemologies. For positivists, the objective and non-personal attributes of sense data provided reliable and solid contact with "empirical reality" and thereby an openness to, and knowledge of, phenomena. For Voegelin, experiences are reliable because of their ultimate rest in the true order of the soul. In Voegelin's words, "the true order of the soul . . . furnishes the standard for measuring and classifying the empirical variety of human types as well as of the social order in which they find their expression."[2]

Some of the difficulties with these epistemologies can be briefly noted. Is not the structure of an explanation the same in both cases: i.e., that there is a presumed unproblematic base for openness to phenomena? Is not Voegelin's using of experience epistemologically privileged in the same sense that sense data were once claimed to be? One inescapable difficulty with such explanations is that the foundational categories of sense data and experience are porous and imbued by the philosophic and cultural themes of an age.[3]

It is only fair to note that Voegelin did not write a retrospective in which he reworked these earlier epistemological formulations. However, he did continue to explore the nature of consciousness, the precondition of experience, however defined, and this topic would therefore seem to present a more fruitful topic for analysis. Accordingly, I will address the nature of consciousness in Voegelin's thought. Voegelin famously said that his followers should "get on with it," by which, as I understand it, he meant spending less time explicating him and more time doing analyses that follow in Voegelin's philosophical footsteps. Professor Cooper's many works are admirable examples of getting on with it. In this spirit, my essay will probe the questions of how well Voegelin's philosophy can handle the problem of consciousness. Can it provide greater clarity? Does it explore dimensions of the problem not visible before? Is his solution more adequate and fruitful than others? To aid in this examination, I have chosen the work of the contemporary philosopher, John Searle, who has written extensively on the mind, intention, and consciousness.[4] While Searle is the most famous of contemporary philosophers in this area, he does represent a minority position within philosophy. Nevertheless, he is not a materialist or functionalist, and this means that a philosophic conversation between his work and Voegelin's is indeed possible without having to start from the very beginning.

To set the stage for an examination of Voegelin's potential contribution to this issue, I will give a brief summary of the various positions that have been taken, a longer explication of Searle's own position, and finally a look at whether Voegelin's philosophy of consciousness can be of much use in approaching this issue.

I

The vast literature on the philosophy of mind that has developed since Descartes can be broken into two groups: property dualists and materialists. The latter group includes their first cousins, behaviorists and functionalists. Dualism in various forms dominated the first three centuries of modernity, but, starting in the twentieth century, materialism and its variants are in a clear ascendancy.

Initially, Descartes appeared to have established that there are two sub-
stances in reality (ignoring for the moment the eternal substance of God):
"the one of created substance which thinks, the other of corporeal substance, provided we carefully separate all the attributes of thought from
those of extension."[5] We humans, then, are body and mind, but, as everyone knows, Descartes proceeds to view us as united in some fashion. We
are embodied minds in the sense that the mind operates on the body
through the brain. As Descartes reasons, from the *cogito* we can indisputably establish the existence of the mind, self, and consciousness.
Moreover, each of these three features of our nature is affected by, but
independent of, our body.

Although dualism was a persuasive theory, there have been many objections to it. I will give only three major ones that have pushed most philosophers to some variant of materialism. First, Wittgenstein, in *Philosophical
Investigations*, refuted the idea of a private language and by so doing dealt a
deadly blow to key features of the Cartesian theory of mind. There are features of Descartes's model of the mind that, Wittgenstein argues, are incoher-
ent. Descartes's mind is a non-corporeal substance, known through introspection, and standing in a privileged relationship with the self, soul, and
body. If the mind were so constituted, how could one speak of sensations and
feelings? Each person would have his own language for labeling what was
going on in his or her mind. A private language, in short, would be necessary. Wittgenstein, through a famous thought experiment, shows how a private language cannot communicate and, strictly speaking, cannot even exist:

> Suppose everyone had a box with something in it: we call it a 'bee-
> tle.' No one can look into anyone else's box, and everyone says he
> knows what a beetle is only by looking at *his* beetle.—Here it
> would be quite possible for everyone to have something different
> in his box. One might even imagine such a thing constantly chang-
> ing.—But suppose the word 'beetle' had a use in these people's
> language.—If so it would not be used as a name of a thing. The
> thing in the box has no place in the language-game at all; not even
> as a *something*: for the box might even be empty.—No, one can
> 'divide through' by the things in the box; it cancels out, whatever
> it is.
>
> That is to say: if we construe the grammar of the expression of
> sensation on the model of 'object and designation' the object drops
> out of consideration as irrelevant.[6]

Perhaps even more telling is the fact that a private language could not even function as a language since there are no rules for determining if the usage is appropriate or not. Private language could not communicate with oneself. Not to belabor the point, language requires public rules and practices in which others can enter.

A second set of objections to dualism centers around the connection between mind and body. These objections flow from the sharp distinction between material bodies and events and mental phenomena. Simply put, material bodies have mass and space; consequently, force and motion can cause change. How can a physical body cause change in phenomena—mental states—that do not have space or mass? How can there be cause and action in either direction? Moreover, there seems to be no empirical way in which one could even study such a purported connection. There simply can be no plausible theory providing a connection between mental states and objects with space or mass, although many attempts have been made.[7]

A third objection to dualism is less a set of objections than the accumulated force of modernity itself. It seems impossible to have an epistemology that would be acceptable to science and to argue simultaneously for some kind of property dualism. Dualism often is accused, for example, of being an ersatz duplicate of the real "thing" epistemologically: the empirical and logical methods of science provide knowledge of the external physical world; this knowledge can be expressed in third-person, neutral, and testable language. It is not persuasive to argue that introspection also provides a kind of "empirical" knowledge of mental phenomena. Soul-stuff, mind-stuff, and, as we shall see, even consciousness-stuff are held to be only the stuff of ridicule and incompatible with a scientific world-view. In Searle's words, there is "a terror of falling into Cartesian dualism."[8] The result of these and many other objections to dualism has been a turn to materialism, in particular to functionalism and behaviorism. Most philosophers believe that there are only two choices, property dualism or some variant of materialism. Not surprisingly, the last half of the twentieth century has witnessed an enormous amount of energy and cleverness spent on developing a plausible material theory to account for consciousness.

There is a configuration of positions surrounding materialism, regardless of the variant, which enables it to be at home with modernity and to escape the philosophic schizophrenia associated with property dualism. One of these positions is that the mind and consciousness are ontologically subjective. In contrast, reality is objective and can be studied using impartial, non-personal, third-person language. Since this conception of reality is held to be true, it follows that the only way in which the brain can be studied is by examining its functioning and by examining human behavior. In both cases, third-person observations are possible, and mental phenomena can be treated in a fashion consistent with our understanding of reality and of science. The connection between mental phenomena and our physical nature is still viewed as an area requiring a plausible theory and further research. But there is the great hope among many scholars that a new scientific breakthrough is possible. Materialists of all stripes take comfort in the future of cognitive science and in the evolution of computers. Indeed, William Lycan, a functionalist, puts the question: "What moral rights would an intermediate or marginally intelligent machine have?"[9] These machines will be used as labor-saving devices, and, therefore, there will be questions of exploitation.

Searle attacks such triumphant materialism, but he claims that his arguments against materialism are nevertheless consistent both with a scientific world-view and with an acknowledgment of the reality of consciousness. He calls his position biological naturalism.

Except for Searle and a minority of others, materialism in some guise or other appears to be the only option, given the obvious inadequacies of property dualism. This, it should be added, is a materialism with no place for any ontological status to consciousness and mind. Searle has to address two tasks: he must show the inadequacies of the dominant materialist theories that purport to explain away or to refute the alleged reality of consciousness; he must show how his recognition of the reality of consciousness is consistent with modern science.

Searle examines a large number of theories, but for our limited purposes, a few will be sufficient to outline his major criticisms. All of these theories, as well as Searle's, have to account for certain apparently intractable characteristics of consciousness. Above all, consciousness is subjective, not in the pejorative sense of being a topic that is hopelessly partial or one in which knowledge claims cannot be made. Rather, consciousness has always a first-person existence, which immensely complicates our understanding. It is true that we can recognize mental states in others, but the mental states always belong to someone else. In this sense, the so-called real, natural world itself has an obvious subjective element. We see mental states and consciousness in others but only by their external manifestations upon external behavior. Then, the manifestations can be put in a third-person form. We remain one removed. Our own conscious-ness, too, is not amenable to self-examination or introspection as if it were an external object. Again, an "objective," third-person observation is impossible. As Searle echoes Voegelin: "Any introspection I have of my own conscious state is itself that conscious state."[10]

The great difficulty, in sum, is that the bulk of reality can be known objectively in that all competent observers have equal access to reality and in that explanations can be expressed in a neutral, third-person form, but we simply cannot explain consciousness in the ways that we explain other phenomena in reality, or so it appears to common sense. We have to rely upon manifestations in behavior and relationships with others and with a context. The actual subject of consciousness is not observed. The visual metaphor for knowing is not helpful for consciousness. Introspection can-not be a seeing turned inward. One does not relate to consciousness as if it were an external object to be examined. The spatial metaphor for knowing is equally unsatisfactory: the mind is not a special place to which one has privileged access for knowing. Both metaphors fail. Neither my own sub-jectivity nor that of others can be treated as simply an external object to be observed.

Remarkable ingenuity has been shown by various materialists in try-ing to meet these and other difficulties in forming an adequate theory of consciousness.[11] Searle is critical of all of them. Behaviorism, no longer in vogue, is quickly dismissed by most philosophers, regardless of approach.[12] Searle, too, gives it short shrift. Gilbert Ryle and others had argued that sentences about the mind could all be translated into sentences about behavior and thereby cover all of the phenomena involved: "intelli-gent performances are not clues to the mind; they are those workings."[13] As he says, there are not two things called body and mind. There is no "ghost in the machine."[14] One standard counter, which Searle repeats, is that behavior cannot be explained without resource to one's beliefs, which are mental acts.

> . . . [A]ccording to a standard behaviorist account, to say that John believes that it is going to rain is simply to say that John will be disposed to close the windows, put the garden tools away, and carry an umbrella if he goes out. In the material mode of speech, behaviorism claims that the mind is just behavior and dispositions to behavior. . . .
>
> John's belief that it is going to rain will be manifested in the

behavior of closing the windows only if we assume such additional hypotheses as that John doesn't want the rainwater to come in
through the windows and John believes that open windows admit
rainwater. If there is nothing he likes better than rain streaming in
through the windows, he will not be disposed to close them.
Without some such hypothesis about John's desires (and his other
beliefs), it looks as if we cannot begin to analyze any sentence
about his original beliefs.[15]

Another counter example is to create a Tinfoil Man, a cleverly constructed robot operated by electronic engineers. The Tinfoil Man then
replicates all sorts of human behavior. The "explanation" of the behavior
of such a creation would be the equivalent for a behaviorist of an "explanation" for a human. Such an "explanation" would be absurd, since the
Tinfoil Man is empty.[16] Yet another counter example, used by Searle, is that
of acting: "One can easily imagine an actor of superior abilities who could
give a perfect imitation of the behavior of someone in pain even though the
actor in question had no pain, and one can also imagine a superspartan who
was able to endure pain without giving any sign of being in pain."[17] This
willful reliance only on external manifestations has led critics to characterize behaviorist theory as one "feigning anesthesia."[18] To put it bluntly,
behaviorists have to deny that beliefs and desires, i.e., mental states, cause
behavior.

Behaviorism's inadequacies were the result of adhering in cult-like
fashion to an empirical methodology, which led to a denigration of consciousness and mental acts. Behaviorists dismissed the phenomena of consciousness and mental acts by referring only to their manifestations. These
could be empirically known, were therefore real, and were all that existed.
No mental or ghostly residue was left over needing an explanation.
Cartesian dualism, the argument concludes, was therefore escaped.

Far more reputable than behaviorism is identity theory. This position
is simple: mental states are identical with states in the brain and the central nervous system. Contrary to the behaviorist view, in identity theory
mental states are inner. They are the intermediary between stimulus and
response, and they are the manifestations or measurable inputs and out-
puts of the human body.[19] A common example used is pain. It is held to
be a mental phenomenon resulting from a certain neurophysiological
state. This theory purports to eliminate the independent reality of mental
states by identifying them with physical states. One of many problems

with identity theory is that it is logically impossible to identify a state of the brain as being mental without having a prior identifying mental state. Not only does an infinite regress occur, but identity theory, in effect, is claiming to identify the mental with the non-mental and "without leaving out the mental."[20]

The attraction of identity theory was that it appeared to be a clear improvement over behaviorism. But, it too flounders upon an empirical fundamentalism. The crude physicalism undergirding identity theory could never be shown in any case. The attempt to eliminate consciousness and mental states only leads to a logical reliance on the mental states that are then to be identified with neurophysiological states. Identity theory is not satisfying, logically or empirically.

Functionalism—and it too has many varieties—claims to be an improvement over the simple physicalism found in identity theory. Functionalism maintains that mental states are actually operations of the brain system, which in turn are physical states with causal powers. The following example, used by Searle, shows how to have a functional analysis of the belief that it is raining:

> That belief will be a state of my brain, but a computer or some other system might have the same belief although it has a completely different physical/chemical composition. So what fact about my brain state makes it that belief? The functionalist answer is that a state of a system—human, computer, or otherwise—is a belief that it is raining if the state has the right causal relations. For example, my belief is a state of my brain caused by my looking out the window when rain is falling from the sky, and this state together with my desire not to get wet (another functional state of my brain) causes a certain sort of output behavior, such as my carrying an umbrella. A belief, then, is any physical state of any physical system which has certain sorts of physical causes, and together with certain sorts of other functional states such as desires, has certain sorts of physical effects.[21]

Functionalism of various kinds is now dominant; the development of cognitive science as a discipline and our growing reliance on computers have further increased its appeal.[22]

The chief criticisms of functionalism—echoing criticisms of the other theories—point to its inability to recognize meaning and conscious mental acts. One renowned criticism is Searle's Chinese room argument.

> Simply imagine that someone who understands no Chinese is locked in a room with a lot of Chinese symbols and a computer program for answering questions in Chinese. The input to the system consists in Chinese symbols in the form of questions; the output of the system consists in Chinese symbols in answer to the questions. We might suppose that the program is so good that the answers to the questions are indistinguishable from those of a native Chinese speaker. But all the same, neither the person inside nor any other part of the system literally understands Chinese; and because the programmed computer has nothing that this system does not have, the programmed computer, qua computer, does not understand Chinese either.[23]

The formal, functional system cannot recognize the meaning of any word or sentence. Consciousness and the mind are eliminated in this functional stimulation of human knowing, and, obviously, meaning is lost. The functional program does not duplicate human knowing.[24]

Perhaps a more powerful illustration of the emptiness of functionalism, not used by Searle, is Helen Keller's precise but eloquent description of learning sign language. For some time, she explains in a telling metaphor, she was just making her "fingers go in monkey-like imitation." This was only information recording and processing—to use the language dear to functionalists—but it was not language with meaning. One day her teacher put Keller's hand under a spout of water. In itself, this method of teaching was no different from what the teacher had been doing in the "naming" of all of the other objects the child contacted. Now, however, there was a difference:

> As the cool stream gushed over one hand she spelled into the other the word *water*, first slowly, then rapidly. I stood still, my whole attention fixed upon the motions of her fingers. Suddenly I felt a misty consciousness as of something forgotten—a thrill of returning thought; and somehow the mystery of language was revealed to me. I knew that that "w-a-t-e-r" meant the wonderful cool something that was flowing over my hand. That living word awakened my soul, gave it light, hope, joy, set it free! There were barriers still, it is true, but barriers that could in time be swept away.
>
> I left the well-house eager to learn. Everything had a name, and each name gave birth to a new thought. As we returned to the house every object which I touched seemed to quiver with life.

That was because I saw everything with the strange, new sight that had come to me. On entering the door I remembered the doll I had broken. I felt my way to the hearth and picked up the pieces. I tried vainly to put them together. Then my eyes filled with tears; for I realized what I had done, and for the first time I felt repentance and sorrow.[25]

After Keller's description of her theophany, it is flat and redundant to say that this act of knowing was a conscious act requiring a movement of the imagination linking reality, language, and reason. A machine "detecting" H_2O or quartz on Mars is not doing the same; the only detecting is done by engineers who constructed and are reading the machine's sign language. Wittgenstein says of labeling, i.e., the monkey-like imitation mentioned by Keller, that it is only "preparatory to the use of a word. But *what* is it a preparation for?"[26] Without the ability to use it, it has no meaning.[27] This ability flows from the conscious use of the imagination, for lack of a better phrase, and, to repeat, without this capacity there is no meaning.[28]

Although this is only a cursory description of the many theories of mind and consciousness that now abound, there is nevertheless, as Searle notes, a dreary similarity to their failings. All are driven to be acceptably scientific, as they define the term; all repeat the catechism that they have avoided Cartesian dualism; and all have eliminated even the ghosts of consciousness and mind. We can now turn to Searle's own theory of consciousness.

II

Searle's thesis is that "consciousness is just an ordinary biological feature of the world."[29] We find it enormously difficult to grasp that consciousness is both real and distinct as well as a biological phenomenon. Part of the difficulty flows from the Cartesian frame of thinking from which modernity has evolved. As Searle argues, the Cartesian distinction between *res cogitans* and *res extensa*, mind and body, has been so indisputably useful in the development of science that the distinction has been embedded in, if not branded on, our brains. However useful the distinction might be, Searle contends that it has become a "massive obstacle to a scientific understanding of the place of consciousness within the natural world."[30]

The dominant view that a satisfactory explanation must be in a reductive form and the view that any theory of consciousness must be consonant with the atomic theory of matter in physics and the theory of evolution in biology further impede, in his judgment, grasping consciousness as a bio-logical phenomenon. The basic particles of matter are no longer conceived as Democritus's atoms, or Locke's corpuscular molecules, or Descartes's matter; rather, they are points of energy/mass which behave like waves when left alone. Still, the salient feature of the theory of matter is that these ultimate particles, for lack of a better name, explain higher-level physical systems. The most satisfying form of explanation for modernity, accord-ingly, remains the reduction, i.e., bottom up from the micro to the macro level. This remains the bedrock of material fundamentalism and a massive obstacle for constructing a theory of consciousness.

Searle believes that the theory of evolution, properly conceived, pro-vides the opening necessary for establishing the biological phenomenon of consciousness. Evolutionary theory contains two mutually supportive lev-els of explanation. First is the survival or functional explanation: a species survives because its characteristics have developed to fit it into its environ-ment and survive. Second is the causal level of explanation: the biochem-ical properties within DNA cause certain features to be created, which in turn enable a species to reproduce and survive. The pertinence of evolu-tionary theory is this, according to Searle: "Consciousness . . . is a biolog-ical feature of human and certain animal brains. It is caused by neurobio-logical processes and is as much a part of the natural biological order as any other biological features, such as photosynthesis, digestion, or mito-sis."[31] By conceiving of consciousness as an "evolved phenotypical trait of certain types of organisms with highly developed nervous systems," Searle claims to have developed a theory completely compatible with the scien-tific world view.[32]

Given this explanation of the origin and nature of consciousness, it is not acceptable or necessary to have to talk about spiritual values, immor-tality, mysteries, religion, or God in order to defend the reality of con-sciousness. It also follows that consciousness need not be denied in order to keep a scientific world view. An apposite analogy, he argues, is with liq-uidity: it is constituted by the causal relation of hydrogen and oxygen mol-ecules, but it is also a distinctive feature—not mysterious—of the molecu-lar system. Thus, Searle repeatedly concludes that consciousness "is as much a part of the natural biological order as any other biological feature such as photosynthesis, digestion, or mitosis."[33]

It is Searle's contention that his theory unmasks three key assumptions undergirding other theories of consciousness. First, his theory shows that we need not think of consciousness as a stuff of some kind, the perennial quest of dualists. Consciousness is a feature of the brain, just as—to use his favorite analogy—liquidity is a feature of water. A second assumption found in many theories is that consciousness has a kind of structure that can be known by introspection. This, too, is common among dualists, and the identity theorists have a scientific version of introspection based upon this assumption. Consciousness is not an observable quality found in a certain space. The third assumption is that there must be some sort of link between consciousness and the brain, the continuing obsession of the materialist to the contrary. One does not need either the "ghost in the machine" of the dualists or the brain states that link mental acts in the computer fashion of materialists. One does not look for a missing link to explain water and liquidity either.

To reiterate, Searle's position is that consciousness should be viewed as a "causally emergent system feature" of the brain. In general, properties of the elements of a system within nature can explain some features of a system, but there can be other features of a system that result from the causal relations of the elements that cannot be so explained. As he states, "solidity, liquidity, and transparency are examples of causally emergent system features." Consciousness is of the same nature. It is "an emergent feature of certain systems of neurons in the same way that solidity and liquidity are emergent features of systems of molecules."[34] Similarly, the physical nature of neurons cannot explain consciousness; rather, it is the causal relations among neurons from which consciousness emerges. It would be an inappropriate reductionism to search for the explanatory link between water and liquid; the same holds for consciousness and the physical brain. There is one aspect of the analogy with liquidity that makes the relationship of consciousness to the physical world more complicated. In the world of physical reality, science has shown that a system feature—such as liquidity or solidity—can be explained by examining the causal relations of molecules. As a consequence, this causal reductionism leads to an ontological claim of providing greater objectivity and generality. The problem with consciousness is that the science of the brain cannot make the same explanatory reduction for consciousness. There are certain causal features of molecules that entail the system feature of liquidity or heat or solidity, but, Searle insists, to the annoyance of most philosophers, that consciousness is both irreducible and consistent with a scientific world view.

With respect to irreducibility, Searle argues, with others, that pain, as one illustration, cannot be reduced to nothing but neuron firings, because "no description of the third-person, objective, physical facts would convey the subjective, first-person character of the pain, simply because the first-person features are different from the third-person features."[35] Knowing one's own pain is quite different from knowing someone else's pain. It is here that the asymmetry between liquidity and consciousness can be easily seen. We know what are the molecular movements that cause liquidity or heat or solidity. "Heat" can then be redefined in these terms, and the same holds for liquidity or solidity. Our subjective experience of heat, liquidity, or solidity still exists. The latter experience we tend to call appearance, and the former definition we call reality. Searle then makes the contrast:

> But unlike solidity [or heat or liquidity], consciousness cannot be redefined in terms of an underlying microstructure, and the surface features then treated as mere effects of real consciousness, without losing the point of having the concept of consciousness in the first place.
>
> ... We did not really eliminate the subjectivity of red, for example, when we reduced red to light reflectances; we simply stopped calling the subjective part of light "red." We did not eliminate any subjective phenomena whatever with the "reductions"; we simply stopped calling them by their old names. Whether we treat the irreducibility from the materialist or from the dualist point of view, we are still left with a universe that contains an irreducibly subjective physical component as a component of physical reality.[36]

Searle quickly adds that there are no consequences for the scientific world-view: the irreducibility of consciousness is a "trivial consequence of our definitional practices." It may be the case that there could be a "major intellectual revolution that would give us a new—and at present unimaginable—conception of reduction, according to which consciousness would be reducible."[37] Even in this case, consciousness, however explained, would remain a component of physical reality just as heat, liquidity, or solidity are now.

Searle's arguments for the irreducibility of consciousness are developed at some length, and, indeed, he can rightly cite a variety of respected philosophers who would generally agree. The relationship of his theory of consciousness to the scientific world view, as he calls it, or to the physical world is less developed and more problematic. In the main, his position is a version of the levels argument, i.e., one level of reality may provide the conditions for, and establish boundary conditions of, a higher level, but the lower level does not determine the nature of the higher level, nor is the higher level reducible to the lower level. The interrelationship among the sequence of sound-words-grammar-sentences-style-meaning illustrates this point.[38] The dependence of the higher level on the lower level and the irreducibility of the higher are the characteristics Searle cites for explaining the relationship between consciousness and the neurophysiological. He continually uses his analogy of liquidity and consciousness, which in effect depends on a level argument: liquidity is both "causally dependent on the behavior of molecules, and can also be a feature of the system made up of molecules;" similarly, "my present state of consciousness is caused by neuronal behavior in my brain and that very state just is a higher level feature of the brain."[39]

An explanation of consciousness, Searle suggests, should have the same form as an explanation in biology. If we could do this, many of the problems plaguing the attempts to have an adequate conceptualization of consciousness would be dispelled. Before evolutionary theory, an explanation in biology referred to the intrinsic intention in the plant: "In order to survive, the plant turns its leaves toward the sun." This anthropomorphic explanation has been replaced by a mechanical-physical and functional explanation: "variable secretions of auxin cause plants to turn their leaves toward the sun," and "plants that turn their leaves toward the sun are more likely to survive than plants that do not."[40] Searle's exhortation is to explain consciousness in a similar manner:

> In our skulls there is just the brain with all of its intricacy, and consciousness with all its color and variety. The brain produces the conscious states that are occurring in you and me right now, and it has the capacity to produce many others which are not now occurring. But that is it. Where the mind is concerned, that is the end of the story. There are brute, blind neurophysiological processes and there is consciousness, but there is nothing else. If we are looking for phenomena that are intrinsically intentional but inaccessible in principle to consciousness, there is nothing there: no rule following, no mental information processing, no unconscious inferences, no mental models, no 2 ½-D images, no three-dimensional descriptions, no language of thought, and no universal grammar.[41]

There is no doubt in Searle's mind that consciousness has provided humans "flexibility and creativity" plus "powers of creativity," and that these qualities have clear evolutionary advantages.[42] But, as the long quotation above makes clear, it is a philosophical and scientific mistake to contend with Chomsky that there are unconscious rules of a universal grammar or with Freud that there is a repressed unconscious or any other intentional structure.[43]

Searle is tentative about developing in much detail his own views on the structure and nature of consciousness:

> Two subjects are crucial to consciousness, but I will have little to say about them because I do not yet understand them well enough. The first is temporality. Since Kant we have been aware of an asymmetry in the way that consciousness relates to space and to time. Although we experience objects and events as both spatially extended and of temporal duration, our consciousness itself is not experienced as spatial though it is experienced as temporally extended. . .
>
> The second neglected topic is society. I am convinced that the category of "other people" plays a special role in the structure of our conscious experiences, a role unlike that of objects and states of affairs; and I believe that this capacity for assigning a special status to other loci of consciousness is both biologically based and is a Background presupposition for all forms of collective intentionality. But I do not yet know how to demonstrate these claims, nor how to analyze the structure of the social elements in individual consciousness.[44]

There appears to be a recognition of the need to place consciousness within a larger context in order to understand it. He devotes some attention to the Background by which he means human "hardwiring" capacities, society, and physical reality. Precisely how this Background relates to consciousness is not fully developed, although he does say that "intentional phenomena such as meanings, understandings, interpretations, beliefs, desires, and experiences only function within a set of Background capacities that are not themselves intentional."[45] He does not use the word participate for explaining the relationship. His last sentence in *The Rediscovery of the Mind* is that "we need to rediscover the social character of the mind."[46] He also makes clear that the Background is not wholly determined, since it includes a social dimension. Consequently, consciousness enables humans to establish purpose and meaning in their existence, but all within a Background that can also be altered to some extent by human actions. These seem to be his tentative conclusions.

III

Before examining how Voegelin's philosophy of consciousness might contribute to an analysis of the mind-body problem, let me reiterate three of the key questions. Consciousness has a first-person existence, which means that objective, neutral, third-person forms of explaining can only be of manifestations of consciousness. This applies to consciousness in others and in ourselves. (1) Is such a conception of consciousness irreducible? Equally important is the question: (2) What is the relationship between consciousness and physical reality? In short, it will be necessary to have a theory of consciousness and mind that is compatible with a scientific world view. These two questions state the central dilemma: if consciousness is irreducible, one must be a dualist and face the difficulty of holding a theory that is to most philosophers incompatible with a scientific world view; if one develops a theory consistent with a scientific world view, consciousness and mind must be eliminated, which appears to some philosophers and most others as plain nonsense. A final question, and one only tentatively probed by Searle, is (3) how consciousness relates to humanity's social and historical existence.

Question One
The irreducibility of consciousness is a topic where Searle and Voegelin have considerable agreement. Searle amends William James's views on consciousness in several respects, but he would accept Voegelin's reliance on James's analysis of pure experience.[47]

> In developing his concept of pure experience, James put his finger on the reality of the consciousness of participation, inasmuch as what he calls *pure experience* is something that can be put into the context either of the subject's stream of consciousness or of objects in the external world. This fundamental insight of James identifies the something that lies between the subject and object of participation as the experience.[48]

Searle might quibble over Voegelin's spatial language, but the central point is that consciousness has to be conceptualized as independent of its manifestations. This means for both that there is no self or I behind consciousness who is an agent operating consciousness. Both insist on the primacy of consciousness. In Searle's language: "Ontologically speaking, behavior, functional role, and causal relations are irrelevant to the existence of conscious mental phenomena."[49] Here is a clear and radical disagreement with Descartes. His picture of consciousness always and logically assumes a self behind the consciousness, experiencing the external world, and running the cogito. Consciousness is not primary, paradoxically, in spite of Descartes's dualism.

Both Searle and Voegelin would also deny the existence of inherent or substantive features to consciousness. Voegelin, for example, says that just as there is no hidden I, there is no "flow" to consciousness, and "there is psyche deeper than consciousness, and there is reality deeper than reality experienced, but there is no consciousness deeper than consciousness."[50] Searle's position, already described, can be seen in his analyses of Chomsky, Freud, cognitive scientists, and others.[51] He also repeats Voegelin's statement that there is no ultimate subconsciousness: "Any introspection I have of my own conscious state is itself that conscious state."[52] In Searle's phrase, all models of consciousness which purport to see some intrinsic substantive elements are "observer relative."[53]

Both Searle and Voegelin have stipulated that the irreducibility of consciousness does not entail either substantive dualism or a fundamentalist materialism. For both, consciousness is tied to physical reality and the individual human body. Searle's position has been sufficiently described. Voegelin, too, states that humans are "human beings and not disembodied consciousness," that there is no Hegelian-like "unfolding of the consciousness," and that human consciousness is "always the concrete consciousness of concrete persons."[54] Searle would no doubt find Voegelin's language quaint, but, for all that, the placing of consciousness within physical reality is as much Voegelin's position as Searle's:

> The substantive unity of human existence, which must be accepted as [an] ontological hypothesis for the understanding of consciousness's basis in body and matter, is objectively inexperienceable. That does not mean, however, that there is no such thing. At any rate, the hypothesis is indispensable for grasping the 'ensemble' of consciousness and bodily process in the total process of human existence.[55]

Neither Searle nor Voegelin is a Dualist.[56]
Although Searle and Voegelin are agreed concerning the "purity" of consciousness, its being free from intrinsic and substantive elements, and its

embodiment in the physical world, there are two features of consciousness as conceived by Voegelin that seem incompatible with Searle's theory: the Question and the metaxy. Voegelin argues in several places that humanity exists in a state of unrest:

> The reality experienced by the philosophers as specifically human is man's existence in a state of unrest. Man is not a self-created, autonomous being carrying the origin and meaning of his existence within himself. He is not a divine *causa sui*; from the experience of his life in precarious existence within the limits of birth and death there rather rises the wondering question about the ultimate ground, the *aitia* or *prote arche*, of all reality and specifically his own. The question is inherent in the experience from which it rises; the *zoon noun echon* that experiences itself as a living being is at the same time conscious of the questionable character attaching to this situs. Man, when he experiences himself as existent, discovers his specific humanity as that of the questioner for the where-from and the where-to, for the ground and the sense of his existence.[57]

He proceeds to argue that questioning consciousness is the constituent of humanity. Furthermore, the questioning or the search for meaning takes place within the metaxy, which is between the divine-human poles of existence. The anti-Cartesian import of the metaxy is that no third-person, neutral, objective language, claiming absolute knowledge, is possible about the human quest for meaning. Voegelin prefers to use the word indices: "neither an immanent world nor a transcendent being 'exist'; rather these terms are indices that we assign to areas of reality of the primary experience, as the noetic experience dissociates the cosmos into existing things and their divine ground of being."[58] Searle would not use this language.

A careful attention to Voegelin's language shows nevertheless that he has not made any claim that clearly places him in the camp of substantive dualism. In fact, some of the theological criticisms aimed at Voegelin are directed precisely at his failure to be a clear substantive dualist. The category of indices does not refer to substantive "stuff"; rather it works in the same way as interpretations and meanings work for Searle, i.e., they articulate human consciousness within its social and historical context. While such articulations may be expressed in many ways, some knowledge claims for some articulations are simply incompatible with what we know of physical reality and of human reasoning.

Searle admits that there are "dispositional states of the brain" and, accordingly, that there can be an "unconscious intentionality" with a "latency relative to its manifestation in consciousness."[59] This seems like very thin stuff indeed and an impossible stretch to make compatible with Voegelin's two claims, whatever their epistemological status. To summarize these claims: first, a fundamental human experience of reality leads to a questioning unrest and a search for an ultimate or divine source of meaning, and, second, the articulation of the search and of the ground or source of meaning takes place within the metaxy. One could argue that "ground," even with the adjective divine attached, works for Voegelin like "significant" or "normative" does for Searle when connected in some as yet unspecified way with "disposition" and "latency." Nevertheless, Voegelin's claim is that within consciousness there is a divine encounter. It is a claim that could be added to Searle's theory of consciousness, primarily because of the very sketchiness of Searle's theory with respect to his categories of "interpretation," "latency," and "disposition."

Searle and Voegelin are in agreement on the irreducibility of consciousness. Both are consistently and clearly anti-Cartesian in constructing their views. Voegelin's speculative philosophy—which is not meant in a pejorative sense—clearly goes much further. In fairness, his views are not incompatible with what Searle has written; however, if Searle were to spell out in more detail his own metaphysical views, I have no doubt that the differences would be sharp.

Question Two
The second question was: What is the relationship between consciousness and physical reality? When discussing the irreducibility of consciousness and its independence, it was necessary to note that both Voegelin and Searle insist upon the embodiment of consciousness in physical reality, including human physical and biological nature. Neither thinker separates consciousness from the body. The problem is the nature of the relationship. Searle uses the levels argument, stressing that consciousness is a distinctive non-reducible feature of neurophysiological capacities of the brain in the same way that liquidity is a feature of hydrogen and oxygen molecules. Both liquidity and consciousness are "causally emergent system features." Voegelin's analysis of the relationship is far more problematic. He refers to a traditional model of levels of being, but their interrelationship is never fully developed. He does ground consciousness, as already noted, in physical reality.

Human consciousness is not a process that occurs in the world side by side with other processes without contact with these processes other than cognition; rather, it is based on animalic, vegetative, and inorganic being, and only on this basis is it consciousness of a human being. Man's structure seems to be the ontic premise for man's transcending into the world, for in none of its directions of transcending does consciousness find a level of being which is not also one on which it itself is based. Speaking ontologically, consciousness finds in the order of being of the world no level which it does not also experience as its own foundation. In the "basis-experience" of consciousness man presents himself as an epitome of the cosmos, as a microcosm. Now we do not know in what this basis really consists. . . .[60]

Up to this point, there is nothing at odds with Searle's picture. Voegelin, however, goes on to state that the linkage of the levels is unclear: "Even though the levels of being are clearly distinguishable in their respective structures, there must be something common which makes possible the continuum of all of them in human existence."[61] He concludes with a line that seems totally at odds with his own theory of consciousness and of the role of the metaxy: "Finally, we are related to the transcendent world in the mysterious relation of objective knowledge, a relation which phenomenology has by no means illumined but rather only described from without."[62] It is a sentenced best dropped![63]

Voegelin has nothing like the detailed explanation provided by the levels argument, and the coupling of the transcendent world with objective knowledge only confuses matters. He does insist that the noetic and pneumatic leaps in beings or differentiations of consciousness do not change the cosmos or the world. He is generally critical of pneumatic differentiations precisely because of the tendency to claim that a change in reality has occurred.[64] Rather, differentiations occur in consciousness when the process of reality is experienced and articulated differently. Yet again, Voegelin will use language, unknown to Searle, whereby the meaning or significance of reality is referred to as divine. Such phrases as the "divine depth of the Cosmos" do not change Voegelin's stress on the nature of being, i.e., reality as unshaped or unchanged by human actions, but they do add a level of purported significance and asserted meaning not mentioned by Searle, who would predictably view the phrase as at best irrelevant.[65]

Question Three

There are fundamental agreements between Searle and Voegelin on the irreducibility of consciousness and on the relationship of consciousness with
physical reality, even though in each case Voegelin quickly turns to adding
interpretations about the significance and meaning for human existence.
Voegelin's additions are not entailed, nor are they clearly incompatible with
the common aspects of their answers to the first two questions: Is such a conception of consciousness irreducible? and, What is the relationship between
consciousness and physical reality? The third question concerns how consciousness relates to humanity's social and historical existence. Searle holds
the question to be centrally important for a fully developed theory of consciousness, but he offers only a few tentative suggestions toward answering it.

The contrast with Voegelin is clear. For Voegelin, the active power of
consciousness is a response to the human condition of unrest and to the
context of God-man, world-society; humans seek meaning in some solid
source, a "divine ground of being." The context of our response remains
the world and society. Human history is best described as the differentiations of consciousness whereby humans articulate the process of understanding within the larger process of reality. Order in human existence
flows from differentiating consciousness into society and history, according to Voegelin. Thus, humanity's social and historical existence depends
upon the centrality of differentiating consciousness and the insights, experiences or events that, from time to time, lead to such differentiation:

> What becomes visible in the new luminosity, therefore, is not only
> the structure of consciousness itself (in classical language: the
> nature of man), but also the structure of an "advance" in the
> process of reality. Moreover, the site of the advance is not a mys-
> terious entity called "history" that would exist independent of such
> advances; the site rather is the very consciousness which, in its
> state of noetic luminosity, makes these discoveries. The theophan-
> ic events do not occur *in* history; they constitute history together
> with its meaning. The noetic theophany, finally, reveals conscious-
> ness as having the structure of metaleptic reality, of the divine-
> human Metaxy. As a consequence, "history" in the sense of an
> area in reality in which the insight into the meaning of existence
> advances is the history of theophany.[66]

History is constituted by new perspectives within consciousness, but these
changes occur within the metaxy. In contrast, Searle has no philosophy of

history, and there is nothing in his few tentative remarks that could be extrapolated into a such a philosophy.

The third question is where Searle and Voegelin diverge the most, notably since Voegelin's interest is in the significance and meaning of human existence in history. It was examining this topic that led Voegelin back to formulating a theory of consciousness. Searle proceeded from the opposite direction.

IV

A full assessment of Voegelin's contribution to the mind-body problem and to the nature of consciousness would require a full analysis of his theory of consciousness. Nevertheless, there are a few points that can be made as a prolegomena for a full analysis.

In contrast to Searle's analysis of consciousness, Voegelin's treatment is mainly directed toward the pertinence and significance of consciousness for human existence—personal, social, and historical. Unlike Searle, he devotes little attention to the biological and physical nature of consciousness, although what he does say is consonant with Searle's arguments. Consciousness for both is embodied in our biological and physical nature. Neither resorts to "stuff" talk, nor has either one posited a self behind consciousness. Voegelin also spends little time on the interrelationship between consciousness and the levels of reality. But again, what he does say is compatible in the main with Searle. Both have clearly broken with Descartes, and neither is a philosophical dualist.

Searle stops where the bulk of Voegelin's work starts: the pertinence and significance of consciousness. Searle would be aghast at such formulations as the divine ground of being, transcendence, the noetic and pneumatic differentiations of consciousness, and the Question. An analysis of the coherence of these categories in Voegelin's philosophy of consciousness would require a separate paper.

Serious questions about Voegelin's philosophy of consciousness do need to be addressed in a full-length study. These questions should be analytic and philosophic rather than primarily theological. The area most in need of study, and where there is the greatest need for amendments, is epistemology. John Ranieri has recently asked the question: "While rejecting the positivist claim that knowing is only valid when modeled on the method of the natural sciences, did he not tacitly accept the positivist account of what it is that constitutes knowing in the natural science?"[67] This is correct. In fact, the question points to a deeper problem that needs to be studied. Voegelin continuously resorts to a mode of analysis and a use of language that is in dissonance with his ontology, particularly his claims about the metaxy. As one brief example, the category of consciousness as luminous is problematic in many ways. Consciousness as luminous purportedly is free of the hypostatization of experience by being direct and immediate, unmediated, privileged, and therefore undistorted. This is a remarkable set of descriptors, identical with the claims originally made for sense data from Hobbes and Bacon to the Vienna Circle. Instead of the mechanical-like body as the authenticating receptor for knowing, we now have luminous consciousness. His use of the word symbol reflects the same kind of problem. In contrast to mere concepts, symbols do reflect the originating experience and as such have the authenticating power to persuade and illuminate. But there are no such privileged words by which consciousness and reality are linked; there are only usages within a context. To cite Voegelin's remarks on reflection and the metaxy as immunizations from such criticism is not sufficient. Voegelin's epistemology is not adequate to his task.[68]

In addition to epistemological considerations, one other area particularly needs to be addressed: the relationship between pragmatic history and Voegelin's theory of consciousness. Again, there is a tendency to use dichotomous language where one set of categories is set off from another, just as we saw "luminous" and "symbolic" work with respect to "concepts" and "empirical knowledge." It is a brilliant insight to view history as a history of theophany and to break with volumes one to three in *Order and History*. Serious questions can still be asked: How can society embody the life of reason? What is the relationship between consciousness as luminous and pragmatic history, and how is it constituted?[69]

Let me conclude with a brief recitation of the contribution Voegelin provides to the theory of consciousness and to the mind-body literature. These items are in addition to what he shares with Searle. The significance and meaning of consciousness for human social and historical existence have been Voegelin's unmatched endowment to the end of modernity. It is immensely fruitful to conceive of humanity as participating in the process of reality, as understanding within the metaxy, and as pursuing the Question. To talk about the Background and normative considerations, as does Searle, seems flat and even puerile. At the level of pertinence and significance, Voegelin would have far more in common with those thinkers who stress human powers to seek and to understand. For example, he would surely agree with Nussbaum's characterization of the questing consciousness: "We are all of us, insofar as we interact morally and polit-ically, fanciful projectors, makers of and believers in fiction and metaphors."[70] In a similar vein, Wittgenstein's famous phrase, "to imagine a language is to imagine a form of life," is often laboriously and lugubri-ously explained as an injunction to relate language with a context in order to achieve meaning. The explication, rather, should be aimed at the verb "to imagine." Such again is the power of questing consciousness. In the words of Prospero:

> . . . like the baseless fabric of this vision
> The cloud-capp'd towers, the gorgeous palaces,
> The solemn temples, the great globe itself,
> Yea, all which it inherit, shall dissolve,
> And, like this insubstantial pageant faded,
> Leave not a rack behind: We are such stuff
> As dreams are made of, and our little life
> Is rounded with a sleep.[71]

Such is the context for human existence, this is what humans do with con-sciousness, and the quest opens all reality to our reverent participation and exploration.

Endnotes

1 Barry Cooper, *The Restoration of Political Science and the Crisis of Modernity* (Toronto: Mellen, 1989), 272.

2 Eric Voegelin, *The New Science of Politics* (Chicago: University of Chicago Press, 1952), 63.

3 A striking illustration is the natives' response to Columbus's sailing ships. They were in awe of the long boats which were merely bigger canoes, but they had no response to the sailing ships. So much for sense data and experience.

4 John R. Searle, *Intentionality: An Essay in the Philosophy of Mind* (Cambridge: Cambridge University Press, 1983); *The Rediscovery of the Mind* (Cambridge: MIT Press, 1995); *Philosophy in a New Century* (Cambridge: Cambridge University Press, 2008). For quick summaries of his position, see: "The Myth of the Computer," *The New York Review of Books* (29 April 1982), and "Consciousness and the Philosophers," *The New York Review of Books* (6 March 1997). For fuller explications and interpretations of Searle, see: Nick Fotion, *John Searle* (Princeton: Princeton University Press, 2000); *John Searle and His Critics*, Ernest Lepore and Robert Van Gulick, eds. (London: Basil Blackwell, 1991): *John Searle*, Barry Smith, ed. (Cambridge: Cambridge University Press, 2003).

5   René Descartes, *The Philosophical Works of Descartes* (New York: Dover, 1955), 241.

6   Ludwig Wittgenstein, *Philosophical Investigations*, G.E.M. Anscombe, trans., 2nd edition (New York: Macmillan, 1958), section 293.

7   For a survey of many of these attempts, see James W. Cornman and Keith Lehrer, *Philosophical Problems and Arguments: An Introduction* (New York: Macmillan, 1974), 239–311; Searle, *The Rediscovery of the Mind*, ch. 2; William G. Lycan, *Consciousness* (Cambridge: MIT Press, 1995), ch.1.

8   Searle, *The Rediscovery of the Mind*, 13.

9   Lycan, *Consciousness*, 127.

10 Searle, *The Rediscovery of the Mind*, 97.

11 The term "materialist" is used throughout to mean a philosophic position about reality in which consciousness and mind are given no ontological status. It is conceivable that one could be a materialist in another sense and recognize the ontological status of consciousness. This, as we shall see, is the position of Searle.

12 Lycan, for example is a functionalist who dismisses behaviorism in four succinct pages. *Consciousness*, 3–7.

13 G. Ryle, *The Concept of Mind* (New York: Barnes & Noble, 1949), 58.

14 *Ibid.*, 15–16.

15 Searle, *The Rediscovery of the Mind*, 33–34.

16 Lycan, *Consciousness*, 5.

17 Searle, *The Rediscovery of the Mind*, 35.

18 Behaviorists have had to suffer many jibes: Two behaviorists meet on the street, and the greeting goes, "You're fine; how am I?" Another variant: After making love, one behaviorist says to another, "It was great for you; how was it for me?"

19 The most famous advocate is J.J.C. Smart, *Philosophy and Scientific Realism* (London: Routledge and Kegan Paul, 1963); "The Content of Physicalism," *Philosophical Quarterly*, vol. 28.

20 Searle, *The Rediscovery of the Mind*, 39; S. Kripke, "Identity and Necessity," in *Identity and Individuation*, M. Munitz, ed. (New York: New York University Press, 1971). Wittgenstein analyzes how the language of pain operates and thereby shows the impossibility of eliminating a consciousness and meaning: *Philosophical Investigations*, sections 300–315.

21 "Consciousness and the Philosophers," 43–44.

22 Recent examples are, Lycan, *Consciousness*, and David J. Chalmers, *The Conscious Mind: In Search of a Fundamental Theory* (Oxford: Oxford University Press, 1996).

23 Searle, *The Rediscovery of the Mind*, 45; Searle, *Philosophy in a New Century*, 67–85.

24 Arguments from Wittgenstein are also often used to make a similar point.

25 Helen Keller, *The Story of My Life* (1903); an excerpt is found in *About Language*, Marden J. Clark, Soren F. Cox, Marshall R. Crait, eds., 2nd edition (New York: Scribner's Sons, 1975), 24–25. An exegesis of this extraordinary passage is itself worth a paper.

26 Wittgenstein, *Philosophical Investigations*, section 26.

27 Michael Polanyi has a useful essay on this point: "Sense-Giving and Sense-

Reading," in *Knowing and Being: Essays by Michael Polanyi*, Marjorie Grene, ed. (Chicago: University of Chicago Press, 1969), 181–207.

28 The importance of the imagination is explained and persuasively defended by Martha Nussbaum, *Poetic Justice: The Literary Imagination and Public Life* (Boston: Beacon Press, 1995).

29 Searle, *The Rediscovery of the Mind*, 85.

30 Ibid., 85. With the silo mentality common among academic disciplines, Searle never mentions that this thought could have occurred to many others, even in science. See Michael Polanyi's various works: *Personal Knowledge, Knowing and Being*, and *The Tacit Dimension* (Garden City: Doubleday, 1966).

31 Searle, *The Rediscovery of the Mind*, 90.

32 *Ibid.*

33 *Ibid.*, 93.

34 *Ibid.*, 111–112.

35 *Ibid.*, 117. Searle acknowledges his reliance at this point on Frank Jackson, "Epiphenomenal Qualia," *Philosophical Quarterly*, 32: 127–136; Saul Kripke, "Naming and Necessity," in D. Davidson and G. Harman, eds., *Semantics of Natural Language* (Dordrecht: Reidel, 1971), 253–355, 763–769; Thomas Nagel, "What Is It Like to Be a Bat?" *Philosophical Review*, 4 LXXXIII: 435–450. See also Wittgenstein's analysis of pain in *Philosophical Investigations*, sections 300–315.

36 Searle, *The Rediscovery of the Mind*, 123. One of Searle's most famous antagonists, D.C. Dennett, has argued in *Consciousness Explained* (Boston: Little, Brown and Company, 1991) that consciousness is incorrigible and that therefore consciousness itself is suspect. This view, Searle retorts, is founded on the confusion that any claim about the existence of consciousness (ontology) entails a knowledge claim about what one is conscious of (epistemology). *The Rediscovery of the Mind*, 149.

37 *Ibid.*, 124.

38 This example is from Polanyi, "The Logic of Tacit Inference," in *Knowing and Being*, 154.

39 Searle, *The Rediscovery of the Mind*, 252. His critique of the theory that the brain and consciousness are explainable by using a computer model also depends upon a levels argument. Ibid., 251.

40 *Ibid.*, 230.

41 *Ibid.*, 228–229.

42 *Ibid.*, 108–109.

43 *Ibid.*, 244–245, 151ff.

44 *Ibid.*, 127–128.

45 *Ibid.*, 175.

46 *Ibid.*, 248. See also, "Social Ontology: Some Basic Principles" in *Philosophy in a New Century*, 26–52; Fotion, "Social Reality," 175–189.

47 Searle, *Intentionality*, 89; *The Rediscovery of the Mind*, 135–139.

48 Voegelin, *Autobiographical Reflection*, Ellis Sandoz, ed. (Baton Rouge: Louisiana State University Press, 1985), 72.

49 Searle, *The Rediscovery of the Mind*, 69. See Voegelin, *Anamnesis*, Gerhart

Niemeyer, trans. (Notre Dame: University of Notre Dame Press, 1978): "it seems to me that there is no I that would be the agent of the consciousness. It is doubtful whether consciousness has the form of the I, or whether the I is not rather a phenomenon in the consciousness" (p. 19).

50   Voegelin, "Equivalences of Experiences and Symbolization in History," *The Collected Works of Eric Voegelin*, vol. 12, ed. Ellis Sandoz (Baton Rouge: Louisiana State University Press, 1990), 126.

51   Searle, *The Rediscovery of the Mind*, 228–229.

52   *Ibid.*, 97, 162.

53   *Ibid.*, 211.

54   Voegelin, *Anamnesis*, 180, 200.

55   *Ibid.*, 31.

56   John Ranieri, in his excellent book, *Eric Voegelin and the Good Society* (Columbia: University of Missouri Press, 1995), criticizes Voegelin for having the same dilemma as Descartes in trying to unify body and consciousness. Ranieri's criticisms flow from his own understanding of pneumatic consciousness. In sum, Ranieri is a substantive dualist, and Voegelin is not. It may be the case, as Ranieri implies, that Voegelin's theory of consciousness is not consonant with Christian theology, but this is a different matter and quite independent of the question of the coherence of Voegelin's theory of consciousness.

57   "Reason the Classic Experience" in Voegelin, *Anamnesis*, 92–93; *Order and History*, vol. 4, *Ecumenic Age* (Baton Rouge: Louisiana State University Press, 1974), 326–330.

58   Voegelin, *Anamnesis*, 176.

59   Searle, *The Rediscovery of the Mind*, 161.

60   Voegelin, *Anamnesis*, 27–28.

61   *Ibid.*, 28.

62   *Ibid.*

63   "Eternal Being in Time," in Voegelin, *Anamnesis*, 115–133, does not use such flawed formulations.

64   Several scholars have commented on Voegelin's semi-submerging of the pneumatic into noetic consciousness. See fn. 1. Eugene Webb has recently suggested that Voegelin should add an appetitive consciousness. This suggestion imitates the Platonic triad of reason, spirit, and appetites. I doubt if Voegelin would have agreed. See "Eric Voegelin at the End of an Era: Differentiations of Consciousness and the Search for the Universal," in *International and Interdisciplinary Perspectives on Eric Voegelin*, Stephen A. McKnight and Geoffrey L. Price, eds. (Columbia: University of Missouri Press, 1997), 159–188. Voegelin uses "reality" to include the all-encompassing process, and at other times he refers to the cosmos or world or thing reality. See *Anamnesis*, 63, and *Order and History*, vol. 5, *In Search of Order* (Baton Rouge: Louisiana State University Press, 1987), 15–16.

65   The life and works of Donna Williams are salutary for any treatment of the irreducibility of consciousness and the relationship with physical reality. She suffers from a form of autism, which is to say the mental process operates quite differently from other humans. Yet, through a process of consciousness, as remarkable as that of Helen Keller, she was able to understand her predicament, to survive as a

person in spite of the flaws in the neurophysiological capacities of her brain, and to find meaning and purpose to her existence, i.e., the quest incarnate. *Nobody Nowhere* (New York: Avon Books, 1992); *Somebody Somewhere* (New York: Times Books, 1994); *Like Color to the Blind* (Toronto: Doubleday, 1996).

66 *Ecumenic Age*, 252.

67 Ranieri, *Eric Voegelin and the Good Society*, 31.

68 Porter, "A Philosophy of History as a Philosophy of Consciousness," *Denver Quarterly* 10 (1975): 96–104; Porter, "From the Other Shore: Eric Voegelin's Philosophy of History and Consciousness," *Marxist Perspective* (Summer, 1980), 152–169; Ranieri, *Eric Voegelin and the Good Society*, 27–, 127–136. Ranieri makes some useful suggestions for amending Voegelin's position.

69 John Ranieri has suggested that there is a striking Kantian legacy in Voegelin. To the degree that this should be true, Voegelin's break in Volume Four would have to be recast as a mere shift. This would be a matter of deep regret, in my opinion, since I prefer to think of Voegelin as a true post-modern in the sense of the second Whitehead or Wittgenstein.

70 Nussbaum, *Poetic Justice*, 140. Nussbaum cites her indebtedness to Stanley Cavell, *The Claims of Reason: Wittgenstein, Morality and Tragedy* (Oxford: Oxford University Press, 1979), 329–496.

71 William Shakespeare, *The Tempest*, Act IV.

Chapter Eleven

Eric Voegelin's Workshop:

A Study in Confirmation of

Barry Cooper's Genetic Paradigm

Tilo Schabert

Over the past 25 years, a particular field of studies has been established concerning the work of the German-American political scientist, Eric Voegelin, and the significance of this work for our civilization. Barry Cooper has been a major actor in this process, not only as author of a considerable number of books and articles on the work of Eric Voegelin and as editor of some of his writings, but also, and in particular, by a singular "archaeological" curiosity and perception. With his three books, *Eric Voegelin and the Foundations of Modern Political Science* (1999), *Voegelin Recollected* (2008), and *Beginning the Quest: Law and Politics in the Early Work of Eric Voegelin* (2009), he has developed a genetic paradigm for the study of Voegelin's thought and work and demonstrated its hermeneutic significance.[1] Cooper is currently at work to produce another exemplification of the paradigm. In 1968, Voegelin started to consider a prolongation of *Order and History* "backwards" to the symbolisms of the Paleolithic Age and pursued this project of "Volume Zero" (as I have called it) over the following years. He didn't write the volume, but the idea for it remains, and, indeed, has stimulated Barry Cooper to apply his genetic approach once again. We can look forward to this new book from Barry: *In Search of Volume Zero: Early Historical Symbolism and Voegelin's Philosophy of Consciousness*. A phenomenon becomes visible in this context that is crucially significant for an understanding of Voegelin, namely his workshop.

I

Each text, it might be said, is the death mask of its creation.[2] Once it has been finished and its author has bid it farewell, as it were, the *text* will continue to be contemplated and studied as the existing work of a creative deed that has all but vanished behind it—and this even to the eyes that read it. In the perception of those who now read it, the creative life from which the text originally emerged has been replaced by the finite concreteness, the formal rigidity of a text that endures both in time (being infinitely the authoritative document apart from its author) and in the reading process (being necessarily the normative guide for the act of its being read). Following its creation, the life of the created work begins: an extended and varied life, indeed, if we look at our example and observe the burgeoning literature interpreting the *work* (*Werk*)[3] of Eric Voegelin.

Preceding this existence, of course, was the *generation* of that work. Voegelin's writings originated from the work of a creative actor: *Voegelin at work*. With this expression, my intention has already been formulated. In view of the work of Eric Voegelin, I would like to make a few remarks about its creation, to elucidate the activity from which the texts arose and through which they were formed and which takes place behind the mask-like rigidity of the texts themselves. In particular, I will attempt here to illuminate both the spatial construction and the spatial extension of this activity. For *Voegelin at work* must be imagined as *Voegelin in his work-shop*. Voegelin wrote his work alone,[4] yet he did not create it alone. Voegelin's workshop was part of his creation of his work. It was the intellectual studio (*Geistesatelier*) that he formed while drawing to himself those who could nourish his creative existence and, in particular, those who were able to help him press forward with his work.

The following presentation on Voegelin's workshop draws chiefly upon personal experiences and insights. These go back to the 1960s, when I began to study at the institute where Eric Voegelin worked: the Institute for Political Science on *Konradstrasse* in Munich. Through this study, I became acquainted with his workshop, as I now understand it in retrospect. He had made of the organism of the institute under his leadership (or better—under his inspiration) a workshop that was part of a larger workshop that extended far beyond Munich. I was drawn into this workshop in 1968, as I was finishing the dissertation that I later defended under Voegelin in the winter semester of 1968/1969. During that time, Voegelin turned to me increasingly with requests for information in the areas with which he associated me (theology and French intellectual history). Sometimes smaller research assignments developed from such inquiries—assignments for which, properly, I received a remuneration as a research assistant. I found it absolutely exciting, novel, and instructive to follow a scholar closely at work, to observe how he grasped knowledge as yet unknown, how he hewed himself a path of cognition, absorbed stimuli for his research, dismissed, shoved aside, and could be just as erratic as persistent in doing so. To that point, I had not yet experienced such a thing.

The most lasting impression that Voegelin made upon me at that time was his emotionality. A single citation that one had found somewhere and—as he then saw it—that was of absolutely extraordinary significance (albeit of one that others could not always see) was capable of setting him in high spirits for days afterward, days during which he continually returned to this "find." On a different occasion, a book that one had brought to him, for example, could provoke angry irritation. Here, some-one had used language that was alienated ("ideological") in Voegelin's eyes; and Voegelin no longer wanted to know anything further about what the book was actually about ("what am I supposed to do with it?"). He did this even when he knew—but was reminded in vain—that the materials that had been assembled here were actually of interest to him and could do nothing for the language in which they had been presented.

I fully entered into Voegelin's workshop, however, when I accepted his invitation to assume the position of Research Fellow at the Hoover Institution on War, Revolution and Peace at Stanford University. Voegelin himself was permitted to fill this position, which lasted in my case for two years beginning on October 1, 1970. There was no talk of a "workshop" in the letters that we had exchanged on the subject (his letter of invitation and my letter of acceptance). Rather, with the Stanford Fellowship Voegelin had granted me two years of the freest research and study. No formal responsibilities of any kind were attached to the Fellowship. In place of these, Voegelin took up soon after my arrival something of which I gradually became aware. I became aware of it, because it occurred so regularly—that is: almost daily. For an extended period of time and in a way that was, to a certain extent, even "obligatory," I had become a co-worker in the centre of Voegelin's workshop. In the innocuous way in which "rites" can develop among close friends or partners, Voegelin began to call me at my apartment on Webster Street in Palo Alto every morning from his office at his home on the Sonoma Terrace in Stanford. Never without having discreetly ensured for himself a silently assumed mutual agreement, he would discuss with me, in a conversation of a half—or three-quarters of an hour, what he had written the evening and night before, or what had occupied him in the reading—or better said, the thinking—that was connected with it. In Stanford/Palo Alto, I soon became equally familiar with other such means through which he formed his workshop and worked in it with others. These I came to know either because I myself was involved in them to a varying degree, or simply because I observed them.

With all this, it was inevitable that my own scientific curiosity would be aroused over and beyond the personal experiences. I called this phenomenon Eric Voegelin's "workshop," as I had come over time to understand it. My scientific curiosity was strengthened by two facts that had objectified it. First: as it emerged in Voegelin-researching conversations within the circle of Voegelin's *associates*, my own experience in Voegelin's workshop had been the experience of others as well. Thus did my initial impression crystallize into a general matter of fact. A glance beyond the limits of the discipline into literary studies[5] made it clear to me that the phenomenon of a workshop of the type that Voegelin cultivated for his thinking and writing had been thoroughly analyzed in studies of the process through which literary works are created.[6] This phenomenon has been extensively described in individual cases. Classical studies on this topic bear such titles as *Dickens at Work, Byron's Don Juan: The Making of a Masterpiece,* and *Keats's Craftsmanship.*[7] Such studies show that literary creations originate in the sense of a handicraft, of a workshop: with pieces of paper folded in four with four different versions of text written in ink of four different colors. Or take the example of Charles Dickens at work in a regular writing process that occurred daily between nine in the morning and two in the afternoon. This was accompanied by the author himself, still following the example of Charles Dickens, making, reflecting, and sending reports on the creative process to others in letters. Such letters demonstrate how he prepared his work using writing plans in his writing quarters or how he made it transparent in retrospect.[8]

II

Eric Voegelin had his own working and sleeping quarters in the house on Sonoma Terrace. Here were installed the books with which he worked, whereas the larger and more valuable—more valuable regarded from the perspective of the antiquarian, at least—portion of the Voegelinian library adorned the living room. Boxed files (typical, pale yellow American folders) were piled in and atop the shelves. Here, Voegelin had placed such loose materials as work notices, letters, photocopies (with which he very much liked to work) and manuscripts that had been sent to him. Mixed with these were journals like *Encounter* (which he read regularly) as well as his daily newspapers. For information on the stock markets, he read the *Wall Street Journal* first thing in the morning. Later in the day, he read the *New York Times*, which his wife Lissy always brought him from a newspaper store in Palo Alto (Frans on Lytton Ave.) together with his daily supply of cigars. Voegelin used his office at the Hoover Institute solely for practical business (settling correspondence, making telephone calls, and organizing research trips with the help of his secretary). He by no means worked in the publicly visible, typically American way of spending his workdays on the campus with his office door always open. Instead, he fit the classical image of an Old-European scholar (*Gelehrter*) completely. In Stanford as in Munich—and prior to that, in Baton Rouge—Voegelin withdrew for his creative work into the workshop that had been arranged at home to this purpose. For her part, Lissy Voegelin sheltered him to the extent that he wished it and excellently provided him with all the physical necessities of life.

Voegelin began his day at about eight o'clock. In the hour that directly followed, the calls in which he conversed with me about what he had thought and written the night before took place. If he went to his office, he showed up between nine and ten o'clock; if he stayed at home, he spent the hours before lunch—which occurred at about one o'clock—having further telephone conversations or reading. Sometimes he worked in the yard (where he attacked the "fungi" in the lawn as stubbornly as he did vainly). One of the morning telephone conversations was often a particularly important one: the call to the stock-broker at Merrill Lynch through whom Voegelin made his buying and selling deals in the American stock market. As it turned out, the scholar also regarded himself as a "business man," as he called himself during one of our conversations in October of 1980 when we saw each other for a few days in Florence. At that time, he always carried the *International Herald Tribune* with him; the first thing he discussed when we met was the latest news on the stock market. On this occasion, his intentions in speculating on stocks had been stimulated by the following news: "Did you read about the airplane accident with a Lockheed machine? The value of Lockheed's shares has fallen drastically. Now is the chance to buy! Of course I will stock up on Lockheed shares *now*."

On a usual day at Stanford, the businessman "disappeared" as soon as Voegelin and his wife had concluded their shared lunch, as did the telephone caller, reader and gardener. At this time, Voegelin absented himself for a long afternoon siesta during which he absolutely did not want to be disturbed. (If an unchecked call reached him here, the one who had made it would have succeeded in thoroughly ruining his chances with him for some time.) Voegelin seldom emerged from his siesta before four o'clock and, when he did, he was the scholar (*Gelehrte)* getting down to his work. He prepared for his writing (and his lecturing activity, which was intimately connected with it) with drawings, sketches and drafts; these were then transformed into graphic architectonic schemes for the text that he was about to write. And, of course, he wrote. The hours of the scholar who created in this way extended beyond midnight. On normal days, these hours were broken up by the evening meal, which he ate with Lissy between seven and eight o'clock. From this meal, Eric—supplied once more by his wife with ample amounts of coffee (albeit of the lighter, American kind)—withdrew immediately again into his workshop. In making the transition from working to sleeping, Voegelin often spent a few moments reading one of the crime thriller novels that were piled on the shelves surrounding his bedstead.

Voegelin usually wrote one to one and a half pages daily: typewritten pages, one-and-one-half spaced, equipped with generous margins. He typed his thoughts out directly on an old mechanical typewriter. Converted into words, this would have been approximately 450 to 500, but Voegelin did not calculate in these terms. Naturally, he wanted to make progress in writing a text, but "progress" meant for him above all to be as "true" and "clear" as possible in formulating the insight to be expressed and captured in linguistic terms. He himself was always the first to set this standard on his texts. That is why he wanted to leave so much space on the margins and between the lines of his typewritten pages. Scarcely after he had written them, he began to correct them with a black felt pen—to hone and reconstruct his words and syntax, to strike out concepts and sentence fragments, to fill in, shift back and forth, make the text as a whole more succinct and fluent, and more appealing and elegant. Once he had finished with this activity, Voegelin gave his secretary a version that was already the second" one of the pages he had written, even though "first" and "second" versions were to be found on the same page. She then typed up everything fresh. This then became the "third" version, which Voegelin himself improved, followed by yet another typo-free version. As far as this final version was concerned (speaking here of his habitual conduct), although Voegelin was still open to suggestions for correction, these now had to be accompanied by a commentary that took fundamental issue with his text in general: not merely with its language, but with its content. Thus did Voegelin begin to take leave of what he had written. He then distributed the latest sections of his work to selected persons in the form of photocopies.

In writing the pages that were now distributed, however, he had enlisted much more of his "workshop" than merely himself, his typewriter and his secretary. The work that occurred between the "first" and "second" versions endured a certain period of time—sometimes only a few hours,

sometimes one day, sometimes even several days. It was during this intermediate period that Voegelin brought others into his workshop. Or better
said: through them and with them, he expanded his writing workshop. The
expanded workshop had long and often included Lissy Voegelin; she was
usually the very first. Either she read what Eric wrote immediately, or he
read something to her out loud, or he tried out on her certain sentences that
he had in his head. No one else could protest as freely as she could: "But
Eric, nobody can understand that!" "Once again, you make here a *petition
of principle*" (with this much-loved formula, she meant: "this does not
work, please think it through afresh"). Lissy had a keen intellect and a
highly developed sense for language, which she constantly tended with her
reading of literature in both English and German. Effectively and repeatedly, she brought both of these gifts into Eric's workshop. (Hers, by the
way, was a contribution to Voegelin's work that the Voegelin research has
not yet acknowledged.)

In their shared home, Voegelin could incorporate his wife directly into
his working process. With others, he was forced to expand his workshop in
a more purposive way. I have already mentioned one way in which he
much preferred to take the initiative in this respect: he reached for the telephone receiver and rang up those people to whom he reported his work and
with whom he wanted to discuss the creative activity that had just
occurred. He made such calls with particular frequency during periods of
intensive writing, and above all during the interval between the "first" and
"second" versions, and he seldom restricted himself to calling solely one
person. That he so frequently called me at Stanford was due not least to the
fact that local calls were involved here; despite their length (Pacific
Telephone calculated even local calls according to their temporal length),
they were still inexpensive telephone conversations. Two other telephone
workshop connections that Voegelin valued highly were Gregor Sebba in
Atlanta and Manfred Hennigsen in Hawaii; he rationed both the length and
frequency of his calls to them on account of the considerably higher cost
of long-distance calls.

A second way in which Voegelin drew people into his workshop was
extraordinarily effective as a means to continually to surprise one, if not,
in fact, to cause one to shrink back and become inoperative in speechless
embarrassment. He favored the use of this method whenever someone vis-
ited him at his hotel or guest quarters during one of his trips or guest pro-
fessorships. The meeting—in the mind of the visitor, at least—would have
been assumed to be a visit made out of politesse or friendliness. One

certainly did not reckon with what would then occur: scarcely had mutual greetings been exchanged when Voegelin would take out a few sheets of paper. On these stood, in typewritten, mistake-riddled text or in scrawled handwriting, the sketches that he had drawn up wherever he happened to have been during the prior few days, or even during the prior few hours. He would then unflinchingly hand over these pages with the request to read them immediately. Nor would he make motions of any kind that might make this task easier—something like an inviting smile, some transitional words. He would simply regard one in total suspense and await the response that befit what he had written and what he had thought; and by "befit" we should understand here whatever helped improve the text—ideally, whatever helped *create* it anew.

Sometimes he snagged someone using this method at his home on the Sonoma Terrace. This he did with particular relish at one of the evening dinners to which he and Lissy often invited guests from all over. As soon as Lissy had bidden the guests to move from the dining room into the salon for a Grand Marnier (her preferred *digestif*) or a cognac after dessert had been served, Eric drew some guest or another off to one side. To Lissy's utter distaste, he would then take this person, from whom he usually already knew he could expect to receive some insightful feedback, into his office in order to surprise him with his latest theses.[9]

It was inconceivable to him that the products of his workshop would not have been the most interesting things in the world to those whom he had included within that workshop. Were these people not the mirror? Did they not co-produce through their reflection the image of Eric Voegelin striding through his thought? How, then, could they not have wished, consumed with interest, to absorb this image? Voegelin himself mightily encouraged it, both through the aforementioned telephone calls and through the "letter method" of constituting and maintaining his workshop. He used the latter to an extraordinary degree. One could devote a longer study under the aspect of the "workshop" to Voegelin's correspondence.[10] Extensive in both duration and addressees, it was also highly diverse. I will cite here only one thoroughly typical example of the constitution of his workshop in letter form as through a mirror.

Voegelin wrote to his American colleague and friend, Robert Heilman,[11] on June 19, 1996, shortly after the publication of *Anamnesis*.[12] The letter is framed by some introductory news and comments on Voegelin's activity in Munich and in Germany in general and by a few concluding pieces of information on plans for travel and the summer. As the centerpiece of the letter, however, Robert Heilman received a complete and concise presentation of *Anamnesis*, his friend's latest book. This came from his own pen; it was as though Voegelin sought to offer his work to Heilman in the mode of a confession, a kind of self-revelation of its creator. The two pages of the letter in which Voegelin introduces *Anamnesis* are a *self-portrait of Eric Voegelin at work*. In this self-portrait, presentations of the various stages of this work, hence, of Voegelin the creator, are layered upon one another. If we regard them as such, then the layers can be read in different ways (each individually and then combined); as a text of self-commentary in which Voegelin interpreted his work after having concluded it; as a description of contents in which he presents what is going on in his work in terms of material; as a memorandum on the history of thought in which Voegelin historically classifies and interprets both the course and the results of his work; and as a plan for his work that Voegelin may have had in mind during the process of the work's generation or might perhaps have committed to paper only in retrospect.

"It is my philosophy of consciousness," the letter stated about the book at the beginning. And: "I wanted to experiment with a new literary form in philosophy." "Let me explain," Voegelin immediately added, and then wrote further as summarized here: Heraclitus was the first thinker to have equated philosophy with the exploration of the soul *(psyche)*—its tensions, its dynamic, its structure—in its depths. From this point onward, interpretation *(exegesis)* of the soul or of consciousness remained the central concern of philosophy. Historically, however, philosophy in the secondary sense—communication of both the results of the interpretation and the logical speculative consequences—has been superimposed upon this concern. This is why philosophy in history occurs as an alternation between the exegeses of consciousness on the one hand and the formulation of its results as dogma on the other; the latter is followed by a return to the original consciousness, then by new dogmatization, etc. Presently, we are confronted with the tasks of ridding ourselves of a considerable accumulation of dogmas and of retrieving the original experiences of the tension of the human being toward the divine ground of its existence. Yet an authentic exegesis of consciousness can assume the form solely of direct observation accompanied by a meditative retrieval of the structure of the psyche. For its part, this structure is not a given that might be described using theoretical statements, but is itself a psychic process for which language symbols can be found only as the process occurs—a process that occupies a human life-span in any case.

From this arose the problems of the form of presentation. Heraclitus is said to have discovered the form of the aphorism. Another is the *via negativa* of Christian meditation, a form that was still used by Descartes. He himself, thus Voegelin continues, has proceeded along the path he describes in what follows. He then sketches the sequence of his own exercises in the exegesis of consciousness. Having begun with them in Baton Rouge in the fall of 1943, he concluded them—so he states—in the second half of 1965. Eight historical studies are built into this sequence, which forms one section of *Anamnesis*. As the second part of his book, these studies demonstrate how the historical phenomena of order have led to the kind of analysis that culminates in the meditative exploration of consciousness. The entire book, therefore, is pervaded by a dual empirical process: by a movement that begins with the historical phenomena of order and leads to the structures of consciousness from which it arose, and, conversely, by a movement that begins with the analysis of consciousness and leads to the phenomenon of order.[13] The latter occurs insofar as the structure of consciousness is the instrument through which the historical phenomena are interpreted. "Well," Eric Voegelin concludes his explication with qualifications that were certainly important to him and with self-established comparisons that are indeed very telling, "we'll see how the public will take to this novel form which is neither pre-Socratic, nor classic, nor Christian, though it has certain affinities to the mysticism of Plotinus and of Dionysius Areopagita—not to forget *The Cloud of Unknowing*."[14]

III

Voegelin was present in his workshop like a scholar-prince (*Geistesfürst*). He did not merely press onward with his creating; he *governed* it.[15] Creatively. On the one hand, then, he was suffused with the authority that flowed into him, the creator of his work, and rendered him in the eyes of others the *authority, Eric Voegelin,* in the kingdom of thought.[16] (This had useful consequences for his workshop.) On the other hand, however, he was utterly free with regard to his own work. As one who was not subject to it, he was always free of it: free to be able to think away again from that which had been created and to conduct himself, in his perceiving, experiencing and thinking, in a divergently curious, even a subversive way. Thus did Eric Voegelin confront his work as two figures at once: as the intellectually powerful prince of thought (*geistesmächtiger Denkfürst*) who was simultaneously the rebel that irreverently provoked respect and radically raised his fist. This occurred within the contexts both of his own thought and, with great relish, the perception of others.

In this way, dinners in a restaurant at which Lissy and Eric Voegelin convened with others could take on experimental features, sometimes for the larger part of their duration. In my recollection, such dinners occurred at the Peking restaurant on the Camino Real located on the edge of the Stanford campus or at the more elegant Mandarin restaurant in Palo Alto. Voegelin preferred these and several other Chinese restaurants. Sometimes they took place at the Tadich Grill in San Francisco, which Lissy Voegelin preferred on account of the excellent seafood it offered. After initiating a conversation, and without considering whether what was to follow would interest all who were present or would even be acceptable to them, Voegelin would present the latest ideas that had come to him in the course of his thought, of his work. Manifestly, these were ideas that he wanted first to "test." They were delivered in the manner he always maintained: one of presenting them as conceptual discoveries that were absolutely unfamiliar, shocking and unorthodox, yet of a far-reaching significance. Voegelin usually proceeded in precisely the same way in lectures and presentations, especially during the discussion round. On such occasions, he appeared as the figure of the experimental mind that rebelliously probed to the furthest, least expected limit.[17] The effect upon his audience was palpable: it brimmed with creative excitement as well. Voegelin regarded his lectures as a manifestation of his workshop that had no parallel anywhere else. As a matter of particular note, it was at just such lectures that Voegelin won others over to his thought and gained them for the study of his work.

In his workshop now, we see it just as he did it: before him at all times and in all places. But how did he summon it to shape his creative work with him? Would this not be the sight that we should wish to take in last of all? But how? In what follows, let us attempt to do so by way of the perspectives that are described.

In October 1968, at a congress of the *Istituto Accademico di Roma* in Rome, Voegelin met a researcher of prehistory and early history, Marie E. P. Koenig. From this encounter arose a scholarly relationship that both parties experienced as being exceedingly stimulating and beneficial to their work—and they tended it accordingly.[18] Voegelin, Marie Koenig later reported on the encounter that had initiated the relationship, "held a lecture at the *Istituto Accademico di Roma* and so did I. He came to me immediately and said: 'We must work together.'"[19] Why? In his understanding of the recent and quickly accumulating knowledge of pre-history and early history (especially of the Old Stone Age), Voegelin saw something he found to be very exciting. In the petroglyphs and drawings carved in the stones that had been left behind by the people of the Paleolithic Age, he saw a "further" symbolic order alongside the human symbolic orders that had been relevant for him during the conduct of his work on *Order and History*, his universal history of human symbolic orders. In a letter that he wrote to Marie Koenig shortly after their encounter in Rome, Voegelin stated:

> Your essay is of great value to me, because it shows that an histor-ical picture can indeed be crystallized out of the most diverse spe-cial prehistoric archaeological sciences that goes back at least to the beginnings of Homo sapiens. You can understand the impor-tance such an account has for me from the fact that the prehistoric symbols are the same as those that are found in the earliest written texts on political symbolism, i.e., in the Egyptian texts of the 3rd millennium B.C. Through comparison of these Egytian texts with the symbolism as you have presented it, the decisive step in sepa-rating the remnants of tradition from those symbols specific to an imperial civilization becomes possible.[20]

Volume IV of *Order and History, The Ecumenic Age*, was published in 1974 and Volume V, *In Search of Order*, in 1987. As he was working on these—those volumes of *Order and History* that had not yet been finished and were supposed to *follow* the three that had already been published—it became increasingly clear to Voegelin that a Volume "0" devoted to the symbolism of the Paleolithic human culture might *precede* Volume I, *Israel and Revelation*, published in 1956. On November 22, 1971, he sent a let-ter on behalf of Marie Koenig to the director of the *Gebr. Mann Verlag*, the publisher in Berlin to whom Marie Koenig had submitted the manuscript of her book on the petroglyphs in the Paleolithic Age.[21] In explaining the significance of Marie Koenig's work, Voegelin pointed out that this work permitted now to "prolong" the relationship between Neolithic-Mycenaean and Greek cultures "backwards" up to the "Paleolithic symbolism":

> I am writing to you in the matter of Mrs. Marie Koenig's manu-script on Paleolithic symbols.. . . . Mrs. Koenig's work is of great scientific importance since to date there has been no similar inter-pretive study on this subject at all. The prehistories that occupy

themselves with these problems are almost all historical positivists and hardly have any eye for the meaning of symbols. Mrs. Koenig's manuscript is all the more important since the research on Neolithic and Megalithic cultures makes more and more clear the connections of this pre-imperial layer of culture to the genesis of Greek culture. . . . Through Mrs. Koenig's work it is possible to extend the connections between the Neolithic-Mycenian and the Greek cultures backward into Paleolithic symbolism.[22]

The latest research had yielded increasing knowledge about the Paleolithic symbolism, and Voegelin quite energetically engaged in "backwards" research of his own.[23] This, in addition to her own unorthodox path as a private scholar who was bound solely to her own original ideas, was why Marie Koenig became Voegelin's highly treasured guide into the world of the Paleolithic Age. She advised him on the research literature and especially on his own research trips to sites of Paleolithic culture in Spain, England, Malta, and Hawaii. At her house in Saarbrücken, she acquainted him with her own research material. In 1977, she personally led him through the caves near Milly-la-Forêt in Ile-de-France (central France), where she was able to show him her insights into the symbolism of the Old Stone Age directly.[24]

During one of the morning telephone calls that I received from Voegelin at Palo Alto —this was in March of 1971—he abruptly posed the following question to me: "do you know the concept, *egophany*?" "No," of course, was the answer, and certainly the one to be expected, since, prior to the preceding evening, no such concept had existed. "You know," Voegelin continued, "I established the concept yesterday evening, as the opposite of the concept of theophany." He explained further: the revolt of the modern human being against God culminates in the phenomenon of the "absolute ego." In claiming the "absolute ego" as the status of his existence, the modern human being sets himself in the place of God. *Seeks to set himself* in the place of God, I objected immediately: for the modern human has not succeeded in doing so, and we were, of course, in agreement that he never could succeed in doing so. Voegelin did not dispute this; he himself constantly stressed that the revolt of modern thought against the reality of the divine is a pure illusion and not a reality. No matter how often and persistently the "ego" posits the divine status of the human being, it does not exist; thus, it cannot "appear" in the event of an "egophany." Voegelin offered no counters to objections of this type. Neither did he say that he would do better to give up his latest conceptual invention, nor did he declare that he would stick with it. The "test," in any case, had been conducted, and Voegelin drew *his* conclusions from it. He formally introduced the concept of "egophany" in *The Ecumenic Age* and presented it as a new linguistic symbol by which to analyze the "egophanic revolt," as he now called it, of modern thinkers.[25]

Upon reading two new texts he wrote, "Wisdom and the Magic of the Extreme" and "The Beginning and the Beyond," I wrote Voegelin a letter on February 27, 1981.[26] His answer arrived in a letter that was dated March 11, 1981. "I would agree with most of your critical questions," Voegelin informed me kindly, "especially because I am now working on an answer to them in Volume V [*In Search of Order*]."[27] If he did not answer them earlier, it is because he believed that I took a serious problem "too lightly" in posing my questions. He then seemed to be preparing to offer a critical corrective of what he understood to be my "posing of critical questions." In this workshop conversation in letter form, however, Voegelin ranged afield to address something entirely different. The letter became a self-declaration in which he methodically unveiled his mode of creating: his duty to the absolutely creative, his boundless openness to the empirical materials, his subversive curiosity and his work on concepts. This last was to a certain extent sculptural, seeking to construct symbolic complexes that could be visualized graphically and that were at once "beginning" and "end" in the process of his creating. These structures served both as the theoretical work that preceded the writing and as the theoretical plan once the writing had begun. Voegelin was painting a self-portrait in his intellectual studio (*Geistesatelier*):

> My analyses of consciousness go so far—and no further—than the historical material analyzed in a given case permits. I have no finished 'theory' that I apply. Each unjustified generalization might lead to conflicts with historical symbols of consciousness that I do not yet know or have overlooked. With Augustine, for example, I have just noticed the symbol of the *sacrificium confessionis*, which throws overboard all the boasts in the literature about the *Confessiones* being an autobiographical work and demands a new classification of a kind that I have not to this point considered.
>
> You are absolutely correct, however, when you note that the series of symbols of consciousness that have been developed are not isolated, but call for the formation of chains. I call such chains of symbols 'complexes' that cannot be isolated from one another.

I began to assemble catalogues of such complexes in Florence and enclose for you one such first attempt. Since then I have already come much further with this problem in my work on Volume V. But still: nothing without justification in the historical phenomena of consciousness.[28]

The following two pages bear a reproduction of the sheets of paper upon which Voegelin worked out, in the fall of 1980, his "complexes" of symbols for writing *In Search of Order*. These pages also serve as the conclusion of my contribution. If one turns in Voegelin's fifth and final volume of *Order and History* to pages 15 and 29 and begins reading from the respective pages, one can—comparing these to the pages that follow in the present chapter containing the "complexes"—trace a literary creation history back to the point of its very genesis (*Schöpfung*).[29]

[Eric Voegelin]
October 4, 1980[30]

COMPLEXES

1. *Consciousness* Reality   Language
    Intentionality   Thing-R.   Concepts &
    Luminosity   &   Symbols (participatory)
    (Refl. Dist.)   It-Reality   " (reflective)

2. *The Meditative Complex*
    Zetesis – Kinesis – Existence in the Metaxy
2a. *Expansion of Meditative Complex by Plato*
    Into an Order of Being   *(Philebus)*
    To hen – apeiron – measure

3. *The Hierarchy of Being*
    From Apeiron to the Nous (the Noetic Beyond)
    (With relations of Foundation & Formation)

4. *Partners in Being*
    Divine – Personal – Social – World

5. *Dimensions of Existence*
    Person – Society – History

6. *The Beginning and the Beyond and Time*
   Time & Beyond Time & Ambiguity

Beginning	—	of the Story	—	in Time
"	—	of the Story	—	beyond Time
End	—	of the Story	—	in Time
"	—	of the Story	—	beyond Time

   (No beginning *in* Time unless beginning *out* of Time . . . & no end *in* Time unless end out of Time)

7. *Being beyond Being*
   i.e., beyond being-things (including gods!)

8. *Mytho-speculation*
   Beginning & Beyond speculation (in compact form)
   Cosmogony – Theogony – Anthropogony – Historiogenesis

9. *The Historiographic Complex*
   Spiritual Breakthrough – Imperial Expansion – Historiogenesis
   (Note parallel in Renaissance)

10. *The Historical Process*
    (a) Compact Symbolization
    (b) Differentiations
        Noetic (ethnic differences)
        Pneumatic
    (c) Analysis of Consciousness

11. *"Theology"*
    (a) Compact "gods" – of *both* Beginning & Beyond
    (b) Creation and Salvation
    (c) Psychodramas
        i) exclusively salvational God – Gnosticism
        ii) identifying creator & savior God – Xtian Incarnation
        iii) psychodrama of the *mache athanatos* – Plato
    (d) The "It"

12. *The Ambiguous Psyche and Pneuma*
    Plato – Laws X
    Matthew – chapters 3 to 4

13. *Doctrine*
   Negative propositions - Positive propositions
   "Solution": Meditative Analysis

Endnotes

1   Barry Cooper, *Eric Voegelin and the Foundations of Modern Political Science* (Columbia, MO: University of Missouri Press, 1999); *Voegelin Recollected: Conversations on a Life,* Cooper and Jodi Bruhn, eds. (Columbia, MO: University of Missouri Press, 2008); Cooper, *Beginning the Quest: Law and Politics in the Early Work of Eric Voegelin* (Columbia, MO: University of Missouri Press, 2009).

2   I arrived at this formulation through the expression, "death-masks of conception," which can be found in Louis Hays's essay, "Die Dritte Dimension der Literatur: Notizen zu einer 'critique génétique,'" *Poetica*, Vol. 16 (1984), 307–323 (310).

3   As this essay originally was written in German, a few key terms will be noted in that language (Tilo Schabert, "Die Werkstatt Eric Voegelins," *Zeitschrift für Politik*, März 2002, 49(1): 83–95). For this English version the original German version was revised and enlarged.

4   On Voegelin's process of thought (*Denkweg*) and his method of working (*Arbeitsmethode*) compare Thomas Hollweck, "Gedanken zur Arbeitsmethode Eric Voegelins", *Philosophisches Jahrbuch* (Band 88, 1981), 136–152.

5   For which, as so often before, Ina Schabert was the guide.

6   Remarkably, such studies hardly exist in the fields of philosophy and political theory. In a review article published in *Le Monde* ("De l'atelier d'Arendt à l'établi de Badiou," March 24, 2006) Roger Pol-Droit typically asked at the beginning: How do philosophers work? What are the processes they use to elaborate their writings? He added that, curiously, there were only a very small number of elements for giving an answer to such questions. The theorists, Pol-Droit remarked, almost always furnish finished results. One doesn't know much about their "kitchen" (*cuisine*). There are no traces of any groping, of paths pursued or abandoned. One should, though, note one exception, he added: Hannah Arendt's *Denktagebuch*. But then, this is an intellectual diary of the author, Arendt herself, and not a study of her creative work in her workshop.

7   John Butt and Kathleen Tillotson, *Dickens at Work* (London: Methuen, 1957); Truman Guy Steffan, *Byron's Don Juan*, Vol. I, *The Making of a Masterpiece* (Austin and London: University of Texas Press, 1957); M. R. Ridley, *Keats' Craftsmanship: A Study in Poetic Development* (Oxford: Clarendon Press, 1933). Compare further the literature cited in Louis Hay, "Die Dritte Dimension der Literatur."

8   See John Butt and Kathleen Tillotson, *Dickens at Work*, 19, 25–27.

9   In his article, "Eric Voegelin: Reminiscences" (*Southern Review*, Vol. 32 (1994), 147–165), Robert Heilman reports: "During visits to the Voegelins in Palo Alto, we [Ruth and Robert Heilman, Lissy and Eric Voegelin] might, as I have said, dine together, or we might chat" (164). However, something else might happen too, as

Heilman reports: "Occasionally Eric would say, making a rare dip into colloquialism, 'Bob and I must have some boy-talk.' Off we would go to a restaurant, and by way of boy-talk Eric would hold forth on whatever topics he was currently exploring in his reading and writing." (Ibid.).

10   An exemplary illustration and "material" (to use a term Voegelin liked to apply) for such a study would be the extensive and intellectually very substantial correspondence with Alfred Schütz. See *Alfred Schütz. Eric Voegelin. Eine Freundschaft, die ein Leben ausgehalten hat. Briefwechsel 1938–1959*, Gerhard Wagner and Gilbert Weiss, eds. (Konstanz: Universitätsverlag, 2004). English edition: *A Friendship that Lasted a Lifetime: The Correspondence between Alfred Schütz and Eric Voegelin*, William Petropulos, trans., Gerhard Wagner and Gilbert Weiss, eds. (Columbia, MO: University of Missouri Press, 2011).

11   *Letter from Eric Voegelin to Robert Heilman*, dated June 19, 1966. See Hoover Institution (Stanford), *Eric Voegelin Papers*, Box 17, Folder 9. This letter has been published in *Robert B. Heilman and Eric Voegelin: A Friendship in Letters, 1944–1984*, Charles R. Embry, ed. (Columbia, MO: University of Missouri Press, 2004), 240–244 and in Eric Voegelin, *Selected Correspondence, 1950–1984, Collected Works of Eric Voegelin*, vol. 30, Sandy Adler, Thomas A. Hollweck, and William Petropulos, ed., trans. (Columbia, MO: University of Missouri Press, 2007), 503–506.

12   Eric Voegelin, *Anamnesis. Zur Theorie der Geschichte und Politik* (Munich: Piper,1966). – Edition in English: *Anamnesis. On the Theory of History and Politics*, M. J. Hanak, trans., David Walsh, ed., *The Collected Works of Eric Voegelin*, Vol. 6 (Columbia-London: The University of Missouri Press, 2002).

13   As to Voegelin's strictly empirical method of study, in particular with regard to consciousness, see the chapter, "Eric Voegelin, Empirical Political Scientist" in Barry Cooper's book *The Restoration of Political Science and the Crisis of Modernity* (Toronto-New York: Edwin Mellen Press, 1989), 271–282. On the place of Voegelin in the development of his own work, see Barry Cooper's account, "Weaving a Work," *Canadian Political Philosophy. Contemporary Reflections*, Ronald Beiner and Wayne Norman, eds. (Don Mills, Ont.: Oxford University Press, 2001), 374–385.

14   Voegelin, *Selected Correspondence, 1950–1984*, 505.

15   On the connection of the "creative" and "governing," compare Tilo Schabert, *Die zweite Geburt des Menschen. Von den politischen Anfängen menschlicher Existenz* (Freiburg: Alber, 2009); also Tilo Schabert, *How World Politics is Made. France and the Reunification of Germany*, John Tyler Tuttle, trans., Barry Cooper, ed. and abr. (Columbia-London: University of Missouri Press, 2009; American edition forthcoming, Chicago UP 2014).

16   In the obituary that appeared in *The Times* (London) on February 5, 1985, after Voegelin's death on January 19, it was noted: "As the heir to metaphysical and phenomenological traditions little understood in the Anglophone world, Voegelin's work was widely misunderstood by his contemporaries, though upon those many scholars whom he influenced, in political philosophy and theology, the influence ran very deep indeed. To say this is to suggest that he was a scholar's scholar of limited significance to the wider world. But this would be misleading. In recent

years the circulation of his work among dissident intellectuals who live under totalitarian regimes of Central Europe testified to his capacity to illuminate the experience of those who endure the regime of ideology triumphant." Worthy of additional attention is Voegelin's relationship to Hegel, which is manifestly competitive in his work.

17　"A formidable combination of scholarship and *prophetic passion*" (my emphasis, T.S.) characterized Voegelin, in the view of Robert Nisbet. See his article "Eric Voegelin's Vision," *The Public Interest* (Spring 1983), 110.

18　See here the correspondence between Eric Voegelin and Marie E. P. Koenig, *Eric Voegelin Papers*, Box 21, Folder 15; and: Gabriele Meixner, "Marie E. P. Koenig— ihre Konzepte und ihre Bedeutung für die feministische Forschung," *Vom Knochenmann zur Menschenfrau. Feministische Theorie und archäologische Praxis*, ed. Sigrun M. Karlisch, Sibylle Kästner, Eva-Maria Mertens (Münster: Agenda Verlag, 1997), 140–160; Gabriele Meixner, *Auf der Suche nach dem Anfang der Kultur. Marie E.P. Koenig. Eine Biographie* (Munich: Frauenoffensive, 1999), especially 139 ff. English translations of letters are published in Voegelin, *Selected Correspondence, 1950–1984*, 576–577, 621–622, 668–669, 747–748, 828.

19　Meixner, *Auf der Suche nach dem Anfang der Kultur*, 139. Translation by present author.

20　*Letter from Eric Voegelin to Marie E. P. Koenig,* dated October 14, 1968, Voegelin, *Selected Correspondence, 1950–1984*, 576–577.

21　The book was accepted by Gebr. Mann Verlag and appeared in 1973 under the title, *Am Anfang der Kultur: Die Zeichensprache des frühen Menschen.*

22　*Letter from Eric Voegelin to Dr. Peters*, dated November 22, 1971 (*Eric Voegelin Papers*, Box 21, Folder 15). The editor of Voegelin, *Selected Correspondence, 1950–1984*, dates this letter in 1970 (month and date are not indicated). The translation is taken from the published version in this volume (641). Emphasis added by present author.

23　Voegelin's research efforts on Volume "0" endured through the years. See the numerous letters in which he reported on and explained them. This is just a selection: *Letter from Eric Voegelin to Wilhelm Hennis*, dated November 2, 1972: "I have worked now for two years on the results of archeological research concerning the Paleolithic and Neolithic to make them useful for political science. I have just returned from a research trip to Ireland and England, where I have seen most of the excavations (*Ich arbeite jetzt seit zwei Jahren daran, die Ergebnisse archaeologischer Forschung betreffend Palaeolithikum und Neolithikum für die Politische Wissenschaft brauchbar zu machen. Eben komme ich von einer Forschungsreise nach Ireland und England zurück, wo ich die meisten Ausgrabungen gesehen habe.*)" (*Eric Voegelin Papers*, Box 18, Folder 1, translated by editors); *Letter from Eric Voegelin to the author*, dated April 4, 1973: "The travel plans for this fall have not yet been entirely worked out. If it is somehow possible, I would like to see the new excavations in Iran. Unfortunately, they are very difficult to access, and the preparations require a good deal of time." (Archive of the author and *Eric Voegelin Papers*, Box 33, Folder 1); *Letter from Eric Voegelin to Cleanth Brooks*, dated April 20, 1973: "In the recent years I have been working on prehistoric and archaeological materials that have become suddenly of acute importance, because of the revision of the radio-carbon dates since 1966. Our whole picture of history has been radically changed. In the pursuit of these problems we have taken trips to Hawaii, Yucatan, Malta, Crete and Greece. . . . For the coming fall I am hesitating between Iran and Turkey on the one hand, and the Megalithicum of the Bretagne and Spain on the other." (Voegelin, *Selected Correspondence, 1950–1984*, 764); *Letter from Eric Voegelin to Friedrich Engel-Janosi*, dated June 4, 1973: "In the last few years I have conducted studies on Neolithic civilizations that have led us to Hawaii, Yucatan, Malta, Crete, Greece, and Ireland. This year, if possible, we want to investigate the Megalithic of Bretagne and perhaps also Spain. . . . At the moment I am most interested in the Neolithic cultures, since the historical picture has completely changed since 1966 due to the revision of the C-14 dates. It is now certain that there was a series of Neolithic civilizations that temporally preceded the Sumerian and the Egyptian. For instance, the Maltese temple culture existed about 1000 years before the time of the pyramids. " (Voegelin, *Selected Correspondence, 1950–1984*, 770). Voegelin also supplemented his library throughout the seventies with a large number of books on primordial and early history.

24 On October 4, Voegelin wrote Marie Koenig a letter of thanks, stating quite in accordance with his empirical way of working: "It became once again apparent that one has to see things on location, if one wants to understand them correctly" (*Letter from Eric Voegelin to Marie Koenig*, dated October 4, 1977, Voegelin, *Selected Correspondence, 1950–1984*, 828).

25 Eric Voegelin, *The Ecumenic Age, Order and History*, Vol. 4 (Baton Rouge: Louisiana State University Press, 1974), 260.

26 These two works have been published as: "Wisdom and the Magic of the Extreme: A Meditation," in *Published Essays, 1966–1985, Collected Works of Eric Voegelin*, vol. 12, Ellis Sandoz, ed. (Columbia, MO: University of Missouri Press, 1990), 315–375, and "The Beginning and the Beyond: A Meditation on Truth," *What is History? And Other Late Unpublished Writings, Collected Works of Eric Voegelin*, Thomas Hollweck and Paul Caringella, eds., 173–232 .

27 *Letter from Eric Voegelin to the author*, March 11, 1981, *Selected Correspondence, 1950–1984*, 864. The translation reproduced here is by the author.

28 Ibid.

29 Voegelin, *In Search of Order, Order and History*, vol. 5 (Baton Rouge: Louisiana State University Press, 1987).

30 Translated from German, in collaboration with the author, by Jodi Bruhn.

Chapter Twelve
Hope Does Not Disappoint[1]
David Walsh

When hope is lost, then it is needed most of all. It is only when the situation has become hopeless that hope comes into its own, for we cannot lose hope. The very meaning of hope is bound up with this paradox by which the more it is lost the more deeply it is retained. This is evident in the ordinary meaning of the word, for we would hardly consider it a mark of hope if it was present merely when everything was going well. On the contrary, we are inclined to think, it is precisely when the whole world has fallen apart that hope rises to sustain us. It is in this sense that hope does not disappoint. Everything else may disappoint, but hope cannot, because it has already reached its goal. This is what it means to hope, that we cannot be disappointed. Nothing that happens can dislodge us from our hope, because that is precisely what hope is, a warrant against disappointment. That is not the same as success. Hope does not carry a guarantee that we will accomplish or reach the objectives we set for ourselves. But it does immunize us against abandonment of the struggle. Without giving us the sure possession of our goal, hope provides us with the only sure pathway toward it. Through hope we lay hold of our goal and thereby become capable of reaching it. Put another way, we might say that we have already arrived at the goal at which we still have yet to arrive. Hope is what spans the work of life. We may think that it is up to us to hold onto hope but it is really hope that holds onto us. In the end this is why hope cannot disappoint. We may disappoint, but hope, by definition, is what cannot disappoint. Hopelessness is only our failure to hope. It is not a failure of hope itself.

All of this dynamic comes vividly into view at times when hope itself is under strain, when we can discern few reasons for hope. In the absence of hope we become aware of its deeper undertow. We realize, not only that hope does not depend on reasons, but that it is most manifest when the reasons for hope have disappeared. The crisis of confidence that has gripped the world financial markets and pervaded the global economy is such an instance. Hope in the ordinary reliability of contracts has evaporated, while the clothes of optimism are in tatters. Acceptance of the normal ups and downs of business transactions has been replaced by the paralysis of a globalized distrust of exchange. Metaphors of machines seizing up hardly capture the sheer panic of the prospect that cash would no longer be available when we sought to withdraw it from our machines. The terror that induced money managers to accept, even for a short while, a negative return on US Treasury bills is a more telling indication. When no repository can be relied upon funds must be parked in the only repository that can be relied upon. It was a moment of acute awareness of the insubstantiality of all of the arrangements so routinely taken for granted. The world economy rested, we saw, on evanescence. Collectively we experienced that unmistakable jolt with which our feet pound the floor when we thought we still have one more step to descend. Instantaneously we are alert to what we had scarcely been aware of only moments ago. We saw with searing clarity that the whole vast network of interlocking transactions was in reality nothing more than a web of hope. Would it endure?

The global shudder that pervaded world financial markets and has now rippled through the real economic relationships of our lives has yet to encounter an answer to that question. Recession is merely recognition of the absence of an answer. That is, the cascading effect of myriad individual choices to withdraw from circles of exchange in order to hoard all that is of value. Without hope, our global economy spirals downward without a break against its descent. This is what is unusual about our present moment. There is no source of a counterthrust. All are caught in the same downward inexorability. Yet even this global character of the decline seems less a cause than a symptom of an underlying deficit that is more than economic. The mere absence of money does not betoken a lack of it, only an extreme aversion to circulating it. Everything remains as it was in the real world of those tangibles on which human existence and flourishing depends while, at the same time, everything has changed in the way we regard them. Value has declined because demand has dried up. Now, such corrections, we know, are normal in the course of any economy in which supply and demand get out of balance. Indeed, price changes are the main signal and mechanism by which such adjustments are effected. Here, however, we seem to have entered onto a persistent preference for withdrawal that, if it were to continue, would have catastrophic consequences. Whatever the hazards contemplated from global warming, the effects of prolonged recession would be far more detrimental to the billions sustained by systems of global exchange. It is the possibility of a world economic collapse on top of the narrowly avoided financial meltdown that concentrates our attention. We begin to see the real scope of the danger if our present moment extends beyond a temporary readjustment to become a continuing aversion to the very dynamism of economic growth through which our world has been built. Such a turn can become more than an economic downturn. It carries within it the darkest possibility of a turn against life itself.

We are not, of course, at that point, but the sharp reversal of our fortunes has brought into view the extent to which we have lived on hope. A self-fulfilling prophecy that the future will be better than the past has no other basis for its fulfillment than the prophecy itself. Once alerted to the insupportability of such a faith, the headlong pace of descent accelerates. It is only if we can somehow regain the anchor of hope that there is any possibility of arresting the momentum. We know that all we have achieved has been made possible by the powerful dynamic of hope and yet we also know that such achievements can hardly underpin the hope that has made them possible. Somehow hope must be rediscovered as the momentum that enables us to stay aloft so long as it is not questioned too closely. Our situation is reminiscent of the bumblebee whose flight is predicated on its unwillingness to listen to the animadversion that its wings are too slight to support it. Everything works out fine for the bumblebee so long as it eschews such self-doubt. Abrupt economic descent seems to originate in a similar moment of self-debilitation. Yielding to the proliferating uncertainties that afflict every possible transaction, we reflexively turn aside from the imponderables of risk through which action takes place. Instead, we hold back from existence thinking we can thereby regain the mastery we have lost. Such a step is fatal. It is the deliberate turning away from the dynamic of life by which we are drawn beyond ourselves to forge bonds of mutual responsibility. The fatality is made evident by its impossibility for, far from achieving a new position of mastery over the whole in which we find ourselves, we have only thereby managed to shrink existence into a nullity. Withdrawal is not an alternate form of existence, but merely the definitive form of non-existence. No more than any living thing can we choose to enter a state of suspended animation; the economy cannot opt to suspend the dynamic of growth by which it is sustained.

Political Infusions of Hope

What has been instructive in the current upheaval is that even when economic institutions have been inclined to effect such a preference, they have not been permitted to do so. Much has been made of the parallels to the Great Depression of the 1930s and no doubt there are such. But the one decisive difference has been in the political responses. In contrast to the aversion against energetic economic intervention in the earlier era, now we are more likely to suffer from an excess of political intrusion. The one thing that policy makers cannot be accused of is inaction. Governments around the world have been highly solicitous of the capital requirements of the financial markets and of the stimulative spending mandated for economic recovery. All have pursued the same policy directions, while diverging only on the levels of commitment indicated. So far, too, governments have displayed a remarkable degree of coordination, extending even to the need for revitalization of the developing world. At this point no one can tell what the outcome of such abundant ministrations will be, whether they will have the intended benefits or will lead to yet unexpected consequences. What has become clear, however, is the principle of the priority of politics over economics that remained in doubt during the 1930s. This is indeed the outcome of that bitter experience of the Depression and its unfolding into the great totalitarian convulsion of the Second World War. Now, no government is prepared to stand aside while its economy spirals downward and, to the extent that all national economies have become interdependent, that predetermination has become universal. Taken as a whole, such initiatives constitute an impressive affirmation of the communal or social reality that, while normally unnoticed, nevertheless undergirds a system of free economic exchanges.

Private property that is communally produced, Marx declared, cannot simply be owned by individuals. All have a share in its production and therefore a claim on its benefits. But Marx's is still an excessively materialist perspective, suggesting that wealth is a physically fixed quantity. In reality, as we see in the current asset deflation, the very meaning of wealth is socially constituted. Diamonds and houses remain what they were, as useful or as useless as previously, only now they have declined in value because demand for them has shrunk. What we thought was owned individually turns out to have a very significant component of social recognition built into it. Not only is the very idea of property socially constituted, for ownership is primarily what other people regard as my possessions, but much of the value of such commodities is inextricably tied to the estimates and exchanges that take place in the minds of others. Use value is constant, but that is by far the least significant component of value. It has been the precipitous decline in socially constituted wealth that has had such depressive effects in prompting a flight from leverage and risk. Who would want to buy or borrow when the same things may be had more cheaply in the future? Why assume risk when everyone is heading for safety? Such are concerns not just of individual decision-making but of the social whole from which individuals take up the cues to which they respond. An economy is made up of multiple individual centers of decision, but its dynamism derives from the mutuality of interconnection that is more than a product of separate wills. For better or worse we are bound together for better or worse. Even our individual calculations are premised on the sustaining dynamism of the whole that is nowhere reducible to the sum of its separate constituents. When pressed to identify the source of that overarching confidence or hope, we can only suggest that it comes from outside ourselves. We are not simply individuals; we are members of a social whole. That is why the collapse of confidence must be socially or, more precisely, politically addressed, since it is through political organization that societies take action.

The interesting question is, what gives the political community the confidence that it can recapture the hope that has been lost at the economic level? How is it possible for governments to inject the trust that must be present before the cycle of exchange, buying and selling, can even begin? Can political action compel what cannot be compelled? What is noteworthy about the present energetic interventions from the political side is that they have been undertaken only reluctantly, with full recognition that they must also recede at the earliest signs of economic reawakening. Government knows that it cannot substitute its direction for the initiatives of the free market. We are not in any danger of a political overreach that would supplant the vitality of private enterprise. Consensus revolves around the recognition that free markets are the prodigious generators of wealth; government can only offer a pale substitute for their dynamism. Even countries, like China, with the institutional capacity to return to a command economy show not the slightest inclination to do so. They seek only to restore the market to its full vigor, albeit with whatever regulatory mechanisms might be indicated for its future enhancement. Interventions are, in other words, largely premised on the necessity of making markets work better. Government aims at restoring, not abolishing, economic liberty. No doubt there will be some resistance to the devolution of political powers assumed within the crisis, but the temptation would have to overcome the longstanding objection of the unsuitability of government to the generation of wealth. So what then is the nature of the interventions undertaken by political communities? They have been nothing less than a redirection of the markets toward their own social nature. There is no incompatibility between the political and the economic, because the economic already points toward the political. Markets are only apparently constituted by a privileging of private decisions. Their reality is that they constitute a public order. Participants may generally ignore that larger good that sustains their pursuit of private profits, but they cannot, as we have seen, utterly disregard the consequences of their actions on the system as a whole except at their peril. The logic of markets is that they are sustained by what is not reducible to the terms of the market.

Profit and loss may seem to be defined by the perspectives of the particular entities involved, but the possibility of their interrelationship derives from considerations that are beyond measurement in terms of profit and loss. It is well known that there are many factors that make market exchanges possible that are not susceptible to being bought and sold in the same way. Honesty and reliability, as well as the rule of law and the enforcement of contracts, cannot simply be priced. They are not for sale. Buying and selling are possible only because of the presence of such transcendent commitments. This is also why we cannot buy and sell human beings, or in any way discount the dignity of their humanity, because their engagement in commercial exchange is possible only by virtue of their full spiritual reality. Markets, far from diminishing the stature of human beings, imply their non-reducibility to the finite terms of their transactions. This elevation of human dignity was entirely overlooked by Aristotle and much of the traditional disdain of commercial grubbiness, a prejudice refuted in the sheer human exuberance that exceeds the boundaries of virtually all economic transactions. But over and above such individual transcendence of the marketplace, there is also the living dynamism of the systems of exchange as a whole. It is not just that individuals and their virtues are beyond negotiations of the market, but that markets themselves are somehow more than they appear to be. In themselves markets are a testament to hope in a future that does not arise from any particular contract. Nothing in what has happened fully justifies the virtually limitless confidence with which they confront the future. Even risk assessment seems to be premised on the faith that risk might be defeated. However dubious such an effort of containing what cannot be contained is, we nevertheless persevere within the hope, because we know that without such hope there would be no possibility of overcoming the unpredictabilities that can be overcome. The difficulty is that the economy has no way of recollecting what it had never made articulate to itself. Hope does not disappoint, but it can be forgotten.

Politics Constituted by Hope

Recollection of hope is the function of the political community. We might say, along the lines of Hegel, that the community that is implicitly present between participants in the marketplace becomes explicit in the mutual recognition that constitutes the political community. It is at that point that hope comes into view, since the political community is its historical invocation. No one asks whether there will be a market; it is simply taken for granted, except on those occasions when its collapse raises the question. But the political community stakes its existence on a promise toward the future that cannot occur without express acknowledgment of the order of time in which it finds itself. When the political community comes to the aid of the beleaguered economy, it makes explicit what is merely implicit in the latter. Politics is the truth of economics. Hegel understood this rather well, for he was probably the first thinker to recognize that the economic system, while it follows its own autonomous dynamic, cannot subsist without the political umbrella. As a system of mutual cooperation, albeit operating through the invisible hand of self-interest, the economy could not be sustained without acknowledgment of its political culmination. That is, the pursuit of private profit is only one side of economic reality and not by any means its most significant aspect. Deeper even than the participants are aware is the community that makes the rounds of exchange possible and that in turn is sustained by them. Politics, too, may lack the full linguistic evocation of the priority of hope, but it cannot evade the awareness that it is more than the sum of its parts. Individual citizens are bearers of responsibility toward a good greater than their individual well-being, while that fidelity is itself the product of a faith without which their individual efforts could neither be initiated nor sustained. It is in the political community that the spiritual reality of human life is finally acknowledged. We are not the source of that larger dynamic of existence by which we are lifted beyond ourselves. It is rather the case that our self-transcendence is merely the point at which the spirit of hope is apprehended. Hope in this sense is not ours for, strictly speaking, we belong to it.

This may seem a rather elevated conception of politics and indeed it is, but it leads directly to some crucial practical consequences. Governments, it turns out, can raise virtually unlimited money on the world capital markets. It has been through this process that governments have been able to undertake such vigorous measures to arrest the financial and economic declines. When great multinational companies that had for years bestrode the globe either could not access or could not afford the terms of credit markets, mere governments have been able to raise as much as they desired on extremely favorable terms. Now while the "b-word" has been mentioned in reference to some governments, none have come anywhere near the precipice over which the great investment banks and other corporations have fallen. To date, at any rate, no government entities have found the capital markets irrevocably closed to them. Besides, what would it mean for a country to go bankrupt? Insolvency is a condition that attaches only to those entities that are reducible to their parts. Bankruptcy proceeding is merely the legal process by which that dismantling is effected. For a political community, that is not just unthinkable; it is impossible. The political community is so elusive, as Aristotle discovered, that it cannot even be identified with its constitutional form. Always there is what is over and above every change through which it passes. There are no parts to be sold off, because the political community scarcely exists in such transient expressions of its reality. Indeed it cannot go bankrupt because it is never truly and fully present at any time in its history. It is this historical existence that at once insulates the political community from the mortality of all mere enterprise associations and at the same time ensures its capacity to call on virtually unlimited resources. To the extent that the civil association exists in an indeterminate time horizon, it is not shackled by the determinate commitments within which all other entities must live. The state can mortgage not just the present, its pledges can include the future. Just as the present generation has honored the debts incurred by the past, so it can, in turn, make commitments that entail future generations. Of course, that does not mean that the political community can draw on unlimited resources or presume on the forbearance of its successors, but it does mean that the limits are more elastic than those of all other corporations. States alone do not have to amortize their debt, since they are more than mortal.

They do go into and out of existence, but even when they are no longer present they seem to retain an attenuated presence. Despite the solidity of the instruments of state power and the firmness of the trappings attached to it, we know that this fierce reality is in many ways the least substantial aspect. Expressions of political might are only the temporary manifestations of a vitality that reaches back into a remoteness beyond memory and stretches toward a future that is all but invisible. Swords and tanks eventually rust, nuclear warheads decay, and all the accumulated economic might drains away, but the community from which they spring endures through generational renewal. The inexorability of death is defeated, not just through the miracle of biology, but through the even greater miracle of the spiritual bond of union. A state cannot die, because it literally does not exist, at least not in the sense of any physical entity in space and time. Its real existence is through the community that spans space and time and therefore escapes their vicissitudes, to a very considerable extent. The language of a contract has been invoked to denote this spiritual condition through which the political community exists. But there has always been something too specific in such a notion, as contract theorists themselves always conceded. Edmund Burke perhaps came closest to the core of the political community when he described it as an "eternal contract" between the ages and the generations. In other words, the state is founded not through the actions of its founders, but through the founding that has already occurred before they or any of their successors come on the scene. Perhaps it would be more accurate to say that founding is made possible by the pre-founding that happened before they began. We do not make contracts, contracts make us. It is this constitution outside of space and time that is the source of the formidable power of the political community both to maintain itself and to shelter us from the disasters that befall us.

The resources on which the political community can draw are beyond the limits of all other entities, because the political community emerges from beyond those limits. In this sense we may say that the political community is the pure sign of hope, the hope that does not disappoint, because it has already reached its goal. If the contract that constitutes it is eternal, then it has already surpassed the uncertainties of existence. The ups and downs through which the state may pass cannot erase what is there as the condition of possibility for the unending struggle of its existence. In each generation we play our part in transmitting the community in which we find ourselves before we even begin. At one level, this imposes an awesome responsibility on us to preserve and pass on all that we have received; at another level we have nothing to pass on but what can never be passed on because it always remains untouched. We are bound together in mutual responsibility within and across the generations, but there would be no possibility of being bound if we were not already in a community of mutual responsibility. It is, of course, up to us to build up and provide for the future as an act of homage to those who cared for us from the past. But there would be no possibility of such an undertaking if we were not from eternity already related across and within time. Responsibility is ours, but the condition of responsibility does not depend on us. It has already been given, and it cannot be taken away. A political community can only be built up by those who are already in community with one another, even though they may not even know it yet. This is precisely the relationship we have with those who came before us and who follow after us. We do not know one another, yet we are known to one another. It is possible for us to join together because we have already been joined together before our lives have begun or ended. Not only is failure not an option, it is not even possible.

All of this was no doubt only dimly intuited in Burke's striking formulation of an "eternal contract," but such intimations are an inarticulate source of its evocative power. His formulation perfectly captures the faith that is needed for a political community to persevere through the vicissitudes of history, because the faith itself is not exposed to the same deviations. Nothing about this faith guarantees that it will reach its worldly goal, but it does inure it against abandonment of the effort. States will still disappear from history, but even when they do, their idea, that which sustained them from eternity, remains unimpaired. Burke himself was familiar with lost causes, having backed more than his fair share over the course of his public career. But he also knew that practical defeat affected the moral principle that was at stake not one whit. He was very much like Plato, who knew that the actual Athens with its corrupt self-destructiveness did not in the slightest impair the true Athens he beheld within himself. Unfortunately, the association of this true city with the term "idea" has proved to be a major obstacle to apprehending its real status. Western political thought has struggled to overcome the association of what is known inwardly with all forms of private, imaginary, and subjective connotations. Largely overlooked in the discussion has been the derivation of all real historical cities from this ideal reality. It has been difficult to unravel the paradox of the Platonic heritage in which the ideal city is the most real, while the real city is the least real. It is only with Hegel that the issue begins to be resolved, although even he has far from won universal assent to his claim that the opposition is entirely redundant. The exhortation, he explained, by which the actual city is pressed to conform to the ideal makes no sense unless the latter is somehow contained in the former. There may, of course, be a tension between the two, but it is premised on their deeper affinity, for we cannot be exhorted to become what we are unless we are somehow what we are to become. It is within that irremovable tension that history unfolds.

The formidable power by which states make history, nowhere more vividly on display than the switch by which governments became debtors and creditors of last resort, arises directly from their historical existence. When credit markets had suddenly closed to all other entities, governments had little difficulty in raising capital that they in turn lent back to all the recently rebuffed borrowers. Overnight governments had been entrusted with the wealth of the world, not because they were judged to be better managers of it, but simply because they could not disappear. General Motors or Citigroup have revenues larger than many states, but they can only call on the finite resources of their current shareholders. There are no future generations of owners ready to honor the debt incurred for the sake of the corporation's survival. Yet even the smallest state can summon the loyalty of citizens not yet present in time. There will always be an Iceland but the same cannot be said for Lehman Brothers. The relationship of the participants to the larger enterprise is markedly different. Owners of joint stock companies are by definition willing to put a limited amount of capital at risk for the sake of their projected gains, while citizens find themselves placed under a limitless obligation only remotely connected to the benefits they may expect to receive. The one can calculate the limit of his indebtedness in advance, while the other may not know when he will be called upon to exceed the full measure of devotion. The reason for the astounding durability of associations of the latter sort is not hard to see. They are formed on the basis of a debt that cannot be fully repaid, so that it is not surprising that they are prepared to shoulder burdens whose limits cannot be known in advance. This is the very meaning of the historical existence of political communities. They are constituted by a readiness to sacrifice that, because it is indeterminate, is prepared for every eventuality.

Obligation as Hope

An eternal contract is one to which our name has been affixed even before we have been named. Far from being a mere aspiration or ideal to which we might choose to lend our support, the obligatory force of the political community is of a primordiality that outweighs all else within our existence. It is for this reason that the unreal, that which is not yet, is the most real, that which underpins everything else. Before there is political action, there is the obligation that propels it. Our moral language, like our political language, has suffered from an excessive individualism, beginning with the Greek discovery of mind as the seat of decision-making. As autonomous, as self-legislating, we seem to be always there before the decision has to be made and therefore enjoy a distance stretching infinitely away from us. But this is completely the opposite of the concrete moral life, where duty imposes itself upon us with a brutality that is far from welcome. Obligation leaves us with no choice. That is its very meaning. Our freedom has been abolished once we find ourselves under obligation. That, of course, does not mean that we ever lose our freedom to walk away, to abandon our responsibility, but it does mean that such freedom is tantamount to the abandonment of its highest calling. What does freedom mean when it has been turned against itself? This is a familiar question within the kind of liberal discourse that marks our modern moral reflection. While we may not have unraveled the conundrum of freedom, we have not by any means despaired of the attempt. The crucial insight we have yet to absorb is that freedom is not something we can comprehend, for it comprehends us in our entire existence. Only the freedom inextricably woven into our prior obligations is worthy of the name. The force of such obligations may initially strike us as a diminished reality—they are, after all, still to be determined by our free choice—but in hindsight we realize that they encompass the whole reality of our being. Obligations are not an unreal possibility, but the very real ground of all possibility. It is we that are in danger of becoming unreal if we fail to live up to them.

Despite his reputation as an idealist, Kant is the point at which this primordiality of the moral life begins to find its appropriate formulation. His elevation of duty to a primacy that supersedes all other considerations is, however, only a beginning, because he still did not manage to identify the full existential import of that prioritization. For Kant, it is still we that make duty possible, rather than the other way around. It is only when attention is shifted to the political level that the generative and regenerative force of duty becomes fully apparent. Duty makes historical existence possible, to wit, the persistence of political communities bound together over time by nothing more substantial than that transcendent imperative. This is what has been in evidence in the impressively elastic borrowing capacity of governments of late. Over and above the daily gyrations of markets is a readiness for responsibility that arises from depths hitherto unsuspected. It is that possibility of shouldering responsibilities beyond pragmatic calculations that impresses us with the reality in depth from which our lives have always emanated. The pull of obligation is deeper than we are ourselves. It is almost as if we are the latecomers who must take up the call of duty that has preceded us. In this regard, exhortation is beside the point, for there would be no point in exhorting us to step up to the call of duty if we had not already heard it. Those who cannot sense its imperious pull can hardly even be candidates for such homiletics. By contrast, those who hear such an appeal have already heard it as the very condition of their hearing. The moral undertow of existence is so close to us that it is nearer to us than we are ourselves. It is this closeness that has been the reason we have so often overlooked it, for we can scarcely gain the distance needed to see it apart from ourselves. A rupture is required to open us up to the glimpse of what it is that makes our moral existence possible. In sacrificing ourselves, we see that we are not our own but are rather carried along by a goodness that is greater. All moral action is an enlargement of the self, but its possibility is rooted in the transcendence of the self that is prior to even being a self. It is what we are not that enables us to become what we are.

The eternal dimension is what makes time possible. History is a possibility only for beings that are not historical, at least not in the sense that their reality is wholly contained within history. With us it is precisely the impossibility of encapsulation within finite expression that makes the unfolding of all conversation possible. There is something inexhaustible, we know, about every human being, an unfathomability that makes it impossible to finally know him or her, or even ourselves. No matter what is said or done, the sayer or the doer escapes all tangibility. This mystery at the core of the person is not something incidental but the central possibility of our existence. Only occasionally do we brush up against the abyss of unattainability, yet it is palpable in every moment through which we pass. When pressed to name it, we are incapable of giving it a definition, for all definitions arise out of the indefinable. But we do know that it is the mystery of the beyond in which we participate without ever knowing what it is. Even more than what is accomplished, it is who we are. It is this possibility of communication beyond all that is said that makes it possible for us to join with one another in the formation of political communities bound together through time. We know one another before we even know one another, because we have already responded to the call of the other before we have even met. Responsibility, that by which we are connected with those we do not know, is what makes it possible for us to bridge the separations of space and time. History is merely the path along which responsibility is enacted. The capacity of political communities to undertake commitments indefinitely into the future is testament to their transcendence of all purely temporal origins.

They aim, not at success, but at the eternal principles from which all action springs. In this sense they have always already reached the goal which still has to be attained through the struggle with the vicissitudes of time. Whether the target is hit or missed is not the most crucial aspect, for there would be no possibility of action unless it were first kept in mind. Already our minds have leapt ahead to that goal as the very condition of the whole uncertain undertaking. The possibility of reaching it lies in the priority of having reached it. Failure appears incidental to the trial. What counts is fidelity to the beginning that can be lost, not by the inabilities and adversities that block our way, but by deviation from the principle itself. It is the possibility that we might fail to hold on to the principle by which we are held that is the great danger. Even when the exercise of responsibility is prevented from reaching the intended beneficiaries, the very fact of its having been undertaken already means that it has been exercised. The others know it too, for they do not hold the unpreventable failure against us. Only the refusal to undertake the effort is culpable. Those who have expended their best have been absolved of blame by those who are joined together with them in a community built on the supererogatory. Historically, there is nothing to be accomplished, because it is already there in the beginning. All that remains is the adventure of discovering the degree to which our efforts bear temporary fruit, since nothing remains within history except the witness to impassable goodness from which all good action springs. Eternal truth cannot be wiped away by the mere passage of time.

This is what is meant by the phrase "hope does not disappoint." It appears in Romans 5:5 with an all-important ground of explanation, "because the love of God has been poured into our hearts through the Holy Spirit who has been given to us." Within the context of St. Paul's letter, the principle and its justification flow seamlessly into one another. Yet their mutuality can also be separated or, perhaps, so deepened that they silently include one another. Then "hope does not disappoint" stands on its own. The "because," we discover, was already embedded in hope as that which cannot fail. We may disappoint hope, but hope cannot disappoint us. We may lose hope, but hope can never lose us. We may become hopeless, but hope cannot. Hope abides, because it is hope. Not only does hope spring eternal, but it is eternal as that which cannot turn away from itself. It is for this reason that we live in hope and from hope, as the vital wellspring of all our actions. Hope never ceases, not only in the conceptual sense that it is fixed, but in the pre-conceptual opening that includes our whole existence. We live in hope as the very possibility of living. There is nothing prior to hope or, more accurately, there is nothing for which we have to hope before we arrive at hope. We cannot get back to what is there before there is hope, for then we would need hope for that. There is nothing more hopeful than hope. We are contained and embraced by hope.

To speak of hope as a virtue is not inaccurate, but it still suggests that we are the bearers of hope, as a quality that resides within us. Absent from this traditional formulation is the existential priority of hope that is better captured by its acknowledgement as a gift. We do not, indeed cannot, make any special efforts to obtain hope, for the whole possibility of making efforts cannot depend on a prior effort. A beginning must always be found in what is purely and simply given, behind which we cannot go. Hope is in that sense the gift of being that makes all existence possible. Again contrary to a traditional notion, we do not move from existence toward being, to that which is more fully than ourselves, but from preeminent being to the transitory unfolding of existence. The Platonic idea of recollection defines our orientation toward a fullness we have lost, but the truth is that we could only seek that which we have never really lost. All seeking is within the horizon of finding. Not only do we know that for which we search but, more importantly, the possibility of searching is provided by that for which we search. From our perspective, we move from potency to act, but from the perspective of potency, there is only act. Nothing more remains to be accomplished, since all possibility of accomplishment is contained within it. The finitude of the language of potency and act in this sense is already well highlighted by St. Thomas's observation that God is all act and no potency. There is nothing that remains to be actualized in God. Now we begin to see how such a glimpse of God might be possible, from within our own movement from potency to act that is already transparent for the condition of its own possibility. Only by virtue of that which fully is do we gain the possibility of attempting to be. Hope is the thread by which we are held. Its durability surpasses all our expectations.

Optimism may be lost but hope cannot, for it is most manifest when the situation has become hopeless. Expectations of success or failure closely track the oscillations between optimism and pessimism. Hope floats serenely above such vacillations or, more accurately, below them as the anchor that is its artistic symbol. Optimism and pessimism are sentiments blown about on the surface that provide no basis for human action. They are more like the attitudes we take up when we have distanced ourselves from the imperative of action. We ask about how we feel in regard to the future, a question that is utterly irrelevant when we are called upon to assume responsibility for it. Action cannot be held hostage to endless speculation on its prospects for success, most of which involve a myriad of factors beyond our control. All that we know is that the likelihood of success is zero unless we undertake the effort. That is under our control, or at least the beginning of action is. What provides the possibility of beginning cannot be provided by us, for it is the gift of hope that itself has no beginning, for every beginning presupposes hope. A baby is not a sign of optimism, but of hope. No one can know what the future will hold, but we do know that there will be no future without hope. Quite apart from success or failure, or even how we measure them, there is the guarantee of a future, which is life itself. Optimism and pessimism are each deviations from hope that tilt dangerously toward despair. Postponement of life for the sake of something more is already a turning away from life. The complete withdrawal from action, the fall into depression, is not an option, least of all for a whole society. It has been this refusal to commit what Kierkegaard termed the only original sin, the sin of depression as the turn away from existence, that has been on display in the impressive political initiatives of late. Economic life may have declined, but political life has reasserted itself. No one knows what the outcome will be, and there are good reasons to be dubious about the merit of various initiatives, but we cannot doubt the determination to do something. Even in the Great Depression, this was really all that was achieved.

Persons as Opening of Hope

Whether the political realm preserves the economic is not the most decisive point. What counts is that it preserves hope. That is in the end its signal contribution to an economy that has seemed to lose hope. But more than that, it has brought hope into view as the horizon of our existence. This may in turn bring about a deeper account of what the political itself is. As the community that is constituted by hope, it exists in the point of intersection of the timeless with time, not in the seemingly solid embodiments of power and presence with which it is readily identified. This is something we have always known. Certainly it is familiar to the wielders of public power who cannot quite eliminate the nagging possibility that their writ might one day go unheard and unaccomplished. Perhaps now we can admit the fragility of power without the heightened anxiety that usually accompanies it. For we have seen that it is precisely this fragility, its eruption from depths immune from evanescence, that is the source of the prodigious strength and durability of political communities. Mere changes of government, even extra-constitutional ones, do not touch its underlying dynamic, for the political community is already present in the hope that precedes its formation. All that is needed is the assent by which possibility is affirmed. Free government is merely its most explicit realization but all governments are based on consent. It is simply that the less free varieties cannot be certain of their foundation and thereby must resort or be ready to resort to the uncertainty of coercion. A genuinely free polity is an awesome expression of strength. It is the most compelling testament to the power of hope that bridges the separation between human beings. Assent may be the means by which they are united, but its possibility is provided by the hope in which they are already united before they begin.

There is no foundation before hope, nor is there historical access to any point before it. This is why the formation of states is a mysteriously impenetrable process. It is not defined by constitutional conventions or ratifications, because they already presuppose a community for whom such events are authoritative. What is crucial is perhaps most noticed through its absence, when trust has suddenly collapsed as it did in the recent financial crisis. No one knows whether the other party is truthful or reliable; suspicion distances each from engagement with the other. How, Thomas Hobbes asked in the midst of the English civil war, is it possibly for such mutually suspicious individuals to come together in the formation of a civil society? The answer that he gave of an agreement or covenant has colored our perception of political community ever since. Its individualistic premise avoids the most decisive aspect. That is that individuals could never come together by way of an agreement if they were not already within some relationship of readiness to form agreements with one another. Hobbes knew this and, for that reason invoked the priority of natural and divine law, but his formulation placed all of its weight on the necessity of individual decision. That precarious commitment of individuals to the formation of a commonwealth is precisely what leaves modern societies prone to periodic collapses of mutual trust and confidence, until they discover that what they thought they had lost has never really been lost because it was never simply there. How can we lose what furnishes the condition of our existence? Or how is it possible for what provides the dynamic of our lives to become completely present within them? Crises of confidence are themselves only a possibility for beings that can never so fully incorporate the hope from which they live nor ever so fully lose it that they cannot even remember it. Hope does not disappoint, because it is what we live within.

The problem has been that we have lacked a model or metaphor that would enable us to grasp this about ourselves. That in turn has made hope that much more inaccessible. We may be held by hope, but we cannot hold onto hope without knowing that we are held by it. This is the big philosophical revolution underway since the time of Hobbes as we discover that the language of entities and fixed quantities does not apply to human beings. A very different mode of discourse was needed to break the hold of objectification. The breakthrough occurred in the realization that the model or metaphor we had been searching for has literally been under our noses all along, for it is as persons that we are capable of becoming what we are not and of discovering that we are more than we thought we were. It is not that this awareness of persons has failed to inform our whole liberal political tradition. We might even point out that the centrality of persons, entitled to limitless concern and respect and at the core of liberal political thought, arises from just such awareness. A person, we know, is a source of inexhaustibility in the universe, each one incapable of reaching the limit of what he or she is. Most of all, we know this about the people we know and love. Our political practice has been built around this elevation of persons as ends-in-themselves never to be used, as Kant insisted, as a mere means. The problem is that we have lacked the adequate linguistic means of conveying this, because all our language references entities of a relatively fixed nature. How can we talk about persons who are distinguished by the impossibility of fixing them in any particular status? The answer must begin from the recognition that such a question can only arise from persons and that we are capable of answering it only because we ourselves are persons. Not only do we not have to abstract from our own existence as persons, but we must not, if we are to have any possibility of grasping the reality of persons. Indeed, it is only through the horizon of the personal that we have any chance of grasping what can be known about the whole within which we find ourselves.

We discover that we are not isolated monads wandering aimlessly through the universe, but are borne along by a trust in what is trustworthy before we even become aware of ourselves. Even Hobbes's solitary individuals eventually yield to that predisposition as the possibility of creating a Leviathan. The loss of trust only comes later in response to bitter experience, but it cannot eliminate the priority from which it recedes. Our recent collapse of financial confidence is just such a moment and it has, interestingly, been followed by a robust reaffirmation from the political level, although it is a reaffirmation that cannot fully account for the source of its own confidence. That more delicate reflection entails an enlargement of perspective to include the condition of the possibility of political community that only becomes visible in the mutuality of persons. It is only possible for persons to form such enduring associations across space and time because that is what persons are. Never simply confined to what they are, persons are the movement out of non-existence that is never exhausted in existence. The possibility of forming community has in principle no limits, because there is never a point where responsibility for the other has reached its limit. I carry every other human being within me, including all that have ever lived or will live. This is what underpins the possibility of communication between us. Barriers of language and circumstance are only incidental. I can know each other as a unique other. That is as a person. Indeed, there is a sense in which we have not really met until we have met in person. All other forms of communication, including mass communication and the myriad possibilities of contact available to us, are all derivative from that primacy of persons to one another. The hope through which we reach out to one another is what it means to be a person.

The mistake within political thought was to think we could comprehend it, to render it intelligible in terms of some more elemental factors of need or interest. Overlooked in this assumption of an easy mastery over the conditions of our own existence is the degree to which we have ourselves already eluded them. Calculations about need and interest are only possible because we are not simply reducible to need and interest. Indeed the political arrangement by which such elemental imperatives are served are viable because we are already joined within a community beyond need and interest. A community of persons exceeds a community of drives. They become capable of considering and cooperating in the satisfaction of their desires through the freedom in which they are already related to one another. The whole premise of the contemplation of necessities is that we are not captured by them. If we were simply the sum total of our impulses, there would never be any need to name and reflect upon them; their imperious demands would render any self-reflection irrelevant. The cooperation of an anthill does not have any theoretical underpinning. For us, by contrast, the whole point of the acknowledgment of our primary drives is to construct a mode of satisfying that attests to our transcendence of them. A political community is by definition a free community for it exists, as Aristotle insisted, not merely for the sake of life but for the good life. Strictly speaking we might say that there are no untranscended drives within human existence, that is, none that have not already been seen through the eye of the other whose needs come before my own. The moral community of persons is always prior to the urges of animal life. We cannot understand the former in terms of the latter without defeating the very possibility of a free community and rendering the very idea of understanding impossible. Hope is not just the horizon within which the political unfolds, but is also the horizon in which all thinking about it is possible.

Reductive thinking is itself a forgetting of thought. Only those who are not reducible to their elementary impulses can ponder the possibility of such, but only so long as they fail to recall the impossibility of their pondering it if it were so. To understand hope, therefore, requires us to concede that it is itself the horizon of our thinking. We cannot understand hope in terms of anything else, but rather everything else within the light of hope. We cannot think outside of hope. This is what it means to say that hope does not disappoint. Not only can we not live without hope, but we cannot even think about it without hope. The movement of thought toward its object is a movement that is sustained by the hope in the possibility of reaching it. To the extent that everything is understood in relation to hope, we cannot, for that reason, understand hope. All that we can do is stand within hope, thereby gaining the only perspective that is possible for us. Through hope we glimpse hope. To stand outside of hope is to lose hope or at least our connection with hope. We cannot reduce hope to something else without eliminating hope from the frame of our thought. If it were possible for us to do that, then we might be seriously in trouble. The truth is that we can only forget about hope, a hope that now endures by way of forgetting. Even when it is forgotten, hope is present in the mode of its absence. We can even question the possibility of hope, but the questioning itself occurs within hope. It is by means of hope that we can ask about hope. How is it possible to understand such a vertiginous dynamic? We seem to be at the limit of thinking, a limit that early modern political thought thought it could surmount, although we now realize that it is through such limits that the unlimited is glimpsed. Even the effort to find a way of rendering hope more certain, to include it within what we control, cannot dispense with hope itself. There is no stepping outside of hope. Not even by losing hope do we lose hope, for hope does not lose us. Hope remains. To say that hope does not disappoint is appropriately redundant, for that is the very meaning of hope.

Endnote

1   This essay originated in a lecture delivered at the Quinn Business School, University College Dublin, in April 2009, at the invitation of its chaplain, Fr. John McNerney, who suggested the topic of Hope. Prepared at the height of the financial crisis in the winter of 2008, it was presented at the moment when world markets had reached their nadir. As a document from that time I thought it preferable to retain the present tense of global uncertainty.

Publications by Barry Cooper

Books

It's the Regime, Stupid! A Report from the Cowboy West on why Stephen Harper Matters. Toronto: Key Porter, 2009.

Beginning the Quest: Law and Politics in the Early Work of Eric Voegelin. Columbia: University of Missouri Press, 2009.

Editor. Tilo Schabert, *How World Politics is Made: France and the Reunification of Germany*. Translated by John Tyler Tuttle. Columbia: University of Missouri Press, 2009.

With Jodi Bruhn. *Voegelin Recollected*. Columbia: University of Missouri Press, 2007.

Editor, with Charles Embry. *Philosophy, Literature and Politics: Essays Honoring Ellis Sandoz*. Columbia: University of Missouri Press, 2005.

New Political Religions: An Analysis of Modern Terrorism. Columbia: University of Missouri Press, 2004.

Editor, and translator with Peter Emberley. *Faith and Political Philosophy: The Correspondence between Leo Strauss and Eric Voegelin*, 2nd ed. Revised. Columbia: University of Missouri Press, 2004.

French translation. *Faith and Political Philosophy*, 1st ed., by Sylvie Courtine-Denamy, *L. Strauss-E. Voegelin: Correspondance, 1934–1964, Foi et Philosophie politique*. Paris: Vrin, 2004.

With Lydia Miljan. *Hidden Agendas: How Canadian Journalists Influence the News*. Vancouver: University of British Columbia Press, 2003.

Editor and translator, with Jodi Cockerill. *The Collected Works of Eric Voegelin*, vol. XIII, *Selected Book Reviews*. Columbia: University of Missouri Press, 2001.

With Mebs Kanji. *Governing in Post-Deficit Times: Alberta in the Klein Years*. Toronto: University of Toronto Press, 2000.

Eric Voegelin and the Foundations of Modern Political Science. Columbia: University of Missouri Press, 1999.

Editor. *The Collected Works of Eric Voegelin*, vol. XXIV, *The History of Political Ideas*, vol. VI, *Revolution and the New Science*. Columbia: University of Missouri Press, 1998.

Editor, with Jürgen Gebhardt. *The Collected Works of Eric Voegelin*, vol. I,

The Form of the American Mind. Baton Rouge: Louisiana State University Press, 1995.

The Klein Achievement. Toronto: University of Toronto Press, 1995.

Sins of Omission: Shaping the News at CBC TV. Toronto: University of Toronto Press, 1994.

With David Jay Bercuson. *Derailed: The Betrayal of the National Dream*. Toronto: Key Porter, 1994.

Editor, and translator with Peter Emberley. *Faith and Political Philosophy: The Correspondence between Leo Strauss and Eric Voegelin*. University Park: Penn State University Press, 1993.

Action into Nature: An Essay on the Meaning of Technology. Notre Dame: Notre Dame University Press, 1991.

With David Jay Bercuson. *Deconfederation: Canada Without Quebec*. Toronto: Key Porter Books, 1991.

French translation of *Deconfederation: Good-Bye...et bonne chance! Les Adieux du Canada anglais au Québec*. Montreal: Le Jour, 1991.

The Restoration of Political Science and The Crisis of Modernity. Toronto and New York: Edwin Mellen Press, 1989.

Editor, with Allan Kornberg and William Mishler. *The Resurgence of Conservatism in Anglo-American Democracies*. Durham: Duke University Press, 1988.

Alexander Kennedy Isbister: A Respectable Critic of the Honourable Company. Ottawa: Carleton University Press, 1988.

The Political Philosophy of Eric Voegelin. Toronto and New York: Edwin Mellen Press, 1986.

The End of History: An Essay on Modern Hegelianism. Toronto: University of Toronto Press, 1984.

Michel Foucault: An Introduction to the Study of His Thought. (Studies in Religion and Society, Vol. II.) Toronto and New York: Edwin Mellen Press, 1982.

Translator. Jean Baechler, *Suicides*. New York: Basic Books, 1979.

Merleau-Ponty and Marxism: From Terror to Reform. Toronto: University of Toronto Press, 1979.

Translator. Raymond Aron (Gifford Lectures), *History and the Dialectic of Violence: An Analysis of Sartre's Critique de la Raison dialectique*. Oxford: Basil Blackwell, New York: Harper and Row, 1975.

Translator. Jean Baechler, *The Origins of Capitalism*. Oxford: Basil Blackwell, 1975.

Articles and Chapters

An Analysis of "Jihadist" Militancy, Political Extremism, with Martha Lee (Waterloo: Wilfrid Laurier University Press, December 2011), in press.

"Raymond Aron and Nuclear War," *Journal of Classical Sociology*, 11:2 (May 2011), 203–224.

"Wikileaks and the Dream of Transparency," *The Dispatch* (April 2011), 15–16, www.cdfai.org

"Voegelin, Strauss, and Kojeve on Tyranny," in *Eric Voegelin and the Continental Tradition: Explorations in Modern Political Thought*, Lee Trepanier and Steven McGuire, eds. (Columbia, MO: University of Missouri Press, 2011), Eric Voegelin Series in Political Philosophy, 218–239.

"Political Order and the 'Culture of Entitlement': Some Theoretical Reflections on the Gomery Commision," *Political Cultures and the Culture of Politics*, Jürgen Gebhardt, ed. (Heidelberg: Universitätsverlag, 2010), 45–68.

"The Failing Greek Economy," *The Dispatch: Newsletter of the Canadian Defence and Foreign Affairs Institute*, 8:2 (June 2010), 8–9.

"Voegelin, Eric," *Encyclopedia of Political Thought* (April 2010).

"Freedom of Religion and Terrorism in Canada," in *Faith in Democracy? Religion and Politics in Canada*, John Young and Boris DeWiel, eds. (Newcastle: Cambridge Scholars Publishing, 2009), 151–166.

"Recollecting the Personal in Voegelin's Political Science," in *Politikos— Vom Element des Persönlichen in der Politik: Festschrift für Tilo Schabert zum 65. Geburtstag*, Karl-Heinz Nusser, Matthias Riedel, Theresia Ritter, eds. (Berlin: Duncker und Humblot, 2008), 417–426.

"'Jihadists' and the War on Terrorism," *The Intercollegiate Review*, 42:2 (Spring, 2007), 27–36.

"Aron's Clausewitz," in *Political Reason in the Age of Ideology: Essays in Honor of Raymond Aron*, Daniel J. Mahoney and Bryan-Paul Frost, eds. (New York: Transaction Press, 2007), 75–104.

"Ethics and National Security in an Age of International Terrorism," in *The*

Ethics of Foreign Policy, David B. MacDonald, Robert G. Patman, Betty Mason-Parker, eds. (Aldershot: Ashgate, 2007), 53–66.

"Terrorism and Globalization," *Perspectives on Global Development and Technology*, 4:3–4 (2005), 543–575. Reprinted in *Globalization and Political Ethics*, Richard B. Day and Joseph Masciulli, eds. (Leiden: Brill, 2007), 293–325.

With John von Heyking, "'A Cow Is Just a Cow': George Grant and Eric Voegelin on the United States," in *Athens and Jerusalem: George Grant's Theology, Philosophy, and Politics*, R.P. Peters, ed. (Toronto: University of Toronto Press, 2006), 166–189.

"Understanding Jihadist Terrorism after 9/11," in *The West at War*, Bradley C.S. Watson, ed. (Lanham: Rowman and Littlefield, 2006), 41–52.

"Some Implications of the Embedded State in Canada," in *Insiders and Outsiders: Alan Cairns and the Reshaping of Canadian Citizenship*, Gerald Kernerman and Philip Resnick, eds. (Vancouver: UBC Press, 2005), 104–116.

"Hunting and Political Philosophy, An Interpretation of the Kynegetikos," in *Philosophy, Literature and Politics: Essays Honoring Ellis Sandoz*, Charles Embry and Barry Cooper, eds. (Columbia: University of Missouri Press, 2005), 28–53.

"The Sadism of Moralizing Canadian Multilateralism," in *Independence in an Age of Empire: Assessing Unilateralism and Multilateralism*, Graham F. Walker, ed. (Halifax: The Centre for Foreign Policy Studies, Dalhousie University, 2004), 284–292.

"A Solid Foothold," *The Review of Politics*, 66:4 (2004), 683–685.

"Classical Western Political Philosophy," in *Comparative Political Philosophy*, 2nd ed., Anthony J. Parel and Ronald C. Keith, eds. (Lanham: Lexington Books, 2003), 29–44.

"Modern Western Political Philosophy," in *Comparative Political Philosophy*, 2nd ed., Anthony J. Parel and Ronald C. Keith, eds. (Lanham: Lexington Books, 2003), 45–70.

"Limitations and Ambiguities," in *Fixing Canadian Democracy*, Gordon Gibson, ed. (Vancouver: The Fraser Institute, 2003), 117–150.

"Some Limitations to Digital Democracy and Networks in Canada," *Zeitschrift für Kanada-Studien*, 43:2 (2003), 96–112.

"Lun gudian zhengzhi zhexie," (On Classical Political Philosophy) in Ma Depu, ed., *Zhengzhi wenhua lung ong* (Series on Political Culture) (Tianjin: Tianjin renmin chubanshe, 2002), Vol. 2, 175–190 (in Chinese).

"Canadian Discourse on Peacekeeping," in *International Intervention: Sovereignty versus Responsibility*, Michael Keren and Donald A. Sylvan, eds. (London: Cass, 2002), 126–46. Reprinted in *Calgary Papers in Military and Strategic Studies*, 2 (2007), 75–98.

"Cultural Myths and Political Realities or Why Quebec Will Never Separate," *Review of Constitutional Studies*, vol. 7 (2002), 231–254.

"The Spiritual Structures of Contemporary Terrorism" in *Im Schatten des Terrorisimus: Hintergründe Strukturen, Konsequenzen des 11 September, 2001* Petra Bendel and Mathias Hildebrandt, eds. (Wiesbaden: Westdeutscher Verlag, 2002), 131–149.

"Two Tellurian Themes in Plato's *Republic*" in *Politics, Philosophy, Writing: Plato's Art of Caring for Souls*, Z. Planinc, ed. (Columbia: University of Missouri Press, 2001), 80–121.

"Regionalism, Political Culture and Canadian Political Myths," in *Regionalism and Party Politics in Canada*, Lisa Young and Keith Archer, eds. (Toronto: Oxford University Press, 2001), 92–112.

"Quebec Nationalism and Canadian Politics in Light of Voegelin's *Political Religions*," in *Politics, Order and History: Essays on the Work of Eric Voegelin*, Glen Hughes, Stephen A. McKnight, Geoffrey L. Price, eds. (Scheffield: Scheffield Academic Press, 2001), 208–232.

"Zur Entwicklung von Voegelins Politischer Wissenschaft," *Zeitschrift für Politik*, 48:3 (2001), 243–256.

"The Unfounded Country" in *Great Questions of Canada*, Rudyard Griffiths, ed. (Toronto: Stoddart, 2000), 55–60, 65–71. Revised edition in *Great Questions of Canada*, Rudyard Griffiths, ed. (Toronto: Key Porter, 2007), 73–77; 83–90.

"Weaving a Work" in *Canadian Political Philosophy*, Ronald Beiner and Wayne Norman, eds. (Toronto: Oxford University Press, 2000), 374–385.

"Canadian Political Myths" in *Politik und Politeia: Formen und Probleme politischer Ordnung: Festgabe für Jürgen Gebhardt zum 65 Geburstag*, Wolfgang Leidhold, ed. (Würtzburg: Köningshausen und Neumann, 2000), 269–280.

"Surveying the Occasional Papers" *The Review of Politics*, 62:4 (2000) 727–751.

"Agency Law and Governance: Some Theoretical Considerations," Law Commission of Canada, *Occasional Papers* (2000), 1–37.

With Lydia Miljan. "Censorship by Inadvertence? Selectivity in the Production of TV News," in *Interpreting Censorship in Canada*, Klaus Petersen and Allan C. Hutchinson, eds. (Toronto: University of Toronto Press, 1999), 318–333.

"Canadian Discourse on Peacekeeping," in *Philosophical Designs for a Socio-Cultural Transformation: Beyond Violence and The Modern Era*, Tetsuji Yamamoto, Edward G. Andrew, Roger Charter, Paul Rabinow, eds. (Tokyo: Ecole Des Hautes Etudes en Sciences Culturelles; Boulder: Rowman and Littlefield, 1998), 751–768.

"French Philosophy and Contemporary North American Society," *Iichiko*, 42 (1997), 70–85. Translated by Tomohiro Tanaka into Japanese.

"Does Canada Need the CBC?" in *Crosscurrents: Contemporary Political Issues*, 3rd ed., Mark Charlton and Paul Baker, eds. (Toronto: Nelson, 1997), 459–465.

"W.J. Stankiewicz's Search for a Philosophy of Ideology" in *Holding One's Time in Thought: The Political Philosophy of W.J. Stankiewicz*, Bogdan Czaykowski and Samuel V. La Selva, eds. (Vancouver: Ronsdale Press, 1997), 237–250.

"Theoretical Perspectives on Constitutional Reform in Canada" in *Rethinking the Constitution*, Tony Peacock, ed. (Toronto: Oxford University Press, 1996), 217–232.

"Political Science in Canada: 1970–1995" *Political Science Reviewer*, 25 (1996), 100–26.

"Eric Voegelin's Analysis of the Deformation of Consciousness in Voltaire," *Lumen*, 15 (1996), 37–55.

"The End of History: Déjà-vu all over again," *History of European Ideas*, 19 (1994), 377–383.

"Looking Eastward, Looking Backward: A Western Reading of the Never-Ending Story," in *Constitutional Predicament: Canada After the Referendum of 1992*, Curtis Cook, ed. (Montreal & Kingston: McGill-Queen's University Press, 1994), 89–108.

"Modernity, Postmodernity, and Culture" in *Reflections on Cultural*

Policy: Past Present and Future, Evan Alderson, Robin Blaser and H. Coward, eds. (Waterloo: Wilfrid Laurier University Press, 1993), 163–171.

With David Bercuson, "From Constitutional Monarchy to Quasi-Republic: The Evolution of Liberal Democracy in Canada," in *Canadian Constitutionalism: 1791–1991*, Janet Ajzenstat, ed. (Ottawa: Canadian Study of Parliament Group, 1993), 17–27. French version in *Le constitutionalism Canadien: 1791–1991*, Louise Massicotte, ed.

Foreword to Y. K. Umar, ed., *George Grant and the Future of Canada* (Calgary: University of Calgary Press, 1992), ix-x.

"Did George Grant's Canada Ever Exist?" in *ibid*, 151–164.

"Classical Western Political Philosophy," in *Comparative Political Philosophy: Studies Under the Upas Tree*, Anthony J. Parel and Ronald C. Keith, eds. (New Delhi: Newbury Park; London: Sage, 1992), 29–43.

"Modern Western Political Philosophy," in *ibid.*, 45–69.

With David J. Bercuson, "Electoral Boundaries: An Obstacle to Democracy in Alberta," in *Drawing Boundaries: Legislatures, Courts and Electoral Values*, John C. Courtney, Peter MacKinnon, David E. Smith, eds. (Saskatoon: Fifth House, 1992), 110–127.

"Comment: What Liberalism and Civic Humanism have in Common: The Rejection of Classical Thought," *The Journal of Canadian Studies*, 26 (1991), 44–45.

"Plato and the Media," in *Public Policy & the Public Good* Ethan Fishman, ed. (New York: Greenwood, 1991), 15–28.

"Can Political Science Think Through the Crisis of the Age?" in *Papers in Comparative Political Science* Manuel J. Pelaez, ed. (Barcelona: Gráficas Cometa, 1990), 4543–4562.

"George Grant and The Revival of Political Philosophy," in *By Loving our Own: George Grant and the Legacy of Lament for a Nation*, Peter Emberley, ed. (Ottawa: Carleton University Press, 1990), 97–121.

"Defining the Larger Context of Aboriginal Rights," *Canadian Journal of Law and Society*, 5 (1990), 127–140.

"A Key to Voegelin," *Review of Politics*, 52 (1990), 648–650.

"On the Professionalization of the Intellectuals," *University of Toronto Quarterly*, 58 (1989), 451–454.

"Nihilism and Technology," in *Nietzsche and the Rhetoric of Nihilism*, Tom Darby *et al.*, eds. (Ottawa: Carleton University Press 1989), 165–181.

"Action into Nature: Hannah Arendt's Reflections on Technology," in *Democratic Theory and Technological Society*, Richard B. Day, Ronald Beiner, and Joe Masciulli, eds. (London: Sharpe, 1988), 316–335.

"George Grant, Political Philosopher," *The Political Science Reviewer*, XVIII (1988), 1–33.

"The Meaning of Technology at the End of History," University of Minnesota, Center of Humanistic Studies, *Occasional Papers*, No. 7 (1986), pp. 31. Translated by Guy Laforest, "Le Sens de la technologie à la fin de l'histoire," *Génitif*, 8:3–4 (1987), 111–146.

"Hegelian Imperialism," in *Sojourns in the New World: Reflections on Technology*, Tom Darby, ed. (Ottawa: Carleton University Press, 1986), 25–67.

"What is Post-Modernity?" *Canadian Journal of Social and Political Theory*, IX:3 (1985) 77–89.

"Alexander Kennedy Isbister in England," *Canadian Ethnic Studies*, XVII:2 (1985), 44–63.

"The West: A Political Minority," in *Minorities and the Canadian State*, Neil Nevitte and Allan Kornberg, eds. (Toronto: Mosaic, 1985), 203–220.

"Western Political Consciousness," in *Political Thought in Canada*, Stephen Brooks, ed. (Toronto: Clarke Irwin, 1984), 213–238.

"Ideology, Technology and Truth," in *The Ethical Dimension of Political Life: Essays in Honour of John H. Hallowell*. Frances Canavan, ed. (Durham: Duke University Press, 1983), 138–155.

"Ideology and Technology, Truth and Power," in *Ideology*, A. Parel, ed. (Waterloo: Wilfrid Laurier University Press, 1983), 93–109.

"An Introduction to Voegelin's Account of Western Civil Theologies," in *Voegelin the Theologian: Ten Studies in Interpretation*, (Toronto Studies in Theology, vol. 10), John Kirby, William M. Thompson, eds. (Toronto and New York: Edwin Mellen Press, 1983), 253–289.

"Reduction, Reminiscence and the Search for Truth," in *The Philosophy of Order: Essays on History, Consciousness and Politics, for Eric Voegelin on his Eightieth Birthday, January 3, 1981*, Peter J. Opitz and Gregor Sebba, eds. (Stuttgart: Klett-Cotta, 1981), 316–331.

"Hermeneutics and Social Science," *Philosophy of the Social Sciences*, 11:1 (1981), 79–80.

"Phenomenology and Political Science," *Canadian Journal of Social and Political Theory*, 5 (1981), 99–111.

"The Politics of Performance: An interpretation of Bolingbroke's Political Theory," *Interpretation*, 9: 2/3 (1981), 245–262.

"Reason and Interpretation in Contemporary Political Theory," *Polity*, 11:3 (1979), 387–399.

"Hermeneutics and Political Science," in *Recent Approaches to the Social Sciences*, H.K. Betz, ed., Vol. II, Social Sciences Symposium Series (University of Calgary, 1979), 17–30.

"Nihilism and Modernity," *Canadian Journal of Political and Social Theory*, 2:2 (1978), 97–103.

"On Reading *Industry and Humanity*: A Study in the Principles Underlying Liberal Management," *Journal of Canadian Studies*, 13:4 (1978), 28–39.

"Ab Imperio usque ad Imperium: The Politics of George Grant," in *George Grant in Process: Essays and Conversations*, Larry Schmidt, ed. (Toronto: Anansi, 1978), 22–39.

"Voegelin's Concept of Historiogenesis," *Historical Reflections/Reflexions Historiques*, 4:2 (1978), 232–251.

"A Fragment of Voegelin's History of Western Political Thought," *Political Science Reviewer*, 7 (1977), 23–52.

"Hegel and the Genesis of Merleau-Ponty's Atheism," *Studies in Religion/Sciences Religieuses*, 6 (1977), 665–671.

"The Literature of Medical Ethics: A Review of the Writings of Hans Jonas," *Journal of Medical Ethics*, 2 (1976), 39–43.

"Culture and Anarchy: The Politics of Matthew Arnold," in *The Prospects for Constitutional Change, Festschrift for Taylor Cole,* John H. Hallowell, ed. (Durham: Duke University Press, 1975), 21–35.

"The Civil Theology of Matthew Arnold," *Eglise et Théologie*, 6 (1975), 365–385.

"Hegelian Elements in Merleau-Ponty's La Structure du Comportement," *International Philosophical Quarterly*, 15 (1975), 411–425.

"Rhetoric and Violence," in *Thinking About Change*, David Shugarman, ed. (Toronto: University of Toronto Press, 1974), 71–78.

"Recent Studies on Marx," *The Political Science Reviewer*, 2 (1972), 35–74.

"Values and the Methodology of Political Science: A Comment," *Canadian Journal of Political Science*, 4:11 (1971), 119–122.

"Vallières Confession," *Journal of Canadian Studies*, 6:2 (1971), 3–17.

With Allan Kornberg. "Procedural Changes in The Canadian House of Commons: Some Reflections," *Journal of Constitutional and Parliamentary Studies*, II (1968), 1–18.

Non-Academic Writings

Small Wars and Democracies (Calgary: Canadian Defence and Foreign Affairs Institute, 2009), 1–49.

"Geopolitics Today," *The Dispatch: Newsletter of the Canadian Defence and Foreign Affairs Institute*, 7:2 (Summer, 2009), 13–14.

"What's Wrong with the Libertarian Case Against the War in Afghanistan?" *C2C*, 3:1 (2009). Available at www.c2cjournal.ca

"ITARS," *The Dispatch: Newsletter of the Canadian Defence and Foreign Affairs Institute*, 6:2 (Summer, 2008), 11–13.

"Green Shift or Green Shaft?" *China and Canada Exchange*, 2 (September, 2008), 11–12.

"New Thinking on Islamist Terrorism," *The Dispatch: Newsletter of the Canadian Defence and Foreign Affairs Institute*, 5:1 (Spring 2007). Available at: http://www.cdfai.org/newsletters/newsletersspring2007.htm

CFIS: A Foreign Intelligence Service for Canada. (Calgary: Canadian Defence and Foreign Affairs Institute, 2007).

Baeri Kupo, "Canada-a-so Pon Korea: Seoul-a Dok Cha Chok Kuk Ik Chu Ku-Pyongyang-a Kun Sa Chok Do Par," *Cha-Yu Gong-Ron*, No. 476 (November, 2006), 96–103. In Korean. (Barry Cooper, "A Canadian Perspective on Korea: With Special Reference to Military Relations with North Korea," *Liberty and Culture*, No. 476 (November, 2006), 96–103.)

"The Historical Experience with Proportional Representation in Canada," *Fraser Forum* (February, 2005), 5–7.

With Alex Moens. "Canadian Participation in North American Missile

Defence: A Cost-Benefit Analysis," *Fraser Alert: Military and Security Series* (February, 2005).

With Mercedes Stephenson. "Ballistic Missile Defence and the Future of Canada-US Cooperation," *Fraser Forum* (March, 2005), 9–11.

With Lydia Miljan. "The Canadian 'Garrison Mentality' and Anti-Americanism at the CBC," *Studies in Defence and Foreign Policy*, No. 4 (Vancouver: The Fraser Institute, 2005).

With Lydia Miljan. "Measuring Intangibles: Some Forms of anti-Americanism are Emotional rather than Rational," *Fraser Forum* (July/August, 2005), 30–31.

With Ray Szeto. "The Need for Canadian Strategic Lift," *Studies in Defence and Foreign Policy*, No. 5 (Vancouver: The Fraser Institute, 2005).

"Adam Smith's Defence of Capitalism," *Fraser Forum* (November, 2005), 4–5.

"Bureaucrats in Uniform: The Politicization of the Royal Canadian Mounted Police," Fraser Institute Digital Publication, 96 pp. Available at: http://www.fraserinstitute.ca/shared/readmore.asp?sNav=pb&id=833

With Mercedes Stephenson and Ray Szeto. "Canada's Military Posture: An Analysis of Recent Civilian Reports," *Critical Issues Bulletin* (Vancouver: The Fraser Institute, 2004).

"Privacy and Security in an Age of Terrorism," *Studies in Defence and Foreign Policy*, No. 3 (Vancouver: The Fraser Institute, 2004).

"North American Military Relations: How can Canada help?" *Fraser Forum* (June, 2004), 19–20.

"Rebalance the Federation by Rebalancing the Spending Power," *Fraser Forum* (October, 2004), 4–6.

With David de Groot, "MPs Hide behind Judicial Robes," *Fraser Forum* (October, 2004), 11–13.

"Like Lipstick on a Pig . . . The Politics of Kyoto," *Fraser Forum* (January, 2003), 4–5.

"Canada's Unlikely Freedom Fighters," *Fraser Forum* (January, 2003), 19–20.

"Should Airline Pilots Carry Guns to Stop Terrorists?" *Costco Connection*, 16:1 (January-February, 2003), 12–13.

With Mercedes Stephenson. "The End of Canadian Sovereignty?" *Fraser Forum* (March, 2003), 10–11.

With David Bercuson. "Helicopter Replacement Fiasco," *Fraser Forum* (June, 2003), 28–29.

With Royce Koop. "Policing Alberta: An Analysis of the Alternatives to the Federal Provision of Police Services," *Public Policy Sources*, No.72 (Vancouver: The Fraser Institute, November, 2003).

"Could the Alberta Provincial Police Return by 2012?" *Fraser Forum* (November, 2003), 5–7.

"Unholy Terror: The Origin and Significance of Contemporary, Religion-based Terrorism," *Studies in Defence and Foreign Policy*, No. 1 (Vancouver: The Fraser Institute, 2002).

With David Bercuson. "New Policies for War and Peace," *Fraser Forum* (February, 2002), 17–18.

"Why We Need a Continental Security Perimeter," *Fraser Forum* (March, 2002), 4–5.

With Sylvia LeRoy, "Commanding Identity? Canadian Cultural Policies Within the American Perimeter," *Fraser Forum* (April, 2002), 27–28.

"Foreword" to Jason Clemens, Joel Emes, and Nadeem Esmail, "Saskatchewan Prosperity: Taking the Next Step," *Public Policy Source*, No. 58 (Vancouver: The Fraser Institute, May, 2002).

With Jason Hayes and Sylvia LeRoy. "Science Fact or Science Fiction? The Grizzly Biology Behind Parks Canada Management Models," *Critical Issues Bulletin* (Vancouver: The Fraser Institute, 2002).

With Mebs Kanji. "Shifting Priorities: From Deficit Spending to Paying Down the Debt and Lowering Taxes, Evidence from the Alberta Advantage Surveys, 1995–2000," *Public Policy Sources*, No. 46 (Vancouver: Fraser Institute, 2001), 1–31.

With Shainoor Virani and Mebs Kanji. "Moving Beyond the Status Quo: Alberta's 'Working' Prescription for Health Care Reform, Evidence from the Alberta Advantage Surveys, 1995–2000," *Public Policy Sources*, No. 49 (Vancouver: The Fraser Institute, 2001).

With Sylvia LeRoy. "Room to Experiment: Seizing Alberta's Advantage for Reform," *Fraser Forum* (October, 2001), 13–14.

With Sylvia LeRoy. "Co-opting Voluntary Service: Canada's State-

Sponsored Version of Civil Society," *Fraser Forum* (December, 2001), 17–19.

With Sylvia LeRoy. "Off Limits: How Radical Environmentalists are Shutting Down Canada's National Parks," *Public Policy Sources*, No. 45 (2000), 1–55.

With Shainoor N. Virani & Mebs Kanji. "Why Bill 11 Won't Hurt Ralph Klein," *Policy Options Politiques*, 21:4 (May, 2000), 36–41.

With David Bercuson. "Anne of Green Gables in the Twenty-First Century," *Fraser Forum* (November, 2000), 30.

With David Bercuson. "A Constitutional Expert's Last word," *Fraser Forum* (November, 2000), 11–12.

"Shoddy Pamphlet or Great Man's Thesis? Barry Cooper on John Ralston Saul," *The Literary Review of Canada*, 7:3 (1998), 16–18.

"Taylor-made Canada," *The Literary Review of Canada,* 5 (February, 1996), 19–22.

"Red Tories No More," *From the Right,* 2 (1996–1997), 4.

"The Political Significance of Technological Action," *National Forum,* 74:2 (Spring, 1994), 32–36.

"Class Action," *Saturday Night,* 107 (September, 1992), 26–33.

"Thinking the Unthinkable," *West Magazine* (May, 1990), 22–28.

"How to Watch TV News," *The Idler*, 28 (May, 1990), 17–22.

"International Affairs: Defence and Security," *On Balance,* 2:3 (March, 1989), 1–7.

"After the Comets," *The Idler* 18 (July/August 1988) 49–53.

With Senator Lorna Marsden. "What is a Fair Share?" in *Equality in the Economy*, Emer Killean, ed. (Montreal: IRPP, 1987), 1-5.

"Eric Voegelin's Early Career," in *The World and I*, II: 1, Morton A. Kaplan, ed. (February 1, 1986), 696-703. Reprinted as the Introduction to Voegelin's *Political Religions*, III, translated by T.J. DeNapoli and E.S. Easterly, (vol. 23, Toronto Studies in Theology) (Lewiston: Edwin Mellen, 1986), v-xxvi.

"The Dark Side of Employment Equity," *Choices* (April 1986), n.p.

"The Politics of Apocalypse," *Canadian Forum*, 51 (1971), 603-604, 636-638.

Tabula Gratulatoria

Janet Ajzenstat

Edward Andrew

Mamie Angus

David Bercuson

Ken Boessenkool

Alison Bowes

Jodi Bruhn

Paul Caringella

Mark Castelino

Jason Clemens

Leon Craig

Tom Darby

Jim Doak

Peter Emberley

Tim Fuller

Gordon Gibson

Hugh Gillis

Fraser Gordon

Evelyn Guichon

Gary M. Guichon

Lorne Gunter

Nigel Hannaford

Stephen Haigh

Glenn (Chip) Hughes

George Hungerford

Beverly Jarrett

Jake Kerr

John Kirby

Royce Koop

Terry Lauder

Martha Lee

George Leitch

Carol McMahon

Kathleen McNally

Lydia Miljan

Kenneth Minogue

Mark Milke

Marco Navarro-Genie

Bradley Nemetz

Walter Nicgorski

James O'Donnell

John O'Neill

Morten Paulsen

Anthony A. Peacock

Charles Pentland

Jacqueline Pfeffer-Merrill

Brendan Purcell

James Rhodes

Shawna Ritchie

Robert Roach

Ellis Sandoz

Tilo Schabert

Trevor Shelley

Robert Sibley

Sandy Soutzo

David E. Smith

Rouven Steeves

Melanie Timmons

Fred Wall

James L. Wiser

Catherine Zuckert

List of Contributors

Janet Ajzenstat taught Canadian politics and public law at McMaster University for several years. Among her most recent books is, *The Canadian Founding, John Locke and Parliament* (McGill-Queen's University Press, 2007), which won The Osgoode Society's John T. Saywell Prize (2009) for the best book in Canadian legal and constitutional history in the years 2007 and 2008.

Richard Avramenko is a displaced Albertan who teaches political philosophy at the University of Wisconsin-Madison. He is the author of *Courage: The Politics of Life and Limb* (Notre Dame, 2011) and co-editor of *Friendship and Politics: Essays in Political Thought* (Notre Dame, 2008).

Leah Bradshaw is Professor of Political Science at Brock University in St. Catharines, Ontario. Much of her scholarly work owes a debt to the philosophy and common sense of Hannah Arendt, and a further debt to Barry Cooper, in whose classes at York University in the late 1970s she first encountered the formidable triad of Hannah Arendt, Leo Strauss and Eric Voegelin.

Peter C. Emberley is Professor of Philosophy at Carleton University. His publications include *Zero Tolerance: Hot Button Politics in Canada's Universities* (Penguin, 1996), *Values Education and Technology: The Ideology of Dispossession* (University of Toronto Press, 1995), *Bankrupt Education: The Decline of Liberal Education in Canada* (University of Toronto Press, 1994), *Faith and Political Philosophy: The Correspondence Between Leo Strauss and Eric Voegelin* (Penn State University Press, 1993), *Divine Hunger : Canadians on Spiritual WalkAbout* (HarperCollins Canada, 2002), and *Suspended Disbelief: The Spiritual Searches of Canada's Babyboomers* (HarperCollins Canada, forthcoming). In 1994, he designed a core curriculum in the humanities at Carleton University, resulting in the College of the Humanities, of which he was the Founding Director. His current research interests are comparative religion and the impacts of globalization on traditional life in India.

Tom Flanagan is a professor of political science at the University of Calgary. He is Fellow of the Royal Society of Canada and a former national campaign manager for the Conservative Party of Canada.

Michael Franz is professor and chair in the Department of Political Science at Loyola University Maryland. He is the author of *Eric Voegelin and the Politics of Spiritual Revolt: The Roots of Modern Ideology*. Franz also edited and wrote the "Introduction" for *The Ecumenic Age*, by Eric Voegelin, Vol. IV of *Order and History*, Vol. 17 of *The Collected Works of Eric Voegelin*. He is the author of numerous scholarly articles and reviews concentrating on problems of political violence and fanaticism in the light of philosophical anthropology.

Jürgen Gebhardt is Professor Emeritus of Political Science at the University of Erlangen-Nuremberg. His research focuses on political theory, political philosophy and comparative politics. His publications include the volumes *Politik, Hermeneutik, Humanität* (2004) and *Americanism* (1993) as well as numerous articles on the history of political ideas, systematic political theory and comparative politics. He is a member of the board of directors of the Bavarian-American Academy and chairman of the board of the Bavarian-American Center at the Amerika Haus in Munich.

Thomas Heilke is Professor of Political Science and Dean of Graduate Studies at the University of Kansas. He is the author, editor, or co-editor of several books, including: *Voegelin on the Idea of Race: An Analysis of Modern European Racism* (1990); *Nietzsche's Tragic Regime: Culture, Aesthetics, and Political Education* (1998); *Eric Voegelin: The Quest for Reality* (1999). He has authored numerous of articles and chapters in the areas of political theory, religion and politics, Protestant political thought, and international relations. He is at work on a co-authored book with Brent Steele: *As for the Gods: Religion in International Politics*.

John von Heyking is Professor of Political Science, University of Lethbridge in Alberta. He is the author of *Augustine and Politics as Longing in the World* (2001), and co-edited *Friendship and Politics: Essays in Political Thought* (2008) and *Civil Religion in Political Thought: Its Perennial Questions and Enduring Relevance in North America* (2010). He is currently working on a book on friendship and political philosophy.

Rainer Knopff, Professor of Political Science at the University of Calgary, has written widely in the areas of public law, human rights, and Canadian political thought. His books include *The Charter Revolution and the Court Party* and *Charter Politics* (both with F.L. Morton), *Human Rights and*

Social Technology: The New War on Discrimination (with T.E. Flanagan), and *Parameters of Power: Canada's Political Institutions* (with Keith Archer, Roger Gibbins, and Leslie A. Pal). He is currently pursuing projects on land use and hunting policy, and on current Canadian constitutional politics. Visit his website at http://poli.ucalgary.ca/knopff/.

Zdravko Planinc (Religious Studies, McMaster University) has published three books on Plato, the most recent of which is *Plato through Homer: Poetry and Philosophy in the Cosmological Dialogues.* His studies of Shakespeare have been published in *Interpretation, Shakespearean Criticism, Humanitas,* and the *Journal for Cultural and Religious Theory.* His articles on modern subjects include analyses of Hegel, Marx, George Grant, Eric Voegelin, and Canadian constitutional law.

Jene Porter is Professor Emeritus from the University of Saskatchewan. He has published books and papers primarily in the areas of political philosophy, from the history of political philosophy itself (with John Hallowell) to works from Luther to Voegelin and of public science.

Tilo Schabert is Professor Emeritus of Political Science at the University of Erlangen, Germany. Among his recent publications are: *How World Politics is Made: France and the Reunification of Germany* (University of Missouri Press, 2009), and *Die zweite Geburt des Menschen. Von den politischen Anfängen menschlicher Existenz* (Freiburg-Munich: Alber, 2009; American edition forthcoming Chicago University Press, 2014).

David Walsh is Professor of Politics at The Catholic University of America, Washington, DC. He is the author of a three-volume study of modernity addressing the totalitarian catharsis, the resurgence of liberal democracy, and the philosophical revolution of the modern world. Intended as a guide to the multiple facets of the age in which we live, the volumes appeared as *After Ideology: Recovering the Spiritual Foundations of Freedom* (1990), *The Growth of the Liberal Soul* (1997), and *The Modern Philosophical Revolution: The Luminosity of Existence* (2008). Three other books provide tangential perspectives on this modernity project: *The Mysticism of Innerworldly Fulfillment: A Study of Jacob Boehme* (1983), *Guarded By Mystery: Meaning in a Postmodern Age* (1999), and *The Third Millennium: Reflections on Faith and Reason* (1999). He is presently working on an account of the person that will appear as *Politics of the Person.*